From Joseph Bensman

On the cover: Portrait of Joseph Bensman by Lydia Csato Gasman, reproduced with the permission of Marilyn Bensman, in association with the art gallery Les Yeux du Monde and the Lydia Csato Gasman Archives, both in Charlottesville, Virginia. Photograph by Lindsay Ann Nolin.

The artist's inscription reads: "With gratitude. I'll always remember you Joe. Lydia Csato Gasman. 1976."

From Joseph Bensman

Essays on Modern Society

Edited and introduced by

Robert Jackall and Duffy Graham

Newfound Press
THE UNIVERSITY OF TENNESSEE LIBRARIES, KNOXVILLE

Digital version at newfoundpress.utk.edu/pubs/bensman

Newfound Press
University of Tennessee Libraries
1015 Volunteer Boulevard
Knoxville, TN 37996-1000
newfoundpress.utk.edu

ISBN-13: 978-0-9846445-9-9
ISBN-10: 0-9846445-9-8

Bensman, Joseph.
From Joseph Bensman : essays on modern society / edited and introduced by Robert Jackall and Duffy Graham. Knoxville, Tennessee : Newfound Press, University of Tennessee Libraries, ©2014.
1 online resource (vi, 696 pages)
Includes bibliographical references and index.
1. Bensman, Joseph -- Political and social views. 2. Sociologists -- United States – History – 20th century -- Biography. 3. Sociology. I. Jackall, Robert. II. Graham, Duffy. III. Title.
HM585 .B465 2014

Book design by Jayne W. Smith
Cover design by C. S. Jenkins

Contents

Acknowledgments

The editors wish to thank Marilyn Bensman, David Bensman, Miriam Bensman, Rhea Bensman, and the Willmott Family Professorship at Williams College for supporting this project. Special thanks also to Peggy Weyers of Williams College and Jayne Smith of Newfound Press for outstanding technical assistance.

Creator and Disturber

Robert Jackall and Duffy Graham

In "Crime and Punishment in the Factory,"[1] Joseph Bensman and Israel Gerver analyze the use of a simple tool, the tap, in the wing-assembly unit of a military airplane manufacturing plant in 1953-54. The authors bring to life complex and contradictory social behavior across the factory floor and up the hierarchy of corporate management. In doing so, they elucidate the moral rules-in-use typical in bureaucracy, the central institution of our epoch.

The essay introduces the tap with a straightforward description. "The tap is a tool, an extremely hard screw, whose threads are slotted to allow for the disposal of the waste metal that it cuts away. It is sufficiently hard so that when it is inserted into a nut it can cut new threads over the original threads of the nut." Plainly, by design, the tap is a destructive tool.

But if recognizing the tool's inherent subversiveness raises the reader's eyebrows, then understanding its role in wing assembly triggers an alarm. Large-scale mass production of complex machines presents special challenges and, inevitably, is perfect only on paper. There is, for example, the problem of alignment of parts. "In wing-assembly work, bolts or screws must be inserted in recessed nuts, which are anchored to the wing in earlier processes of assembly.

The bolt or screw must pass through a wing plate before reaching the nut." These alignments between nuts and plate-openings can be off. Solutions to the problem of failed alignment include returning the wing plates to an earlier stage in the manufacturing process for adjustment or even returning to the drawing board for an entirely new design. Another solution lies in the tap. "When the nut is not aligned with the hole, the tap can be used to cut, at a new angle, new threads in the nut for the purpose of bringing the nut and bolt into a new but not true alignment. If the tap is not used and the bolt is forced, the wing plate itself may be bent." The solution achieved by the tap, however, deviates from design specifications. "On the basis of engineering standards true alignments are necessary at every stage in order to achieve maximum strength and a proper equilibrium of strains and stresses." The use of the tap, in other words, overrides design to achieve a tenuous, superficial, and dangerous solution. It compromises the structural integrity of the aircraft. It conceals defects. It also creates maintenance problems for another day. Moreover, it is grounds for termination of employment for individual workers and of business relationships for the company. It is, in short, a threat to the entire enterprise.

The authors are explicit: "The use of the tap is the most serious crime of workmanship conceivable in the plant." Officially, with obvious good reason, the tap is contraband, its use forbidden, its mere possession grounds for dismissal. Yet, the authors observe, wing-assembly workers widely, even routinely, use the tap. At least half of the workers in a position to use a tap have at least one in their toolbox.

The intellectual problem that arises from this paradox is, why and how does this airplane factory accommodate the use of the tap? Or, more generally, why and how does an organization accommodate criminal conduct?

The answer, Bensman and Gerver explain, is that production demands use of the tap and compels individuals and occupational groups within the factory to strike bargains amongst themselves to set the terms of its use. Factory work is classically segmented and layered, broken into parts vertically and horizontally. One part has no control over, and indeed little knowledge of, another. Each part focuses on its own task, not on the whole. At the apex, the factory's obligation to the military is to produce a certain number of airplanes at a certain rate according to certain specifications. At the bottom, individual workers have discrete, routine tasks. In between, for office managers, for plant managers, and not least for foremen on the plant floor directly in charge of groups of assembly-line workers, the obligation comes down to ensuring that fixed amounts of work get done in fixed amounts of time at predetermined costs, so that the product can come together in a timely way, each unit ready to forward finished work and to receive incoming work on schedule. This obligation takes the form of workload requirements, monitored by production charts. Failure to meet unblinkingly the constant demand of the production chart jeopardizes the factory's commitments to the military, the ability of other departments or units to meet their obligations on time, the standing of one's bosses, and one's own employment. This pressure is felt at every level in the factory and the business office. Accordingly, failed alignment poses a serious, material problem. To cope, experienced workers apprentice new workers in the use of the tap and, crucially, accompanying etiquette; foremen authorize workers to use the tap in coded, often nonverbal language; inspectors and workers choreograph their interactions to avoid confronting the problem—all while strictly maintaining the official, public condemnation of the tap. Breaches of these agreements are opportunities, never wasted, to censure publicly the use of the tap while covertly reestablishing the terms of the agreements. For the individual, these bargains constitute an ad hoc reconciliation of competing and contradictory demands: the tap is forbidden, but the tap is required; one must "get the work out" but also respect the rules of craftsmanship; one fosters collegial relationships, not least because of the protection they provide, or one insists on proper but inevitably contentious relationships with the risks these carry.

Thus, one engages in behavior that is officially criminal because it is essential to satisfy bureaucratic imperatives. Those affected accommodate this moral ambiguity through a series of specialized social transactions. These transactions are complex, provisional, subject at all times to renegotiation, and feature public and private dimensions involving "coercion, sanctions, genuine cooperation, and altruism," as well as ritual, ceremony, and the invocation of situational moral rules-in-use. So understood, use of the tap is not an act of rebellion, not a departure from norms, not "unethical"—and certainly not a crime. One does right by doing wrong. In this context, the crime is to refuse to act illegally, to refuse to use the tap according to rules agreed upon and worked out within the factory, to refuse to compromise.

"Crime and Punishment" is one of Joseph Bensman's earliest essays, first presented in 1955 and first published in revised form in 1963. It bears his trademark habits of mind:

- An analytical stance rooted in the work of Max Weber, fundamentally objective and dispassionate

- A vigilant awareness of the reach and vitality of bureaucracy in shaping individual character and consciousness as well as social behavior

- An ability to discern intellectual problems in superficially unremarkable phenomena and to penetrate face-value and made-for-public-consumption presentations of reality

- Faithfulness to empirical data, not to abstract preconceptions

- An elegance of thought, specifically in its accommodation rather than rejection of the messy reality, the fundamental chaos, of social behavior

- An appreciation of irony and of unintended consequences

- A sense of the connectedness of social behavior

When these habits of mind come together to analyze particular instances of social life, the result is electrifying. "Crime and Punishment" does not simply explain the use of an obscure tool or illuminate the workings of a factory in the mid-1950s. It transforms the reader's understanding of the world.

No small part of the enduring brilliance of "Crime and Punishment" is that it examines a subversive instrument to such subversive effect. Bensman and Gerver frame the essay as a comment on structural-functional theory, a sociological approach dominant in the mid-twentieth century and still in currency in various forms today. Briefly, the proponents of structural-functional theory argue that the social system consists of an interrelated set of structures that work together to produce a given social order or equilibrium. Individuals play prescribed roles that, taken together, function to further the social order of the system. The social system operates independently of interpersonal relationships, social improvisations, and individual consciousness.

Structural-functional theory is seductive in its tidiness. But, as Bensman and Gerver demonstrate, it ignores or distorts the social realities it purports to analyze. It disregards behavior that does not immediately function to create equilibrium, defining it as "deviant" or "dysfunctional." The authors establish that the use of the tap is deviant in the factory only in the most narrow, formal sense. Contrary to the public pronouncements of factory bosses, it is essential to factory operations, the only means to satisfy bureaucratized production goals. This analysis emerges from field data that Bensman collected in a year working in the airplane factory, not from the ungrounded definitions and abstract models that characterize structural-functional theory.

In this sense, "Crime and Punishment" becomes a critique of all theory that attempts to model the world based on a priori assumptions and definitions, instead of grappling with the ambiguities of the world itself. This critique is central to Bensman's intellectual work.

Joseph Bensman was born in 1922 to a Jewish immigrant peddler-turned-shoemaker father in Two Rivers, Wisconsin. He was the youngest of ten children. From his earliest years, he felt marginal and out of place, not least because of then-commonplace midwestern anti-Semitism, but also because he was simply brighter than the lower- and working-class boys he ran with. He read voraciously and quickly exhausted the local library. From his unlettered but sage father, Bensman internalized an abiding resentment against middle-class pretentiousness of any sort, a downright hostility toward "stuffed shirts" or businessmen on the make, guys with "knife-edged pressed pants, shined shoes, holes in the toes of socks, and dirty underwear."[2] He became a debater in high school and delighted in demolishing his opponents' arguments by virtue of his vast reading. After two years at a local junior college, he ended up at the University of Wisconsin at Madison where he met New York Jews and Hans Gerth. In the politically radical New Yorkers, he found his first intellectual community, though Bensman himself eschewed the communist ideologies that many in that circle embraced. Indeed, he became "an open enemy of the Communists," a stance reaffirmed in the 1950s as the truth of Stalin's slave-labor camps became known. In Gerth, Bensman found a great teacher, a man whose unique, idiosyncratic synthesis of Marx and Weber shaped an entire generation of sociologists.[3] Bensman's own deepest affinity was always for Weber's critique of bureaucracy, the profound significance of which only became clear to him during his service in the United States Army during the Second World War. Bensman coped with the total institutional regimen of army life by becoming a good soldier Švejk, complying "with every rule in such a way as to make a mockery of it."

Bensman returned to Madison after the war, wrote his master's thesis under Gerth,[4] and then went to New York City where he enrolled in the doctoral program at Columbia University. There, he worked as a research assistant for C. Wright Mills, an earlier Gerth protégé, although Bensman regarded Mills's work as shoddy sociology. He was unengaged with Columbia's sociology program and most of its professors, though he finished his course requirements in record time. But he became entranced with New York City's multiple artistic worlds. He haunted the city's galleries and museums, concert halls and dance spaces, and theaters on and off Broadway, developing a refined cultural eye and sensibility. After a two-year sojourn teaching at Syracuse University, he returned to New York where he landed a job at Voice of America (VOA) doing surveys of all sorts in the research division headed by Leo Lowenthal, a distinguished sociologist of literature. Here, the relentless sanitization of all internal documents to produce for employees a public face of organizational harmony—even as the VOA, like all bureaucracies, was riven with internecine rivalries—furthered Bensman's intense interest in propaganda and public relations that Gerth's teaching had prompted. The VOA job, like the Syracuse job before it, ended for budgetary reasons.

After a year's work as a mechanic in the airplane factory discussed earlier, Bensman had the opportunity to utilize the survey research know-how he had learned at VOA. He took a job in the research division of one of the many large advertising agencies in New York. The firm specialized in packaged-goods advertising. For ten long years, he figured out the target audiences for commodities like toothpaste, beer, toilet paper, pet food, tobacco, and cleaning materials. He also developed techniques to measure the effectiveness of the slogans and images that copywriters and art directors crafted to sell those goods. During this time, he hired as consultants many of his sociological colleagues, especially Arthur J. Vidich, to run focus groups. They discovered that consumers, when asked why they consumed particular products, often repeated verbatim advertising slogans, such as "Winston tastes good like a cigarette should."

Bensman considered his ten years in advertising to be meaningless work, and it took a great personal toll. He suffered an intense psychological crisis. But he worked his way out of that maelstrom by seizing the opportunity to write a cathartic essay about the peculiar occupational ethics of advertising work, published initially under a pseudonym.[5] That essay helped lead to his appointment as a professor at the City College of New York (CCNY). During this period, Bensman also did extensive consulting work for nascent "community action programs" where he got a firsthand look at the vast corruption and racialized ideologies that characterized President Lyndon Johnson's signature Great Society initiative. Bensman went on to become Distinguished Professor of Sociology at the Graduate

Center, City University of New York, and the formal and informal mentor of scores of young scholars, including one of the editors of this volume.[6]

Throughout his career, Bensman wrote regularly with colleagues. His most important collaborators were Arthur J. Vidich,[7] Robert Lilienfeld,[8] Bernard Rosenberg,[9] and Israel Gerver.[10] Like his mentor, Hans Gerth, Bensman thought out loud, developing his ideas in long conversations with these and other colleagues. Unlike Gerth, he then wrote out his work in longhand on legal-sized yellow pads, drafts that became the basis for further conversations and debates.[11]

Bensman's principal circle consisted mostly of New York Jewish intellectuals, many of them clustered around the democratic socialist, anticommunist journal *Dissent*.[12] The postwar generation of Jewish intellectuals and other professionals, against the backdrop of the Holocaust in Europe, was still struggling to find its way in the WASP-dominated institutional sectors of American society such as the banking and financial industries, the big corporations, the consulting businesses, the white-shoe law firms, advertising and public relations companies, the inner circles of government agencies, and colleges and universities. Bensman's generation's intellectual stance was therefore generally critical, sometimes sharp-edged, and often ethnocentric, the typical response of talented outsiders to clubby exclusiveness. Much more than most in his large network of friends, however, Bensman welcomed the company of gentile intellectuals, as evinced by his nearly half-century of friendship and collaboration with Arthur Vidich and his embrace of younger colleagues who posed challenging intellectual problems.

What mattered most to Bensman was unlocking the riddles of modernity. He thought that the keys to those riddles lay in the work of Max Weber. Like Weber, a main part of Bensman's own intellectual work revolves around bureaucracy, the quintessential organizational form of modernity. Bureaucracy organizes every institutional sector of modern societies: all industries and businesses; all but a few occupations and professions; all workplaces of any size; all governments, whether national, regional, or local; schools, from kindergartens to universities; religions, from sects to churches; police and all military forces; all health care and welfare; mass media and the vast apparatus of advocacy; and all of the visual and performing arts. Bureaucracy transforms the class structure of capitalist societies by eroding the dominance of the old independent middle classes and giving ascendancy to the new middle classes, the armies of salaried employees wholly dependent on large organizations. It shreds and remakes once-stable communities. It rationalizes almost every aspect of individuals' lives, including their most private experiences, and demands as the price of surviving and flourishing that individuals rationalize their own selves to conform to bureaucratic premiums. Bureaucracy splinters knowledge through endless specialization; it devalues substantive expertise and exalts interpretive expertise; it separates men and women from the consequences of their decisions and actions, fracturing ancient notions of moral economy. In eroding personal accountability for decisions, bureaucracy invites the kind of recklessness that regularly produces unforeseen and unintended consequences of action and, consequently, the concomitant public bewilderment that marks our times.

Bensman had a particular interest in how bureaucracy, in general, and bureaucratized occupations and professions, in particular, shape individuals' ethics—moral rules-in-use—and world images. The range of these studies of craft and consciousness (mostly, but not entirely, with Robert Lilienfeld) is remarkable: mechanics, admen, public relations specialists, social workers, urban planners, politicians, visual artists and performing artists, journalists, sportsmen, doctors and other medical practitioners, lawyers, and intellectuals—philosophers, theologians, historians, economists, psychologists, litterateurs, and, of course, sociologists.

* * *

Bensman saw the task of sociology, as variously conceptualized by Comte, Simmel, Durkheim, and Weber, to be the exploration of "the interrelatedness of [the] social, economic, political, psychological, cultural, [and] normative . . . attributes of human existence."[13] His choice of Weber as his master led him not only to the study of bureaucracy and rationalized work and consciousness, but also to a lifelong focus on social/economic class, class interests, ideologies, and conflicts, on status groups, and on both geographical and occupational communities, always approached from a historical and phenomenological standpoint and always through real-world data. One of his great strengths was the ability to frame intellectual problems with profound implications that could be addressed empirically. For Bensman, theory must not be determinative and must be grounded in and responsive to real-world social behavior.

That range, discipline, and art, already in short supply when Bensman died in 1986, has largely disappeared. Sociology today has all but lost touch with its fathers and with the profound historical questions about the nature of modernity that they proposed. The field lacks identity, intellectual rigor, and imagination. With important exceptions, current scholarship in the field and course offerings in undergraduate and graduate programs tend to elevate methodological issues and abstract theory, often undistinguishable from speculation, over substantive examinations of key institutions, such as law, the criminal justice system, religion, politics, the economy, the vast apparatus of advocacy, and the military. Ideological interests and outright advocacy have gained ascendancy over dispassionate analysis. In these respects, sociology today differs little from its sister disciplines of history and political science, or from the many newer programs, such as American Studies, Africana Studies, Latina/o Studies, Popular Culture Studies, and Gender and Sexuality Studies, now entrenched in higher learning. Such programs aim less at elucidating social life than at advancing special interests and garnering resources, often accompanied by demonstrations against some real, imagined, or invented "offense" that thrust whole campuses into frenzied bursts of religious-like zeal and self-righteous outrage that terrify administrators. Bensman witnessed the beginnings of such phenomena in the late 1960s at City College—developments that undermined that once-great institution. He predicted then that things would get worse.

Still, opportunity remains, as always. Bensman's existential response to the turmoil and drift of his own times was his work, some of the best of it republished in this volume. With Arthur Vidich, he argued:

> Only the individual scholar working alone—even in the midst of a bureaucratic setting—has the possibility to raise himself above the routine and mechanics of research. . . . The work of the individual scholar, no matter where he is located, and no matter how he is financed, organized, constrained, or aided, is perhaps the sole source of creativity.[14]

Bensman's work endures not just for its remarkable substance, but also for demonstrating how to be a sociologist.

Notes

1. "Crime and Punishment in the Factory," in this volume. The relevant materials in quotes here come from that essay.

2. This biographical sketch, complete with most of the phrases quoted, is drawn from Joseph Bensman, "The Sociologist on the Cutting Edge," in this volume.

3. See Joseph Bensman, Arthur J. Vidich, and Nobuko Gerth, eds., *Politics, Character, and Culture: Perspectives from Hans Gerth* (Westport, CT: Greenwood Press, 1982).

4. "Max Weber as a Social Psychologist: A Critical Study," University of Wisconsin, Madison, MA thesis in the Department of Sociology, 1947.

5. Ian Lewis, "The Advertising Man and His Work," in *The Human Shape of Work: Studies in the Sociology of Occupations*, ed. Peter L. Berger (New York: Macmillan, 1964), in this volume.

6. See Robert Jackall, *Moral Mazes: The World of Corporate Managers* (New York: Oxford University Press, 1988). Jackall dedicates the book to the memory of Joseph Bensman, as well as to two other mentors. Jackall notes at page ix: "As I began fieldwork for this book, I got to know Joseph Bensman. Our many conversations over the next few years were invaluable in helping me grasp and articulate my data. And even his last ravaging illness did nothing to deter his relentless editing."

7. Arthur J. Vidich was Professor of Sociology & Anthropology at the Graduate Faculty of Political and Social Science at the New School for Social Research. See Arthur J. Vidich and Joseph Bensman, *Small Town in Mass Society* (Princeton, NJ: Princeton University Press, 1958; rev. ed., 1968); Joseph Bensman and Arthur J. Vidich, *The*

New American Society: The Revolution of the Middle Class (Chicago: Quadrangle, 1971), as well as a great many cowritten essays, some in this volume. Bensman and Vidich also edited *Metropolitan Communities: New Forms of Urban Sub-communities* (New York: Franklin Watts, 1975); *Reflections on Community Studies,* with Maurice R. Stein (New York: Wiley, 1964); and *Politics, Character, and Culture: Perspectives from Hans Gerth*, with Nobuko Gerth (Westport, CT: Greenwood Press, 1982).

8. Robert Lilienfeld was Associate Professor of Sociology at the City College of New York. See Joseph Bensman and Robert Lilienfeld, *Craft and Consciousness: Occupational Technique and the Development of World Images* (New York: John Wiley and Sons, 1973; 2nd ed., New York: Aldine de Gruyter, 1991). See also Joseph Bensman and Robert Lilienfeld, *Between Public and Private: The Lost Boundaries of the Self* (New York: Free Press, 1979). Bensman and Lilienfield also wrote several important articles together. See, for instance, "Psychological Techniques and Role Relationships," *Psychoanalytic Review* 58 (1971), no. 4, and "Friendship and Alienation," *Psychology Today* 13 (October 1979).

9. Bernard Rosenberg was Distinguished Professor of Sociology at City College of New York and the City University Graduate Center. See Joseph Bensman and Bernard Rosenberg, *Mass, Class, and Bureaucracy: The Evolution of Contemporary Society* (Englewood Cliffs, NJ: Prentice-Hall, 1963), and Joseph Bensman and Bernard Rosenberg, eds., *Sociology: Introductory Readings in Mass, Class, and Bureaucracy* (New York: Praeger, 1975), as well as many essays, one of which is in this volume.

10. Israel Gerver was Associate Professor of Sociology at John Jay College of Criminal Justice, City University of New York. In addition

to "Crime and Punishment," he coauthored Bensman's first published essay, "Towards a Sociology of Expertness," a crucially important theoretical article, and "Art in the Mass Society." All of these essays are included in this volume.

11. According to a great many oral accounts, first recounted at the American Sociological Association meetings in Boston in 1978 shortly after Gerth's death, Gerth was first and foremost a teacher. Students gathered at his house near Madison on Friday nights. Gerth greeted them in the middle of a discourse that he had already begun. The discourse continued throughout the evening, through Saturday, and into Sunday, without interruption. The students departed exhausted on Sunday evening with Gerth still talking. Only C. Wright Mills was able to harness Gerth and get his insights down on paper. See Guy Oakes and Arthur J. Vidich, *Collaboration, Reputation, and Ethics in American Academic Life* (Urbana: University of Illinois Press, 1999).

12. *Dissent* began in 1954. Among its founders were Irving Howe, Lewis A. Coser, and Meyer Schapiro. Over the years, the editorial board included Daniel Bell, Marshall Berman, Paul Berman, Isaac Deutscher, Paul Goodman, Robert Heilbroner, Alfred Kazin, Deborah Meier, and Michael Walzer, among many other important Jewish, and occasionally gentile, intellectuals.

13. *Craft and Consciousness*, 147.

14. "The Springdale Case" in this volume.

Autobiographical Essay

The Sociologist on the Cutting Edge

Joseph Bensman

I'm the son of a shoemaker who spent sixty years in middle America, never really learning English but conducting his business exclusively with a non-Jewish clientele by communicating with an idiosyncratic assortment of words and gestures. He came to New York in 1900 and worked a year in garment shops. Some *landsleit* (immigrants from the same community) were located in Sheboygan, Wisconsin; he saved enough money to move there and then became a peddler. He traveled in the outskirts of Sheboygan, selling and sometimes exchanging fruit for junk. He came to Two Rivers (where I was born in 1922) and discovered a town with no shoemaker! He went back to Sheboygan and bought shoemaking equipment. The salesman ostensibly taught him how to repair shoes. He could be called a religious man; however, he worked on Saturdays. He drove to Sheboygan for the holidays. He existed in spite (or because) of almost no contact with the town, a man who got along with his customers but, underneath, harbored real resentment against "beer-drinking and time-wasting goyim."

Published originally in a slightly different form in *Creators and Disturbers: Reminiscences by Jewish Intellectuals of New York*, drawn from conversations with Bernard Rosenberg and Ernest Goldstein (New York: Columbia University Press, 1982), 368-87. Republished in print format by permission from Columbia University Press. Republished in digital format by permission from Deena Rosenberg Harburg.

I was the youngest of ten children living in a house my father would not relinquish in the thirties so that we could qualify for relief like most of our neighbors. He wanted the welfare, but evidently wanted even more to keep the house. Whenever I wandered beyond its immediate confines, and at least through high school, I continuously experienced anti-Semitism in ways that I suspect the New Yorker can't imagine. I had no supporting group for me in my Jewishness. So I was a kike and a Christ-killer. My nickname was Yosky—their distortion of Yaseha, which my mother called me. From four through twelve, I belonged to delinquent gangs whose activity ranged from raiding gardens to breaking and entering railroad cars and stealing aluminum and other metals. At one point, we were as close to the reformatory as you can get without actually being thrown into one. Yet I was always marginal, never wholly accepted, *in* but not *of* the group. I was the gang's "intellectual." If they needed me to figure out a way of planning a break-in, I was good for that.

I lived in a working-class neighborhood. In school, I met middle-class kids. My brothers and sisters taught me how to read before I went to school, and, from kindergarten on, my nose was always in a book. There was no cultural or educational tradition in the family, although they had the notion that if I turned out to be smart they'd *shep nachas* (gain prestige) from it. My bookishness did not exactly endear me to the neighborhood kids. I remember one stealing my hat and then beating the hell out of me because I was a lousy kike. At least, that was the reason he gave. In one case around 1937, my assailant was a German kid. One of the parents of my best friend was a Bohemian who, whenever he got drunk, would call me a Christ-killer. I surely knew that I was Jewish.

I went to *cheder* for a while but did not get bar mitzvahed. Attending the *cheder* cost fifty cents a day—and in my eleventh year, we couldn't afford that sum. The family lived on fish and potatoes. Two Rivers was a fishing town, and we grew our own potatoes.

I kept reading away, cultivating my father's kind of resentment, which I directed at middle-class kids who comprised the gangs our gang fought. Within a working-class gang, one developed class consciousness, particularly in the form of hostility toward well-mannered snobs. I suppose I always resented kids whose stock-in-trade was manners, poise, and a feeling that they owned the world. From the age of four on, I knew I was smarter than most of those kids, but I simply could not discover a sensible basis for their self-confidence, the poise and the manners that allowed them to think they could push everyone else around. I must have been thirty-five before I realized that they were just as nutty as I was, but covered themselves with a facade of manners I had not been able to penetrate.

By the time I reached seventh grade, I was half-mockingly called "the professor" by my classmates. Since I had emerged from a lower-class environment, I became a hero of working-class kids. I could put down the middle and upper class just by virtue of my vocabulary. In eighth grade, I had committed the minor offense of throwing a pen at a pupil's foot and missing it by half an inch. The teacher was so shocked at this that she made me memorize the Constitution. As a result, I recited the Preamble in class and thus became a boy orator. This thrust me into a political and social science tradition I had not previously known to exist. I went out for debate and for extemporary speaking, which made me a big *macher* (big shot) in the high school. I depleted the city and the school libraries. Their books enchanted me much more than homework. I did well, I think, as an act of defiance against the system.

When I became a boy orator, my picture began appearing in the local press, and with that, I got hints of recognition at home. The habit of my family was, and my habit also is, never to let the other person know that you're impressed. So I was teased and put down for my accomplishments, but even in that act I recognized that they were praising me.

I learned at an early age that my father had a brilliant mind with absolutely no possibility of using it in his American ambience. He was far more original than any of the teachers I had. Once when we were debating the issue of unicameral legislatures in state governments, he asked me about it. It was clear that he didn't know these words. I spent twenty minutes telling him what we were debating. It was totally outside his experience. Just the same, in his broken amalgam of languages, he remarked, "Well, when you got legislators in two houses of different size, in the large one you can get local interests represented that you couldn't get in the small one." Now, that was brilliant. We had batted this problem around for six months, and in minutes, he presented a stronger case than any of us could formulate.

But my father's greatest influence on me consisted of his resentment of the stuffed shirts and middle-class "respectables." On one memorable occasion, he talked about a peddler who was the cantor, the most religious man in *shul*. This peddler had a son who owned the local pool hall. He described the son as a typical greenhorn: a man with a five-cent cigar, knife-edged pressed pants, shined shoes, holes in the toes of socks, and dirty underwear. His total image of society lay in that description. He was sure that anybody who made two thousand dollars more than he did had to be a *gonif* (thief). I think I internalized his whole attitude, and that it's as good a basis for sociology as any.

My father was an honest artisan. His ambition for me was to be a tailor and to earn a respectable living in the local tailoring shop. Of course, I had no interest in it. I was a high-flying debater, who had been reading at such a high level that what to do next was altogether unclear.

While I was a senior in high school, I thought I might become a village freak, the kind of small-town intellectual at whom everyone else laughs and jeers. That year, I joined the community discussion club. We were then debating the third term for Franklin Roosevelt. I was pitted against the vice president of Hamilton Manufacturing Company—the Vice President of Public Relations—a very smooth guy who made all the firm's speeches. Everyone there—whether banker, lawyer, or businessman—thought that Roosevelt was either insane or a Communist. I was well prepared, making an innocent historical speech in which I concluded that Roosevelt had to be elected *because* he was antibusiness. In the question period, I cited numbers, statistics, laws, legislation. I had more evidence than anyone present. To me, it was exhilarating because here I was fighting the whole goddamn establishment. Also, I knew that in the very act of winning, I was done for in Two Rivers. There were maybe half a dozen people there who, although they would not publicly support my argument, congratulated me after the meeting. They would help me get to college, to make something of myself, but would take no risks themselves. This group understood that I did not fit in either the upper- or lower-class life of a small town.

My family as a whole and each member individually had the same problem that I did in matters of sociability. I certainly didn't focus on my Jewishness. I went away from it, to escape it. For instance, I was an honorary Rotarian, which meant that for four weeks I'd go to Rotary meetings. There again, I'd get into political arguments with businessmen. Intellectually, I overcame them, but at all other levels I was still a kike. For example, along with everyone else, they served me a pork dish. I didn't mind eating pork. We were kosher at home, but I ate crabs and bullheads with my friends when we caught our own fish. When they served me pork, I started to eat it. This was the first time I ever had pork as part of a prepared meal. Then these people remembered that I was Jewish. They embarrassed me by ordering something else for me that was equally *tref* (nonkosher). I was humiliated not because they served me pork, but because they reminded me of its religious significance.

That kind of thing happened all the time. The junior college at Manitowoc, which was all of seven miles away, propelled me into the midst of a whole new population. There, my academic accomplishments might have pulled me in the direction of being acceptable in Manitowoc polite society. I was president of the class in my second year and was invited to join the De Molay Society, which, however, struck me as being a *goyishe zach* (a gentile thing). For me, being middle class and being gentile was the same thing. But in those two years, I got some validation of the fact that I was a smart kid. Maybe I needed it. I went to the University of Wisconsin at Madison for my junior and senior years. There, for the first time, I met New York Jews.

Three days after my arrival at university, I was sitting at the Rathskeller when I encountered the Communists—the YCL (Young Communist League) of the University of Wisconsin. Now, I had read Marx. I knew a hell of a lot about revolutionary socialism, but I had never met a Communist, and meeting the real living species did interest me. At that time, the party line was Yalta-Teheran coprosperity. They immediately wanted me to attend the YCL convention. I wanted to talk to them about how their gathering related to Marx and Engels and revolution. But they didn't want such talk; hence, I didn't want to go. I never did get involved with them. But for the first time in my life, I had dealings with an "intellectual" community, and it happened to be pretty heavily Jewish. My qualifications for entry into that community dated at least to high school. But I was all alone until this experience produced contact with an organized group.

At the same time, through a high-school friend from Two Rivers, I joined a YMCA discussion group. The next year, I was put in charge of the group and met another guy who became my roommate. He had a City College BA and was doing his graduate work at Wisconsin. This fellow had been a Trotskyist and was a strong anticommunist. By my senior year, I too was an open enemy of the Communists, joining the ideological war against them. In that same year, I became a protégé of Hans Gerth, a non-Jewish German refugee.

The student-stimulated culture was dominated, like its politics, by Jewish students from New York. I found hostility to the New York Jews almost everywhere for exactly the same reason that I provoked it: bad manners, argumentativeness, being too smart and too radical. They populated a separate world within the undergraduate universe. It was a world of unspecialized intellectuals who avoided narrow academics and concentrated on politics. The New Yorkers made me feel my own limitations. They had theirs, too, but within a context of sophistication, practice, and intellectual competition. I had learned mainly from books, they more from their social milieu.

I knew Marilyn, my wife-to-be, as the friend of a friend at Wisconsin. But after I'd been drafted into the army and came back on a furlough, we had a whirlwind courtship, a war romance. Then I went back to the army, started writing letters, and proposed by mail. Most of the girls I knew represented the eastern radical type. Marilyn was a stunning girl with qualities rather different from those we thought of as eastern and radical. She was athletic, enthusiastic, an outdoors girl, danced well, and was also an egghead.

I supported the war, not just as a Jew but out of hatred for Hitler. We knew about *Kristallnacht* and concentration camps but not about death factories. As a G.I., I wasn't going to take shit from anybody. So, when I had a civilian teacher in the army school who was anti-Semitic, anti-Roosevelt, and antiwar, I denounced him for propagandizing in class and had him put on the carpet. When another guy sounded off with anti-Semitic remarks, I shut him up by saying, "You could get a Section 8 for that." I was a fighter, but not a monomaniac. Lots of personal abuse was built into the system. I understood that, but I also realized that anti-Semitism was illegal.

I had a dream after three weeks of basic training, a magnificent full-color dream in which I was an executioner chopping the heads off all my friends. I, the executioner, was doing this with military precision, discipline, and detachment. I woke up in a sweat and decided: that's enough of this army shit. From then on, I became a kind of special goof-off; that is, I complied with every rule in such a way as to make a mockery of it. In little symbolic acts, I was sabotaging military chickenshit—and getting away with it. A couple of times, people tried to punish me, and I immediately asked for their court-martial because by then I had developed a defense that is part of my permanent character. Basically, it consists of a vast, formal respect for the rules. You do everything legally, you even overdo it, and the more you comply, the more you defy the establishment. I still do that all the time. I use legalism as a means of survival. I perfected my technique in the army. I was frightened by the whole goddamn system. I had read Max Weber on bureaucracy, but I didn't thoroughly understand it until I experienced army life with its mindless precision and caste privilege. After my military experience, I was ready to become a revolutionary.

It never happened. Almost as certainly, my intensive reading of Max Weber made me an antirevolutionary. Bureaucracy, not socialism or capitalism, was the problem. In this sense, I took Weber more seriously than Gerth did. He was a Marxist-Weberian, and I responded to those aspects of Weber that are antiestablishment and antibureaucratic, whether capitalist or socialist. The army is not private enterprise. And what did I see? Stupidity, anti-Semitism, ignorance, and a more-than-incipient form of bureaucratic totalitarianism. I said to myself, "If this is a form of socialism, then socialism is no solution." The lesson I drew is that specific policies, not formed structures, are crucial. The problem wasn't solved by capitalism, and it could be turned into a greater disaster by socialism. The Russians had developed a kind of socialism, and it exhibited every imaginable disease.

And then there was National Socialism, which was not socialism at all but an abomination, an unmitigated evil, an assault on civilization itself. I was aware of the Nuremberg laws from the time of their passage as well as the major events leading up to World War II. But I found the imminence of European war uppermost in my mind. Erich Fromm's *Escape from Freedom* was a very important book for me. Fromm asked, How is it that the most civilized nation on earth could become the most brutal nation? He offered a partial answer, and his question is still important, but in 1942, it was a major concern to me. Anyhow, my interest was focused more on the Germans than the Jews. And with that interest, one expected the worst.

When information on death camps became available, during the war and afterwards, we were appalled, depressed, shocked, and silenced. In its direct and immediate impact, the Holocaust was overwhelming. I had friends who were among the first American soldiers to visit those camps, and after the war, they told us as much as they could. But what they had seen at close range was almost too horrifying to talk about. And yet this obscene culmination was more or less what I had been led to expect. Precisely because somewhere in my mind I had half expected it, I was partly insulated from the shock, the sheer horror of it. But the slave labor camps in Russia took us by surprise. As early as 1936, we had read Ilin's book called *The New Russian Primer*, which described the Russian Constitution as similar to the US Constitution. It carried the promise of liberation and redemption, but turned out to be no more than salesmanship for a document that never got more than lip service.

I had read about the show trials and had become very much of an anti-Stalinist. And yet knowing all about them and Stalin's awful purges and the dispossession of the so-called kulaks, one never expected the death of millions. So when, beginning in 1952, we were exposed to incontrovertible data on Soviet slave labor camps, I was particularly horrified. At some perhaps half-conscious level, one expected Hitler's death camps but not Stalin's massive slave labor camps.

I came back to Wisconsin after the war, completed an MA, and entered Columbia for my PhD. I was a rebel at Columbia, detached from most of the teachers, and only a little closer to C. Wright Mills, who had also been a protégé of Gerth. But I did some work for him, we kidded around, and I generally confirmed my view that he was as shoddy a Marxist as he was a Weberian.

Columbia meant less to me than just being in New York. There, I felt I was *in the world* and that Wisconsin had been hopelessly parochial. I could now enjoy a continuous rediscovery of dance and all the other arts. In Wisconsin, I had known music and painting; I learned literature. I was not altogether unprepared for the riches New York City had to offer. But they were different in kind from the hothouse exposure available on a midwestern university campus. I frequented museums and galleries and concert halls—and I reveled in the absence of any self-consciousness about it. This was different from Wisconsin, where you went to a concert, a gallery, or a show feeling that it was something very special indeed. I used to go to first-night showings at Madison dressed like a bum, unshaven and seedy in old clothes. In New York, I didn't feel the need for striking such poses. What's unique about New York is that you don't have to take a bath just to participate in the arts, even as a spectator.

Yet it didn't take me too long to discover the kind of salon character of much intellectual life in the city. The underside of all that I admired was filled with personal politics, factionalism, intrigues among cultural and intellectual circles and elites. This reality has kept me marginal to most intellectual, academic, and aesthetic communities. They always make me acutely uncomfortable.

I finished the course requirements at Columbia; then, I taught at the University of Syracuse for two years. There, I collided with the academic gentility and parochialism that always make me squirm. I was back in the hothouse. From Syracuse, it took four and a half hours by car to reach New York, where we went as often as we could. We had no extra money, which made it all the more like suffocating in the sticks. Now, *I'm* from the sticks, but after one year in New York, I had the sense that anywhere else was the sticks. In my mind, the sticks came to mean those places in which lace-curtainism predominated. Syracuse was such a place.

After I lost my job in Syracuse, I went back to New York, took six months on the G.I. Bill of Rights, and did nothing much, though supposedly I was working on my thesis. Finally, I got a job at the Voice of America through a college friend who had been Leo Lowenthal's secretary in the Institute of Social Research. By dropping Leo's name to the personnel manager, who was three steps below Leo, I got hired. I worked primarily through people who had been in the

Bureau of Applied Social Research. When I was at Columbia, these people seemed to me to be "soap salesmen," survey market researchers. But I was hired at the Voice to learn the techniques of survey research, which I did, and to work with dopes at the higher levels. This judgment did not apply to Lowenthal: I admired his academic work, particularly his book on the sociology of literature.

Once, I attended a meeting between the heads of our department and those of the Russian bureau of the Voice. I knew the meeting had political overtones; they were jockeying and struggling for position. My job was to write the minutes, designed to help us learn about the larger organization. I wrote a nearly exact summary of the meeting, perhaps heightening the differences and the issues somewhat. It turned out to be a nice sociological document, which was the last thing they wanted. The governing "ethic" was that no one could edit our work without our approval. Another person, two grades higher, was given the job of editing my work, but had to get my okay on it. She took out all of the sharp angles, the conflicts, the differences. I more or less sadistically forced her to explain every change. She sympathized with me, but had her job to do, and she conscientiously performed it. Then, my minutes were moved to a higher level where even more conflicts were removed; the final report was love and roses, consensus, cooperation, and positive accomplishment. I made stabs at bureaucratic sabotage like this one, which, however, had no consequence at all—except to feed my sense of righteousness.

After a budgetary reduction in force, I went to work in an aircraft factory whose environment was anything but strange to me. I'd previously had my share of experiences inside such places. The brutality, the noise, and the playful aggression were familiar enough. I certainly didn't like being there, but I had to make a living, and I had the skills to do it as a result of my army experience. I was there one year, until a layoff.

I then went through "the snowball phase" of job seeking. People would refer me from one place to another place to another. At last, I heard of a job in an advertising agency. I had an interview with a vice president, who reviewed my considerable research experience, while I faked even more. I got the job. In this agency, I was the third Jew they had ever hired. All were employed in the research department. No doubt, we made it as highly trained technicians with a special mystique imputed to us. During my interview, the VP had asked me what kind of work I was doing. "The phenomenology of industrial administration." My interviewer was a PhD in psychology who had never heard the word *phenomenology*. He asked me what it was. I told him that it pertained to the qualities of meaning associated with administration. "Well, does it have any application to advertising?" I modestly replied that I didn't know advertising so well, but would venture to say that all of it had qualities of meaning susceptible to phenomenological inquiry. Hence my second- and thirdhand encounters with the philosophy of Alfred Schutz got me into advertising just as motivational research was sweeping the field. Of course, phenomenology and motivation are not the same thing, but my interviewer didn't know that. His definition of the job I was seeking was that of a psychologist. So I had to use projective testing without ever having studied it. I couldn't wait, with an imminent deadline, to get the standard tests. I "invented" dozens of techniques that already existed, deducing what they must be from shoptalk with friends and peers in other agencies. They all worked better than the standard tests because, lacking the standard tests, I made up new ones to fit the specific problem.

About Jews in advertising: this is a big topic. Briefly: Ad agencies were willing to hire Jews in possession of certain techniques, which by the accident of postwar training, they had. Those techniques were most important to account executives for whom the major problem was and is self-presentation—in other words, how to deal with and sell ideas to WASP businessmen. It must have been 1964, just as I was leaving, when our agency got its first admittedly Jewish account executive. (We were fairly sure another one had been passing as a gentile.) Catholics preceded Jews in top spots by about ten years. We didn't have any Jewish clients, primarily because we dealt only with giant monopolies such as Colgate, Ballantine, and Reynolds Tobacco.

My boss was a five-foot-two tyrant who demanded total subservience and who, as soon as he got it, treated you like dirt. I was constitutionally incapable of being subservient. As with Leo, I treated him like an equal. The difference was that I got the advertising boss out of jams. We worked well together at an official level. He was a good salesman, and I was a good technician. As far as he was concerned, my work was good, but the one thing I would not do was give him deference. And the one thing he had to have was deference. My personal style was not to be hostile, but to be friendly and equal, which he found insufferable. Whenever I made a mistake, my boss, a former colonel, would try to court-martial me. Whenever he made a mistake, I'd remind him of it in a very gentle, pleasant way. We had this battle of wills for ten years. Meanwhile, I got raises, making it hard to leave.

There comes a time when, just on the basis of your salary, you are constrained to take your work seriously, and for me—in advertising—that was impossible. I was expected to act as if our business made sense, and I had something like a breakdown. It came in my tenth year as an adman. Then, when Peter Berger decided to edit a book in the field of occupational sociology, he asked me for an essay on advertising. I delayed doing that essay for about six months. It meant summing up and winding up a whole decade of experience. I was close to 100 percent in the company's profit-sharing plan, after which there would be no unusual premium for staying on. Came the breakdown. During that period, I went briefly into psychoanalysis, but I started writing my essay, which assesses advertising primarily as work with its own peculiar form of ethics. I had an absolutely wonderful, mad, euphoric time writing it. The essay lent an air of finality to one long chapter in my life.

* * *

Then came an offer from CCNY, which I welcomed because it meant liberation from the madness of Madison Avenue. I no longer had a crazy boss, nor was I under constant pressure to produce immediate results. Teaching was easy, even with the full load—twelve hours, four nights a week. For two days a week, I worked as a consultant and wrote a great deal, including half a dozen books and more articles than I can remember. I didn't think too much of City College, but I wasn't required to think too much of it. In my time, the college wasn't a great place that went downhill. It was a crummy place that went downhill. As of, say, 1960-65, one could have said the students were better than the faculty. This would have been even more the case around 1950. After '65, however, the faculty became better than the students, but not because the faculty improved.

In California, where the student rebellion began, the students may originally have had some legitimate grievances. But there and every place else, as soon as the "revolution" erupted, faculty jumped in, first to lead and control it, and then to redramatize their youth. Once these people were rejected by the students as being too old, too ideological, conservative, and dominant, *they* rejected the students. It's important to remember that the students first rejected them. Where I taught, the basic demands were those of the blacks to make City College into *Harlem University*, a term the revolutionaries used. But let me emphasize the point that just as soon as the student rebellion became a national or an international affair, somewhere between '66 and '67, the faculty made it their revolution. Once that happened, professors organized students for their own rebellion. At City, by 1968, we had faculty caucuses whose avowed purpose was to take over the college. Their first objective was to "get" the president. Later on, students were organized partly by the faculty and partly by radical youth organizers. Some faculty members felt that the student rebellion was the wave of the future and that they needed to be brokers mediating between the past and the present by becoming leaders of the institution and of a new society. Many were instant radicals.

At the Graduate Center (citywide headquarters for PhD programs), there were grantsmen who had worked indirectly for the CIA and the military services who, up to that point, had been apolitical. Such people became spokesmen for the student radicals and for the wave of the future. Gutlessness was their common characteristic. These men and women felt sure they were going to be the winners. They jumped on the bandwagon. But, being lousy social scientists, they jumped on the wrong one. Some used it for the sake of promotion, others for tenure or for keeping their jobs. They organized little mobs of students, to use directly and indirectly as a physical threat to other professors. And so we had, in the two institutions that I know directly and in the half dozen I know indirectly, a kind of terrorism practiced by gangs of students sometimes standing outside or in a room next to which a faculty meeting was being held for the purpose of making academic decisions. They were there in order to intimidate the professors.

At City College, demands for open admission, for special black and Spanish ethnic orientation programs exceeded all others. In 1969 or thereabouts, President Gallagher announced a plan for open enrollment that would take five years to implement, bit by bit. The youth rebellion came after the announcement of that plan, by those who expressed impatience over Gallagher's gradualism. In talking to kids after it was all over. I learned that the black caucus was composed of less than a dozen blacks. There was also a white caucus that joined with the black caucus; it was made up of a couple of faculty members and a few students. A white faculty radical would negotiate with the black caucus and present demands to the president and to other faculty as a spokesman for the blacks. His students were almost all white. In addition, another faculty caucus was formed about a year and a half before the outbreak. In this one, there were white radical professors not particularly geared to the black issue who wanted to make City College "relevant." They were out to get Gallagher, who himself had been generally recognized as a good friend of the blacks at City, a pacifist, a liberal who had headed a Negro college in the South. In our department, seven or eight radical professors helped organize student terror. I responded primarily to the terror, real and implied, not to the issue of open enrollment, or black versus white, but simply the threats, the indecency, the lying, and the cheating.

What first shocked me was the mendacity. One guy wanted to negotiate with me. Not that I was in any official position to negotiate with him, but he thought I had influence. Every time he told me anything, it was a lie. I have some instinctive caution or chronic inability to believe unclever lies. So I checked everything he said and found I was being fed a bunch of lies, all in connection with political reorganization of the university. I was offended. The clumsiness of these lies was a blow to my pride. There was also something else. You could sit in a class and listen to a lecture by an activist who had just been radicalized and patently didn't know what he was talking about. He was teaching but hadn't had time to do the necessary reading. Now, I know the material, and my mind is not completely closed to all aspects of Marxism, but it does offend me that young men should passionately preach its problematic tenets without even having done their homework.

Neither was I opposed in principle to open enrollment. I came from a university that provided open enrollment, and I thought it was great. The Wisconsin system allowed anybody to enter the university, but did so without lowering standards. Fifty percent of the freshman class flunked out by midterm. This was open enrollment *with* academic standards. Anybody could enter. Not everybody *did*; but anybody *could*. That's open enrollment. It doesn't mean you have to kidnap people who sorely need remediation and guarantee them college degrees after a four-year period, when they'll need just as much remediation. As it turned out, open enrollment at City College was an immediate boon to the white ethnics. I sensed that it would not be that much of a boon to the blacks, and it never was.

Just before the explosion at CCNY, I had been doing work at Bedford-Stuyvesant on the value of college-bound programs. What we found by analyzing all students in high school was that 50 percent of the black junior class dropped out in the eleventh grade, and 50 percent dropped out in the twelfth grade. So, if open enrollment applied to high-school *graduates*, it wouldn't affect the blacks very much, but it would affect white ethnics. Without something like SEEK (a large-scale remedial program) as a means of qualifying blacks for the equivalent of a high-school diploma, open enrollment wouldn't work to their advantage. Yet City College could not continue to operate as it had in the past for too much longer, partly because as Jews moved up the middle-class ladder their children went to private schools, ideally to Harvard. For them, Harvard became the City College of the seventies.

The next several years at City College were a total disaster. One problem had been the spirit that animated its new students who on account of the hubbub were dragooned into college whether or not they wanted to go. College admission was redefined as a right, and that right existed apart from motivation and qualification. Some students were pushed into college to validate the principle of open enrollment. I would guess that most students did not know why they were there or, once there, what they ought to be doing. The clear, if unstated, demand they made was, "Entertain us. We are here to enjoy our rights." They did not recognize that a certain amount of work might be incumbent upon them. They were not aware of what a college is. Combined with a high degree of militancy, the product is a witch's brew, expressed as follows: "If I'm not getting anything out of this, *you're* doing something wrong." If a teacher says, "You ought to do some reading," or, "You ought to learn to read and to write," he's making an unconscionable demand. So that happened, and a hell of a lot of faculty members were miserable, while "teaching" was turned into a euphemism. Yet I try to find in each class students I can inspire to do some real work and who can learn from that work. I'm not too successful, though I think of myself as a good teacher, in the role of a Shakespearian actor in the Borscht Belt.

I would say that, strangely enough, all of these issues of nine or ten years ago are present right now, beneath the surface. We're still fighting them out. Everybody who participated in the youth revolution on any side is in some way marked for life. At a very subdued and subtle level, the same issues are always being fought. They constitute the battle against inequality, privilege, and exploitation, where there is never a final victory. If you win on one issue, that victory will perhaps produce a new elite that has to be fought again; there is no final resolution. Thus, mine has become a pragmatic approach. I believe that there is no end to the struggle, no utopian final solution, whether that of Hitler or that of Stalin. This means that I'm certainly not likely to be taken in by any radical solution that will solve all problems in one act or by a conservative acceptance of things as they are, which says there is nothing to struggle for.

I was disgusted with those of my colleagues who yielded to short-term pressures for a final solution. In business, you don't expect too much of people, because they have to survive economically; no one professes to do much more than jobs that are presumably designed to increase profits. In the academic world, where higher ideals are emphasized, everybody proclaims them. Once you receive tenure, all you have to do is work along the lines of your self-determined scholarly or academic interest. You're largely free to pursue your own demons. The university, which has greater institutional freedom, might allow one to be an honest man, yet the percentage of honest men in academic life is no greater than anywhere else. Therefore, it's more disenchanting to see crooks, charlatans, operators, and goof-offs in a university than it is to see them in advertising or in any other field. The contemporary college is becoming a sewer, and I would guess most of the faculty have lost even the ability to look above water level. So they mostly seek petty favors and little means of surviving. They may be desperate, but they find a way to dissolve their desperation by beating the system to get out of a course or brownnosing somebody into a promotion. There is a kind of creeping mediocrity so embedded in my college that if I spend more than four hours there at a time I get nauseous. I also get nauseous at those people who know better and let things slide because to act on their knowledge might offend someone.

There are worse things I could be doing, but are there worse things that could be happening to the university? It ain't gonna get better—it'll get worse. Today, it's not only a financial crush; I think this kind of creeping desperation, creeping madness, is cumulative. We've had a president who would reform the world from City College, a sycophantic administration, and a faculty that has adjusted itself perfectly to madness by complacency or by developing countermadness, which is just as bad. It still doesn't mean everyone has to go mad.

At City College, the issues were not primarily nor even largely focused on anti-Semitism. There were, of course, some anti-Semitic graffiti in the toilets, and some black militants have charged that white Jewish professors repressed and discriminated against the black masses and students. There were charges of Jewish elitism. But many of the radicals were Jews. And some of *them* were anti-Semitic.

I don't think I responded to these issues as a Jew. I have never been religious. I do not very often think of myself self-consciously as a Jew, although I am reminded, and all my life have been reminded, that I am a Jew. I cannot escape—and I do not attempt to escape—my Jewish identity. At the same time, the marginality that I have unfailingly experienced, and in which I exult, is partly based on being a Jew and partly based on a lower middle-class background that makes it impossible for me to accept middle-, upper- and, even lower-class things as they are. Nor am I any more receptive to the cant and clichés that justify things as they are. But there is still the experience of being a Jewish ethnic. There is an experience of some kind of Jewish elitism. That is, I can identify with Jews as intellectual disturbers and creators. I accept that, I suppose, primarily because we have all been brainwashed into that position and we've all been victims of our Jewish ethnicity. But this state of affairs is inherent in the Jewish tradition. Georg Simmel could only have had European Jews in mind when he introduced the concept of marginality. We are still wandering Jews in the Diaspora, still in exile, even in America and even in the Middle East.

In 1973, I took my first trip to Israel, which sharpened some ethnic pride and brought old fears to the surface. The pride is in what the Israelis have accomplished while turning a desert into a garden. I've been in other arid areas—southern Yugoslavia, Egypt, and North Africa—and seen forbidding physical environments. I can well imagine what the Israeli pioneers did with their own work, their massive effort, the self-exploitation and the exploitation of world Jewry. Even their will to survive makes me proud.

The fear I share with all Jews is that Israel may not survive. But, here again, any civilization may collapse, from without or from within. In Israel, the dangers are external. In the United States, the dangers are internal, as they were prior to Hitler's Germany and prior to Soviet Russia. The totalitarian states of the left and the right are evidence of this descent into barbarism. The possibility of barbarism and brutalization lies deep in the human psyche, as Freud and Marx have separately taught us. But the pressures that turn that potentiality into an empirical reality are economic, political, and social.

And there's still the problem that for me will always be symbolized by National Socialism. It is easier to understand Hitler than it is to understand the acceptance of Hitler by a plurality of the German people. It is above all the combination of madness, opportunism, and gutlessness that troubles me. Wherever turmoil exists, that combination is deadly. We are always living on the edge of barbarism, brutality, and madness. In Israel, the edge is external. In most countries, it is internal. Of course, Israel has its share of corruption and crime, plus a host of other problems. But the accomplishment remains, and this has given me some sense of Jewish identity.

I am not committed to Israel in any one-dimensional way. I'm committed to this country, at least in the sense that only its stupidities can make me really angry. I'm committed to my work, though I'm critical of my profession; I'm committed to my friends and to the universalism of Western culture and to an intellectual tradition that I see being sold out every day by its practitioners.

In all of these crisscrossing and contradictory traditions, I'm a marginal man who accepts his position. But this acceptance may be the decisive component of my Jewish identity.

PART I

Bureaucracy

1

The Meaning of Work in Bureaucratic Society

Joseph Bensman with Bernard Rosenberg

Conflicts between Bureaucratic Roles and the Personal Needs of the Official

Bureaucracy is designed only as a technical system of administration. In practice, it is much more than that. This difficulty constitutes an inherent cause of organizational problems such as those that are bound to plague bureaucrats everywhere. To the official himself, the bureaucracy is a whole way of life, no less exacting than other ways of life. It makes sharp demands, it imposes rigid codes and stringent standards, and it places a special kind of stress upon him as a *total* individual.

To play his role as a bureaucrat at all adequately is to pay a heavy social and psychological price. The official has to repress certain prebureaucratic sentiments that may have been instilled in him as a youth, and he will invariably be forced to reject or neglect nonoccupational roles that are more continuous with his self than with his profession. When those sentiments and roles having no connection with his job are very meaningful to him, the official becomes less of a bureaucrat; on the other hand, if his bureaucratic role has been

---

Published originally in a slightly different form in Maurice Stein, Arthur J. Vidich, and David Manning White, eds., *Identity and Anxiety: Survival of the Person in Mass Society* (Glencoe, IL: Free Press, 1960), 181-97. Republished by permission from Maurice R. Stein and Joseph Vidich.

deeply internalized, he will be anxious and unhappy about subordinating it to other things. He can attempt to stabilize the conflicting values and roles within himself or deliberately pick and choose among them. When this occurs, bureaucracy may be said to have changed the personality of its officials, and when a large number of officials are affected, it also modifies the dominant character structure of the society.

We will discuss briefly some conflicts generated by the fulfillment of bureaucratic roles, as well as their impact upon the bureaucrat and bureaucracy.

Compulsive Sociability in Bureaucracy

A large number of bureaucrats (scientists, accountants, and other pure technicians) are pure "pencil pushers," men more oriented to abstract symbols than to colleagues or clients. However, by far the majority of bureaucrats are "people-pushing" white-collar employees, for whom association with others is a constant requirement. The ordinary bureaucrat is situated in a fixed and highly structured relationship to the public and to other officials, whether they are superiors or subordinates. Satisfactory performance of his tasks is grounded in his ability to secure their cooperation, goodwill, and support. Furthermore, his chances for advancement depend as much upon whether higher officials like him, trust him, and feel at ease with him as upon his objective qualifications and his technical efficiency.

With respect to subordinates, the bureaucrat's success will hinge, to a great extent, on getting them to "produce" for him. Likewise, he must take care not to let other sides of his personality, especially those revealing his real preferences, his personal likes and dislikes, intrude upon any negotiation with either his equals or with outsiders. Up and down the line, large-scale organization puts a high premium on muted discord and surface harmony, as it does on everyone's being likeable and pleasant.

This emphasis is a recurrent, not a constant, one. To a degree, it matches behavior prescribed for the courtier in handbooks like Castiglione's *The Courtier* and Lord Chesterfield's *Letters to His Son*. Surly behavior was appropriate in aristocratic societies among noblemen close to princes and kings. The courtier had, however, only to please those above him. Bureaucracy, which is so much a matter of "teamwork" and "cooperation," constrains the individual to please all his associates: those equal to and below him, as well as those above him. The English yeoman, the independent farmer, and the frontiersman achieved historical fame for their possession of traits directly opposite to those that shape contemporary officials. The sense that poverty or prosperity depended mostly upon their own efforts gave them a feeling of independence, confidence, and even cockiness. It allowed them to be unpleasant without running any great risk of economic loss. Niceness had not yet become compulsory—or compulsive.

Self-Rationalization in Bureaucracy

In an employee society, "personality" becomes a market commodity, one that has measurable cash value in terms of present and future income to its possessor. Once the alert bureaucrat recognizes this, he sets out to acquire his magic key to success. That quest Karl Mannheim has brilliantly analyzed as a "self-rationalization." In Mannheim's words:

> By self-rationalization we understand the individual's systematic control of his impulses—a control which is always the first step to be taken if an individual wants to plan his life so that every action is guided by principle and is directed towards the goal he has in mind. . . . Modern

> society attains perhaps its highest stage of functional rationalization in its administrative staff, in which the individuals who take part not only have their specific actions prescribed . . . but in addition have their life-plan to a large extent imposed in the form of a "career," in which the individual stages are specified in advance. Concern with a career requires a maximum of self-mastery since it involves not only the actual processes of work but also the prescriptive regulation both of ideas and feelings that one is permitted to have and of one's leisure time.[1]

Self-rationalization appears when the official begins to view himself as a merchandisable product that he must market and package like any other merchandisable product. First, an inventory is necessary. He must ask: What are my assets and liabilities in the personality market? What defects must be banished before I can sell myself? Do I have the right background? If not, how can I acquire it? With such questions, the inventory is converted into a market-research project. The answers give him findings with which to remodel his personality. The bureaucratic personality is molded out of available raw materials, shaped to meet fluctuating demands of the market.

Old habits are discarded, and new habits are nurtured. The would-be success learns when to simulate enthusiasm, compassion, interest, concern, modesty, confidence, and mastery; when to smile, with whom to laugh, and how intimate or friendly he can be with other people. He selects his home and its residential area with care; he buys his clothes and chooses styles with an eye to their probable reception in his office. He reads or pretends to have read the right books, the right magazines, and the right newspapers. All this will be reflected in "the right line of conversation," which he adopts as his own, thereafter sustaining it with proper inflections. His tone is by turns disdainful, respectful, reverential, and choleric, but always well attuned to others. He joins the right party and espouses the political ideology of his fellows. If he starts early and has vision, he marries the right girl, or if he has been guilty of an indiscretion, he may disembarrass himself of the wrong girl. Every one of these procedures is a marketing operation—with *its* own imponderable hazards. If the operation succeeds, our official will have fabricated a personality totally in harmony with his environment; in a great many ways, it will resemble the personality of his coworkers. The drive for self-rationalization implies nothing less than adult socialization, or, in the majority of cases, radical resocialization.

The Organization Man

The pressure in bureaucratic organizations that forces an individual to make himself amiable, sweet-tempered, and bland results in conspicuous conformity, but the standards of conformity vary from organization to organization. Standards for a military officer, an academician, a businessman, a journalist, a medical technician, and a civil servant are obviously not the same, yet they have in common a deeply assimilated inclination to search for external standards, by which their interests, activities, and thoughts can be consciously directed. Each man takes on the special tincture of his organizational environment. Each tends to focus his projected self on those qualities that will be most pleasing to others. Since the others are similarly occupied, everyone's personality is fractionated. Part of it can be seen; the rest is subdued and hidden. Bureaucratic organizations sweeten and soften the visible personality.

The sweetening process, however, requires denying other portions of the self. Officials strive to develop those aspects of their personality that fit the bureaucratic milieu. This makes it difficult for them to develop aspects that are "out-of-phase." Hypertrophy in one direction spells atrophy in another. One consequence of self-rationalization as a technique to control personality is that, after some time has passed, the poseur may find that he is a different person. With much practice, "control" becomes unnecessary; the bureaucratic mask becomes the normal face, and refractory impulses get buried beyond reactivation. Functionaries are then, in the fullest sense, Organization Men.

Special Bureaucratic Stresses

The bureaucratic atmosphere may seem to be warm and friendly; officials are encouraged to call each other by their first names, and, except in the armed forces, "pulling rank" clumsily tends to be offensive. There is an outward show of civility, politeness, and decency. Conspicuous harassment of subordinates is condemned by every efficiency expert and human engineer in America, usually on the ground that it reduces efficiency. Yet tensions are aroused even in the smoothest bureaucracy, and there they cannot be publicly aired. This may make them harder to contain. These stresses can cause officials to violate the norms of their organization and nullify its purposes. The stresses we have in mind are related to impersonality, isolation, and powerlessness.

Let us recall that the principle of uniform administration is based upon specific rules, carried out by those whose duties are rigorously prescribed. Bureaucratic officials are placed in relationship to each other by the rules, and deal with each other—as they do with the outside world—according to fixed regulations. They are not supposed to be influenced by personal preference, affinity, taste, or choice. They deal with and see each other because the situation obliges them to do so. Office contacts of a particular kind are required, and each party to them knows that they are required. Every intraoffice relationship is covered by formal specifications, which, because of their official nature, cannot easily be executed or accepted with spontaneity, empathy, or a sense of personal identification. But, without some degree of warmth, no durable human interaction has ever been observed to take place. Dehumanization is never wholly attainable. On the other hand, human spontaneity knows no bounds; it cannot be safely restrained by offices and rules and is therefore likely to cause trouble. A common compromise occurs in the form of controlled warmth or planned spontaneity; synthetic emotion is meant to pass for real warmth and spontaneity, but it does not actually commit officials beyond the point of involvement formally demanded of them. They act out their parts, performing or discarding them as necessity and convenience require. Such roles are never really internalized.

In the bureaucratic milieu, which is a vortex of togetherness, other-directedness, teamwork, and cooperation, the individual finds it exceedingly difficult to relate or commit himself to his associates. He learns that they respond as shallowly or as deceptively as he does to them. This awareness makes him wary of the apparent camaraderie others offer in their official capacity. Thus, in the midst of endless interaction with clients and other officials, the individual feels isolated, unbreakably tied to, and hopelessly cut off from, those others he will see every working day of his life. Ironically, the greatest measure of social and psychological isolation may be traced to two very different, if not opposite, structures: the city with its extremely loose organization, and the bureaucracy with its extremely tight organization.

The Quest for Identification in Informal Groups

Bureaucratic impersonality bemuses the official at precisely that point where he feels a deep personal need to identify with and relate to people as people. Like almost every other human being, the official has acquired his basic orientation to social life in the family and in other primary groups, where deeper, more intimate, and unpremeditated responses are provided. His formative environment generates expectations that formal bureaucratic organization is not capable of satisfying. Consequently, the bureaucrat improvises patterns of response, calculated to satisfy extra occupational needs by means that go beyond—and outside of—the prescriptions of his official role.

The quest for personal identification often leads one official to seek out others. In defiance of all the proprieties and all the rules, he may make attachments that have no organizational sanction. As this process spreads, the office comes to be reorganized into informal and unofficial friendship groups, cliques whose existence is unrecognized in the table of organization. Such cliques form as the result of physical propinquity, or they sprout from common interests, common ambition, common resentment, or common ethnic origin. Each clique evolves a common core of standards from the initial consensus of its members, and, again, they may clash with those of the organization. Such separate standards include the restriction of output and systematic violation of office procedure (so that the clique punishes what the highest officials reward). Clique control is perhaps most serious when it is informally responsible for promoting policies that lack official authority to back them up. The clique is hospitable to personnel, from different departments and at different levels of authority, who establish their own channels of communication. They have little regard for preconceived blueprints, reaching each other and selected segments of the public without "clearance" from above. In this way, gossip circulates, secrets are revealed, information is leaked—and official policy has been unofficially nullified.

The informal group has its informal leaders. These leaders are men who, through their network of personal friendships and influence, bring other persons into continuous unofficial interaction. A clique leader is not necessarily an official of the highest rank. The situation that then presents itself—in extreme cases—is such that the nominal bosses exert less influence than those without title to authority. There is no other way to gain intimate knowledge of cliques than by joining them—which those on top and those outside are often precluded from doing. When men vested with official authority try to get things done by using the formal administrative machinery, they may find that machinery inadequate and obsolescent. At the same time, those who manipulate the informal network of clique communications do get things done—by breaking all the rules.

The many cliques in a large office are often at odds with each other. Individual bureaucrats compete for raises, promotions, niches, and prestige symbols. To that competition they bring not only their own rivalries, but also such support as can be mustered from friends, partisans, and cliques. Not just separate individuals, but whole cliques choose sides, lining up on a host of issues that pertain to office politics. They reward their friends on the basis of personal loyalty rather than performance, and they hinder or penalize even those enemies who completely fulfill legitimate functions.

In these circumstances, the bureaucratic regime is turned upside down. Despite its outward quiescence, the office becomes a battleground in which "politics" is a potent weapon, and one in which mines and traps are common dangers. An official may unsuspectingly befriend one of his colleagues who belongs to the wrong camp—and thereby consign himself to oblivion. Or he may hitch his wagon to a floundering team: he may be identified with an unstable clique on its way down—and suffer personally for all the failures of that clique.

In sum, the formation of cliques tends to alter operational bureaucracy to something quite different from its ideal type. The uniformity, predictability, and precision built into it are processed out of it by intervening social and emotional factors. For this reason alone, bureaucracy can never be perfectly smooth or absolutely efficient.

Disidentification with the Bureaucracy

The search for personal identity in social relationships that are not wholly purposive and functional is one of several tendencies. Some bureaucrats, overwhelmed by the impersonality of their work, give up the idea that it is meaningful or that it is a suitable medium for self-realization. They turn to, and enlarge upon, other aspects of life, while doing as little work as possible in offices that are distasteful to them. The major locus of meaning lies in the family, a hobby, a satisfying style of consumption, contact with people from other spheres, in philandering, in romantic dalliance, in suburban and exurban affairs, in the affectations of "Upper Bohemia," or in any of several idiosyncratic activities.

By denying the meaningfulness of their work, they become less devoted and less efficient. They minimize their duties and perform them in a routinely competent way, giving no more thought to the office than is irreducibly necessary. They systematically avoid decisions, pass the buck, and take no action whenever possible. In his analysis of the United States Navy Officers Corps, Arthur K. Davis found "avoiding responsibility: the philosophy of do-the-least" or "shunting responsibility upward" both common and complex; it was surrounded by social, personal, and technical conditions, and it could be disastrous. At the lower and middle levels of bureaucracy, officials are strongly tempted "to slide (problems) into their superior's lap by asking advice, requesting instructions, securing approval in advance." But, Davis writes, "For the man at the top there is no such escape from the strains of decision except by a do-nothing policy." Timid or indifferent bureaucrats who pass the buck and who, when on top, avoid decisions are the bureaucrats whose public imagery has fixed itself upon the popular imagination. Here, the man corresponds to the prototype. He has abandoned his initial hope of upward mobility and looks elsewhere for satisfaction.

To achieve positive action and speedy disposition of business, a bureaucracy needs esprit de corps, high morale, and enthusiastic dedication. If an organization is staffed with apathetic bureaucrats, its purposes are less and less likely to be achieved.

Overidentification

The very same sense of isolation that leads one bureaucrat out of the organization to seek his "self" will lead another to "overidentify" with the organization. In this case, the organization as a whole is substituted for other identifications and for various social relationships. A clear and familiar case (not without pathos) occurs when the lowly clerk employed by a large, powerful, and well-known agency, reaches for the halo of his organization to cover his anonymity and powerlessness in it. He speaks knowingly of policies and practices that circulate through the office grapevine but are many times removed from himself. He implies by use of the pronouns *we* and *our* that the organization's policies and practices are his policies and practices, that he somehow had a hand in making them. Since he must conceal his actual position in order to exploit it among strangers, his life is sharply divided between office and home. With a fictitious title and some histrionic ability, an elevator man employed by one of the large communications companies who is domiciled in a fashionable suburb and who looks, dresses, and talks like a Madison

Avenue hotshot, can effectively exploit his connection. This is what the Captain from Koepnig did in Kaiser Wilhelm's Germany when he pretended to be an officer and was accepted as such. The assumption of a false identity is increasingly possible in societies that give higher prestige to the organization than they do to the innumerable individuals who must make it work.

Identification with "The Rules"

Another kind of overidentification manifests itself in inordinate and inflexible adherence to rules. To the outsider, such rigidity looks like senseless obstructionism, and he finds it maddening enough to have changed the word *bureaucracy* from a label into an epithet. To the functionary whose personal identity has been swallowed up by the organization, rules that are precise, orderly, fixed, and certain may represent a source of psychological security not otherwise available to *him*.

In the grip of his passion for legalism, a bureaucratic virtuoso follows the letter of every rule, never deviating, never counting the consequences or considering what possible harm he does to others. Javert, the police official of Victor Hugo's *Les Misérables,* is a perfect example of the legalist. Far beyond the call of duty, Javert remorselessly pursues a man of whose excellent character and good deeds he is fully aware, putting aside his own knowledge and disregarding the sympathy that wells up in him. When confronted with the ineluctable choice between rampant legalism and personal conviction, he takes his life.

Nazi documents, captured after World War II, indicate that, on the day Adolf Hitler committed suicide and Russian troops were marching through the streets of Berlin, officials of the Reichschancellery were too busy to look out of their windows. They were engaged in estimating and ordering paper clips for the next fiscal year!

Legalism, which Davis has called the psychology of affirm-and-conform, and for which he lays down a golden rule, "Follow the book or pass the buck," is perhaps the most dangerous and pathological outgrowth of bureaucratic organization. Davis deals with the seriousness of overemphasis on instrumental devices among naval officers in time of war. He cites two striking examples:

> In one large air unit, even the most trivial correspondence was routed up to the Chief of Staff and often to the Admiral, then down to the appropriate department for action. Here the reply was drafted, typed, routed back to the top for approval and signature (often refused, pending minor changes), and finally routed down to the dispatching office. Mail which a clerk should have handled in and out in 24 hours was thus sent to the top and back two or three times, drawing attention from 8 to 12 persons over a ten-day period.
>
> We cite next the behavior of certain heavy-bomber crews on anti-submarine patrols. Because of their short tour of duty, the infrequency of submarine sightings, and the complexity of anti-submarine tactics, these air crews usually made several errors in the course of an attack. For this they would be sharply criticized by their superiors. Hence arose a serious morale problem. At least three flight crews in one flight squadron began going out for "quiet patrols" by their own admission. Observing the letter of their instructions legalistically, they flew their patrols exactly as charted. If a suspicious object appeared a few miles abeam, their course lay straight ahead.[2]

The use of forms and of standard procedures, the transmutation of mechanics into a Sacred Cow, and the reduction of a task to many phases in which only a few persons (or no one at all) can understand the whole flow of a single operation: these are among the factors that contribute most heavily to legalism. And legalism is widely, subtly, and grossly converted into a means of self-identification.

Inversion of Identification

Consider another kind of overidentification, one that occurs at higher levels of administration. In contrast to the individual who submerges his own identity in the organization, there *is* the top official who conceives of the organization, or the department he heads, as an extension of his own ego. The administrative apparatus—human and material—is seen by him chiefly as a means for his personal action, a machine he can use to execute his will. Thus, a standard army phrase for reporting the number of troops under one's command used to be, "I have (so many units) in my hand."

Such an approach is taken up by some men who have successfully worked their way up the hierarchy and who have developed a healthy respect for their own ability. To the extent that this respect is unwarranted, it may result in a gross neglect of the "mechanical" side of organization, a tendency to ignore educated advice from specialists of lower rank, and the manipulation of an organizational apparatus for personal rather than corporate ends. To regard the organization as an extension of one's own ego is flagrantly to violate that cardinal principle of bureaucracy that separates official existence from personal life.

Powerlessness

The feeling of powerlessness often experienced by modern administrators is fundamentally related to the structure of bureaucracy. That structure is notable for its strict hierarchy and the marked differences—in authority, rank, income, and prerogatives—between men at various levels. Such differences exist in any form of social organization, but they are greatly sharpened in a bureaucracy where each job is as systematically defined as all duties and privileges are clearly delineated.

Structurally, every bureaucrat knows where he stands, who is above him and who is below him. He knows this by direct perception or by informed guesswork. It is possible for him to compare his salary, his benefits, and his chances of promotion with those of others, to notice how others get along with each other and whether they are on the "outs" with key figures. It does not take an unusually perceptive actor to realize that he may be one of those functionaries who actually has little power and no real leverage in the organization.

A second form of structurally determined powerlessness issues from the bureaucracy's segmented and specialized nature. As individuals and departments divide and subdivide the performance of a single operation, there are times when no one person can envisage the total task. More often, it seems chaotic to everyone except the coordinator and those few persons taken into his confidence. The first atomic bomb was produced at Los Alamos in just such an atmosphere; most of those engaged in the Manhattan Project had no knowledge of its real purpose. The everyday conduct of bureaucratic affairs that do not involve top secrets may be quite as mystifying to those who are responsible for them. In the case of almost every bureaucrat, his assignments originate in another department, they are passed on to him, and finally completed in still other departments. He works only on one phase of a job, in accordance with directives from above, which, from his worm's-eye view, may not make sense. To a detailed specialist, facets of the job other than his own are seldom clear, and he may do no more than conjecture uncertainly about them. He sees what look to him like avoidable mistakes made by bosses who do not have his special competence and who are therefore viewed with some disdain. This is stylized into the wry and half-serious belief that the men in charge got there by making mistakes so repeatedly that they had to be kicked upstairs. More serious is the belief that luck, marriage, apple-polishing, and bootlicking make for success.

In almost every bureaucracy, there is a myth of incompetence that lower officials cherish about higher officials. It is assumed that somehow incompetence mixed with smooth talking and aided by "connections" is what it takes to come out on top. The existence of this myth is a rough gauge of the resentment that powerless people feel for their ostensibly powerful superiors. Resentment—that peculiar emotion that begins with striving and is heightened by impotence—is most especially evoked among lower- and middle-ranking officials who cannot realistically expect to attain power. It leads to disidentification from the bureaucracy.

White-collar Sabotage

This disidentification is concretely expressed by the bureaucrat who gossips, complains, and searches for errors. In a more advanced stage, it includes passive resistance and subtle sabotage. One's duty is performed in ways that are procedurally correct and yet make the task impossible to accomplish. With no show of malice whatsoever, one's superiors may be deliberately exposed to the probability of error and ridicule. The claim that messages are unclear, that directives are ambiguous, and that therefore misunderstanding cannot be avoided, is a technique instantly familiar to modern readers as Švejkism—after *The Good Soldier Švejk,* by Jaroslav Hasek. Švejk is an obedient Yes Man and an effective saboteur in the Austro-Hungarian army; he does at once everything the officers tell him to do and nothing they tell him to do. Švejk is prototypic. His methods are still widely employed by enlisted men in armies everywhere. Government bureaus are still subject to Švejkism, as they are to the disloyalty of men who reveal office secrets, leak embarrassing data to the press, or otherwise put higher-ups "on the spot." Private business zealously guards its secrets; for a functionary to betray them would be unpardonable; this is true even when everybody in the industry knows what everybody else knows. According to Raymond Loewy, there is no more significant difference among American automobiles than there is among cake mixes. Loewy, an industrial engineer who designed the postwar Studebaker, explains that this sameness has come about because every company produces "imitative, over-decorated chariots, with something for everyone laid over a basic formula design that is a copy of someone else's formula design." With that, Loewy divorces himself from the automotive industry and, hence, never identified with it, is free to report that:

> Detroit spends an annual fortune to insure its lack of originality. . . . To protect its styling studios, Ford has a force of 20 security guards commanded by an ex-FBI agent. Different-colored passes admit different people to specific different rooms and to those rooms only. Unused sketches and clay models are destroyed. Ford's studio locks can be changed within an hour if somebody loses a key. To pierce such a wall of secrecy, each company employs spies and counter-spies, rumorists and counter-rumorists. Rival helicopters flutter over high-walled test tracks. Ford guards peer at an adjacent water tower with a 60-power telescope to make sure no long-range camera is mounted on it by a rival concern. One automotive company installed a microphone in a blond's brassiere and sent her off to seduce a secret. . . . All secrets are discovered! The shape of a Ford hubcap! The number of square inches of chromium on the new Buick! The final result is that all the companies know all the secrets of all the other companies, and everyone brings out the same car.[3]

To reveal known or unknown secrets is a form of lèse-majesté practiced only by the disaffected and the disidentified. Frontline officials in this condition do not remain unidentified. They reidentify—usually with clients, taking their side, waiving rules, and forgetting standard forms. Into this category fall the relief investigator who grants an applicant's claim without carefully checking it; the insurance adjuster who okays the obviously excessive claim of a policyholder; the foreman who sides with workers in his plant rather than with management; and the supervisor who, instead of correcting his subordinates' mistakes, covers them up. In all such cases, the official who feels powerless in relation to his superiors stretches, bends, or breaks the regulations so that he can give a better break to persons still less powerful than himself. And in all such cases, personal interaction is substituted for impersonal procedure. Powerlessness and impersonality are negated—at the organization's expense. Such behavior frequently elicits sympathy; it is viewed as human—all-too-human—kindness.

Authoritarianism

The public has much less patience with another response to powerlessness, one that motivates the bureaucrat who is hedged in on one side to break out in search of power on another side. A lowly clerk, squelched by his superiors, may redirect the resentment that comes over him. He can do this by abusing his clients. So can the case worker who uses legal and extralegal methods to humiliate or otherwise punish those in need of his help. To them, he represents the awful power of a large agency. The official who has no other source of power, who regards himself as an insignificant part of the organization, is very powerful indeed when he faces outsiders who are dependent upon him. Similarly, a middle-level boss may exult in tyrannizing without mercy over his subordinates precisely because he has so little overall discretion. He may be compulsive and petty about minor matters for the reason that his area of jurisdiction is petty and unimportant. James Jones's novel *From Here to Eternity* is an extended illustration of the fact that such abuse can be torture to its victim.

Every officeholder knows that the petty tyrant who overpowers his underlings is simultaneously capable of meekness and sycophancy to those who outrank him. Such conduct is all of a piece. It may properly be called authoritarian, for it is based on the premise that authority as such, any and every kind of authority, must be respected. The relation of that authority to wisdom or purpose—or even sanity—goes unquestioned, as Herman Wouk argues in his postwar best seller, *The Caine Mutiny.* That novel placed the onus of scorn on a naval officer who disobeyed his deranged captain, thereby evincing illegitimate disrespect for authority, even insane authority.

This pattern of behavior, familiar to psychologists as dominance and submission, is especially common in any bureaucracy. It is no doubt embedded in the individual personality as a trait that makes bureaucratic employment attractive in the first place, but that employment in its objective form accentuates the trait. It produces individual suffering, and, when widespread, it can produce a fundamental weakening of the organization.

Authoritarian Misinformation

As a communications system, bureaucracy transmits information up the line in a stream of data, messages, and reports, and down the line in a stream of orders, instructions, and morale-making propaganda. In its lateral flow, the system conveys gossip and stimulates interdepartmental negotiation. Insofar as it affects the movement of upward communications, submissive behavior has certain negative consequences. A subordinate is, among other things, supposed to function as "the eyes and ears" of his superior. He is supposed to keep his superior informed, to protect him from making errors based on misinformation or ignorance of the facts. He is even required, if necessary, to disagree with his superior and to explain his reasons for disagreeing. Otherwise, he is a poor watchdog. Now, the submissive official is afraid to disagree. On the contrary, he seeks out his superior's opinions and assembles data that will support them. By selective inattention to data that might ruffle established thinking, he isolates his superior, validates mistaken notions, and gives them an expert aura of infallibility. Without accurate information from below, the policy maker is helpless. He is stripped of independent knowledge of the social or political or economic reality in which he operates and about which he is expected to make intelligent decisions.

The judicious and secure bureaucrat avoids sycophantic subordinates, because he knows that they are likely to isolate him from reality. At some levels, he will invite advance criticism of his decisions, even encouraging a systematic statement of objections. Just as an attorney sometimes prepares his opponent's case, the better to refute it, so the efficient administrator faces all weaknesses in his own position, its possible loopholes, contingencies, and repercussions. He can proceed only after many arguments have been presented, by taking them into account and then making his decision with some sense of its many-sidedness. Lately, bureaucracies have institutionalized internal criticism by setting up special departments for that purpose. They may use an "Inspector General's Office," the self-survey, independent commissions, and managerial consultants.

The authoritarian administrator shies away from independent criticism of his work. He demands subservience of lower bureaucrats who feel that it is risky to provide him with unpleasant information. Critical and independent views, like inconvenient facts, are interpreted as personal criticism and as symptoms of disrespect or of impudence. This attitude conditions subordinates to feed him a steady diet of cheerful good news, automatic assent, and insincere agreement. The result is that he increasingly makes his decisions in a vacuum. Such a situation has been known to demoralize the foreign service of more than one country. When diplomats, ambassadors, consuls, and attachés on the spot are too fearful to report what they see, preferring to report what others think they see from a great distance, serious miscalculations are bound to occur. To clog the channels of communication within a foreign ministry or a department of state with intimidated personnel is to invite needless and possibly mortal peril.

Power Seeking and Office Politics

Still another response to the feeling of powerlessness among those below is for those above to urge upon them the desirability of pursuing power. The logic they try to instill dictates that, since a man lacks power by reason of his low rank, he can overcome his lack only by gaining higher rank. Those who accept this logic, the young, the ambitious, the undefeated, are not really daunted by an objective and presumably temporary lack of power, which is parallel to that of children who will one day supplant their powerful elders.

Thus, one bureaucratic segment, particularly in the middle and upper layers, is made up of extremely ambitious individuals strongly motivated to the acquisition of power. From this group come the office politicians, the apple-polishers, the toadies, and favor-seekers, ever ready to betray their equals and their superiors. These are the Machiavellians who organize and lead factions capable of tearing an office apart. When successful, they may purge an organization of unsuccessful rivals and then regroup creating new lines of antagonistic cooperation, until they are once more convulsed by the same tactics. Friends are imported and allies enlisted in the battle to strengthen their hard-won position. Past political debts are paid. Bureaucrats become warriors who, if they are not "fur us," are "agin us" in the battle of all against all. It is possible to overstimulate the appetite for power. If, after much deprivation, men are spurred on primarily by this hunger, the organization's functional objectives exist merely as a setting, wherein the power-starved ravenously wage their battle.

What happens in this setting to the nonpolitical, personally unambitious, and professionally zealous official? At first, he may find the execution of his tasks more difficult, for it is impeded by other officials who are more concerned with jockeying for position than with their occupational roles. Finding that the "politics" his associates practice makes it hard for him to do his job, he concludes that the only way to get it done is to line up "political" support for his "nonpolitical" goals. Regardless of his own inclinations, he is forced to become a politician and to do things he dislikes. Doing them, he sometimes discovers that he is a good politician who can now accomplish things he previously considered impossible. However, he is now less likely to want to accomplish those things. If this transformation takes place, our man may well be destined for a high executive role in which politics will dominate his life. Thenceforth, he must balance and coordinate the divergent factional and political activities within his organization.

The Powerlessness of the Intellectual

Another kind of anxiety is aroused in the bureaucrat who has strong academic and intellectual interests. These interests prompt him to view everyday problems with a broad and total sweep. He experiences the narrowness of jurisdictional limitations only as a bureaucrat. His self-image is that of a thinker employed, far below his capacity, as a technician and a hack by poorly educated ignoramuses. Frequently, his disenchantment with the organization is a sudden one. Ultimately, he either adopts some of the aforementioned responses or resigns. There is much turnover of intellectuals in bureaucracies. Some repair to less bureaucratic pastures; others move from job to job, restlessly seeking a bureaucracy in which their talents can be given fuller scope. If, in the process of experiencing these limitations, they capitulate and accept a greatly circumscribed role, intellectuals can become quite valuable specialists and eventually move into top administrative positions. They have been socialized to the bureaucracy.

A cautionary word must be added. All of our descriptions distort the appearance of bureaucracy as it visibly operates. These conditions exist, but within a context of overwhelmingly routine work, often neither pleasant nor unpleasant. Moreover, there is nothing so psychically burdensome or intolerably harsh about bureaucracy that it cannot be softened by ordinary social activities or sweetened by "seeing the better side of things." If there are economists (in this case, Kenneth Boulding) who warn that "beyond a certain point increase in the scale of organization results in a breakdown of communication, in a lack of flexibility, in bureaucratic stagnation and insensitivity,"[4] who liken the bureaucratic monster to a dinosaur leaving free men breathing space only in the interstices of its path, there are cheerful academicians (in *this* case, Harlan Cleveland, Dean of the Maxwell Graduate School of Citizenship and Public Affairs at Syracuse University) to offer consolation:

> My impression is that "large-scale" organization generally implies loose organization. Precisely because big organizations make most of the vital decisions affecting

> our destiny, more people are participating in those decisions affecting our destiny, more people are participating in those decisions than ever before. . . .
>
> In a household managed by people who can walk and talk, a baby begins to experience a sense of personal freedom when it masters the techniques of walking and talking. Just so, in a world dominated by large-scaleness, it is those individuals who learn to work with and in large-scale organizations who have a rational basis for feeling free. There are, of course, plenty of free men who work for giant corporations or government agencies but they aren't those who are so afraid of them that they scurry into the "interstices" of smallness. I have no doubt that a large number of middle-grade bureaucrats in the Soviet Union have so mastered the system that they are, in a sense, experiencing within its limits a significant measure of personal freedom. The reason is that the Soviet is not, as Mr. Boulding protests, a "one-firm state," but a myriad collection of manageable size bound together by leadership and a sense of destiny in ways not so fundamentally different from other nations as they (and we) like to assume.[5]

Real bureaucracy is neither as efficient as its ideal type suggests, nor as cruel and inefficient as our treatment of its pathologies suggests. Not all people are frustrated by bureaucracy, toward which they may have gravitated by predisposition. No bureaucracy is exclusively staffed with pathological types. The negative tendencies we have sketched are, however, as much a reality as the positive ones. These tendencies pose typical problems and present typical difficulties, which most white-collar workers encounter at one time or another in the course of their careers.

To a certain extent, they are inescapable, simply because bureaucracy is here to stay. As society is more and more dominated by largeness, bureaucracy's share of our total life cannot but grow with it. The future points to ever greater degrees of hugeness. Beyond that, Boulding is correct in saying, "The electric calculator, the punched card, operations research and decision theory all point to a still further revolution in the making"—to still more bureaucracy.

Notes

1. Karl Mannheim, *Man and Society in an Age of Reconstruction: Studies in Modern Social Structure* (London: K. Paul, Trench, Trubner & Co, Ltd., 1940).

2. Arthur K. Davis, "Bureaucratic Patterns in the Navy Officer Corps," *Social Forces*, 27 (1948), 143-53. Reprinted in Robert K. Merton, Ailsa P. Gray, Barbara Hockey, and Hanan C. Selvin, eds., *Reader in Bureaucracy* (New York: Free Press, 1952), 380-95. The block quotation in the text may be found in Merton *et al.*, eds., 389-90.

3. Raymond Loewy, *Never Leave Well Enough Alone* (New York: Simon and Schuster, 1951).

4. Kenneth E. Boulding, "The Jungle of Hugeness: the Second Age of the Brontosaurus," *Saturday Review*, March 1, 1958, 11 ff.

5. Harland Cleveland, "Dinosaurs and Personal Freedom," *Saturday Review*, February 28, 1959, 12 ff.

2

Power Cliques in Bureaucratic Society

Joseph Bensman with Arthur J. Vidich

A central problem in the study of social structure has been the precise relationship between social and economic classes and political power. The unilinear relationship between class and power as postulated by Marx has been denied by almost all uncommitted thinkers. Moreover, Marx's formulation that economic classes are the chief agents in political and social action presumes that classes have a corporate character and are active agents. Actually, even under Marxist analysis, classes are distributive phenomena—that is, collections of individuals responding in roughly the same ways to the same economic situations—and not corporate entities as were the medieval estates.

Even if one were to assume that economic interests are a major basis for political action, intervening agencies must be posited to channel the distributive actions of the individuals that make up the classes. The concept of political parties has been used with some degree of justification to point to a major channeling agency. It is easy to point out, however, that the same economic interests organize a number of class interests, that many class interests are organized in the same party, and that some class interests remain unorganized by political parties. These points are particularly well illustrated in the United States, and they indicate that political parties are less than the sum total of class agencies.

Published originally in a slightly different form in *Social Research* 29 (Winter 1962), 467-74. Republished by permission from *Social Research*.

In addition, with the development of the administrative state, major decisions are made by nonelective executive agencies and by individuals who are relatively anonymous to the public at large. Such decisions are based on highly legalistic and technical documents that do not appear to be substantive in nature, but may result in individual and group advantages and disadvantages involving billions of dollars without appearing to be political. Reaching and influencing the key anonymous individuals making such decisions does not require the vast operations of mass political parties, nor even formally organized pressure groups and associations, which by virtue of their formal organization tend to become publicly conspicuous. Reaching and influencing these key decision makers may instead rest on the exercise of personal influence. It is in this sense that personal influence is a major concept in the understanding of modern society.

To account for at least one major mechanism by which specialized class interests get translated into social and political action, we wish to postulate the concept of the power clique. We do not wish to imply that the conception of a power clique provides an answer to the relationship between class and power, nor do we wish to imply that it encompasses an understanding of the public life of political parties. These are separate problems worthy of attention in their own right. Instead, it appears to us that in a centralized society in which all institutions are typified by centralized administrations, the relationships between class, power, and party are significantly mediated by an intervening dimension of conduct that we subsume under the term *power clique*. Moreover, in this paper it is our intention only to describe and define power cliques (how they originate, are perpetuated, become and remain cohesive, cut across formal bureaucratic divisions, and so forth) and the salient elements of clique functioning in terms sufficiently general as to be characteristic of the underside of any social apparatus. In this respect, our study is not based on any specific case, but represents a synthesis of observations accumulated by experience in a number of organizations.[1] Our analysis is based in part on clues and insights provided by C. Wright Mills in *The Power Elite,* Hans Gerth and Mills in *Character and Social Structure,* Floyd Hunter in *Community Power Structure,* Allison Davis, Burleigh Gardner, and Mary R. Gardner in *Deep South,* Paul Underwood in *Catholic and Protestant,* and Vidich and Bensman in *Small Town in Mass Society.*

Mills suggests that there are three power elites that make the effective decisions concerning the national destiny of the United States. Whether this is true is beyond the scope of this paper. But Mills also suggests that informal power cliques are a basic dynamic in influencing political action. In concentrating his attention on the top power elites, Mills, perhaps for the sake of his central argument, overlooks the existence at every level of society, not just at the top, of similar interlocking cliques that attempt to influence actions in social spheres that are relevant to the position of their members. E. Digby Baltzell in *Philadelphia Gentlemen* highlights the clique nature of a regional elite, and David Reisman through his largely negative conception of power as expressed in the "veto" group comes close to specifying cliques as organized around particular interests. Since the publication of Hunter's *Community Power Structure,* which largely ignores the party and electoral apparatus in decision making, many studies have appeared that point to the central role of personal influence and power cliques. In addition to the existence of power cliques as such, we wish to emphasize that such cliques cut across various institutional boundaries. The membership of any specific clique is apt to be composed of representatives from different economic, political, military, social, prestige, or communications institutions. For this reason, the phrase that best describes them is *interinstitutional power cliques.*

Characteristics of Interinstitutional Power Cliques

We posit as our hypothesis that the major co-coordinators and organizers of societal activities in the area of decision making at any level are the interinstitutional power cliques.

The authors of *Deep South* described the operation of interinstitutional cliques in classic terms when they showed the operation of a clique to be an informal, self-selected grouping of like-minded men and women who by the nature of their association attempted to monopolize prestige within a community.[2] Their description is almost a description of the power clique except that they described it only as related to sociability, social status, and prestige. Essentially the same categories, broadened to include power and noninstitutionalized decision making, describe the essential ingredients of the interinstitutional power clique. The latter's essential characteristics are:

> 1. There is no formal definition of membership, but rather a subliminal recognition of like-mindedness based either on personal attraction or recognition of common personal interest.
>
> 2. There is no precise definition of the limits of membership, but instead, as Hunter has indicated, there are star members and peripheral members who have interlocking memberships in other cliques surrounding other star members. In this respect, they resemble Lewis Yablonsky's "near" groups in the juvenile delinquent gang.[3]
>
> 3. By definition, we exclude cliques that operate only within one organization not because these are not power cliques, but instead because their study is

best suited to studies of industrial organizations and large-scale administration.

4. The specific characteristic of interinstitutional cliques is that their membership is drawn from a multiplicity of agencies, organizations, and institutions and that the origins of the clique members' loyalties arise outside the framework of institutional participation.

The origins of clique members' loyalties to each other rest on personal and extra-institutional considerations. However, the specific origins of the loyalties underpinning individual cliques are diverse:

1. It may include the common members of a graduating class in a college who retain personal friendships or reinvoke personal friendships and contacts as they follow their careers in distinct and different fields. This is the "old school tie" notion that ranges in degree from the brotherhood of the fraternal club to simply having graduated from the same school, even if in different years.

2. It may include an earlier common membership in a given community from which members have migrated to the same city of opportunity.

3. It may include members from the same class in graduate school or a group of graduate students who secured their major training and perspective from a given professor or group of professors.

4. It may be made up of a number of people who previously, in an earlier career stage, worked in the same

office or organization, but later branched off into different industries and different institutional orders.

5. It may rest on common descent or extended kinship ties.

6. It may rest on common wartime experience in combat, in victory, in defeat, in participation in the same military unit at the same or different times, or in a memory of the common real or symbolic bloodletting of war.

7. It may be based on common ties to social, fraternal, or business lodges and associations.

8. It may be based on the invocation of an image of common ethnic, migrant, or religious communities.

Regardless of where these common starting points originate for any individual (and he may have clique contacts arising from more than one of the above sources), his subsequent life experiences place him in positions to become a member of other cliques; this is done by the process of simply introducing friends whom he knows from different areas or life stages of his career. For example, the old "army buddy" may be introduced to the classmate or the friend from the hometown. Thus, a multiplicity of cliques emerge and dissolve and fade into each other; one's personal relations serve as a point of coordination of what could appear to be an infinite interlocking of friendship patterns. What appears to be overlapping sets of friendship patterns, however, are much more than friendship patterns when one sees such patterns acted out in the context of institutional participation.

On the basis of one's institutional position, each individual is in a position to offer institutional rewards to members of his clique who are not members of his institution. And conversely, to the extent that he is identified by other clique members, he is in a position to make a claim on these others for the institutional opportunities they can offer him. Seen within the context of institutional participation, the institutional participant acts in his capacity as a clique member to further the interests of other clique members in other institutions by distributing to them such rewards and resources as he may command.

These rewards can include:

> *Jobs:* Individuals who have jobs to offer will tend to seek out their clique members for prospects and, if they are peers, employ each other's protégés. Thus, a powerful clique may monopolize all jobs in a given area.
>
> *Budgets:* Individuals who have at their disposal the disbursement of funds will tend to distribute such funds to other clique members who are in a position to supply the necessary goods and services. There is no necessity that fraud be practiced; although, at times, well qualified suppliers of goods and services may wonder why they did not receive a contract.
>
> *Policy:* Each individual in a clique, when he confronts his own organization or the community at large, can call on members of his clique to provide him with essential information—sometimes confidential information that would otherwise not be available to him. He can also rely on the direct and vocal support of other clique members and on a clique member who is not directly involved in the issue to apply personal pressure, persuasion, and influence on a third party who may otherwise be antagonistic or neutral. When clique members include members

> of the press or mass media, the attempt can be made to make an issue salient through publicity, to get favorable aspects of one's case presented, and to suppress its unfavorable aspects.
>
> *Third Party Influence:* When a proposal involves the approval of a distant or unknown institutional decision maker, a clique member who has direct and personal relations with the decision maker may be used to secure a favorable decision.
>
> *Support in Depth:* One core clique may be used to mobilize all of the indirect clique brothers in support of a proposition or proposal so that an entire class may be mobilized behind an issue.

Clique Functioning and Bureaucratic Conflict

To this point, we have talked as if institutional power cliques operate from the standpoint of one person or of one clique. It must be recognized that at any given time there are in any complex society an infinite number of cliques whose plans of action may conflict and cut across each other at different axes—or they may be totally unrelated to each other. Membership in one clique may be recognized by others and may therefore disqualify one from membership in other cross-purpose cliques.

Each clique tends to develop an inner structure of loyalties and a rewarding of respective members so that fulfillment of the obligation to one clique means the inability to fulfill obligation to others. Moreover, prestige within a clique is largely based on the actual or potential power to provide more rewards to fellow clique members than one takes. Prestige and power, therefore, have the quality of being a transaction in which support is exchanged for more concrete benefits regardless of personal friendship. The individual who always seeks favors and never reciprocates may be accepted as a clique member, but he tends only to be tolerated. And startling reversals in positions of "pecking orders" occur in a clique when a low-level member secures a position that suddenly gives him patronage, disposable funds, and an opportunity to affect policy or the life chances of others.

Because of the requirement that prestige and power be based on an ability to bestow these forms of patronage, each member of the clique seeks to enlarge his status by enlarging the areas that ultimately come under the control of the clique. As a result, there is an inherent tendency of cliques to expand until they reach limits placed upon them either by: (a) the action of other cliques, or (b) by the institutional officers who in their institutional roles must protect the integrity of their office. Short of this, the institution becomes the happy hunting ground for rival cliques seeking control for personal clique ends.

In his theory of bureaucracy, Weber suggests that the integrity of the formal organization is the essential characteristic of the bureaucracy. But this is only relative to feudalism and can never be absolute because the principle of the interinstitutional power cliques may be as strong as the principle of bureaucracy itself. When conflicts between cliques within bureaucracies come to a head, and a victory of one clique over another results, it is often followed by a liquidation of those defeated clique members who have not made their peace in time; they are then replaced with the clique members of the victorious officials who must be rewarded. It is for this reason that a given bureaucracy may seem to be inundated by swarms of locusts—new position holders with new styles of thought, language, and action—that give a completely new tone and color to an old organization.

The individual clique member in the defeated group must always be sensitive to balances of power within his institution. He must watch to see if his clique will look after him if it loses in an institutional struggle and must be prepared to jump in advance of a defeat.

If a star clique member in an institutional conflict has a second line of defense because of *other* jobs and budgets that he can make available to his protégés, he can command greater loyalties in his battles within that institution. The star member of a given clique may occupy an institutional position that is not the center of battle. The success of *his* clique members in the battle, however, may result in the appearance and actuality of one institution being dominated by another in spite of there being no official connecting link between the two. And, at times, when the star member appears to be particularly successful not so much in his own institution but in the efforts of his clique members in other institutions, it may appear that in a relatively short time his power is growing at cancerous rates.

It is true that as one's successes increase the number of victims of the successes also increases, but this does not mean that success generates its own countervailing limitations. It is rather that as one's successes multiply, the problem of maintenance of supply becomes greater. One must provide personnel who are at least nominally capable of fulfilling the positions created by the success, and one must provide the patronage to keep one's clique members loyal. To a certain extent, success itself generates the means of fulfilling these requirements, for each success means that more budgets and jobs are at the disposal of the cliques and that disaffected members of defeated cliques may become allies.

A limitation on such growth rests on the ability of individuals who are irrevocably committed to defeated cliques to merge and find resources that will enable them to provide patronage for countercliques. This is by no means guaranteed. If the membership of a clique is organized around special abilities to handle technological or institutional processes that are functionally necessary in an emerging society, the counterclique may be irrevocably defeated. The most general way that a triumphant clique can otherwise be defeated is by the weakening of its interpersonal ties by the extension of its lines. Individual clique members may become star members of smaller cliques and fractionate the former victorious clique. It is in this sense that there is some check on the absolute control of the absolute horde.

Finally, a limitation on the success of a clique may occur when a successful clique member by virtue of his success begins to identify more with his organization than with his clique. He may value, in this case, the integrity of the organization more than his status within a clique. In such cases, he will limit clique participation or modify it so that it does not interfere with his formal position.

Regardless of the outcome of clique struggles in any particular place, recognition of the concept of the interinstitutional clique indicates: (a) on one hand, continuous tension between formal position and wider status groups; and (b) on the other, the interpersonal basis of greater coordination between organizations and institutions than can be inferred from the study of their formal connections.

Notes

1. Our experience is drawn from observations on extensive interconnections in the following areas: universities, private philanthropic foundations, and government agencies, particularly in the social science departments; advertising agencies, manufacturing corporations, and the communications industry; interconnections between government bureaus as mediated by civil servants; research and development departments of universities and industrial firms; a management consultant firm and the sugar industry; local, state, and small-town politics; and the United States Marine officer class and social elites in Manhattan. For obvious reasons, we do not wish to make our examples too specific.

2. Allison Davis, Burleigh B. Gardner, and Mary R. Gardner, *Deep South* (Chicago: University of Chicago Press, 1941). See especially chapter 7, "Social Cliques of White Society," 137-70, and chapter 9, "Social Cliques in Colored Society," 208-27.

3. "Delinquent Gangs and a Theory of Near-Groups," *Social Problems* 7 (November 1957), 108-17.

3

Bureaucratic and Planning Attitudes

Joseph Bensman with Robert Lilienfeld

Images of the Bureaucratic Attitude

By now, it is almost a cliché to speak of the bureaucratic attitude. Weber, Merton, Mills, Mannheim, Michels, Blau, and Selznick have presented us with images and models of emerging structures that dominate much of the modern world and that dominate many styles of thought because of their pervasiveness.[1] We will attempt to see if it is possible to go beyond these traditions of modern political and social theory.

Conventionally, the bureaucrat is defined as a paid official employed in a large-scale organization whose work is delimited by relatively narrow, written, legal spheres of competence or jurisdictions arranged in strict hierarchies. The official enters the job as a career and derives his major income from his office. By virtue of training on the job and preparatory education, he becomes a narrow, "technical" expert. He advances through the hierarchy on the basis of examination and merit ratings, which are presumably objective and impersonal. He exercises his function on the basis of standardized, legal, objective procedures that are written down and specified in detail.

Published originally in a slightly different form in Joseph Bensman and Robert Lilienfeld, *Craft and Consciousness: Occupational Technique and the Development of World Images*, 2nd ed. (New York: Aldine De Gruyter, 1991), 325-43. Republished by permission from Transaction Publishers.

In doing so, he is subordinate to bureaucratic law and to the rights, duties, and privileges of offices that are prescribed by the legally constituted codes and tables of organization of his organization. He is enjoined in principle to separate personal considerations, money, and influence from the objective forms and procedures of his organization. He does not provide his own capital, tools, books, office space, or resources, but depends on the organization for them.

He is a cog in a gigantic machine that has an objective character to which he must submit himself. All of this breeds a specific type of social character, or, in our terms, *a set of attitudes.* These include the habits of mind of disciplined obedience to impersonal causes, organizations, and institutions. It includes matter-of-factness or impersonality in dealing with others, the denial of sentiment, personal loyalties and attachments, warmth, and anger. It implies the disenchantment of all that is poetic, myth-oriented, chivalrous, or humane, when such humanity conflicts with the objectivity and impersonality of bureaucratically specified procedures. It implies an emphasis on rationality in action, but a rationality of procedures. In large-scale organizations, the total flow of rationality of action is broken down into thousands of formal procedural acts, each or only a series of which fall within the jurisdiction of any one bureaucrat. No one official may know, or needs to know, the substantive rationality that governs the action of the total enterprise. Formal or functional rationality may be devoid of content as far as any one official is concerned, though that official may have faith in the rationality of the entire enterprise. That faith can be called *morale,* a submission to objective "reasons of state," organizational purposes or mission. Such morale conditions the employee to accept his total dependence on the bureaucracy as a whole and to act as a willing cog in the machine. In addition, this morale is sustained by the fact that one's career will advance with one's willingness to serve and to accept the rationality of the entire enterprise.

Other aspects of the bureaucratic attitude have been criticized. Among other reasons, as his narrow expertness increases, the bureaucrat becomes less and less able to see the overall intentions that govern his actions and the consequences of his action; more and more, he becomes an expert over less and less. As a result, he becomes a "trained incompetent," or exhibits forms of "occupational psychosis." Such a criticism of bureaucracy per se or of the bureaucrat would be unfair from the standpoint of the functional theory of bureaucracy, unless the bureaucracy was so imperfectly organized that the official in his trained incapacity could not exercise the functions that lead to the substantive rationality, the policy purposes of the organization, whether the bureaucrat, in fact, was or was not aware of the intentions that governed that substantive rationality. This criticism might be valid on aesthetic or social-psychological grounds since it portrays man without substance, soul, or heart, devoid of feeling, interest, passion, wisdom, or humanity. Such an image of the bureaucrat as a human being may not be appropriate unless it can be established that the bureaucrat takes over the habits of mind from his work into his nonwork life. The separation of office from domicile, at least in principle, allows the bureaucrat to exist in other, perhaps more human terms, when not on the job. But, certainly, the image of the soulless bureaucrat has become so prevalent, we believe, that it constitutes a major source for the rebellion of youth against possible careers as "clerks" in modern bureaucracies. Beyond this, there is sufficient evidence by now that, despite or perhaps because of the very formal nature of bureaucracies, individual bureaucrats at all levels conspire (perhaps unwittingly) against the bureaucratic system to violate its formal nature. Thus, bureaucratic environments are interlaced with cliques, friendship groups, informal organizations and procedures, which tend to make the environment (at times) more human, personal, warm, and frequently, for these very reasons, less efficient. It is perhaps because of the violation of the formal nature of bureaucracy that complaints on the grounds of inefficiency equal complaints against bureaucracy on the grounds of inhumanity.[2]

At another level, bureaucracy is complained about because, despite its rules, bureaucrats exceed their authority. The very powerlessness of the bureaucrats, a powerlessness caused by strict delimitation of jurisdiction and by standardized procedures, causes some bureaucrats to attempt to enhance what minor powers they have in dealing with less powerful officials, and with their bureaucratic clientele. Thus, petty sadism, obstruction, and delay are standard complaints made against bureaucrats by clients who must deal with them even when the latter are bureaucrats who are not acting in their role as bureaucrats themselves.[3] In a society that is highly bureaucratized, the proportion of people who are not bureaucrats must necessarily be low. But, of course, the opposite complaint is also made, that bureaucrats, in their subservience to bureaucratic and class superiors are often subservient to the point where they confirm the sense of omnipotence of their superiors and deny superiors access to necessary but often unwelcome information. But in both cases—bureaucratic subservience and bureaucratic authoritarianism—the bureaucrat, in overcompensating for powerlessness, or in expressing it through subservience, responds primarily to the dimension of power and subordinates other aspects of his social relationships to power relationships.

At still another level, the bureaucrat is charged with being a legalist, a pettifogger, fully aware of all of the procedures and limits on jurisdiction that make it impossible for him to act in any positive way. He thus becomes an expert in inaction, buck-passing, and in bureaucratic obstruction. At the same time, he is able to insist on his own officially defined rights, privileges, precedents, rank, and exemptions from obligations, agreements, or work demands. Such charges alternate with charges of exceeding one's bureaucratic authority, abusing one's position, power grabbing, and expanding one's prerogatives. Both charges may be true with variations in major orientation being related to bureaucratic level. Bureaucratic expansiveness is more likely at the higher levels, and bureaucratic intransigence or immobility more prevalent at lower levels. Length in grade and mobility aspirations may be another significant variable, with the least aspiring being given most to bureaucratic intransigence.

Dependence on procedure in bureaucracies has led to the charge that bureaucracy results in the development of ritualism: that forms, procedures, and methods of bureaucracy result primarily in the multiplication of paperwork that has no other function than itself. Bureaucratic inefficiency is a by-product of such ritualism.

The very conflicts between bureaucracy as a formal means of carrying out action, its dependence on rules, procedures, paperwork, and the necessity for fast, immediate, efficient action at times lead to a contradiction between the appearances of bureaucracy and its reality. Regardless of whether the action undertaken by bureaucrats is legal or illegal, personal or impersonal, oriented to substantive action or purely ritualistic, the action so undertaken is always presented publicly in legalistic, formalistic, "ritualistic" procedures, language, and form. This is true even when the action of the bureaucrat is generous, personal, malevolent, or illegal. The bureaucrat must follow the bureaucratic form at the expense of his personal generosity or malevolence in order to escape charges that he violates bureaucratic law, jurisdictions, and procedure. The bureaucratic milieu always conveys an aura of hypocrisy. It is always more legalistic than the actions it undertakes, more proper than honest, more impersonal in form than in content, and more righteous than right. The atmosphere of hypocrisy offends laymen who enter the ambience of bureaucracy. But because bureaucracy is "hypocritical" in its form, it is not as legalistic, impersonal, and inhuman as the form suggests.

Other charges against bureaucracy are more serious. At a societal level, bureaucracies are charged with an inevitable tendency toward expansion. The very esprit de corps, the reasons of state, and the ideologies necessary to create the sense of disciplined morale within a bureaucracy result in the tendency for each bureaucracy to see its mission or function as indispensable. An alleged absence of funds, personnel, and jurisdictional limits are seen as impediments to the complete fulfillment of the original mission or of carrying out that mission in related fields or jurisdictions. Almost all bureaucracies tend to find reasons for expanding and to find objective bases for such expansion. Expansion creates new jobs, new opportunities for advancement, and validates the original service ideal. Such expansionist tendencies are further promoted by the fact that the specialization and expertise assembled in a bureaucracy as a whole provide the bureaucracy with access to information that justifies its case. Moreover, the withholding of information by the same bureaucracies may weaken the power of the political overseers of the bureaucracy or, in political bureaucracies, the electorate, so that the only sources of information operate in favor of the bureau. Such withholding of information protects the bureaucracy from evidence of its own incompetence and allows bureaucrats to escape responsibility for actions that are illegal or incompetent. But even more important, the central position of the bureaucracy results in the assumption of policy powers by bureaucrats, resulting in the conversion of elected officials to figureheads. Bureaucracy tends to result in a centralization of power and the usurpation of power over policy by those who legally do not have such powers. Bureaucracy, it is argued, is fundamentally authoritarian, not only in its internal structure but also with respect to its external relations.

The Functional Indispensability of Bureaucracy

The original Weberian discussion of bureaucracy was based on a number of premises. The first of these was that bureaucracy as a means of administration replaced such other forms of administration as feudalism, patrician rule, and boss rule in urban political machines. In comparison with these other forms of administration, there is no doubt that bureaucracy is faster, cheaper, and more efficient. All the inefficiencies of bureaucracy must be understood in comparison with the still greater inefficiencies intrinsic to the other systems of administration. On this basis, there is no doubt that bureaucracy with all its imperfections still remains that most efficient means of administration. Moreover, all large-scale organizations, and all pressures within society that are based on increasing the scale and efficiency of organizational operation result in further extensions of bureaucracy. Most attempts to reform bureaucracy focus on humanizing it, making it more acceptable and tolerable. Few of these attempts alter its fundamental structure.

Some recent attempts at decentralization and community control are aimed at making administration more responsible by breaking up large-scale bureaucracies into smaller units and subjecting these smaller units to local political control. It is not clear at this time whether such attempts will result in the reinstitution of local boss rule or whether the subdivided units are in fact so large as to result in merely smaller bureaucracies.[4] Certainly, the much celebrated decentralization of General Motors in the early forties resulted in the creation of five gigantic bureaucracies subjected only to the financial controls of a central board of directors in place of the one gigantic bureaucracy that was being "controlled."

From a technical point of view, the growth of bureaucracies has largely been a product of the expansion of those functions that are most efficiently administered by bureaucratic organizations. Some inefficiencies of coordination, control, and integration become central when bureaucracies grow so large that the constituent units and officials lose awareness or knowledge of who their colleagues are and of the functions that they jointly manage. At this point, hosts of problems emerge. Problems of communication, record keeping, filing, coordination, processing of paperwork, and transmitting of orders become so large that mechanical errors in the carrying out of routine functions, as well as bureaucratic sabotage caused by poor "morale" and inadequate training, can cause large-scale error and inefficiency simply because the bureaucracy as a whole is so complex and delicately balanced. At the same time, the very complexity of bureaucracy depends on the willingness of lower-ranking officials to be punctilious in processing the flow of paperwork, in filing, and in observing detailed bureaucratic codes. Some social scientists have suggested that segments of this officialdom, penetrated by a new consciousness, by rising expectations, and by disdain for the petty clerical work that constitutes the lifeblood of bureaucracy, engage in positive acts of sabotage or develop unreflective attitudes of indifference, carelessness, or repugnance and, in doing so, weaken the very basis of bureaucracy at the level of mechanical efficiency. To the extent that these are simply problems of scale, of the scope and complexity of the functions involved, decentralization of the bureaucracy may not be a solution, since it may not be possible to divide complex interrelated functions among a number of separate organizations. Thus, it may be difficult to subdivide the functions of a telephone company in any one metropolitan area even though at times it appears that that telephone system as a whole is decreasing in efficiency. If the problem of efficiency is to be solved, it appears that it has to be solved in terms of more perfect coordination, more effective personnel policy and administration, greater knowledge of the internal communications of the system, better planning, and provision for the balanced growth and coordination of functions. More carefully planned bureaucratic extension may be the solution to such problems, not the elimination of bureaucracy itself.

Suprabureaucratic Policy Formation

A second major aspect of the growth of bureaucracy is that regardless of technical function, bureaucracy is a power instrument. The development of state bureaucracies grew as a means of controlling and limiting the power of local feudal lords; military bureaucracies were an answer to a decentralized mercenary or feudal army, and industrial bureaucracy was a means of centralizing economic power. Yet, in all these cases, beyond the bureaucracy were political and economic overlords. While bureaucracy is primarily a means of administration, it is not necessarily the goal of administration. The tendency to confuse the internal authoritarianism of bureaucracy with its external ends is far too easy a solution to the theoretical problem of bureaucracy.

Bureaucracies have existed within totalitarian states and within democratic states. Totalitarian states have rejected the theory of bureaucracy, as in Nazi Germany, in which the Fuehrer principle was used as an alternative to stable bureaucracies, and as in Italian fascism, which was notably weak in its administrative effectiveness.

Bureaucracy as a technical instrument of administration thus is subject to political, economic, and social pressures emerging from sources other than the particular bureaucracies. As modern societies become increasingly bureaucratized, individual bureaucracies provide part of the political pressures that constitute the framework for policy making that govern bureaucracies other than the one in question. Thus, the totalitarian aspirations of any one bureaucracy are limited by the plurality of pressures created by all the bureaucracies that govern the actions carried out by any one. But individuals and pressure groups in a society can be organized by political parties and by other groups that are not organized primarily as bureaucracies, or if so, that cut across the jurisdictions of a particular bureaucracy in such ways that the pressures and interests represented by a pressure group cannot be conceived of as being bureaucratic in nature. Though oil companies, for example, are organized internally on bureaucratic lines, the political interest of these companies is not particularly bureaucratic but rather reflects their interest in oil, markets, taxes, privileges, government regulations, pipelines, etc. In such cases, the struggles of interest groups to dominate or control the formulation of social policy in a given area goes on almost as if bureaucracy were not a factor in the given area. To be sure, the central bureaucracy carrying out the policy in that area will have bureaucratic interests of its own, but these will be limited by the activities of numerous other interest groups, which, while themselves bureaucratically organized, will not make, in the given area of interest, its bureaucratic interests the central focus of concern.

Substantive, Formal, and Functional Rationality

But all of this has consequences for our very image of bureaucracy. The theorists of bureaucracy, notably Weber and Mannheim, have emphasized the rationality of bureaucracy; bureaucracy can be conceived of as having substantive, formal, and functional rationality.[5]

Substantive rationality is defined as the relationship between means and ends. *Formal* and *functional rationality* refer to the procedures by which the means lead to an end. By *formal rationality* is meant the use of systematic, legal procedures in an objective and impersonal way. *Functional rationality* refers to the integration of jurisdictions and procedures so that they interlock in a consistent and organized way, despite the fact that not all bureaucrats need be conscious of the relationship of their function to the ultimate end of action. The notion of substantive rationality, however, implies that there is a clear-cut set of goals that are consciously articulated in a consistent and rational manner and that these goals can be implemented to produce a desired effect. The notion of rational planning, consistency, and harmony of goals all imply a higher rationality than merely the formal or functional rationality of bureaucratic procedures, means, or internal operations.

We do not argue with notions of formal or functional rationality. But our previous discussion of the pluralism of bureaucracies, interest groups, and pressures that operate on the formulation of social policy for a particular bureaucracy opens the question whether substantive rationality in fact governs bureaucratic or other forms of the modern planning of social policy. The discussion of bureaucracy in its traditional forms assumed that bureaucracy is capable of developing centralized planning within its jurisdictional area. It viewed bureaucracy as an institution within a nonbureaucratic world. It did not envisage either the competition between bureaucracies in a bureaucratized world, nor did it fully envisage the state machinery above the level of a single bureaucracy, the legislative or policymaking organizations, as being fully subject to pluralistic pressures. In short, planning functions were seen as artifacts of a single set of hierarchical values that were assumed to be logically interrelated. In fact, one of the major ideologies for modern planning has been that planning introduces order. Implicit in the assumption that planning is rational may be the notion that the planners operate within the framework of a coherent set of values at the political level, perhaps symbolized by the state or the nation, in which national goals are assumed to be clear and unified. Taking place within the framework of such clarified goals, planning becomes a technical means to realize goals that are outside the planning process. Yet if one were to conceive of the state, the nation, as a collectivity of individuals and groups, classes, organizations, political parties, each of which may have goals, interests, ideologies, and structures of relevance that are sometimes unrelated to each other and often in conflict, then the goals within which planning takes place are not to be regarded as given and are often defined and articulated only within the process of planning itself.

The Planning Attitude

Planning may involve more than an ideology of order. It may emerge from the desire to extend the jurisdiction of an existing bureaucracy over a wider and wider sphere of operations, and in doing so subject them to the order given by that bureaucracy. It may arise out of the expansion of the sense of felt needs, new functions, services, and goals that arise out of a sense of ideological changes, political pressures, and the emergence of new groups and interests in society, whose needs can only be met by the development of planning and the expansion of bureaucracy. The failure of existing institutions, bureaucratic and nonbureaucratic, to meet needs that were already present or newly emerging needs may call for the extension of bureaucracy and planning or, alternatively, the reconstitution of existing bureaucracy and planning.

But wherever planning occurs, it is the end product of usually a long period of ideological, institutional, and interest-group pressure, propaganda, bargaining, and policy determination. The need for planning in this sense is never self-evident except to ideologists and interest groups of particular forms of planning and policy. The specific content of the plan is never self-evident to those involved in the development and articulation of planning. That specific content emerges only during the process of planning.

The above discussion allows us to state systematically the elements and ingredients necessary to conceptualize bureaucratic planning. Most of the manifest classical features of bureaucracy, as described above, refer to its internal operation below the level of policy making and planning. Bureaucratic planners must take into account the existence of other bureaucracies, their interests, ideologies, jurisdictions, resources, potential rivalries and competitions, and their capacity to deflect, inhibit, or advance policy in a given area. In doing so, the bureaucratic planners must treat these other groups, though bureaucracies, in virtually the same way that they treat nonbureaucratic interest and ideological groups. These other groups may include political associations and parties, journalistic specialists, formal and informal voluntary associations, and other powerful leaders in the area for which planning is contemplated. The process of constructing a plan or a new or changed policy must envisage in advance or anticipate the interests and ideologies of all groups relevant to the policy or planning area. This is necessarily so, since the adoption and implementation of the plan rests upon the ability to anticipate the resistance of these other groups to the contemplated plan or policy. Successful planning also depends upon the ability of the planners to secure support for the adoption of the plan, and, if adopted, support in the implementation of the plan. Technical planners are frequently forced to call into consultation all groups who have an ideological or interest relationship to the area of planning or policy under consideration. Consultation may be direct and immediate and informal. When informal, the groups consulted are usually considered to be an "establishment." An establishment is the self-selected, relevant, and powerful representatives of the dominant institutions in a given area. At other times, the planning process involves the more formal assemblage of commissions or committees. Committees are usually selected to represent all the relevant and powerful agencies and organizations involved in the planning area. Even when such formal processes are not adopted, planners must take into account the existence of relevant establishments by anticipating their response, their possible support, their resistance, and the bases of such support and resistance. If they do not take these groups, interests, and ideologies into account, they can expect that their plan will generate its own opposition.[6] As a result of these processes, planning as a social process involves the following:

1. The process is highly formalized.

2. Major groups who would respond to the plan are brought into the planning process before the plan is actually formulated.

3. Their perspectives, interests, and ideologies, are taken into account in the planning process regardless of whether their perspectives, interests, and ideologies are consistent with the intention of the plan. Ignoring these other perspectives is possible only when:

    a. The area being planned is too unimportant to be worthy of notice by otherwise potentially impeding groups, or

    b. The planning group has sufficient power and authority to be able to ignore the resistance of the potentially impeding groups.

    c. All other bases for ignoring relevant publics and interest groups must be classified as oversight, ignorance, and incompetence.

Planning Functions

In incorporating the ideologies, interests, and perspectives of the potentially supporting and impeding groups into the planning process, the planning function becomes less the formulation of a substantive plan and more the organization of interests, ideologies, consent, and support for a plan that will emerge only after the outside groups in question have been organized. The planning function, at least at the highest political and professional levels, consists of organizing the interest groups in question, rather than manifestly constructing a plan. It includes discerning what are the relevant interest groups in question. This is no mean task since the relevance of a potential responding group to a planning operation is in part a function of the plan, which at early stages is unknown. Yet there is sufficient experience in all planning operations for planners to realize that the neglect or oversight of a particular relevant group may destroy the plan when the relevant group finds either that it has not been consulted or that the plan does not take into account, because of neglect and oversight, its interests and ideologies. Unless sensitivity to the possible effects of a plan or policy on a potentially powerful responding group is continually maintained, major political faux pas, resistance, and opposition can emerge. This is especially true in the later stages of a planning operation when the planners are considering what appears to be the purely technical implementation of the plan. At this stage, their attention is likely to be deflected from the political consequences of what appear to be purely technical considerations. The reemergence of unforeseen political dimensions of planning in the technical stages of planning disrupts the planning process.

After the relevant "publics" to the plan are discerned, then the planning process consists of the solicitation of points of view, consultation, and the mediation and conciliation of different interests, ideologies, and viewpoints to be incorporated into the plan. It includes the creation of agendas for such consideration and the organization of conferences, committee meetings, and joint consultations. In these stages, the technical planners are concerned with mediation, negotiation, bargaining, and the facilitation of compromises between divergent points of view.

To a large extent, planning becomes purely technical facilitation, administration, mediation, and bargaining between interest groups whose ideologies and interests represent the substance out of which the actual plan emerges. The professional planner exercises purely technical functions. Major functions, technical in nature, may have substantive consequences. The planner, first of all, usually assembles the technical information relevant to the area of planning and may have access to information that may not be available to any of the direct interest groups (though the reverse is also likely to be true). In carrying out the mediating and negotiating functions outlined above, the planner may by now have more access to the interests, ideologies, and points of resistance and compromise among the various groups engaged in the planning process than any of these groups may have with respect to each other. Therefore, the planner can arrange compromises or focus the plan in a given area more easily than any one of the parties. By being outside the major ideological and interest areas, the technical planner may have some degree of "objectivity" and distance from such issues and may be able to suggest alternatives that the ideologists and interest groups cannot.

The discussion above indicates that within any area of planning, a broad range of interests, perspectives, and ideologies are operative among a plurality of persons, groups, and agencies, all of which have different amounts of power, influence, and resources to aid or implement the plan. The primary task of the planner is to reconcile these varied interests and ideologies in such a way as to organize a consensus that will enable the drafting of a plan and to organize sufficient support for the plan, once drafted, to gain adoption and implementation.[7]

Since the various groups and agencies that focus on any area under consideration for planning or policy formation have often competing or unrelated policy perspectives and interests, the construction of a plan involves a series of compromises, the adoption of often unrelated and at times contradictory or mutually antagonistic goals and purposes. Some statements of goals may be incorporated only as a sop to neutralize the opposition of a relevant interest group to a plan. Some may be only verbal formulas whose implementation is not intended. Other incorporations may be designed to gratify the vanity of an individual consultant. Still others may be intended to placate the constituency of a co-opted representative of an interest group who want to go along with the plan because of a sense of community, good fellowship, and morale that the planning process creates in its very operation. Beyond this, the prestige offered to a representative of a low-prestige interest group in a high-prestige planning operation may often, at least temporarily, force him to suspend his "better"—or at least narrower—judgment. The plan will embody a vast number of conflicting goals, values, interests, and means. Since separate means are related to individual goals, and since means are often treated or considered separately from ends in any plan, the means to one goal quite frequently contradict or conflict with the means to another goal. Those who understand the political nature of a plan are often aware of the relationship of particular means to particular ends. Those who at later times are given the task of implementing the plan are not privy to such hidden understandings and thus see the plan as a "mess" or as a self-contradictory and self-neutralizing guide to action. Yet all the above is necessary to organize a consensus and to secure the adoption and implementation of the plan.[8]

The Rationality of Planning

But since the planning process emphasizes the rationality implicit in the planning process, the process of drawing up the final draft of a plan requires that the plan be stated as a logical, rational, systematic, orderly scheme for action. Regardless of the inconsistencies, contradictions, congeries, and lack of clarity between means and ends, the form and style of the plan as a document always suggests the kind of substantive rationality that is always present in theories of planning, bureaucracy, and social policy.

So far as we know, there are very few plans that do not involve these elements of planned irrationalities in their hidden scenarios. When they do not contain these irrationalities, they are the plans of a single, monolithic agency dealing with at most very narrow technical problems that do not have an impact on a wide number of audiences and publics.

Once a plan is formulated with respect to its overall goals and means, the problem of technical implementation emerges. At this point, formal or substantive rationality are salient, for the planners must work out the administrative machinery and the jurisdictions by which a plan must be carried out. However, even at these levels the process of functional rationalization involves political considerations, if and when implementation involves the loss of jurisdiction or the realignment of jurisdictions with respect to the bureaucracy entrusted with the implementation of the plan and other organizations on which that bureaucracy impinges. Such conflicts may emerge in the technical implementation of the plan, or they may emerge after the execution of the plan has been undertaken, when hidden and unanticipated implications of the plan become apparent. At this stage, reconsideration of the political dimensions of the plan may take place, or, as is more often the case, a new plan is proposed. Such reconsideration may occur only after years have passed.

In addition, technical implementation of the plan involves pricing out the cost of the operation of the plan, the creation of tables of organization involving the use of personnel, and costing out the salaries of such personnel. When this is done, quite frequently the costs may far exceed anything anticipated in a planning operation. If this does happen, means must be devised to cut back the scale and focus of the plan. Theoretically, this could involve reconsideration of the overall goals and purposes of the plan; but since such reconsideration also involves the reconstitution of the complicated and unwieldy machinery of organizing consent, the tendency is not to tamper with the overall agreements that became the basis for the plan. The tendency is to thin out the resources needed to implement relatively ambitious plans so that few goals are attainable. The process of "thinning out" the implementation of the plan may take the form of cutting back the means of achieving each of the plurality of ends so that the means are below the threshold of effectiveness. The alternative of concentrating all or a major part of the means to a restricted number of ends might result in greater effectiveness in achieving these ends, but such a strategy might involve violation of the agreements that made the planning possible. In working out a strategy of covering all bases, the plan that emerges is often an empty shell. In addition, the implementation of a plan often requires estimates of the technical efficiency of the scientific or technological apparatus on which the plan depends. In areas of innovation, such estimates are only "guesstimates." As a result, the success of the plan as a whole and its technical implementation can only be determined after the fact, even allowing for test operations and contingency plans. When such technological innovations do not produce the estimated effects, then costs may rise at unanticipated rates and the planners, the bureaucrats, or policy makers become subject to criticism. When technological results are better than anticipated, a budgetary surplus may be possible. At this point, the task before the bureaucrats is to use up the funds in such a way as to make it not appear that they made a mistake in planning or estimating.

When technological innovation is not a factor and when the basic costs and administrative implementation rest upon incidence of use of services and facilities, imperfect estimating may result in the same kinds of binds and squeezes that are produced by technological change. Cost estimates must take into account the rate of inflation in the society as a whole and the increasing costs of the goods and services to be required over the length of a plan. Mistakes in estimating costs are a major source of failure and an excuse for the failure of long-range planning. At another level, the competence and efficiency of those entrusted with the execution of the plan must be evaluated. Planners, we suspect, are loath to build into their planning estimates factors such as incompetence, laziness, inefficiency, bungling, and red tape.[9] If such factors are anticipated, they are usually concealed in other budgetary and personnel categories. All too often, people engaged in planning are socially and organizationally far above the personnel engaged in actual execution of the plan. They tend to take execution for granted. Failures in such estimates are usually compensated for in time periods occurring after the initial implementation of the plan and are subsumed under the category of "experience."[10]

Bureaucratic Narrowness

An interesting problem in planning that runs contrary to the image of planners and bureaucrats as power hungry often occurs. At times, the ideological and interest groups pressing for a plan propose planning and bureaucratic operations that appear to be technically unrealizable. Public pressure and ideological interests suggest that certain planning tasks are highly desirable and that not planning to meet felt needs is politically indefensible. Yet the resistance of an area to planning or the lack of resources likely to be allocated for a highly desirable goal will cause bureaucrats to try to avoid responsibility for the planning operation or its implementation. This is especially true when established bureaucracies have already developed a clear-cut, narrow, and stereotyped image of their own operation, based on techniques that do not "fit" the contemplated planning. In such situations, bureaucrats are likely to resist attempts by others to saddle them with new functions and duties, despite the fact that the functions would entail larger budgets, promotions, and expanded jurisdictions. Even when such missions are handed to established bureaucracies under the above circumstances, some are tempted to shrink the mission to performing what already has been done, or to performing the new assignment by using familiar techniques. In such cases, the problem is not bureaucratic "imperialism" but bureaucratic "narrowness."

Social and Advocacy Planning

Planners and others concerned with urban problems have begun to recognize that planning that is conceived in purely physical terms can be disastrous. Lewis Mumford, Jane Jacobs, and Herbert Gans are among those who have maintained that attention to purely physical planning without concern for social relationships can produce plans whose effects are inhuman and that intensify urban problems.[11] Gans described the demolition of Boston's West End as crude and heavy-handed and a decision that resulted in a net loss for the city. Mumford and Jacobs, though in disagreement over what is to be done next, agree on the pernicious results of project housing plans.[12]

As a result, there has been a turn to planning for social policy in terms of a mix of factors other than the purely physical, and in some instances such planning is directed entirely toward such goals as the elimination of poverty, with little or no discussion of physical or urban planning. These plans include programs aimed at increasing earning power, job development, encouraging community action, the invitation of industry into poverty areas, planning for the life cycles of the poor, encouraging local community leaders to participate in the planning of neighborhood services, and so forth. New York City's Model Cities Program is one outgrowth of such planning.[13]

Richard Titmuss's studies of the effect of welfare-state programs in Great Britain suggests distortive and unforeseen results that may prove as disheartening to social policy planners as previous results have proven for the planners of urban renewal. The provision of welfare services to the urban poor may result, Titmuss argues, in a failure to make changes in their real income, inasmuch as the provision of such programs may be regarded as an adequate substitute.[14]

Bureaucratic professionals may promote and encourage the development of new planning jurisdictions and organizations in areas that manifestly compete with their own. This is likely to occur when bureaucrats are asked to take responsibility for problems regarded as unsolvable or for which techniques of solution lie outside of the traditional competence or imagination of the bureaucrats. In creating a new agency to handle extremely difficult problems, established agencies can divest themselves of responsibility for solving problems for which lack of solution might otherwise embarrass them.

Policy making and planning are not as rational a process as is assumed by such terms as *substantive rationality* or by the very word *planning*. Much of what is usually thought to be planning is the rational articulation of the forms of planning. In substance, planning is a highly political operation based on the reconciliation of conflicting interests and ideologies in order to gain consent for policies and programs and to overcome opposition to such policies.

These political processes must be thought of as the primary planning processes.[15] The articulation of planning in rational form is at best a secondary process. But planning as an ideology emphasizes its rational components and tends to de-emphasize the political components, which are neither rational nor subject to the control of the planner as technician or planning ideologist. As a result, one of the persistent and compelling problems facing planners as professionals is how to deal with the violations of the ideology of planning, wherever planning is undertaken.

Another constant problem is that the planner who believes in the ideology of planning as the basis for the creation of an orderly or humane society continuously discovers that he is being used as a tool by vested interests whose interest in planning is only a means to secure what to the planner are narrow, selfish, personal, and jurisdictional ends. The recurrent disillusionment results at times in cynicism, at times in the abandonment of planning ideals, and in the joining of nonplanning "interest establishments." At other times, it results in a professional mobility in which the planner moves from planning field to planning field, hoping to find an area where both his technical talent and ideological commitment can be simultaneously gratified.

Notes

1. Major documents on bureaucracy include Max Weber, "Bureaucracy," in *From Max Weber: Essays in Sociology*, eds. and trans. Hans H. Gerth and C. Wright Mills (New York: Oxford University Press, 1946); Robert Merton, *Social Theory and Social Structure*, rev. ed. (New York: Free Press, 1957), chs. VI and VII; C. Wright Mills, *White Collar* (New York: Oxford University Press, 1959); Karl Mannheim, *Man and Society in an Age of Reconstruction* (New York: Harcourt, Brace, 1940); Robert Michels, *Political Parties* (New York: Macmillan, 1962); Peter Blau, *The Dynamics of Bureaucracy* (Chicago: University of Chicago Press, 1955); Philip Selznick, *TVA and the Grass Roots* (Berkeley: University of California Press, 1949; repr. Harper, 1966). Important studies include F. J. Roethlisberger and J. Dickson, *Management and the Worker* (Cambridge, MA: Harvard University Press, 1939); F. J. Roethlisberger, *Management and Morale* (Cambridge, MA: Harvard University Press, 1947); Elton Mayo, *The Human Problems of an Industrial Civilization* (New York: Macmillan, 1933); William F. Whyte, *Human Relations in the Restaurant Industry* (New York: McGraw-Hill, 1948). Useful readings are to be found in Robert K. Merton, Ailsa P. Gray, Barbara Hockey, and Hanna C. Selvin, eds., *Reader in Bureaucracy* (New York: Free Press, 1952); Amitai Etzioni, ed., *Complex Organizations: A Sociological Reader* (New York: Holt, Rinehart & Winston, 1961); valuable also is Melville Dalton, *Men Who Manage* (New York: Wiley, 1959). A recent study is David Rogers, *110 Livingston Street: Politics and Bureaucracy in the New York City School System* (New York: Random House, 1968), especially ch. VIII. See also Joseph Bensman and Bernard Rosenberg, *Mass, Class & Bureaucracy* (Englewood Cliffs, NJ: Prentice-Hall, 1963), chs. 9 and 10. Our discussion of bureaucracy draws upon and summarizes the material above.

2. Mayo, Roethlisberger and Dickson, Blau, Dalton, and Whyte, among others, have all emphasized the informal as part of bureaucracy, and by now they are part of the dominant tradition in the field. For other aspects of the bureaucratic character, see Arthur K. Davis, "Bureaucratic Patterns in the Navy Officer Corps," *Social Forces* 27 (1948), 143-53, reprinted in Merton et al., 380-95.

3. See the discussion by Philip Selznick in his "An Approach to a Theory of Bureaucracy," *American Sociological Review* 8 (February 1943), 47-54, reprinted in Lewis A. Coser and Bernard Rosenberg, eds., *Sociological Theory: A Book of Readings*, 2nd ed. (New York: Macmillan, 1964).

4. A current illustration is the ongoing decentralization of New York City's public schools. The *New York Times* of May 8, 1971, carried a story by Emanuel Perlmutter: "Decentralization of Schools Fails, Kenneth Clark Says." Dr. Clark is quoted as seeing those involved in decentralization as having forgotten its original purpose and as having become involved primarily in struggles for power and control. The results to date may not be conclusive.

5. See Weber's "Bureaucracy" in *From Max Weber*, 220. In Mannheim's *Man and Society in an Age of Reconstruction,* see Part I, sections V and VI.

6. Martin Meyerson and Edward C. Banfield, in *Politics, Planning, and the Public Interest* (New York: Free Press, 1955), record this process in their chronicle of public housing plans for Chicago; similar processes and problems for such areas as Minneapolis and St. Paul are recorded in Alan Atschuler, *The City Planning Process* (Ithaca: Cornell University Press, 1965).

7. The difficulties these conditions make for planners who must reconcile their actual functions with the professional ideologies are discussed cogently in Altschuler, 323, 354, 359. See also Robert C. Hoover, "A View of Ethics and Planning," in the *Journal of the American Institute of Planners* 27 (November 1961), 203-304. For other views, see Norman Beckman, "The Planner as Bureaucrat," *Journal of the American Institute of Planners* 30 (November 1964), 323-27; Herbert Gamberg, "The Professional and Policy Choices in Middle-Sized Cities," *Journal of the American Institute of Planners* 37 (May 1966), 174-78. Gamberg argues that planners must learn to play local administrative politics in order to achieve their goals. Beckman suggests a more resigned attitude on the part of planners, who should accept the limitations inherent in their positions. Beckman says (323): "Not everyone is built for the bureaucratic life, and for those planners whose 'idealism' and 'professionalism' make life difficult, [planning] cannot be recommended."

The planners themselves carry a potentially authoritarian, "higher" morality inherent in their ideologies and in their roles, at least earlier along in the history of planning. Contact with local politics may serve in part as a sobering experience.

These points and much of the illustration of these points are documented in detail by Maynard Robison, in *The Ideological Development of American Planning in the 1960's*, unpublished Master's Essay, City College of the City University of New York, 1971.

8. Readers may wish to follow, by way of illustration, an issue that, at the time of writing, is in relatively early stages: the New York City Master Plan, which dates back to 1938. See, e.g., Ralph Blumenthal, "Critics Forcing Changes in Master Plan," *New York Times*, May 29, 1972:

> A deluge of community criticism of the city's proposed Master Plan will bring major changes in some neighborhood projects, according to Donald H. Elliott, chairman of the City Planning Commission. However, he said, critics who have denounced the plan . . . have misunderstood its function as a guideline. The concept of the massive document itself will not be changed, he added. . . . "We have been pushed—and I like to think we have pulled a little," said Mr. Elliott, the city's top planner, who was good-humored but tired after what he called the "physically punishing" series of night-time hearings that ended last week. . . . In addition, Mr. Elliott said, the hearings have helped to foster some changes already. . . . Mr. Elliott's publicly stated eagerness to seek changes in the plan was in contrast to his comment in an interview in February. Asked then whether the hearings until that time had brought any significant issue to his attention for the first time or had forced a change of view, he replied: "I think the answer would have to be 'No.'"

Students of planning as a bureaucratic process will follow its history with interest.

9. The need of the planner to reconcile contradictory goals, and to count on waste in his plans, is discussed in F. Stuart Chapin, *Urban Land Use Planning* (Urbana: University of Illinois Press, 1965), 62 ff. A certain "resigned opportunism" on the part of planners is also suggested by Robert T. Daland and John A. Parker, "Roles of the Planner in Urban Dynamics," in F. Stuart Chapin and Shirley F. Weiss, eds., *Urban Growth Dynamics* (New York: Wiley, 1962), 188-225. It is possible that regional planning in underdeveloped countries may serve as outlets for the idealism (and latent authoritarianism) that some planners try to retain. See Lloyd Rodwin, ed., *Planning Urban Growth*

and Regional Development (Cambridge, MA: MIT Press, 1969), and also his *Nations and Cities: A Comparison of Strategies of Urban Growth* (Boston: Houghton Mifflin, 1970). The hazards described above, however, are no less present, albeit in different form.

10. None of the above necessarily "proves" that plans are not adopted, that "plans do not work" or are stillborn, but we believe it does prove that virtually all implementations of planning result in something other than that intended by the planners at the time of the inception of the planning. As a matter of fact, at the time that plans are adopted, it is most often necessary to forget or conceal the aspirations and intentions that governed the plan. If the planning is reasonably acceptable to its audience at the time of its realization, the audience will tend to forget a major part of the extremely complex steps, adjustments, and readjustments that took place between conception and delivery. If the plan is conspicuously so successful that it surprises the parties involved, then awareness of the planning process will be salient and celebrated, though all the confusion, conflict, misunderstandings and inefficiencies will be "repressed." If the plan, when implemented, is a sudden, conspicuous, and important failure, then awareness of the planning process becomes an object for historical research. The intentions here are usually to distribute and redistribute the blame and to create the confidence that such disasters will not reoccur. When this is done, it is possible to undertake new planning ventures. See, for elaboration, Arthur J. Vidich and Joseph Bensman, *Small Town in Mass Society*, rev. ed. (Princeton, NJ: Princeton University Press, 1968), Part IV, "The Reconciliation of Symbolic Appearances and Institutional Realities," and Part V, "The Findings, Methods, Theory and Implications of a Community Study." See also Joseph Bensman and Israel Gerver, "Crime and Punishment in the Factory: The Function of Deviancy in Maintaining the Social

System," *American Sociological Review* 28 (August 1963), 588-98. Planning can be reasonably successful when the planning agency rests upon grants of authority from outside groups or agencies or opinions that are relatively strong, focused, and clear. The necessity of compromising mutually exclusive and contradictory ends and means is not overwhelming. In this sense, planning is most likely to be effective when the planners are subject to authoritarian constraints.

11. Lewis Mumford, "Home Remedies for Urban Cancer," in *The Urban Prospect* (New York: Harcourt, Brace & World, 1968); Jane Jacobs, *The Death and Life of Great American Cities* (New York: Random House, 1961); Herbert Gans, *The Urban Villagers* (New York: Free Press, 1962). On the fate of plans, see also Gans's "Politics and Planning," in *The Levittowners* (New York: Pantheon, 1967), ch. 14.

12. This history of St. Louis's Pruitt-Igoe housing project is a case in point.

13. Edward M. Kaitz and Herbert H. Hyman, *Urban Planning for Social Welfare* (New York: Praeger, 1970); Leonard Duhl, *The Urban Condition* (New York: Basic Books, 1963); Harvey S. Perloff, "New Directions in Social Planning," *Journal of the American Institute of Planners* 21 (November 1965), 297-303; Lyle C. Fitch, "Social Planning in the Urban Cosmos," in Leo Schnore and Henry Fagin, eds., *Urban Research and Policy Planning* (Beverly Hills, CA: Sage Publishing, 1967), 329-58. See also Peter H. Rossi and Robert A. Dentler, *The Politics of Urban Renewal* (New York: Free Press, 1961), and Martin Anderson, *The Federal Bulldozer* (New York: McGraw-Hill, 1967). Also valuable here is Charles E. Silberman, *Crisis in Black and White* (New York: Random House, 1964), especially ch. 10, "The Revolt Against Welfare Colonialism."

14. Richard Titmuss, *Commitment to Welfare* (New York: Pantheon Books, 1968), Part III, "Issues of Redistribution in Social Policy"; also Richard Titmuss, *Essays on "The Welfare State,"* 2nd ed. (London: George Allen & Unwin, 1963), ch. 2, "The Social Division of Welfare: Some Reflections on the Search for Equity."

15. The decision to escalate and de-escalate the war in Vietnam was in part a very carefully planned operation, and in part it represented a conflict of a variety of different governmental pressure groups, in part the normal operations of both optimism and inefficiency, and the unwillingness of subalterns to question the political authority of their superiors; all these factors contributed to the planned chaos that ensued. In a similar sense, John F. Kennedy's decision to invade Cuba, and later Lyndon Johnson's decision to invade the Dominican Republic, were all highly planned operations, in the sense that we have described above.

PART II
Crime and Morality

4

Crime and Punishment in the Factory

Joseph Bensman with Israel Gerver

Functional and structural-functionalist theories represent attempts to describe ongoing social systems as operating units. Instead of describing factors, parts of systems or "single causes," the theorist attempts to describe the total system. The social system is a complex system of reciprocal actions and social relationships involving a plurality of individuals. In short, it is the abstracted actions of a "group."

Functional theory requires the following: (a) specification of the system, actors and actions involved, including some clear notion of the boundaries of the system; (b) specification of parts of the system (the structural elements); and (c) specification of the interrelation (function) of the parts of the system to each other and, thus, to the system as a whole.[1]

The concept of function includes (though not exclusively) concepts of motivation, "ends" or purposes.[2] Even though they are not often called "ends," ends are attributed to the system as a whole. These usually include the end of maintaining the system as an ongoing social system itself. These system-maintaining ends are sometimes called the functional prerequisites of the social system or of group life.

Published originally in a slightly different form as "Crime and Punishment in the Factory: The Function of Deviancy in Maintaining the Social System," *American Sociological Review* 28 (August 1963), 588-98 [revised version of paper originally presented at the annual meetings of the American Sociological Association, Washington, DC, September 1955].

Thus, the structural units are evaluated for their contribution to maintenance of the systems as an operative unit. *Functions,* then, are more than interrelationships of structural elements; they define and describe how a particular structural unit contributes to the maintenance of the system. Dysfunctions are defined as actions and interrelationships that operate against the maintenance of the ongoing social system.[3]

The problem of *ends* in functional and structural-functional theory remains one of the most difficult problems in the theory. If *ends* (especially the end of maintaining itself) are attributed (no matter how indirectly) to the system as a whole, then there are relatively few problems. By and large, the problem becomes one of selecting, defining, and analyzing the ends of the system. If this is done, the system has the attributes of a person; it has ends of its own, provides goals for its members, means for achieving such goals, and rewards for successful achievement of goals by the approved means. It distributes these goals, means, and rewards throughout its structural units and its membership. If it performs these functions efficiently and intelligently, it will be a closely integrated, tightly functioning system. If it provides competing goals or insufficient means for attaining socially valued rewards, it creates anomie; dysfunctional elements develop.

If one takes the opposite tack, that "systems" do not have ends, that only people do, and that the collective behavior of persons in a stable group or organization represents an accommodation of differing individual (but socially developed) ends and interests, in which "cooperation" is an implicit transaction, containing elements of coercion, sanctions, genuine cooperation, and altruism, then the entire problem becomes a different one.[4]

There is no requirement for the system as a whole to have "ends"; functions are only the "deal," the transaction that brings people together. "Dysfunctions" represent either the attempt "to make a new deal" or the dissatisfactions of some individuals with the deal they are forced to make, short of withdrawing from the system. With this alternative set of assumptions, it is necessary neither to attribute a functional prerequisite of the system for maintaining itself, nor to attribute to "functions" the requirement of contribution to the maintenance of the system.

Norms, under such a model, are not the "norms" of a system but rather the rules that determine the nature of socially permissible actions and transactions. They are established either in the past or in the present by the participants themselves and by those who achieve or have achieved authority under whatever system, power, or authority prevails at a given historical moment.

"Deviancy" is thus simply the acceptance or nonacceptance of these rules in terms of implicit or explicit estimates of consequences of conforming to or rejecting the norms of others, especially the norms of those who have authority. Since social life involves acceptance and rejection of proffered norms *or* expectancies, "deviancy"—that is, deviant action—is the expectable action of individuals who have divergent ends and of individuals who do not comply exclusively with others or with those in authority but who sometimes comply with their self-expectancies.

Deviant action thus is not a separate category of action, defiant of the central ends of a total system, but simply part of the totality of action that makes up the hundreds of individual transactions in an organization. With such a conception of "social systems," it is unnecessary to have a "clear definition" of the system or its parts. It is only necessary to describe the actions and interrelations of persons with respect to a common enterprise. Analytical description thus results in a different type of functionalism.

This paper is a case study in the internal law of one organization. The social functions of the violation of one "law" are treated in detail, in order to ascertain which of the two conceptions of function are operative in an "actual social system." The violation of "law" is specifically a rule of workmanship. For the sake of simplicity, the rules and their violations relevant to one instrument—the tap—are the subject of study. This is because the study of the tap summarizes an entire area of rules of workmanship and their violations. One could also have selected other violations of workmanship rules such as countersinking dimples, rolling of edges in fairing, stretching of metal skins, or greasing and waxing screw threads. The tap was selected as a major example because of its frequent usage and because using the tap is the most serious violation of rules of workmanship.While suggesting the engineering complexity of the data, our theoretical interest is in the social function of crime, particularly violations of private organizational law.

The research was carried out in an airplane factory employing twenty-six thousand people in the New York metropolitan area. Joseph Bensman was a participant observer from September 1953 through September 1954. He gathered his data in the daily course of work while working as an assembler on the aileron crew of the final wing line. No special research instruments were used; the ordinary activities of workers along the line were observed and noted as they occurred and were recorded daily. Factory personnel were not aware they were objects of study; the use of the tap was discussed with them in the context of the work situation.

The Tap and Its Functions

The tap is a tool, an extremely hard steel screw, whose threads are slotted to allow for the disposal of the waste metal that it cuts away. It is sufficiently hard so that when it is inserted into a nut it can cut new threads over the original threads of the nut.

In wing-assembly work, bolts or screws must be inserted in recessed nuts, which are anchored to the wing in earlier processes of assembly. The bolt or screw must pass through a wing plate before reaching the nut. In the nature of the mass production process, alignments between nuts and plate openings become distorted. Original allowable tolerances become magnified in later stages of assembly as the number of alignments that must be coordinated with each other increase with the increasing complexity of the assemblage. When the nut is not aligned with the hole, the tap can be used to cut, at a new angle, new threads in the nut for the purpose of bringing the nut and bolt into a new but not true alignment. If the tap is not used and the bolt is forced, the wing plate itself may be bent. Such new alignments, however, deviate from the specifications of the blueprint, which is based upon true alignments at every stage of the assembly process. On the basis of engineering standards, true alignments are necessary at every stage in order to achieve maximum strength and a proper equilibrium of strains and stresses.

The use of the tap is the most serious crime of workmanship conceivable in the plant. A worker can be summarily fired for merely possessing a tap. Nevertheless, at least one-half of the workforce in a position to use a tap owns at least one. Every well-equipped senior mechanic owns four or five of different sizes, and every mechanic has access to and, if need be, uses them. In fact, the mass use of the tap represents a widespread violation of this most serious rule of workmanship.

The tap is defined as a criminal instrument primarily because it destroys the effectiveness of stop nuts. Aviation nuts are specifically designed so that, once tightened, a screw or bolt cannot back out of the nut under the impact of vibration in flight. Once a nut is tapped, however, it loses its holding power and at any time, after sufficient vibration, the screw or bolt can fall out and weaken the part it holds to the wing and the wing itself.

In addition, the use of a tap is an illegal method of concealing a structural defect. If, for example, the holes were properly drilled and the nuts were properly installed, the use of the tap would be unnecessary, since specifications calling for alignment would be fulfilled. Whenever a tap is used, there are indications of deviations from standards. Furthermore, such deviations make subsequent maintenance of the airplane difficult since maintenance mechanics have no records of such illegal deviations from specifications. Taps can be used in certain cases by special mechanics when such usage is authorized by engineers and when proper paperwork supports such use. But such authorization usually requires one to three days for approval.

The tap, then, is an illegal tool, the use or possession of which carries extreme sanctions in private organizational law, but which is simultaneously widely possessed and used despite its illegal status. The problem of such a pattern for the meaning of private organizational law is to account for the wide acceptance of a crime as a means of fulfilling work requirements within a private organization, the aircraft plant.

The Socialization of the Worker

To most workers entering an aircraft plant, the tap is an unknown instrument. Dies that thread bolts—that is, the process opposite to tapping—are relatively well known and are standard equipment of the plumbing trade. The new worker does not come into this contact with the tap until he finds it impossible to align the holes in two skins. In desperation and somewhat guiltily as if he had made a mistake, he turns to his partner (a more experienced worker) and states his problem.

The experienced worker tries every legitimate technique of lining up the holes but, if these do not succeed, resorts to the tap. He taps the new thread himself, not permitting the novice to use the tap. While tapping it, he gives the novice a lecture on the dangers of getting caught and of breaking a tap in the hole, thereby leaving telltale evidence of it use.

For several weeks, the older worker will not permit his inexperienced partner to use a tap when its use is required. He leaves his own work in order to do the required tapping and finishes the job before returning to his own work. If the novice demonstrates sufficient ability and care in other aspects of his work, he will be allowed to tap the hole under the supervision of a veteran worker. When the veteran partner is absent and the now initiated worker can use the tap at his own discretion, he feels a sense of pride. In order to enjoy his newfound facility, he frequently uses the tap when it is not necessary. He may be careless in properly aligning perfectly good components and then compensate for his own carelessness by using the tap.

He may forego the earlier illegal methods (which are viewed as less serious crimes) of greasing and waxing bolts or enlarging the misaligned holes and indulge himself in the more pleasurable, challenging, and dangerous use of the tap. Sooner or later, he inevitably runs into difficulties with which he is technically unprepared to cope. When his partner and mentor is not available, he is forced to call upon the assistant foreman. If the situation requires it, the foreman will recommend the tap. If he has doubts about the worker's abilities, he may even tap the hole himself. In doing this, he risks censure of the union, because as a foreman he is not permitted to handle tools.

At the time the research was conducted, there were four levels of foremen. These were: assistant foreman (one star); foreman (two stars); assistant general foreman (three stars), and general foreman (four stars). The stars on the foremen's badges are their insignia of rank. The assistant foreman is the immediate supervisor of a work crew. The four star is the shop supervisor. The two- and three-star foremen have authority over increasingly larger sections of the assembly line. In the following discussion, the foreman refers to the one star, assistant foreman, unless otherwise noted.

While the foreman taps the hole, he lectures on the proper and technically workmanlike ways of using the tap: "The tap is turned only at quarter turns . . . never force the tap . . . it has to go in easy or it's likely to snap . . . if it snaps, your ass is in a sling, and I won't be able to get you out of it." The foreman warns the worker to make sure "not to get caught, to see that the coast is clear, to keep the tap well hidden when not in use, and to watch out for inspectors while using it." He always ends by cautioning the worker: "It's your own ass if you're caught."

When the worker feels that he is experienced and can use the tap with complete confidence, he usually buys his own, frequently displaying it to other workers and magnanimously lending it to those in need of it. He feels himself fully arrived when a two-star foreman or even an assistant general foreman borrows his tap or asks him to perform the tapping. The worker has now established his identity and becomes known to the higher-ups.

Once the right to use the tap is thus established, the indiscriminate use of it is frowned upon. A worker who uses a tap too often is considered to be a careless "butcher." A worker who can get his work done without frequently using a tap is a "mechanic." But one who doesn't use the tap when it is necessary does not get his own work done on time. Proper use of the tap requires judgment and etiquette. The tap addict is likely to become the object of jokes and to get a bad work reputation among workers, foremen, and inspectors.

Agencies of Law Enforcement

The enforcement of the plant rules of workmanship devolves upon three groups: foremen, plant quality control, and US Air Force quality control. The ultimate and supreme authority resides in the latter group. The Air Force not only sets the blueprint specifications, but also, and more importantly, can reject a finished airplane as not meeting specifications.

Furthermore, the Air Force inspectors reinspect installations that have been previously "bought" by plant quality control. If these installations do not meet Air Force standards, they are "crabbed"—that is, rejected. When this happens, the plant inspectors who bought the installations are subject to "being written up"; that is, they receive disciplinary action for unintentional negligence that may lead to suspensions, demotions, or in extreme cases loss of jobs. The Air Force inspector has the absolute right to demand that any man be fired for violating work rules.

There were only two Air Force inspectors to a shop at the time of these observations, so that it was almost impossible for Air Force inspectors to police an entire shop of over two thousand men. As an Air Force inspector walks up the line, it is standard procedure for workers to nudge other workers to inform them of the approach of the "Gestapo." When tapping is essential and when it is known that Air Force inspectors are too near, guards of workers are posted to convey advance notice of this approach to anyone who is actively tapping. This is especially true when there are plant drives against the use of the tap.

In all instances, when the Air Force inspector is in the vicinity, workers who have a reputation for open or promiscuous use of the tap are instructed by the assistant foreman to "disappear." Such types can return to work when the "coast is clear."

Despite the Air Force inspectors' high authority and the severity of their standards, they are not sufficiently numerous to be considered the major policing agency for detecting and apprehending violators of the rules of workmanship. Plant quality control is the actual law enforcement agency in terms of the daily operations of surveillance. There are approximately 150 plant inspectors in a two-thousand-man shop. They work along the assembly line along with the workers. In some cases, a panel of inspectors is assigned to inspect the work done by a number of crews who are supervised by a two-star foreman. In this system, a call book that guarantees the equal rotation of inspections is kept. When a worker has completed a job and requests an inspection, he enters his wing number and the requested inspection in the call book. The inspector, after completing an inspection, marks the job as completed and takes the next open inspection as indicated in the call book.

A result of either type of inspection setup is the free and intimate intermingling of inspectors and workers. In off moments, inspectors and workers gather together to "shoot the breeze and kill time." Inspectors, unlike workers, may have long waiting periods before their next assignment. During such periods, out of boredom and monotony, they tend to fraternize with workers. This causes conflict between the role of "good egg" and the role of policeman. A cause of leniency on the part of inspectors is intrinsic to the relationship between mechanics and themselves in circumstances not involving the tap. There is a sufficient amount of mechanical work that is not easily and immediately accessible to inspectors. This is particularly true if the inspector does not want to spend several hours on a fairly simple inspection. In order for the inspector to complete his work and make sure that the work he "buys" will be acceptable to later inspectors, he must rely on the workmanship of the mechanic. In brief, he must have faith not only in the mechanic's workmanship, but also in his willingness not to "louse him up." If the inspector gets the reputation of being a "bastard," the mechanic is under no obligation to do a good job and thus protect the inspector. Since the penalties for the use of the tap are so severe, no inspector feels comfortable about reporting a violation. A number of subterfuges are resorted to in an effort to diminish the potential conflict.

There is a general understanding that workers are not supposed to use a tap in the presence of plant inspectors. At various times, this understanding is made explicit. The inspector frequently tells the workers of his crew, "Now fellas, there's a big drive now on taps. The Air Force just issued a special memo. For god's sakes, don't use a tap when I'm around. If somebody sees it while I'm in the area, it'll be my ass. Look around first. Make sure I'm gone."

At other times, the verbalization comes from the worker. If a worker has to use a tap and the inspector is present, he will usually wait until the inspector leaves. If the inspector shows no signs of leaving, the worker will tell him to "Get the hell outa here. I got work to do and can't do it while you're around."

If the worker knows the inspector, he may take out the tap, permitting the inspector to see it. The wise inspector responds to the gesture by leaving. Of course, a worker has already "sized up" the inspector and knows whether he can rely upon him to respond as desired.

When there is an Air Force-inspired drive against the tap, the inspector will make the rounds and "lay the law down." He will say, "I want no more tapping around here. The next guy caught gets turned in. I can't cover you guys any more. I'm not kidding you bastards. If you can't do a decent job, don't do it at all. If that SOB foreman of yours insists on you doing it, tell him to do it himself. He can't make you do it. If you're caught, it's your ass not his. When the chips are down, he's got to cover himself, and he'll leave you holding the bag!"

For about three or four days thereafter, taps disappear from public view. The work slows down, and, ultimately, the inspectors forget to be zealous. A state of normal haphazard equilibrium is restored.

Other types of social relations and situations between workers and inspectors help maintain this state of equilibrium. An inspector will often see a tap in the top of a worker's tool box. He will pick it up and drop it into the bottom of the box where it cannot be seen easily. He might tell the worker that he is a "damned fool for being so careless." The inspector thus hopes to establish his dependability for the worker and creates a supply of goodwill credit that the worker must repay in the form of protecting the inspector.

Another typical worker-inspector situation occurs when a mechanic is caught in the act of tapping, and the inspector does not look away. The inspector severely reprimands the mechanic, "throw[ing] the fear of God into him," holding him in suspense as to whether he will turn him in, but then letting him go with a warning. Generally, this happens only to new workers. Occasionally, when a worker has a new inspector and no previously established trust relationship, the same situation may arise. In both cases, these situations are an integral part of the socialization of the worker to the plant or, rather, to a specific phase of its operation.

The Role of the Foreman

Another type of ceremonial escape from law enforcement through pseudo-law enforcement involves the foreman. In rare cases, an inspector will catch a worker using the tap, reprimand him, and turn him over to his foreman. The foreman then is forced to go through the procedure of reprimanding the errant worker. The foreman becomes serious and indignant, primarily because the worker let himself get caught. He gives the worker a genuine tongue lashing and reminds him once again that he, as foreman, has to go to bat to save the worker's neck. He stresses that it is only because of his intervention that the worker will not lose his job. He states, "Next time, be careful. I won't stick my neck out for you again. For god's sakes, don't use a tap, *unless it's absolutely necessary.*"

The worker is obliged to accept the reprimand and to assume the countenance of true penitent, even to the extent of promising that it won't happen again. He will say, "Awright, awright. So I got caught this time. Next time I won't get caught." Both the foreman and worker play these roles even though the worker tapped the hole at the specific request of the foreman. The most blatant violation of the mores in such a situation is when the worker grins and treats the whole thing as a comic interlude. When this happens, the foreman becomes truly enraged: "That's the trouble with you. You don't take your job seriously. You don't give a damn about nothing. How long do I have to put up with your not giving a damn!"

The public ritual therefore conceals an entirely different dimension of social functions involved in the use of the tap. It is inconceivable that the tap could be used without the active or passive collusion of the foreman. As noted, the foreman instructs the worker in its use, indicates when he wants it used, assists the worker in evading the plant rules, and, when the worker is caught, goes through the ritual of punishment. These role contradictions are intrinsic to the position of the foreman. His major responsibility is to keep production going. At the same time, he is a representative of supervision and is supposed to encourage respect for company law. He is not primarily responsible for quality, since this is the province of plant quality control—that is, inspection. He resolves the various conflicts in terms of the strongest and most persistent forms of pressures and rewards.

The work requirements of a particular foreman and his crew are determined by the Production Analysis Section, another staff organization. Workers call it *Time Study* although this is only one part of its function. Production Analysis determines, on the basis of time studies, the number of men to be assigned to a specific crew, the locations of crews on the line, and the cutting-off points for work controlled by a particular foreman. Having done this, they determine the workload required of a foreman and keep production charts on completed work. These charts are the report cards of the foreman. At a moment's glance, top supervision can single out foremen who are not pulling their weight. In aviation assembly, since the work cycle for a particular team is relatively long (four to eight hours) and since a foreman has relatively few teams (usually three) all doing the same job, any slowdown that delays one team damages the foreman's production record in the immediate perceivable terms of the report card. Moreover, delay caused by the inability of one crew to complete its task prevents other crews from working on that wing. The foremen of these crews will complain to the two- or three-star foremen that they are being held up and that their production records will suffer because of another foreman's incompetence.

As a result, the pressures "to get work out" are paramount for the foreman. There is a relatively high turnover among foremen, even at the two-star level. Production records are always the major consideration in supervisory mobility. All other considerations—for example, sociability, work knowledge, personality, and so on—are assumed to be measured by the production chart.

In this context, the foreman, vis-à-vis the ticklish question of the tap, is compelled to violate some of the most important laws of the company and the Air Force. Crucial instances occur at times when the Air Force institutes stringent anti-tap enforcement measures. When key holes do not line up, it may be necessary, as an alternative to using the tap, to disassemble previous installations. The disassembling and reassembling may take a full eight hours before the previously reached work stage is again reached. The production chart for that eight-hour period will indicate that no work has been done. In such a situation, the worker may refuse to tap a hole because he risks endangering his job. The foreman also may be reluctant to request directly that the worker tap a hole. To get the work done, he therefore employs a whole rhetoric of veiled requests such as "Hell, that's easy . . . you know what to do . . . you've done it before," "Maybe you can clean out the threads," or "Well, see what you can do."

If the worker is adamant, the foreman will practically beg him to do the *right* thing. He will remind the worker of past favors and will complain about his own chart rating and how "top brass doesn't give a damn about anything but what's on the chart." He usually ends his plea with "Once you get this done, you can take it easy. You know I don't work you guys too hard most of the time."

If the veiled requests and pitiful pleadings don't produce results, the foreman may take the ultimate step of tapping the hole himself. He compounds the felony because he not only violates the rules of workmanship, but also violates union rules that specifically state that no foreman can use a tool. To add insult to injury, the foreman furthermore has to borrow the tap in the midst of an anti-tap drive when taps are scarce.

From the viewpoint of production, the use of the tap is imperative to the functioning of the production organization, even though it is one of the most serious work crimes. This is recognized even at official levels, although only in indirect ways.

Taps, being made of hard steel, have the disadvantage of being brittle. If not handled carefully, they may break within the nut. This not only makes further work impossible, but makes for easier detection of the crime. To cope with such a problem, the tool crib is well equipped with a supply of tap extractors. Any worker can draw an appropriately sized tap extractor from the tool crib. All these are official company property. He can do this even amidst the most severe anti-tap drives without fear of the danger of punishment.

Crime and the Social System

Deviancy, in the sense that it implies a rejection of the norms of a social system or behavior outside of a system, is not a useful concept for analyzing this type of crime. Instead, the use of the tap is literally a major crime that is intrinsic to the system. The conception of a social system as a tightly knit series of interlocking functions, mutually supporting each other and contributing to the support and continuance of the system, is not at all applicable to an understanding of this case.

Crime as defined by the use of the tap (and the other crimes of workmanship subsumed under our discussion of the tap) supports in its own way the continuance of the system, just as the avoidance of the use of the tap contributes to the perfection of the system. The notion of deviancy or of "patterned deviancy" as a residue of systemic analysis—that is, action not conforming to the demands of the system or resulting in dysfunctions of the system—does not adequately describe the system. One reason for this inadequacy is that deviance as thus understood derives from a prior postulation of some primary, but not specifically located end that the analyst himself attributes to the system. The "deviant" action may be as central to the system as the norm it allegedly deviates from.

On the other hand, if one considers the actions called "deviant behavior" as intrinsic to the system, deviant behavior contributes to and supports the system just as does conformity, simply because the system is composed of its interrelated parts. From the standpoint of the past, any change is dysfunctional; that is, it represents a disruption of the system as it was. From the standpoint of the present, those same changes, when adopted, can be viewed as functions, since they become for the moment intrinsic parts of system.

In terms of the above analysis, the conceptualization of deviancy as functional or dysfunctional reduces to a semantic problem. Attributions of function and dysfunction are artifacts of the mode of analysis and are based on the analyst's assumptions of ends for a system, rather than on attributes of the actual collective behavior. The resolution of problems concerning the interrelations of specific social phenomena can best be performed by dealing with substantive data rather than at the level of the verbal pyrotechnics of formal model and deductive theory building. The real problems lie in relating data and concepts and not in the preoccupation with how concepts are related to each other.

Verbal play, however, is a less important concern than the problem of the assumption of ends. A system is imputed to have ends. The functions of its structural elements contribute to these ends and the maintenance of this system. The problem for research is to *locate* and *specify* these ends. It is, in principle, though not necessarily in practice, fairly easy to locate and specify the ends of specific individuals as related to their social actions, but the ends of social systems and collectivities are much more difficult to locate. There is a prevalent tendency to succumb to an ever-present danger of selecting some one set of social ends as primary and then to attribute them to the system as a whole. In such cases, the "objective world" becomes a projection of the personal values of the analyst or the values of some group of individuals in the system, to which the analyst is consciously or unconsciously linked.

If these considerations are applied to our analysis of the tap, a new level of analysis is brought into focus.

Obviously, profit making through production is the major end of the company; that is, profit making is the goal of its stockholders, board of directors, officers, and supervisory staff. Even here, though, there is a complex problem related to conflicts of ends, for example, between reinvestment and distribution of profits, expansion and profit taking. These are considerations that probably complicate the picture, but they are not treated here.

For the Air Force, the major end is a high rate of production of high quality planes at low cost. Reducing costs and maintaining quality are secondary ends or, if one wishes, the means to the primary end of producing efficient aircraft. For the individual foreman, maintaining his job, gaining a promotion, or staying out of trouble may be his primary private ends. The maintaining or exceeding of his production quota, while a major end for the "company" as a whole and as defined by the executives, is the means of attaining the private goals of the foreman.

Similarly, the primary ends of plant inspectors are to get along with workers, to avoid buying jobs that will be rejected in later inspection, and in some cases to achieve a supervisory position. Again, the actions of inspectors in developing a mutual trust situation and in protecting themselves and workers in the tap situation represent a compromise between different private ends. Similarly, the ends of workers are to get their work done with a minimum of effort, to get along at least minimally with foremen and inspectors, to stay out of trouble, and to avoid being fired. The semisecret use of the tap, then, represents a compromise between these complexes of ends.

Taking these means-ends situations together, we find that what are means for one group are ends for another. In all cases, means and ends can be defined as either public or private attributes. Public ends are means to private ends, and private ends are in some cases limited by "public"—that is, organizationally sanctioned—ends and means. In brief, the empirical situation is extremely complex, and not analyzable in a priori terms. The complex of public and private means and ends constitutes a specific research problem insofar as it accounts for an overall operation of the organization.

In terms of the specific problem of the tap as an instrument and its relationship to means-and-ends relationships within the organization, we find that use of the tap is a private means to publicly stated ends. But those ends to which the use of the tap is oriented are, from both the standpoint of the abstraction called "the company" and from the standpoint of its members, only one of a number of possible ends. It is the plurality of ends that accounts for "deviant behavior" instead of the conflict between means and ends. Production is a major end, and quality is a necessary condition for the attainment of that end. Moreover, as individuals are distributed at different levels and in different lines of the status hierarchy, different ends become more salient to individuals occupying different positions. The relationship of means to ends at both the public and private levels is different (in fact, is some times reversed) for individuals in different positions in the organization. The statement of "public ends" attached to the organization or the social system describes the ends of a limited number of particular and publicly accessible or visible positions in the system.

Thus, any theoretical model that accepts as an initial postulate the dominance of an ultimate end and that conceptualizes disorganization as a conflict between means and ends overlooks the possibility that conflicting means and ends are actually conflicts between means to one end with means to another end.

Moreover, in any complex organization where plural ends are distributed in different ways among officeholders, the conflict of ends and the conflicts between means and ends are institutionalized as conflicts between various departments or segments in the organization. Thus, from the point of view of production supervision, quality control is a major obstacle to the achievement of its ends. From the standpoint of quality control, sloppy workmanship is a major crime that may result in sanctions to the inspector. The tolerance of the tap is a means by which workers, inspectors, and production supervisors attempt to achieve their respective ends in a mutually tolerable manner in a situation where they are forced to work together according to directives, which, if closely followed, would result in mutual frustration. For the worker, the inspector, and the foreman, the development of a satisfactory social environment, the minimization of conflict, and the development of tolerable social relations become a major end. Crime, and the toleration of crime within the limits of avoiding extreme sanctions, becomes a means to these social ends and also to the publicly recognized ends of the organization.

In sum, a large part of behavior, visible to an insider or to a sophisticated observer, is "criminal"; that is, it violates publicly stated norms. But since such behavior is accepted—in fact often stimulated, aided, and abetted by the effective on-the-spot authorities—the criminality of such behavior has limited consequences.

Conclusion

The resolution of the "means-end conflict" results in crime. But such crime often becomes fairly acceptable behavior and is stabilized as a permanent aspect of the organization. Crime becomes one of the major operational devices of the organization. As such, it is hard to consider it as a form of anomie. The use of the tap is neither an innovation, a form of rebellion, ritualism, nor retreatism. It is more aptly described as a permanent unofficial aspect of the organization. It is not an innovation because, for almost all of the personnel in the plant, the use of the tap in the plant precedes their knowledge of it. It is not rebellion because it is a means to a company end—that is, quantity production. It is neither a ritual nor a retreat since it is in some sense functional to all concerned. It is a crime only in that there is an official ruling against its use and a wide range of ceremonial forms of law enforcement and punishment. With respect to the

Air Force, use of the tap still remains a serious crime. But, in this area, the wide range of cooperative behavior between workers, foremen, and plant inspectors combines to reduce the importance of Air Force law enforcement as a significant factor in this situation.

The ceremonial aspects of law enforcement are, however, of importance. These include secrecy in the use of the tap to avoid embarrassing the inspector, the reporting of tap violations by the inspector to the foreman who initially requested the use of the tap, the rhetoric used by the foreman in requesting the use of the tap, the mock severity of the foreman in reprimanding the reported violator, and the penitence of the apprehended criminal before his judge, the foreman.

All of these are serious social accompaniments to the use of the tap. They enable the personnel involved to maintain the public values, while performing those actions necessary to attain the public or private ends appropriate to their evaluations of their positions. Thus, a form of institutional schizophrenia is the major result of the conflict of ends and the conflict of means and ends. Individuals act and think on at least two planes, the plane of the public ideology and the plane of action. They shift from plane to plane, as required by their positions, their situations, and their means-end estimations. In a sense, it is a form of doublethink. And doublethink is the major result of means-ends conflict.

From the point of view of the actors involved, and in the light of the doublethink mechanism, the major definition of *deviancy* takes on another dimension. The major crime for the actors involved is the lack of respect for the social ceremonialism surrounding the tap. The worker who allows an inspector to see him possessing or using a tap threatens the defenses of the inspector and is likely to be reprimanded for not being careful. He is likely to find it harder to "sell" his work to that inspector. He gets a bad reputation and is thought of as a "character." Similarly, in talking to an inspector, the worker who casually mentions illegal workmanship is told by this inspector not to mention it. Finally, a worker who grins while being reprimanded for the use of the tap is likely to be bawled out for lack of awareness of the seriousness of his act and his flippant attitude. The foreman is likely to threaten him with a withdrawal from the circle of protection given by the foreman to apprehended criminals.

Thus, lack of seriousness in adhering to the ceremonial forms of law violation is defined as a case of inappropriateness of affect and lack of reality orientation to which serious forms of informal social control are addressed. The major crime, then, is the violation of the *rules* of criminal behavior.

The fact that tapping is a crime, a violation of an inoperative public ideology, does not mean that it is uncontrolled anomalous behavior. On the contrary, the very pervasiveness of the use of tap and its functional indispensability result in a relatively close control of tapping by supervisory authority.

The worker is taught the proper techniques of tapping and the situations for which use of the tap is appropriate. Misuse of the tap (using the tap as a substitute for lining up holes and for careless workmanship) is frowned upon by supervisors. Using the tap as a substitute for less severely defined illegal techniques of workmanship is also frowned upon.

The worker who uses the tap promiscuously is subject to a wide variety of informal controls. He is kidded and teased by other workers. Inspectors become sensitive to his actions, and when he is caught, he is reported and bawled out, primarily because of his reputation and not so much for the use of the tap in a specific situation. The foreman rides him unmercifully and tends to become more sensitive to all his faults of workmanship. If he persists in abusing the use of the tap, he ultimately gets transferred to another foreman who is short of men. The floating worker is presumed to be a botcher by the very fact of his being transferred.

In no case, however, are formal actions that involve the possibility of dismissal taken against the worker. This is because, in writing up a worker for abusing the tap, the foreman risks the danger of bringing into the open and into official and public channels the whole issue of the use of the tap. In punishing promiscuous tappers by official means, the foreman might risk losing opportunities to have the tap used in situations that are advantageous to him. Moreover, in bringing serious charges against the deviant tapper, the foreman might find that workers necessarily would be hesitant to use the tap in situations that the foreman regards as necessary.

For these reasons, foremen and inspectors do not use the formal channels of law enforcement, but rely instead on informal controls. The informal controls tend to limit the use of the tap to necessary situations. In addition, the use of such controls results in a new definition of *crime* and its function at the behavioral level. A "crime" is not a crime so long as its commission is controlled and directed by those in authority toward goals that they define as socially constructive. A violation of law is treated as a crime when it is not directed and controlled by those in authority or when it is used for exclusively personal ends.

The kind, type, and frequency of crime are functions of the system of authority. The ranges of "socially permissible crime" and the degree and severity of punishment are determined by the ends and interests of those who are responsible for law enforcement. Severe law enforcement limits the freedom of leadership groups in attainment of their own ends. Loosening the fabric of law enforcement enables these groups to have greater freedom of action in the attainment of their ends, but also permits a greater amount of crime at lower levels.

Notes

1. Any one of the whole host of books and articles can be used to illustrate systematic attempts to state the methods of functional analysis. Typical attempts are to be found in Robert K. Merton, *Social Theory and Social Structure* (Glencoe, IL: Free Press, 1951). A fairly complete bibliography on functionalism is provided by Harold Fallding, "Functional Analysis in Sociology," *American Sociological Review* 28 (February 1963), 5.

2. Merton, 19. Emile Durkheim, *The Rules of Sociological Method* (Chicago: University of Chicago Press, 1938), 95.

3. Harry C. Bredemeir, "The Methodology of Functionalism," *American Sociological Review* 20 (April 1955), 173-79; and Kingsley Davis, "The Myth of Functional Analysis," *American Sociological Review* 24 (December 1959), 765-66.

4. This "alternative" approach represents nothing new or novel, but is rather the standard method of approaches to sociology such as *Verstehen* sociology, symbolic interactionism, or almost all "non-functional" sociologies. The approach is explicit in Weber's *Wirtschaft and Gesellschaft,* as translated in *The Theory of Social and Economic Organization* (New York: Oxford University Press, 1947), 118. Similarly, it is implicit in all work stemming from George Herbert Mead's *Mind, Self and Society* (Chicago: University of Chicago Press, 1934). This approach is made explicit by John R. Commons, "A Sociological View of Sovereignty," *American Journal of Sociology* 5 (1899-1900), and presented in textbook form by Ernest Theodore Hiller, *Social Relations and Structures* (New York: Harper, 1947), and Robert M. MacIver, *Society: Its Structure and Changes* (New York: Ray Long and Richard R. Smith, 1932).

5

Official and White-Collar Crime in the United States and the Soviet Union

Joseph Bensman

In *The Soviet Way of Crime*, Lydia Rosner presents a fascinating picture of crime in the Soviet Union and of how Soviet émigrés continue their criminal behavior in the émigré community in Brighton Beach, New York.

Crime is an essential ingredient of the way of life of virtually all Soviet citizens, Rosner reports. Top party leaders, NKVD leaders, state officials, regional party leaders, plant managers, and other officials loot state-operated industries for their personal and institutional gain. The ability to gain personal wealth, privilege, dachas, and diamonds rests on control of goods and services that can be illegally diverted from the state in exchange for other illegally diverted goods and services in vast and complex patterns of bribery and corruption and in subsequent mutual blackmail. The blackmail keeps the system in place: exposure of crime in one area of the system necessarily leads to exposure of the entire system. Thus, it is understandable that Yuri Andropov and Mikhail Gorbachev have been concerned with official crime, bribery, "goofing off," and with the hoarding of labor and government supplies to meet phony standards.

Published originally in a slightly different form as the Introduction to Lydia S. Rosner, *The Soviet Way of Crime* (Hadley, MA: Bergin & Garvey, Publishers, 1986), xiii-xvii. Republished by permission from Lydia S. Rosner.

Rosner reports that the level of official crime in the Soviet Union is so great that entirely illegal private industries have been created outside the Communist system. These industries supply unofficial services to the official servants of the state.

But the pattern of crime is not confined to the elite. At every level, those who can steal or divert official supplies do so. The salesgirl at GUM, the largest Soviet department store, may steal gloves to exchange them on the black market for fur hats, chocolates, oranges, or fountain pens. Ill people use stolen state property to bribe doctors to treat them quickly. Parents bribe teachers to "look after" their children. Taxi drivers bribe supervisors to assign them cabs that run. Officials bribe butchers to provide them with unauthorized choice meat. Complex patterns of bribery exist for the exchange of apartments and the purchase of used cars.

The amount of time spent dealing and trading goods and services stolen from the Communist state in the black and grey market may make the Soviet Union one of the great exponents of classical capitalism. The entrepreneurial activity at the interstices of state-owned industries may make those interstices larger than the industries themselves.

Rosner reports that, in order to survive in the Soviet Union at more than the minimum intake of calories, one must become a "necessary criminal." One must develop a "specialty" or trade that provides one with goods or services that cannot be obtained in legal markets. Rosner does not explain, however, the failure of those regular markets, except by noting that the fact of large-scale theft from the state machinery makes that machinery inadequate in providing the goods and services that would make the theft unnecessary. An alternative explanation might be that the vast state investment in military production and security services (14 percent of the Soviet

GNP, compared with 11 percent of the American) deprives the population of civilian goods and services. Also, the Soviet policy of controlling legal prices leaves billions of rubles that can only be spent on the black market.

For the Soviet citizen, the consequence is that honesty results in deprivation. Some individuals, dissident intellectuals and religious believers, do remain honest, but at their own and their families' expense. Apart from these "innocents," vast numbers of Soviet citizens engage in crime. Their crimes include falsification of documents, forgery, and counterfeiting—the paper crimes that reflect a bureaucratic society. Rosner notes, however, that Soviet bureaucracy is not exactly the kind of bureaucracy that Max Weber described.

The paper crimes involve not only a class of necessary criminals, but also a group of more professional criminals, whom Rosner calls connivers. The connivers are experts in forgery, counterfeiting, and the manufacture of documents. Necessary criminals, or survivors, and connivers are Rosner's major categories in her analysis of Soviet and Soviet émigré crime.

Rosner also argues that the Soviet system imposes other peculiarities on the crime conducted by its citizens. Since the major criminals are party members, state officials, and law enforcement officials, the boundaries between enforceable legal norms and ordinary "necessary" crime are indistinguishable. When someone is charged with violating the law, the arrest is often the result of other circumstances, such as political, ethnic, or religious differences. In the absence of external standards of what constitutes illegal behavior and with few internal standards to guide him, the necessary criminal is forced to develop a code of behavior and the ability to interpret nuances and minimal cues to understand who is observing him and what pattern of illegality is being followed. This heightened awareness is a necessity, even if one is honest, in coping with a society in which the majority are criminals and in which prosecution for crime is arbitrary and unpredictable.

Given all of the above, the Soviet émigré comes to Brighton Beach with a predisposition to beat the system through crime. He purchases unnecessary papers such as a forged driver's license, thus providing a market for connivers already skilled in the production of illegal documents and other forms of counterfeiting. The émigré also feels entitled to apply for all state benefits, whether he is legally entitled to them or not. Though well off, he may apply for welfare, housing assistance, food stamps, and other forms of aid. He provides doctored papers that make him eligible for such benefits, while concealing his true assets.

In short, Rosner reports that a large proportion of Soviet émigrés bring to Brighton Beach social and psychological patterns of behavior and expectations imposed upon them in a crime-ridden society. They act out their homeland psychology in behavior that is gratuitous in Brighton Beach. In addition, American law enforcement agencies have found that the Soviet Union has deliberately exported with its Jewish dissidents a large number of professional criminals, spies, and NKVO operatives. It is not clear from these reports whether the professional criminals among them are totally organized or are organized in "families" that have a coordinating committee called the Soviet Mafia of Brighton Beach.

It is clear that, at all levels, the Soviet criminal, whether necessary or conniver, is no unsophisticated peasant arriving in an urban society unprepared to cope with urban complexities and crowded ghettoes and carrying with him attitudes that make him and his children victims of the city. Like almost all immigrant groups that have arrived since the Immigration Act of 1965, the Soviet émigrés are urbanites prepared to deal with the problems of beating the system, especially its bureaucracy. They do, however, have blind spots: they do not understand due process, the rule of law, or the "coddling" of street criminals by the police. They also do not understand the multiple jurisdictions that govern law enforcement in the United States. As a result, Soviet émigré professional criminals use the airplane as a mode of conducting crime along with cooperation among geographically dispersed crime families, as they did in the Soviet Union, to beat the dispersed jurisdictional system in the United States. They are, however, surprised when interjurisdictional crime control agencies use computers to catch up with their dispersed crimes.

Rosner notes that all of these criminal activities exceed what we have come to expect from the basis of American theories of crime. She notes that Soviet crime is not the crime of peasants forced into alien and crowded ghettoes, but that of urbanites, sophisticated and knowledgeable in beating the system. It is the crime of citizens who know that the homeland official system is much more crooked than they ever were. American criminological theory, even before the rise of sociology and professional criminology, blamed the immigrant, the peasant, especially the most recent group to arrive here, and his children, for violent crime, street crime, and professional crime. But one could argue that the major criminal in the United States since the Okefenokee land scandals and redemption of Revolutionary war-pay scrip has been the WASP establishment itself. Certainly, since the American Civil War, the railroads, banks, trusts, lumber interests, and other environmental plunderers were the chief thieves of the resources of the United States. Entire legislatures have been bribed, sometimes repeatedly, by rival interests. Rosner reports that corporate criminals imported elements of the Sicilian Black Hand to break strikes, thus helping to create the Mafia in the United States. But white-collar criminals have rarely been the object of sustained public attention.

Edwin Sutherland developed the concept of white-collar crime in 1930. He charged that virtually every major corporation is a professional criminal, as defined by the MacNaughton rule that defines one convicted of three felonies as a professional criminal. But Sutherland's concept of white-collar crime never really took hold. Instead, *white-collar crime* has been redefined as the crime committed by white-collar employees against the corporation. The corporation has, by definition, become virtually immune.

From time to time, Americans are shocked by great scandals. In Watergate, the attorney general, like Vautrin in Balzac's *Comédie Humaine*, turned out to be not only chief of police, but the chief of all organized crime. Vautrin was not entirely Balzac's invention; he was a composite of two actual figures in early nineteenth-century France.[1] Attorney General John Mitchell was different in becoming the fall guy for a higher-level but unprosecuted criminal.[2]

We have also been shocked when manufacturers of electrical generators conspire to fix prices, when automobile companies bribe legislatures, and when the chief executive of an automobile company forms a private company to cheat the company of which he was president. We have been shocked, too, when the chief suppliers of the Pentagon are charged with systematic cheating on costs and prices. But we grow accustomed to the fact that individual white-collar criminals get a slap on the wrist, while the corporations as criminals are virtually immune from prosecution. Perhaps, despite President Reagan's clamor for the spirit of individualism, the interpenetration of the military bureaucracy and defense supplier bureaucracies is so great that both kinds of white-collar criminals are immune from prosecution.

All of this relates to Rosner's examination of Soviet crime. Rosner reports that the major source of Soviet crime is the regime and the Party. I have emphasized her point that the original source of

American white-collar crime is the corporations, aided by a corrupt government.

Do I overdraw the parallel between the two systems? Rosner stresses the reserve of Protestant morality that causes Americans to be shocked and outraged when highly placed Americans are caught cheating the system. This latent reserve of morality is, she argues, the balance wheel against total corruption. But the Communist ideals of egalitarism and of the "withering away of the state" are equally absolute and, in principle, ought to be equally strong counterbalances to official crime. I suspect that the difference between the United States and the Soviet Union is not in the moral basis of their ideologies, but in the nature of their respective systems of law.

In the United States, the provisions in the Bill of Rights that protect a free press and offer some minimal resistance to government (despite episodes such as McCarthyism and the Palmer raids) provide the basis for a tradition that includes the investigation of official and establishment crime. Investigative journalism "pays," and moral crusaders like Senators George Norris and Robert LaFollette, Sr. were elected because they opposed the establishment. One wonders if this is still true in the present, at least to the same extent.

In the Soviet Union, by contrast, a repressive official establishment has stifled all criticism of the Party and the state since the Revolution. The existence of official and petty corruption is thereby protected from exposure insofar as corruption is the reason for prosecution. The foxes guard the chicken coop.

Nevertheless, Rosner has raised a host of issues regarding white-collar and immigrant crime. Since the 1965 Immigration Act, a great number of immigrants from all shores have been urbanites well equipped to subvert the law enforcement bureaucracies, whether these agencies be criminal or honest. Many of the new immigrants have participated in organized criminal activities in their homelands.

We have Colombian, Dominican, Cuban, and Peruvian cocaine connections that supplement the American-Italian, American-Sicilian, and American-Corsican connections of traditional stripe. The South Korean émigré, so far, has not to any large degree imported the currency manipulations perpetrated to get here. Only the South Korean government, the KCIA, and the South Korean Consul General's Office have engaged in crime, which is usually directed at Koreans living in the United States. It is too soon to tell whether Koreans will follow traditional immigrant patterns and produce their share of criminals along with the scientific, mathematical, and musical geniuses they are already producing.

South Vietnamese refugees are in the same position: it is too soon to tell whether they, necessary criminals in their homelands, will develop that kind of marginality that produces geniuses, crooks, or both.

As for the Soviet émigrés in Brighton Beach, it may be too soon to tell whether the necessary crime they now engage in is a means toward gaining the wherewithal to become respectable citizens and white-collar criminals or whether it is to become the basis for a new, permanent criminal underclass in American society.

Notes

1. It's now generally thought that Balzac's inspiration for Vautrin was Eugène François Vidocq (1775-1857), a former thief, forger, army deserter, fraudster, and fence, who eventually became an informer for the Paris police and eventually the founder of the Sûreté Nationale, which he headed 1812-1827.—Eds.

2. Bensman refers here to President Richard M. Nixon.—Eds.

6

The Advertising Man and His Work

Joseph Bensman

Advertising, more than any other institution in contemporary society, symbolizes and concentrates in its image all that is considered both good and bad in present-day commercial and industrial capitalism in America. The importance attached to advertising by laymen, businessmen, and advertising men themselves far outweighs its numerical importance. Only 65,000 people are directly employed in advertising agencies in this country [1967—Eds.], a small number compared with, let us say, the number of doctors (230,000), public school teachers (1.5 million), or plumbers (333,000).

Nevertheless, advertising men do have important economic functions. In 1965, about $15.3 billion was spent on advertising. This money was actually spent by American businessmen, not by advertising agency executives. At the most, advertising men consulted, recommended, and advised businessmen on this expenditure. Only a small part was directly spent by advertising men in the preparation of print advertisements, television and radio commercials, car cards (advertisements on buses, subways, trains, and trucks), and

---

Published in a slightly different form in Joseph Bensman, *Dollars and Sense: Ideology, Ethics, and the Meaning of Work in Profit and Nonprofit Organizations* (New York: Macmillan, 1967), 9-68. Originally published as "In the Courts of Power—The Advertising Man," under the pseudonym Ian Lewis. See Peter Berger, ed., *The Human Shape of Work* (New York: Macmillan, 1964), 113-80. Republished by permission from Marilyn Bensman.

billboards. For advising on the total expenditure and for preparing these advertisements, advertising agencies received commissions that are approximately 15 percent of the total outlay by the clients. Thus, the net commissions of advertising agencies are approximately $1 billion, 100 million, which, compared with the size of the gross operating income of the automotive industry, ($12 billion, 700 million)[1] or of the steel industry ($8 billion, 400 million), can be described only as small potatoes.

Yet advertising as an industry is as much a cynosure for American society as are the automobile and steel industries. All three form the backbone of our industrial economy. Still, advertising always has been and remains a controversial institution in American society.

At the simplest levels, academic, aesthetic, intellectual, and cultural leaders continually attack advertising for being the source of all of the moral, cultural, and intellectual depravity and bad taste in American mass media. Such an attack overstates the cases because, in the first instance, advertising men only recommend the shows, programs, and placements of advertising to their clients. The final responsibility rests with the client, but, when criticism is made, advertising men are the public scapegoat. They are paid to be so, and many wish that they had the actual influence or power that the critics attribute to them. Advertising is charged with stressing only the material, sexual, and vulgar lower values in the human personality. It is charged with stimulating the sense of individual inadequacy by reminding individuals of their imperfections and their unattained goals and with raising hopes for the achievement of unattainable goals.

At a more sinister level, advertising men are attributed the powers of a Svengali, the sinister deus ex machina, who by devious and highly developed psychological, linguistic, and artistic devices brainwashes the American public. It is charged with controlling the foci of the public's attention, feeding the public lies, and operating on its unconscious and irrational faculties so that people cannot make rational decisions. In fact, the most serious charge made against advertising is that it destroys the capacity for rational behavior, makes men infants, and by creating these habits of thought destroys the psychological and intellectual capacity for democratic decision making and for self-government.

As compared with the severity of this charge, direct or indirect charges aimed at the media-selection functions of advertising appear to be secondary. Advertising men, insofar as they are advisers for their clients, are charged with bringing about the demise of numerous magazines and of weakening the strength of independent newspapers and radio as media, simply because their impersonal concern (correctly or incorrectly assessed) for economic efficiency has resulted in the shift of much agency advertising money (34 percent) to television. Whether advertising agencies had the power to make these decisions, or whether the decisions made were simply objective recognition of inescapable facts, is for the moment beside the point. What is central is the fact that advertising is the object of scorn and criticism for possessing in a high degree precisely those characteristics for which our entire society is criticized.

In a peculiar way, however, advertising men are romanticized and envied for possessing the same characteristics that are criticized. They are seen as supermen or superidiots who live in Ivy League or "gray flannel" suits. They are pictured as leading glamorous lives over expensive lunches, entertaining either fatuous or overdemanding clients, and indulging in sexual promiscuity for business reasons or as an escape from the frustrations of business. They are described as leading barren but exciting lives in suburbs or exurbs, with alcohol and their own and other people's wives, neglecting their children and, by ill-thought-out political gestures, upsetting the politics of their sterile but expensive communities.

Advertising men are articulate and do not take their criticism in silence. They add to the controversy by attacking the long-haired, irresponsible, negativistic, brainless professors, aesthetes, and "faggots" who never met a payroll and who would undermine the American way of life out of envy of the success of their superiors.

They answer the specific charges by "proving" that advertising provides an essential function for an ever-expanding American economy by stimulating new needs and new wants, which only an expanding industry can satisfy. It accelerates the process of "creative destruction," which, in Joseph Schumpeter's terms, provides capitalism with its dynamism and growth.

Advertising, it is asserted, creates markets for new products and expands the markets for old ones. It forces the research and development departments of major manufacturers to experiment continually and to achieve scientific miracles that enable one competitor to raise the quality of its brand over that of another. For advertising, the argument goes, is the soul of competition, and competition is the heart of American enterprise and its free enterprise economy.

On the cultural front, advertising via the mass media is allegedly an important vehicle for the dissemination of serious culture and political awareness. Advertisers support, when it is economically feasible, the production of Shakespeare on radio and television, the ballet, the symphony, and the opera on television, together with news programs, documentaries, and "specials." Moreover, advertisers support newspapers and serious magazines, as well as entertainment in magazines. And, finally, they make it possible, it is reasoned, for newspapers to educate and inform the American public.

Advertising per se informs the public, the argument continues, of the range of brands available, provides information as to the virtues of these brands ("You can't expect advertisers to knock their own products") and makes it easy for individuals to make "consumer choices."

We expect the controversy to continue indefinitely, to wax and wane, as journalists, moralists, politicians, and intellectuals mount new attacks and are repulsed, or when the issues die for a time because of the exhaustion of the protagonists and of a weary public to whom all of the words are too familiar.

The controversy over advertising and advertising men will probably never be resolved at the ideological level. Nor can advertising be understood at that level. Advertising is an industry, composed of separate firms, agencies, each of which has a highly organized internal structure and distinctive but not uniform methods of dealing with its separate clientele, subsidiary organizations (media agencies and subcontractors), the government, and the public. Surrounding the individual agencies are associations of advertising agencies (the "four A's"—Association of Advertising Agencies of America—the Advertising Council, and professional associations composed of the respective technical and professional specialists, employees of a wide variety of agencies). To complete our schematic outline, there are personal and informal cliques that make up a series of interlocking friendship and acquaintance patterns that cut across agency lines, departmental lines, and in some cases, client, agency, and subcontractor lines of communication.

In all the above formal respects, the advertising business does not differ from other businesses. Our discussion will therefore be confined to those aspects of the advertising business that are either unique or that are accentuated much more than is usual in other businesses. We shall, therefore, describe the structure of the advertising industry in order to set the stage for a more detailed discussion of advertising as a drama in which some of the ethical and moral dilemmas at work in our society are acted out.

Economic and Structural Characteristics of the Advertising Agency

1. Advertising is a labor-intensive and capital-extensive industry. The advertising agency makes no great investments in capital goods. Its major capital investments are in typewriters, calculating machines (and, in a few large agencies, the rental of computers), duplicating equipment, and office furniture. The rental of office space is the major fixed cost of an agency. By and large, labor costs—primarily salaries—are the single largest item in agency costs. Labor costs on average constitute 70 percent of the annual operating costs of an advertising agency.

Because of the absence of an elaborate machine technology and the corresponding presence of labor intensiveness, advertising is properly called a service industry. Advertising men emphasize this service feature of the agency until the truth becomes a cliché. The composite cliché is as follows: "All we have to offer our clients is a service—our skill, our knowledge, our brains, our talent, our know-how, and our judgments of words, pictures, sounds, and symbols. To the extent that we execute these functions well, and only to the extent that our clients have need for these functions, are we entitled to the high fees, commissions, and salaries we earn."

If an agency can succeed in convincing a prospective client that these claims are true (and they are claims until proved or disproved by subsequent actions), the agency can make a powerful case. For American business has a continuous need for "brains," ideas, judgment, wisdom, counsel, and know-how. It is by now a truism that most major brands of consumer goods are not distinguishable from one another to the consumer when he tests them by means of blind product tests. If this is true, the tremendous differences in the sales success of various competitive brands are primarily due to differences in the marketing effectiveness of the competitive manufacturers, including advertising.

In a number of industries, the marketing organizations of the manufacturers (the sales and distribution organizations, the financial reserves, the dealer relations programs, merchandising and sales promotion programs) are considered to be at parity. However, some companies have made tremendous sales successes with the introduction of new brands and the revitalizing of declining brands, while the equally well-marketed competitive brands (aside from advertising) have suffered declines or only moderate gains in sales. Thus, slogans like "Winston tastes good like a cigarette should" or "Be sociable, have a Pepsi" have been worth hundreds of millions of dollars to their respective manufacturing companies.

However, since the advertising agencies' claim for their value to business is based on the intangibles of skill, talent, knowledge, know-how, and so on, and not on objective technological processes, the client can at anytime reject the claim, especially since every advertising agency makes substantially the same claim in attempting to seduce accounts from other agencies.

2. While we have stressed that the operating income of agencies is relatively small, the number of persons engaged in advertising is still smaller. The labor intensity of advertising thus consists of a relatively small number of highly paid specialized technicians and managerial officials.

A large-sized but not gigantic agency with billings of approximately $100 million will have an operating income of $15 million. If we allow all costs but labor costs and profits not to exceed $3.5 million, then direct and indirect payments to personnel will amount to $11.5 million. Such an agency, if well run, may employ from six hundred to seven hundred people. The average agency income available for profits and payments to personnel is thus in the neighborhood of $16,000 to $18,000 per employee. Since at least 60 percent of the employees of an advertising agency are relatively low-paid clerical, bookkeeping, and stenographic help, the average amount of money available for the professional, creative, and managerial staff is estimated at (depending upon whether the agency employs six hundred or seven hundred persons in total) from $27,000 to $34,000 per professional employee. Since many agencies are owned by their professional, creative, and managerial staffs, salaries, profits, and profit-sharing funds can at times be considered as part of the same pool.

Of course, not all agencies are as profitable as our hypothetical but not improbable agency. And, of course, we have been dealing with averages—averages in salaries and an equal distribution in stock throughout the professional staff. Both of these assumptions are contrary to fact. There is great range in the salary levels of various professional, creative, and managerial officials of an agency. And even while many agencies are "employee-owned," the chief officers and executives are likely to own the lion's share of stock with middle and lower-level officials owning just enough to satisfy the Bureau of Internal Revenue (that the company is employee-owned and not a proprietorship) and the implicit or explicit demands of these lower-ranking officials for equity. These latter demands are granted either to keep valued employees happy or to seduce them from a competitive agency.

The table below[2] indicates the average salary range of a number of typical positions in a relatively large advertising agency according to the director of the largest employment agency servicing the advertising business. Salaries, per se, cover only part of the perquisites of the advertising man. Profit-sharing plans allow the agency official to accumulate a retirement fund or a separation allowance that may result in a yearly deferred income of up to 20 percent of his annual income, which, when collected, is taxable at capital gains rates.

Stock options and increases in the value of stock in the agency (whose prices are artificially pegged by the company) provide additional capital gains. The opportunity to acquire stock, however, is more than a capital gain, a way of evading taxes when one moves up the income ladder. Stock acquisition is a genuine method of becoming wealthy, based on talent alone, as the agency defines talent. Since the advertising agency is a capital-extensive and labor-intensive industry, the physical assets of an agency do not constitute a limit to stock acquisition. One does not "water" the stock (physical assets) by issuing more stock (equity shares), since the physical assets are of little value in themselves. The issuance of stock to an individual simply means that his "services" represent an important part of the service that the agency sells to its actual or prospective clients. Of course, if an individual makes known to his bosses his estimate of his own worth, they are more likely to calculate the value of that individual's services in terms of the total matrix of the agency's total income-earning services and to reward him accordingly.

All of this means that valued individuals can easily acquire stock, and can do so at a very young age. Stock acquisition is made easy by issuance of new low-price issues, by options, and by deferred payment plans. The ease of stock acquisition means that in advertising, the American dream of rags-to-riches can be realized in a sufficient number of cases to serve as goad and pull to thousands of young men in advertising who may be on the make.

That the agency president and majority stockholder of a $100 million (billing) corporation is the son of Italian immigrants, or that another may be the son of a Jewish rag buyer, is both a reality and a myth. The reality is one that can be illustrated by thousands of examples, and everyone in the advertising business has his own favorite illustration. The use of this reality becomes the myth for these thousands of others and enables them to sustain the pace that advertising demands of them.

The countermyth that advertising opportunities are reserved for "bright" young men from Ivy League schools is also true, but less true. Bright young men from Ivy League schools are especially valued to the extent that their lack of enough imagination to know the difficulties inherent in their work enables them to act with poise, confidence, and with sufficiently good manners to charm and gain the confidence of clients. Such charm, poise, self-confidence, and manners are as important as skill and talent in gaining and retaining clients.

Despite all this, the agency approach to rewarding its personnel is to reward those whom it must (nothing is given away) for whatever talents appear to be necessary. Thus, Ivy Leaguers and non-Ivy Leaguers, Catholics, and Jews, are rewarded. Since a wide variety of types of ability can be used to justify an agency, a wide variety of talents is rewarded. On the whole, this works in favor of the able, regardless of origin.

Becoming a millionaire is thus the major promise that the myth of advertising offers to the able. It is not the only promise. To those who know they will be moderately successful but will not become wealthy, the opportunity to live as if one were rich is almost as seductive. This is done through "fringe benefits."

Advertising men are the customers of the media representatives (television and radio networks and stations, newspapers, magazines, and outdoor advertising), of television and commercials production companies, of graphic arts firms, of research firms, and of thousands of would-be suppliers of services. The standard way of selling one's services is to wine and dine the agency representative who is reputed to have even a minor voice in a "buying decision." Thus, an agency official (in New York) with an $8,000-a-year salary, or more, will be wined and dined at one of the hundreds of "expense accounts" restaurants or hotels. He will eat and drink at the Plaza, the Waldorf-Astoria, the Commodore, the New Yorker, or the 21 Club. If he is deemed really important, he then receives the supreme accolade by dining at the Chauveron, the Four Seasons, or the Forum of the Twelve Caesars. The ubiquity of the free lunch reflects the lack of centralization in advertising. Almost anyone can influence the buying decision. In manufacturing, purchasing is centralized.

At the same time that he is being wined and dined, the agency official may read magazines that come by free subscription, drink whiskey that is part of his Christmas loot, or present his children with toys that are given to him as promotion pieces to advertise a product. If the agency man is truly unscrupulous, and if he has or can convince a prospective supplier that he has great buying power, the gift he receives may be a car, a boat, a European vacation, or sexual access to starlets, models, or television beauties. The public image of the advertising man is not entirely wrong.

The other side of the wining-and-dining complex is almost equally attractive (if one is attracted). The agency man is the supplier for the advertiser or the client. As such, his job is to wine and dine the client. Everything that advertisers do for the agency man can be and is done for the client. There are some differences, however. The amount spent on entertainment is expected to be appropriate both to the position of the agency man and to the position of the entertainee in the client organization. One is not expected to take an office worker to the Chauveron, nor is an officer worker expected to entertain the president or the advertising manager of the client firm. If he does, he appears to be arrogating the position of his bosses.

There are other differences. When entertained by the suppliers, a low-level agency official can be gay, carefree, and expansive, even to a high-ranking official in the supplier firm. When he entertains the client, a high-ranking agency man must, if necessary, pretend deference even to a low-ranking official in the client firm. Thus, mobility in temperament becomes a role requirement for the advertising man.

The expense account thus becomes a major way for a man of modest income to live, during the day, as if he were rich. And this quality of life is far more important psychologically than any increment in income the agency man can gain by cheating on the expense account.

There is some prestige attached by one's peers to having a legitimate reason for eating "for free" frequently; and peers will "keep score" on the size of the tab and the number of times one does so. For agency men accept the myth of the glamour of advertising as much as does the lay public. The poignancy of this acceptance is illustrated at the time when the luncheon appointment is canceled at the last moment and the agency man finds himself eating hamburgers at Nedick's instead of pâté de foie gras at the Chauveron. (No discussion will take place here on the response of the wife who, after preparing a fancy dinner, discovers that her husband is not hungry because he has had a three-hour lunch at the Chauveron.)

We have described the favorable economic and romantic myths and realities surrounding advertising that spring essentially from its labor intensity. The economic disadvantages also spring from this labor intensity. Whenever an agency loses an account, or whenever it is deemed necessary to cut operating expenses, the largest single pool of expenses is the pool available for salaries and wages (since over two-thirds of all agency expenses are in this category). Similarly, since the major concentration of labor costs is the high salaries offered to creative, technical, and managerial staffs, the major opportunities for cost cutting are in this area. To state it differently, firing clerks and secretaries to cut costs is not particularly effective, since the salaries for these categories do not contribute much to costs.

This potential vulnerability of the upper management in the agency business is from time to time made an actuality when accounts shift. The agency that loses a major account (from $2 million to $25 million) finds itself in a cost-income squeeze. If the account lost represents a sizable proportion of its billings, the other accounts cannot bear the burden of maintaining the salaries of the executives. Wholesale firings are likely to ensue. However, since many account personnel work on more than one account, if they are fired because of the loss of one account they are unavailable for work on other accounts. The clients of these other accounts may resent the loss of favored copywriters, account executives, commercial producers, or media planners and take their accounts out of the agency. Thus, the loss of one major account may start a vicious cycle that in a number of specific instances has resulted in the sudden demise of large and profitable agencies.

Account shifts in the agency business are fairly frequent. In 1965, 484 accounts shifted, representing $384 million of billings, and approximately $57,600,000 in commissions. The loss of a $2 million account is likely to result in the loss of ten jobs with an average salary of $20,000 (unless these jobs are absorbed by other accounts in the agency losing that account); the loss of a $25 million account is likely to lead to the loss of 188 jobs (assuming the same conditions).

When such losses occur, the job market becomes flooded with applicants, including many individuals who have the same general qualifications. Whether such enforced mobility constitutes an asset or a liability to the career aspirations of an individual depends on the opportunities available at the time of loss of job. In advertising, the loss of job by competent, capable, and blameless men constitutes a major career obstacle.

Theoretically, when an account shifts, just as many new jobs are created as are lost. This is not true in fact since the agency to which the account shifts will attempt to maximize profits by "doubling up," using hitherto untapped "capital resources" before it employs new people.

Moreover, even if an agency has to "staff up" to absorb a new account, the permanent staff of that agency will view the new acquisition as an opportunity for advancement to new positions, new titles, and salary and stock acquisition benefits. It is for this reason that the individual who had a good position with the agency losing the account is not likely to be desired by the agency gaining the account. Moreover, since an account shifts because the client is "unhappy" with his former agency, the most visible officials in the losing agency (with some exceptions) are likely to be personae non gratae to the client and thus to the gaining agency.

Thus, it frequently happens that precisely those people who have been most successful in the past, and who appeared to be most worthy of the high salaries they were earning prior to the involuntary loss of job, have the most difficulty relocating. As a result, every individual in advertising knows a person or knows of a person who was "near the top" and who has become unemployable through no fault of his own. Such individuals may go into the consulting business, sometimes profitably and sometimes using the fiction that being self-employed justifies the absence of any substantial income. Others retire at a young age and live modestly off the gains from profit-sharing plans and the capital gains from the forced sale of their stock in the company that let them go. Still others become stock and mutual fund salesmen or real estate agents, attempting to sell to their former colleagues.

Some, the younger ones, may become school teachers—a profession that is continuously enriched by talented, able, but unfortunate victims of the economics of the mass media. A few go into family businesses, if they are fortunate enough to have a family business available. Some relocate at salaries that may range from one-third to one-half of their former salaries; these may recoup their losses if they do not become embittered in the process. Some, especially if their skills are used in the creative departments (art, copywriting, musical composition, and so on) may shift jobs without penalty.

Thus, the great opportunities in advertising are offset by the equally great opportunities for total defeat and loss. A job on Madison Avenue appears to be a game of chance, perhaps roulette, or even Russian roulette. In fact, for a time, the phrase *Madison Avenue roulette* meant that the last man to lose his nerve was the man who would win. A job on Madison Avenue is a tontine, a last-man's club, where the victims are the living dead, embarrassing reminders that "it could happen to you."

The atmosphere of gambling that characterizes all aspects of the agency business is reinforced by the defenselessness of the agency and its personnel in the face of the whim, fancy, and even perhaps of the wisdom and ability of the client. This ambiguity is the opposite side of the coin from the confidence, assertiveness, and brazenness that advertising men exhibit in making a pitch, when they claim that advertising can do anything and everything.

The ambiguity that represents the greatest opportunity and menace for a specific agency is simply based upon the inability, in all but extreme situations (as previously specified), to measure the value, efficiency, and effectiveness of a specific advertising idea, advertisement, or campaign. Sales may go up fantastically, and sometimes both the agency and client may be in a frenzy to know why. This becomes a problem because, if one does not know what one is doing to make sales go up, any change may be disastrous. Second, if one's gains are thought to be due to chance, then chance can convert the gains to losses just as easily. Similarly, sales losses do occur even after it appears that every step taken by the agency and the client has been thought out carefully, planned, researched, and pretested and when all concerned have been convinced they have a winner.

The "irrationality" of the marketplace is a source of anxiety, despite the fact that every step may be taken to rule out chance. Research, surveys, pretesting, test markets, controlled experiments—all are attempts to eliminate this ambiguity and irrationality. But the failure to anticipate—to prevent one's "best laid plans" from going astray—is part of the very structure of the market. So many things go into the marketing operation, of which advertising is only a small part, that it is almost impossible to isolate the contribution of a single commercial, slogan, campaign, piece of artwork, or media plan. One can specify all the factors that might conceivably lead to sales success, but one recognizes that each factor applies to one's own brand and one's own marketing operation (including advertising) and also applies to each of a dozen competing brands and to each of a dozen product classes that do not compete directly but do constitute substitute methods of consumer income disposal. Thus, a brand of beer may compete with all other brands of beer in its sales area (though all brands do not compete uniformly throughout the entire sales areas), with whiskey (by brands and types), with other types of nonessentials, and with, as in the case of shoes, brands and types of necessities.

For each competitive situation, then, there may be several hundred factors that affect the success of the advertised brand. Several thousand factors, therefore, may affect sales success. As if this were not bad enough, it is almost impossible to isolate each factor as it operates in the marketplace. The marketing operation is so complex that each factor is simply one small element in a causal chain, but unusual success or failure in any one factor can affect the total chain.

A further complexity is introduced by the fact that it is extremely difficult to measure each factor separately or to measure two or more factors together in terms of a common scale of values. In the latter case, it is as difficult to measure the relative importance of each factor as it is to measure the factors themselves. Moreover, the factors involved in any "marketing chain" are continuously changing. Each successful or unsuccessful attempt at measurement may become ancient history before the measurement is completed.

All research—marketing, sales, copy, product, package, consumer, motivational, media, merchandising, test market, image, and operations research—represents attempts by the client or agency to narrow the ambiguity or to reduce the risk in making decisions. And all these methods must confront the difficulties of action in a complex "irrational" and uncontrolled market for which there are limited and imprecise measures. Over $400 million is invested in marketing research in one year by agencies and by clients in their anxious attempts to overcome the irrationality of the marketplace.

The feeling of anxiety and powerlessness held by top executives in the face of the tremendous responsibilities placed upon them for sales and advertising success constitutes the largest single opportunity for both missionaries and charlatans in the field of advertising research. There is a cycle in research that begins when a "charismatic" hero discovers a new approach—the large-scale sample survey, program analyzing, the store audit, image research, motivation research, operations research, semantic differential, scales, scaling research, computer simulation, or linear programming, to name a few. After each such "discovery," there is an intensified assault on the sales resistance of top agency and client officials to prove conclusively that once the new method is adopted, rationality and "science" will govern marketing. Many of the methods and services are "bought," and the new crusade begins. After the results of such research are in, the method is either discarded or absorbed as a minor tool in the inventory of available methods for research. The method, when absorbed, develops its defenders, who now resist the claims of new crusaders who possess another final solution. The failure of such methods to allay the sense of powerlessness and anxiety in the face of an irrational market is attested by the fact that each new discovery is superseded by a newer one which, in time, will be superseded.

This does not mean that research methods are universally useless. It does mean that, in the light of the complexity of marketing, research works best when there is a clearly defined, specific problem stated so that a specific research finding can, in advance, be interpreted as offering a solution to the problem. Thus, small, undignified, and inelegant studies frequently are the most useful, simply because there was a reason for undertaking them. However, these small studies do not have the grandeur and the elegance of large, theoretical, highbrow studies that appear to solve all problems except the specific one that evoked the study in the first place. Advertising men, in and out of research, want to fly before they can walk.

The irrationality of the marketplace and the lack of ability to specify what is good or bad advertising constitute a major source of job insecurity for the advertising man. If sales are up, it can be claimed (by the client) that they should be even higher. If sales are down, it can be claimed (by the agency) that only the advertising kept them from going even lower. Since no one "really knows," skill at persuasion, at use of pressure tactics, at politics, and at "human relations" becomes as important in gaining and keeping an account as the "objective reality."

The organizational and personnel problem this presents is decisive. Since the client is the source of all benefits to the agency and its personnel, and since agency personnel are usually better paid than officials in corresponding positions in the client firm, the burden of proof of the agency's efficiency is placed on the agency.

It is unusual when client personnel do not resent the "excessive salaries," the glamorous expense accounts, and the claims of infallibility that agencies make in their initial solicitation for an account. Clients' resentment is expressed in excessive demands upon the agency. Tight deadlines, impossible workloads, and unreasonable tasks are presented to the agency as a matter of course. This is often expressed in the phenomenon of the "exercise." The client will present a real or hypothetical marketing or advertising problem to the agency. A short deadline is given, and the implicit or explicit threat is made that retention of the account requires a satisfactory solution to the problem. The agency personnel are then compelled to work day and night, weekday and weekend, under fantastic costs of money, time, and energy to prove the agency worthy of keeping the account. After all the work is done and the agency has demonstrated its loyalty by dancing to the client's tune, the final report is frequently left unread for weeks or filed away without ever having been read. The agency has, for the time being, paid for the commissions it earns from the largesse of the lower-paid client. In rare instances, agencies will resign accounts because of the physical or mental breakdown of key personnel (lower-ranking personnel count less) or because the excessive demands by one client prevent their giving full attention to other, more profitable or less demanding accounts.

The philosophy of the exercise and the attitudes it engenders in agency management are major determinants of relationships within the agency. This is precisely so because the anxiety, powerlessness, and pressure placed upon the agency and its personnel by clients are linked to the extremes of success and failure that are possible because of labor intensity, the claims for infallibility, and the inability to measure successful advertising.

The Occupational and Skill Structure of the Agency

The agency, to repeat, is a service industry that provides intangible skills and counsel to a manufacturing or marketing company. Its product—advertising—is not a standardized product that is mass-produced and sold at low cost to a large number of widely distributed consumers. On the contrary, the final product of the agency—a radio or TV commercial, a print advertisement, or a billboard—is made in somewhat the same way as any other piece of art. The difference between genuine art and advertising (as production and not as aesthetics) is that advertising art involves committee planning, consultation, strategy, research, and the coordination of a wide variety of artistic and nonartistic specialists. This includes writers, audio technicians, painters and graphic men, photographers, engravers, cameramen (cinematic or still), musicians, animators, film editors, TV directors, stage designers, and producers. Art in advertising thus may resemble art in architecture or art under a patronage system in which the patron and his minions determine a great deal of the content and execution of the final art product.

Perhaps the only routine and semiautomatic work in advertising is in typing, billing, and other clerical work. Production work in the sense of semiskilled or unskilled factory work is almost entirely absent. As estimated earlier, almost 40 percent of total agency personnel are engaged in creative, administrative, professional, or high-level staff work. While it is true that there is a wide variety of higher skills assembled in one relatively small enterprise (six hundred to seven hundred people), it is also true that the number of people who professionally exercise any one skill is relatively small.

The account supervisor is a man whose major responsibility is to represent the agency to the client, to receive instructions from the client, to make agency recommendations to the client, and to coordinate the efforts of the agency in preparing plans and advertising for the client. The account supervisor is in charge of overall supervision of the account and is concerned with policy, while the account executive is placed in charge of administering the internal operation of the agency as it relates to a particular client.

Working for and with the account supervisor and executive is the account group. The account group consists of creative, technical, and staff specialists, media planners and buyers, researchers, merchandisers and sales promotion men. Each account group thus is a miniature advertising agency that has a full range of specialists attached to it and is capable of rendering a complete servicing of the account. There are as many account groups in an agency as there are accounts. When the account is a large one, the staff assigned to that account may be employed exclusively on the account in question. When the account is a small one, members of an account group may divide their time among a number of accounts.

Thus, the agency usually has a double organization. One set of "bosses" consists of the account supervisor and executive. The other set consists of the heads of individual departments—that is, research director, copy chief or creative director, media director, art director, and so on. Each set of "bosses" has the same employees, and each set has at times different vested interests in the distribution of its employees' time and efforts. The overall agency officers—the president and chairman of the board—are the referees when conflicts occur, and the board of directors offers the formal representation of the various vested interests of both types. Their meetings are the official stage where conflicts are acted out and, if possible, resolved.

Typical conflicts are as follows:

1. When account personnel work on more than one account, their account supervisors may feel that the "part-time" help are spending

too much time on other accounts. The account supervisors almost always feel that their account is understaffed. In terms of pressures on the account supervisor, this is probably true.

2. The "part-time" staff usually feels that account supervisors are too demanding. Instead of having two, three, or four part-time jobs, they feel they have that many full-time jobs.

3. The account supervisors quite often feel, especially if their account is not a huge or major one, that the creative and technical staff assigned to them are the rejects, misfits, and incompetents who have been assigned to their account on the basis of lack of ability.

4. Most service personnel are technicians, artists, or specialists, while the account supervisor is either a "business administrator," with no specialized, creative knowledge, or an ex-specialist. As a result, the creative or technical specialist feels that nincompoops, politicians, and incompetents meddle unnecessarily in business they know nothing about. They tend to feel that incompetents among their own bosses and at the client's shop force them to do countless revisions of perfectly good work or even force them to execute ideas that are so badly conceived or undefined that perfect execution only makes apparent the stupidity of the plans. Thus, they feel that most of the work done is totally unnecessary.

5. The account supervisors, on the other hand, feel that the technical specialists are "purists," academicians—temperamental, obstreperous, and difficult. Moreover, they resent feeling that the technical and creative specialists communicate a sense of being superior and of treating the account executive as if he were a dope.

6. Department heads resent the account heads, frequently feeling that the latter make excessive demands for their accounts on department personnel. They tend to feel that account heads want to tell the service heads and personnel how to do the work that the latter

are especially qualified for. They also feel that account heads, to save their own necks, will risk the necks of the service personnel by forcing them to do inferior, dishonest, or unnecessary work. They feel they are obliged to be cat's-paws, rescuing the chestnuts from the fire caused by the negligence and incompetence of account heads.

7. The account heads reciprocate this feeling, justifying their attitudes in terms of the jealousy and intransigence of the heads of the service departments.

8. All the above conflicts are expressed quite often in private gossip, in conflicts over salaries, and over the amount and availability of agency stock. The account executive feels that he is the businessman whose job it is to deal with the client, keep him happy, and keep the account in the shop. He must have tact and must lie to, flatter, and drink, eat, and live with stupid people in order to keep an account. He must do this by being self-effacing, polite, and deferential even under the pressures of the conscious and unconscious needling and resentment of the client. This entitles him to a lion's share of the rewards.

The technical or creative specialist feels that he does the actual job of planning, creating, and executing the final product (the advertisement) and/or its placement in a medium. Since this is the manifest job of the agency, the lion's share of the reward should be his.

9. In addition, each specialist group develops a special theory of advertising that just happens to make its function supreme. Copywriters insist that the slogan or apt phrase, the play on words, is the particular ingredient that sells a product. Art directors will stress the symbol and the mood as being especially creative of positive brand images that lead to sales. When images become passé, art directors may insist upon humorous animation ("You can get across unprovable claims by exaggerating them so much that even

if the viewer consciously disbelieves them, he unconsciously accepts them").

Television producers sell "realistic" and "atmospheric" mood photography, montage effects, use of succession of still shots of puppets to produce "animation"—all techniques designed to transport the viewer out of his normal, hardheaded buying attitude into a world that, because of the suspension of belief, is more "real" than the real world, and within which buying the advertised brand is linked to the fulfillment of the viewer's idealized self-image. Thus, the television producer, too, can make a claim for greater salary and more stock on the basis of attainment of this ideal.

The research director knows no limits to his megalomania except those that he encounters in the resistances that all other departments offer to the inquisitive snooping of research. Research enables the research director to "know" the audience, the customer, the sales personnel, and to "know" the action that will lead to success. He can research everybody's area of competence except his own and can thus tell everyone else how to do his work. Every other department is forced, in the face of the self-aggrandizing research director, either to limit the operations of research or to control them to serve the special purposes of that department.

Research *does*, however, sometimes provide answers to specific questions, *does* provide an aura of knowing for the agency as a whole, is useful to specialists in providing them with viable alternatives, and is helpful to the account supervisor in keeping an account and to top management in acquiring accounts. This utility constitutes the claim of the research director and his department for higher salaries and a greater share of profits.

10. The assignment of technical and creative specialists to distinct and separate account groups has additional consequences. While all copywriters, for example, are members of the creative department,

each copywriter actually works with only a few other copywriters on an account or group of accounts. He does not work with copywriters other than those assigned to his own account, though his office will be in the creative departments, next to the offices of all other copywriters.

His working partners, aside from the few other copywriters on his team, are account heads, artists, television producers, media planners and buyers, researchers, and so on. Thus, each specialist works primarily with other specialists who have different specialties from his own. Each is competent to judge only his own specialty, and each is required by the working relationship to make judgments about work he is not especially qualified to judge.

Since each has the vested interest of his craft, the trained incompetence, or the occupational psychosis that characterizes almost all specialists, each attempts if he can to impose his own perspective on his account group. But each specialist has some vested interests in his account group, as opposed to that of his service departmental peers. The value of his services is measured by the way his account group has served to attract and maintain clients. His claim for salary increase and stock benefits is in part related to the success of his account group. Thus, each specialist at times competes against his occupational peers and his service department.

The pattern of using small numbers of occupational specialists on an account group, together with other types of occupational specialists, tends to isolate each from his peers, to turn specialists into rivals, and to cause them to compete with one another for greater income. Thus, the fractionization of the agency into occupational specialties tends to be supplemented by a fractionization of each occupational specialty into account specialties. The individual specialist is thus almost always placed in a cross pressure between specialty and account. In the short run, he might find it profitable to align himself with his account group. If he does this too obviously or too defiantly, he may risk incurring the enmity of his service department head or of his occupational peers. Thus, each service department head would like to insist on the integrity and loyalty of his department in the face of continuous undermining by account supervision.

The competition within a service department is best illustrated by the "creative" competition when a new account enters a shop or when the client requests a new campaign ("The old one is tired"). A number of creative groups (copywriters and artists) are asked to prepare a series of alternative campaigns. Each group is briefed in the background of the account, its past history, its overall marketing, sales, and advertising strategy, and the relevant research background. Each group is given a deadline and prepares prototype advertisements in semifinished form that embody its creative effort. When the deadline has passed, the prototype advertisements are judged by the account supervisors and top agency management, as well as by the client. The creative group that submits the campaign closest to the one finally adopted usually is assigned to the account. Losers, especially if they were previously assigned to the account in question, are relegated to less important accounts. If one gets the new account assignment, one has a further claim to income and prestige. If one loses too many competitions, one becomes a drifter and is sooner or later forced to find another job.

In such competitions, therefore, the tension is deadly. Each creative group attempts to keep its major slogan, theme, or strategy a secret, and some groups attempt to ferret out the secrets of other groups in order to steal them, modify them, or develop, by implication only, a neutralizing theme or antidote. Each creative group attempts to "lobby" for its campaign, even though the campaign may exist only as a glimmer in a copywriter's eye; each may attempt to influence any department that is to evaluate or judge the competition.

All relevant parties are drawn into the competition, and each is used as a tool, even if heedless, of the aspirations of the competing creative groups.

This competition is only an extreme illustration of the normal competition between occupational peers. To some extent, such normal competition exists within all departments, and each department member is thus isolated from his peers. To be sure, temporary alliances do exist, based upon common assignments in the present or upon the prospects of profitable assignments in the future. But each man knows that his organizational position can change overnight, that his friends can become his enemies, and vice versa. Thus, to walk carefully and watchfully is a sine qua non of handling oneself.

11. Since all departments have their sets of rival theories and claims for functional indispensability, the adjudication of such claims is the central function of generalized management. Advertising agencies organize, disorganize, and reorganize constantly in order to solve the problem of control. In some agencies, account supervision is dominant; in others, service departments have major responsibility; and in still others, one service department may be supreme. In the latter case, the agency may be known as a "research agency," an "artwork agency," a "copy agency," specializing in either "hard-sell" or mood commercials. Other agencies, usually the colossi, sell "total advertising" or total marketing, a claim for excellence in all departments and in all services.

A second function of agency management is to control the account groups. If the account supervisor becomes too strong and has complete control of the client's affections and billings, he can either "blackjack" the agency or walk off with the account. The agency president, board chairman, and service departments are thus forced to develop independent channels of communication to the client that limit the influence of the account supervisor.

Skill Requirements for Agency Personnel

To be successful in agency work, artists, copywriters, designers, and other creative personnel need to be talented, trained in the exercise of their skill, and, if possible, creative. Talent and training are attributes that can be judged (if not measured) by qualified experts, if these are available. Creativity in advertising can be judged only under pressure, if it can be judged at all.

A talented copywriter, without ideas, can go far if he is able to develop the necessary appearances of creativity. Thus, when the "Be sociable, have a Pepsi" idea made Pepsi-Cola a major competitor of Coca-Cola, hundreds of brands in all product classes launched advertising that pictured the consumers of these brands as young, modern, carefree, sophisticated, fun-loving, sociable, prosperous, upper-middle-class suburbanites. This image became in a short time a cliché but a highly successful cliché—successful in raising the unspoken wishes of millions of Americans into a self-conscious "model for the millions." The cliché had such wide distribution and penetration that those copywriters and agencies who indiscriminately copied it were not able to establish any distinguishing characteristics for the brands they advertised.

To copy early in the copying cycle may be profitable; to copy late is suicidal. To copy a campaign that is so old that everybody has forgotten it may be a stroke of near genius. To create a genuine concept, a totally new idea that works, requires as much creativity in advertising as it does in other fields of art, letters, and sciences. Unfortunately, the collective character of the creative enterprise in advertising, and the speed at which both good and bad ideas are copied, make it almost impossible to recognize the original creator.

It is relatively easy to judge the skills of technicians in research, film editing, audio departments, and camerawork because there are established techniques in these fields. But even in technical fields, the mechanical application of technique results in dull, plodding work. Insight, imagination, the ability to apply technique to the solution of a "business" or aesthetic problem require, even in advertising, the same kinds of artistry that are required of creative personnel. And in these aspects of the work, the criteria for judging a man's work become just as subjective as those used for judging the creative artist.

Media planners, time and space buyers, and buyers of television programs usually develop a great deal of detailed knowledge of their respective fields merely by working in them. No special training is required of the neophyte to enter the field. But once he is in such a field, special talents for detail work, administration, and ability to exercise "good business judgment" are qualities that bring a good man to the fore.

These nontechnical business and administrative requirements resemble those appropriate to the account. The account executive and supervisor are required to be "good businessmen," good administrators, and to have "good business judgment." In addition, the account administrators are required to be tactful, likeable, charming, and to have, to a very high degree, all the qualities of successful salesmen. The similarity in the personal qualities required of the media buyer and the account man frequently results in the promotion of the time and space buyer to account executive, thence to account supervisor, and finally to agency president.

This career pattern is not fixed. Creative personnel, research men, media men, and a wide variety of other occupational types can become account executives; all types can become agency presidents. But if a specialist is to become an account supervisor or an agency president, he must first exhibit the qualities of the general administrator, businessman, and man of judgment. He has the opportunity to develop these qualities as a department head and administrator, as a member of the board of directors, or in making an impression on important representatives of the client in agency-client meetings or at lunch and after-hours meetings.

Yet a description of the above qualities does not come near to setting forth all the qualities necessary to success in occupational mobility. As indicated above, talent and technical knowledge are desirable qualities for creative and technical personnel. But possession of such qualities results only in the acquisition of rank and position as a staff official. *Administrative skill*, *judgment*, and *business sense* are the terms used to describe the special talents of the nonspecialized businessmen of the agency, who include media and program buyers, account executives and supervisors, and general agency officials. Such lists of qualifications, however, represent only the *public* side of an occupational description. Other, more personal qualities are necessary to complete the description.

Nerve is a central quality that any agency man must possess in order to survive the pressures. Since much of agency work is done under the constant pressure of volume, deadlines, possible criticism, and the ever-present image of total failure, men who cannot "stand the grind" are quickly recognized. Those who can are selected as "comers" and are pushed along as long as they can keep the respect of those who do the pushing.

Nerve means more than the ability not to crack under pressure. It means the capacity to exhibit, regardless of the pressures placed on one, calmness, tact, proper deference, good humor, and loyalty to the right people. But these latter qualities are independent of nerve. The ability to exhibit calmness, tact, deference, good humor, and loyalty to the right people is considered to be a basic personality requirement for any account officer, agency officer, or any creative or technical specialist who wants to move upward, for these qualities are client-pleasing qualities. They are also boss-pleasing qualities. Being in a business where one's very existence depends on the "favors" bestowed on one by the client gives advertising a courtlike atmosphere. The chief officer of the client is the "king," and the agency personnel are only one set of his courtiers. But the courtiers on each level, by virtue of their acceptance by the throne and by individuals who have access to the throne, receive deference in relationship to their imputed proximity to the throne. Ability to be successful as a courtier becomes objectified, is treated as a psychological trait in and of itself, and becomes the basis for further success in courtsmanship.

The quality of likeability (other-orientedness with a purpose) is subject to limitations. In a business where costs are a factor and where pressures are greater than one can absorb by oneself, the ability to resist pressures that are destructive to the individual is a necessary trait for success and for survival. For instance, a client may make demands that are too expensive, too time consuming, or impossible to fulfill. The account executive in this case must either talk the client into modifying his demands or convince him that his demands have been fulfilled when they have not. At times, he may be able to convince the client that the demands are totally unreasonable. But whatever he does, the account executive must do so in a manner that gains the respect or the liking of the client. If the account executive gives in to such demands, he may embarrass the agency and its profit structure, overload the technical, administrative, and creative staffs who have to meet the demands and find himself in trouble with his own bosses. Moreover, if the account executive indicates to the client that he can be pushed around, he invites the resentful or sadistic client to do just that. Finally, some clients expect top agency personnel to have convictions, policies, and beliefs of their own. They are paid to have these attributes. The account executive who is so likable that he accedes to whatever the client wishes is simply not doing his job. He is not providing the client with counsel, which is part of the service of the agency. If he does disagree, however, he must be tactful and, above all, he must know when to stop disagreeing. This *realistic toughness* is the third major quality necessary for success in an agency.

The three major personality traits so far discussed become the basis for types of agency personnel. The types are as follows:

Type 1. The Creative Genius. This is the official who creates or attempts to create the impression that his technical knowledge or creative ability is so great that he can ignore the other realities of the agency business. If he succeeds (by being almost as good as he claims to be), he can go far toward a top staff position. He is usually viewed as irresponsible in positions that require "judgment" or administrative ability.

Type 2. The Likable Chap. He works hard and is continually on the run. He is pleasing, amiable, entertaining, and quite frequently provides more services than the client or account supervisor asks for. He is perfectly eager and willing to handle all details for his superiors, or to get someone else to do so. But he is at a total loss when two or more superiors disagree, or when he is asked to have an opinion before an official opinion exists. He lacks nerve. Such a person is not likely to reach a position higher than account executive because he finds it difficult to work without lines and because he is likely to give away his own, his subordinates', and worse, the agency's shirt in the desire to please. He needs to work under Type 3.

Type 3. The Tough Realist. He may not have creative or technical ability, but he knows how to please when that quality is necessary. He knows when to get tough with his subordinates, with himself ("discipline"), and with the client. He knows in any given situation what his self-interest is, what the client's interests are, and what the agency's, account groups', or service department's interests are. No matter what the social situation is, he knows how to juggle these interests so that he, in the final analysis, will come out on top. Of course, such results do not always occur. When two or more tough realists come into open conflict, one may be forced to go (even if this means his occupational demise). One can make an error in judgment, such as cultivating and supporting an important official in the client firm, only to discover later that this "personal" client has been squeezed out. The enemies of the personal client may now be running the client firm, and the agency man is persona non grata. If this happens, the tough realist may be out of a job. A tough realist may spend a decade cultivating a particular individual in the client firm, nursing him up the ladder of success in his own firm. Shortly after the client "arrives," he dies. The tough realist then loses his "contact" and may have no other assets of value when he faces his own agency.

These are polar types. Most personnel in an agency, however, exhibit combinations of the traits of the three polar types. The creative genius can also be a likable chap or a tough realist (if he is willing to suppress his needs for personal recognition), but he cannot be both. The likable chap is likely to be a pure type. However, a likable account executive, after achieving that position, may suddenly begin to sound like a tough realist. If he can maintain that attitude under pressure or adversity, he may grow up to be a genuine tough realist. The tough realist may have had, in the earlier years of his career, creative or technical ability which, by and large, he is not able to exercise in the present because of the pressures of other work. He can always be likable when necessary. But the quality that accounts for his success is his realistic toughness.

The "Meaning of Work" in an Advertising Agency

Our discussion of the economic, occupational, social, and psychological structure of the advertising agency defines much of what can be said of the "meaning of work" in an agency, for the very framework and operation of the agency constitute a set of limitations and opportunities for the individual. What these limitations and opportunities are to a particular individual is a function of the nature of the social structure within which he works; his particular needs, motivation, and personality; and the particular way his personality is linked to that social structure.

The phrase *meaning of work* is an ambiguous term. "Meaning" can be conceived of as the immanent set of meanings that attach to an *objective* event, situation, or social structure. In this sense, work can be conceived of as being meaningful in and of itself, without the support of external rewards and gratifications that are a product of the work but are not in the work. This immanent meaning can be contrasted to instrumental meanings in which the "meaning" (the satisfaction one gets from the work) is not in the work itself, but in what the work enables one to do in other areas of life. Thus, dull, routine, or painful work—work that contains no joy—can be meaningful if, by doing it, one achieves an economic gain, prestige, power, or even the perfection of a skill that is useful for the attainment of some other goal. With these distinctions in mind, we can pose the question. What are the internal and external meanings attached to work in an advertising agency?

It is simplest to discuss external meaning. As we have previously indicated, advertising work is extremely well paid, has tremendous opportunities for mobility, and in a high-tax economy offers a capable man great opportunities to acquire wealth. Such economic motivations need not necessarily imply that the advertising man is a crass materialist. The acquisition of wealth, in a society that is heir to the Protestant ethic, is simply a means for a man to legitimate himself in terms of the only standards that may be meaningful to him. Certainly, economic and social mobility through success in advertising may mean to an individual that he is on his way to fulfilling the American dream. His efforts, his manhood, his ideals are affirmed by his success. The successful man can hold his head up high in his community and can gain the respect of his wife, friends, and neighbors, if they happen to share his dream. He develops confidence, poise, assertiveness, and even arrogance in his relationships with others outside the industry, no matter how timid and "likable" he is in the agency. Moreover, the upwardly mobile agency man earns almost sufficient income to acquire a lifestyle that conforms to his image of what middle- and upper-class life is like. He can play at being a solid citizen, an upper bohemian, or an English-type country squire. Each type of play is a further affirmation of his version of the American dream and therefore must be taken seriously. But mobile advertising men are usually intelligent, articulate, educated, and expert at seeing through false appearances, including their own. They have this ironic talent because they are marginal men and because their occupational selection and function require them to construct "artificial worlds" that can enchant and seduce outsiders. This talent for analysis cannot be "turned off" when it comes to the analysis of oneself. Thus, in playing the solid citizen, the upper bohemian, or the English country squire, advertising men tend to burlesque themselves, doing so half with tongue-in-cheek and half seriously. This comic aspect of one's private life is frequently presented to friends in the profession, but a more serious demeanor is presented to outsiders.

The thousands of jokes about advertising men, the satires of the language of advertising ("Let's put it [an idea] on at New Haven and see where it gets off" or "Let's get down on our hands and knees and look at it from the client's point of view") are inventions of successful advertising men who cannot genuinely understand their own success because that success appears to be based on so little.

Self-deprecation is one of the prices one pays for what is thought of as unearned success.

Part of this ironical attitude, which is based on the notion of "pinch me—it may not be so," derives from the fact that it may not be "so" tomorrow, for the mobile advertising man realizes, perhaps not openly, that a single job failure at the age of forty-five or over by a man with a salary of $20,000 and over may make it all "not so." Thus, he can never accept fully, at all levels of his consciousness, the success he might otherwise believe in. To outsiders, he may act the role of the successful executive. To the few insiders whom he feels he does not have to "sell," he may confide his anxieties or ironies. The anxieties emerge in pressure-cooker situations, and the ironies in success situations.

An additional set of supporting external meanings is found in the idea that the advertising man makes important decisions for big companies, representing hundreds of millions of dollars of annual sales or billions of dollars of corporate wealth. The young advertising executive, and even an older one, may confide to his wife or friend that he sat in a meeting with the president of a giant corporation and perhaps even said something. He may point to a commercial that is on the air and say, "See that commercial? I wrote one line of it!" or he may say in irony, "I recommended against it." He can speak knowingly about the inner affairs of gigantic American corporations to his male friends or speak even more knowingly about soaps, detergents, floor polishes, foods, and sauces to his wife and his wife's friends. When "the business of America is business," being close to business and to the thrones of the monarchs of business is enchanting.

To the successful advertising man who is himself the son of a successful father, success in advertising has different meanings. Success means the validation of one's birthright, the proof that one has lived up to the task handed down by one's father or family. Success, then, is both a right and a duty; failure is a disgrace. The upper-class advertising man is less likely to develop the ironic self-mockery of the upwardly mobile man. He is likely to take the surrealistic atmosphere of advertising seriously, to accept its rituals, and act unselfconsciously. He is likely to be reliable in dealing with clients because he does not let the mask slip; he has no mask. Therefore, he is capable of genuine sincerity in an industry where sincerity is a major stock-in-trade. The sincere upper-class advertising man is not likely to understand the ironic, sardonic, and self-deprecating mobile man. He feels that such a man will befoul his own nest, will risk upsetting the client, and will regard him as being "thick" or stupid.

These mutual feelings of lack of admiration, however, are usually not expressed; they are kept behind the facade of deference and authority that reflect the respective positions of the individuals in question. Occasionally, they are expressed directly; more often, they are expressed between two individuals of similar class and occupational position. Most often, they result from the fact that individuals of diverse backgrounds do not understand each other.

A third external meaning of advertising work comes from the enjoyment of the glamour of advertising. This includes enjoyment of the food and drink in fancy restaurants, the enjoyment being more a function of the expense than the quality of the food, the drink, or the company. The idea of air travel, with sudden and long trips for short conferences, stays at expensive hotels, and living on the expense account all make life exciting when discussed with outsiders or with the less fortunate. One quickly becomes an authority on exotic foods, restaurants, hotels, and cities, and can compare notes with the equally fortunate. The glamour of advertising supports the feeling of success that mobility may bring, and it sometimes provides a substitute for more tangible success. One frequently hears of newly graduated college students who, in applying for an advertising job, cite as their reason the glamour of the job, along with the economic opportunities or the chance to come close to what they regard as the sources of power and the throne.

Another form of external meaning can come from acceptance of the public ideology. Hypothetically, this meaning pattern would be stated as follows: "Advertising is a service not to me personally or to the clients only, but to the economy as a whole. It keeps the economy going, creates new products, new jobs, makes industry competitive, and helps to bestow the advantages of free enterprise on our economy." This ideology is the basis for the theme and rhetoric of after-dinner speeches, interviews with and articles by distinguished leaders of the advertising industry, advertising and marketing professors, and industrialists speaking or writing for public consumption.

We have described this service ideology as a hypothetical system of meaning. It is hypothetical because it represents a possibility but not an actuality. Advertising men simply do not speak in these terms in personal conversation. At most, a top official will express such a view in an informal group when practicing for a speech or in writing a paper for public consumption. If he does this among his peers, they are likely to interject wry comments. They may well document his speech with examples of conspicuous waste, stupidity, or mismanagement, conducted either by advertising men or by their clients. Even upper-class top officials who take advertising seriously are not likely to indulge in "speech-making" in intimate circles, if only to avoid such wry comment.

On the contrary, most advertising men compile and treasure the conspicuous boners, the waste and fatuousness that advertisers and their agencies commit. Stories circulate about the most sensational television buy of the decade, bought by a company that was so late in reaching a buying decision that it had to buy the only show available, against its inclinations—a show that all other companies and agencies who had been offered it had turned down. Other such stories concern the successful man who moves upward and onward by ruining everything he touches: the company that researches a product so long and so well that, by the time it is done with its research, its competitors have preempted the market; or the company whose advertising and marketing policies and operations can be turned into a casebook on how not to advertise or market a brand. Advertising men have discussed the Cold War with the hope that the Russians have a number of marketing and advertising men in their top ranks to balance the odds a little. It is hoped that the Russians can foul up at least as often as American industry.

Ideology, as it is publicly expressed, then, does not provide meaning in a sense that may sustain the motivations of individuals. At best, it provides a claim for the respectability and legitimacy of the industry, a claim made by individuals who do not believe the claim in any operative sense. Very few advertising men, however, will deny in public the ideology of advertising. To do so would rock the boat, result in a public squabble, and invite clients to withdraw their advertising from agencies that employ controversial characters.

The operative external meanings of work can be conceived of as those surrounding economic gain and the glamour and self-importance achieved by working in an important industry, but not an ideology of service.

Internal Meanings of Work in Advertising

As previously indicated, internal meanings derive from joy in performing an activity for the sake of the activity itself, and not for the external products of that activity. At first glance, this category of meaning appears to be most applicable to creative personnel and to technologists. The writer, the artist, the designer, the musical composer, the trained researcher—all enter the agency with specialized interests, talents, and training in their respective fields. Working in advertising gives the artist or technologist an opportunity to be paid for exercising his creative ability, his craft, or his specialized methodology on "real, live problems" where his art and science can have some effect.

If this is the hope that brings a talented individual into advertising, he is doomed to quick disappointment. For the creative artist or technologist discovers almost immediately that advertising writing, art, and science are not for the small magazine, the gallery, or the scientific journal (except marketing journals). The problems he works on are selected by others. The strategy he works on is the product of countless, boring meetings with artistic or scientific nincompoops. At each stage of his work, the Philistines make suggestions and otherwise interfere. When a work is done, the Philistines reject the already compromised mess because it does not meet the specifications they were unaware of when they commissioned the work. So back the creative artist goes to the drawing board to start all over again under much the same conditions.

The creative man or technologist begins to arrive at a genuine understanding of advertising when he realizes that his work is a tool, a means of achieving goals that lie outside the work itself. Such goals consist of getting the job done on time in a manner that is satisfactory to someone else (if not to his former self), of helping his boss, his department, his agency, and his client to do the job they were assigned, and of getting properly rewarded for successful completion of his work. All these meanings may be admirable, but frequently they are meanings that an individual discovers after he has been in advertising for some time and after he has been disappointed or broken in the attempt to do what he regards as more creative, scientific, or serious work.

Individuals who enter advertising with less grandiose aspirations are less likely to be disenchanted, but they are also less likely to do creative work in advertising. This is because even burned-out ideals and creativity, when not accompanied by bitterness, allow the creative or scientific technician to approach the creation of an advertisement with some of the talent, sensitivity, and techniques that a dedicated artist and scientist can bring to noncommercial work.

Thus, the exposure to agency work tends to turn internal meanings into external meanings. Work tends to lose its meaning-for-itself and to develop instrumental meanings.

There are, of course, limitations to this process. A major limitation consists in the persistence of the "instinct for workmanship," pride in craftsmanship, in doing a sound, workmanlike job. Pride in craftsmanship appears to be as central to the personality of a creative individual as any other trait. It is the last quality to disappear. Thus, most creative and scientific personnel will continue to strive for technical excellence in their work regardless of whether they think the work they are asked to do is badly conceived, is inartistic or unscientific, or essentially is not their own. More conflicts between creative and noncreative personnel take place over techniques than over aesthetics or over ethics. This is because technical virtuosity is the last remnant of a man's pride in his creative ability. To the layman or to a specialist in another field, it is a source of considerable amusement, and at times ennui, to see two creative specialists or technicians fighting tooth and nail (but politely) over minor points of technique that do not appear to affect the strategy, overall design, or imputed results of an advertisement. However, such concern for detail usually results in technically accomplished advertising.

For the noncreative, nontechnical person in advertising, there should, at first appearance, be no internal meaning to his work. His job is primarily administrative in nature. It involves keeping track of the flow of paper through channels and accelerating, stopping, or restarting that flow. It involves "selling" to superiors and clients and manipulating, planning, coaxing, and coercing cooperation and work out of inferiors and peers. He comes to such tasks with no particular interest, talent, or creative genius. By and large, his motivations for getting into the field are: it pays well, it sounds glamorous and exciting, and there is nothing else he really wants to do. Once he becomes an advertising man, he really discovers all the opportunities for advancement, the excitement and the glamour and the possibilities for failure, the pressures, the overwork, the conspiracies, the powerlessness, the isolation, and the anxiety that are recurrent in the course of his career.

Gentle personalities are likely to get out of advertising at relatively young ages. If they are "businessmen," they will try to move to large corporations where, at lower levels and at lower pay, the pressures and crises are less frequent and less turbulent. If they have merchandisable talents, they may try teaching, government, or some other stable field. This process of interindustry mobility results in a shakedown, leaving as survivors those who think they have nerve, toughness, talent, or other personal qualities necessary for the life of a courtier. Those who discover that they do not have these qualities, or do not have enough of them to maintain a career after they are well started on that career, are the genuine tragedies in advertising. They may be too successful to get out, but not strong enough to stay in. Individuals in this situation are the ones who break under pressure.

But to the strong, the nervy, the talented and tough, the very fact of pressure constitutes the strongest set of internal meanings possible. For the difficulties, the pressure, the politics and manipulation, the irrationality, the powerlessness, and the isolation all constitute a challenge to one's manhood. The challenge is, "be crushed or survive." The answer the advertising man gives is, "Throw everything you can at me—work, pressure, senselessness—and somehow I will lick you and force you to throw even more work at me. Each victory will make me more able to survive new challenges, since my nerve and toughness will be greater and my skills will have been tested in more encounters." The response is a Promethean challenge to the gods and the fates.

The satisfaction involved is a sense of delight in knowing that one has succeeded in manipulating others, of "selling" the bosses or the client, of defying the gods and the fates. If nerve and realistic toughness are the supremely valued traits of the tough realist, then awareness of one's exhibition and possession of these traits becomes a value in and of itself. Income, stock ownership, even the glamour of advertising and the way of life derived from advertising, are merely external affirmations of an inner attitude. The inner attitude, not the results, is the chief value that excites the driving, tough businessman.

In literary or philosophical imagery, this meaning pattern can be called "Faustian." The Faustian man seeks goals outside himself that are difficult. His inner goals are to master the difficult, not to possess the goal, and to exercise his strength and talent in overcoming the obstacles. It is the feeling of strength, confidence, pride in mastery, and the recognition he gets from others for his ability that constitute the source of his joy in work.

In psychological terms, this meaning pattern can be called narcissism. It is an intensified form of self-love because the satisfaction derived from activity is a self-conscious pride in achievement. The narcissistic individual, even in the midst of the most difficult work and pressure, keeps an area of his consciousness detached from his work. He becomes his own observer, checking on himself and commenting on his performance, as he manipulates himself and others. He works in a frenzy and praises or condemns himself as he does so. In the sense that the detached observer in his consciousness robs him of the capacity to feel anything spontaneously, none of his feelings are "genuine." Even if he acts or speaks spontaneously, the narcissistic observer makes an ironic or detached analytical commentary on the action, saying, "Nicely done, boy" or "You'll have to do better next time."

The driving ambition of the narcissist, then, is to win the plaudits of his own inner cheering stand. When he does so, the psychological tone he exhibits is euphoria, brazen self-confidence, aggressiveness, and optimism. When he fails, the psychological tone is depression, self-pity, paranoia, and feelings of rejection. But since the narcissist is self-conscious, he knows that if he can generate the attitudes of self-confidence, euphoria, and aggressiveness, he is likely to sound sincere, convincing, and effective.

Thus, one of the most humorous and charming situations in advertising occurs when an account supervisor and his minions are about to make a presentation to the client. After all the work has been done and the presentation, the charts, the film, and the reports are all "locked up" and produced, several days are spent in meetings, rehearsals, and conversations during which each member of the team strokes up the enthusiasm and self-confidence of all the others. Woe unto the hapless observer who wittingly or unwittingly discovers a flaw in operation or throws cold water on it. He destroys the self-confidence of the team, their enthusiasm, sincerity, and capacity for doing effective work. Collective narcissism is a necessary ingredient for teamwork.

Narcissism has other advantages for the advertising man. The source of narcissism is the basic energy of the individual. But with narcissism, all the energy is turned inward and becomes self-love. The individual gives this energy to himself and tells himself to use it in such a way that narcissism can grow and grow and grow. Thus, the narcissist in his euphoric stages has immense reserves of energy, confidence, and aggressiveness that he can direct at narcissistic purposes. He can work at top speed under the worst of pressure for extended periods of time until he collapses either from failure or from physical and psychological fatigue. The demands, the pressures, that advertising work places on the advertising man, then, are appropriate to the narcissist.

However, the narcissistic energy evoked by the man and his job cannot be shut off at will. The energy once released needs an outlet. It will rattle and shake its owner if there is no outlet. In advertising, the flow of work is uneven; in between crises, storms, and drives, there are sometimes extended periods of calm. After the individual has recovered his strength from the last crisis, any further period of calm becomes a threat. The restless energy wants to be released. Advertising men solve this problem in a number of ways. Severe measures to bottle up the energy can be taken at the risk of depression. Narcissistic energy can be released in drinking, entertaining, partying, carousing, and active and demanding vocations and sports. All these are parts of the way of life of many advertising men. Finally, if there is no crisis, one can always be provoked. This can be done consciously, by starting a new round of solicitations for new business, or unconsciously, by starting a fight with a peer, the client, or another department. One can demand an "exercise" to keep one's subordinates busy or can feud and fuss out of lack of interest in routine, calm, peaceful work.

If narcissism is turned into useless burning of unnecessary energy, it becomes self-destructive. The individual wears himself out physically and emotionally, moves from crisis to crisis, and, finally, from breakdown to breakdown. He dies before his time. If he uses his narcissism to provoke crises, feuds, self-dramatizing arguments and quarrels, the narcissist can precipitate crises in others, causing conflict and resentments that can wreck an organization.

Narcissism is a generalized psychological trait that can erupt in anyone. As such, it is not linked particularly to advertising. Narcissism can be linked to any kind of work—it merely means that one is preoccupied with the response to one's self in work rather than with the work itself. Narcissism is likely to be a dominant characteristic in the creative and performing arts where the person releases tremendous energies to act more for an audience consisting of himself than for the audience in the seats. It is likely to be present in politics where the demands on the public personality are so great that only an individual who enjoys his public performance can endure the strain of that performance. It is also likely to be found to a high degree in other industries where the occupational strains and stresses are similar to those of advertising. These include public relations, the mass media, management consulting, and the upper levels of all large-scale organizations.

But it is true that narcissism is found to a very great extent in advertising. Why this should be so can be explained in terms of the structure of advertising. Individuals with creative talent or with scientific aspirations who are intrinsically interested in their work are driven out of the industry if they insist that work be internally meaningful. If they remain in advertising, it is because their work has become instrumental to them. To say that work is instrumental is to say that the work becomes at the same time an object and a means for the individual. The man is separated from his work by intense self-consciousness—that is, narcissism. Advertising thus makes narcissists out of non-narcissists.

In the same way, the noncreative businessman finds that tremendous pressures, difficulties, obstacles, and anxieties are placed in the path of achieving substantial but extrinsically meaningful rewards. The pressures are so great that those who cannot take them leave. Those who remain are the ones who thrive on work and pressure, who enjoy work and pressure for what these enable them to accomplish. Those who remain are the narcissists.

Thus, advertising modifies and selects personalities so that a few predominant types are produced. To the extent that advertising has the public image of being glamorous, exciting, close to the source of power, and frenzied, it attracts individuals who think they might survive in this atmosphere. Even the negative image of advertising serves as a recruiting poster to those who find the "negative image" positive. In this sense, advertising recruits potential or actual narcissists as well as selecting and creating narcissists out of those who unwittingly enter its domain.

Personal Ethics in Advertising

Much of our previous discussion frames the discussion of the role of ethics in advertising. The word *ethics*, however, is an ambiguous term. For our present purposes, "ethics" does not include the following:

1. Rules and regulations governing the competition between agencies, involving such "crimes" as account stealing, speculative unsolicited presentations to secure a new account, and raiding of personnel. We abstain from such discussion because we are concerned with personal ethics rather than with institutional or trade association policies.

2. For the same reasons, we are not concerned with the law, FTC, USDA, and FCC regulations per se. The extent to which individuals regard the law as a barrier to their personal goals is, of course, of some interest.

3. We are not concerned with ethics in an absolute sense, as perhaps expressed by the Golden Rule. The Golden Rule is too severe a standard to judge any industry by and would not distinguish one

industry from another. However, very few people in Western civilization can discuss ethics without thinking about the Judeo-Christian concept of ethics. For our present discussion, we shall leave such a conception of ethics in the back of the mind, allowing it to emerge when and where it must.

The operational definition of *ethics* we use is as follows: those actions or rules for action that, when violated, produce in the violator, a spectator, or a person informed of the action, a sense of moral shock, disgust, or horror. The reverse of this definition also applies: ethics are not operative when an "expected sense of horror" does not follow the commission or the knowledge of the action. In short, an action is viewed as "ethical" when it does not produce a negative judgment on moral grounds. It is viewed as "unethical" when it does.

Ethics in Dealing with the Public

Since the economic function of advertising is to help a manufacturer sell his brand, the evaluation of ethics might start with a consideration of what advertising men believe is ethical or unethical in the claims, promises, and techniques they use toward this end.

Complaints by Newton N. Minow, Chairman of the Federal Communications Commission[3] revealed to the public that a great deal of "fraudulent" advertising is central to the day-to-day operations of an agency and its clients. Fake demonstrations appear in the commercials; fraudulent claims are made; misleading statements are presented as statistical facts. Product weaknesses are covered over—in fact, made into virtues. Certainly, at least some daily advertising operations meet the legal definitions of fraud. But this discussion hinges not on the fact that fraudulent or misleading advertising exists, but on the attitude of agency personnel to commercials that might be construed as fraudulent.

Agency personnel recognize as primary their economic function to help their client sell his brand. Anything that helps is useful, even fraudulent or misleading advertising. This is especially true if the brand has no unusual characteristics to make it attractive to the public. The copywriter or the account executive can paraphrase Winston Churchill, and say, "It is not my duty to preside at the liquidation of my client." This is all the more true when the advertised product is inferior to other brands. In such cases, the copywriter's pride in craftsmanship is invoked ("Anybody can sell a product that sells itself, but it takes art to sell an inferior product!"). Thus, if a hairdressing is too greasy, one inverts the weakness by saying, "A little dab'll do ya . . . or the girls will pursue ya." If the major cleaning ingredient in your client's detergent is so ineffective that it requires twice as much of that ingredient to equal the cleaning ability of the major competitor, you claim "twice the active cleaning ingredients." If your brand needs two or more ingredients to do the work that other products do with one ingredient, you advertise "twinpower" or "just like a doctor's prescription." If your product was inferior and a minor change has been made to make it almost equal to its competitors, you advertise it as "new," "improved," or "25 percent better" (better than what is not specified). You might add just enough of a "miracle" ingredient (lanolin, hexachlorophene, olive oil, and so on) to be able to advertise the ingredient but not enough to affect the cost or the product quality. You might even study the manufacturing process and discover a standard ingredient of all brands in the product class that no one has yet advertised, and then proceed, by advertising, to transform this into a new "miracle" ingredient ("It has sixty-four beans in a cup").

You may employ your research department to use technically accurate and honest surveys that lead, because of the glories of an ambiguous English language grammar, to "dishonest" conclusions:

"Eighty percent of all doctors prescribe the *ingredients* in our brand" (but the vast majority do not recommend the brand—in fact, may recommend against using the brand). Questionnaires are designed so that only one answer is possible, and subsequent research work is similarly scrupulously honest; the results are impeccable and are used to provide the legal basis for an advertising claim.

At each point in this process, pride in craftsmanship enables the creative man to provide the client with "selling" advertising despite brand deficiencies. Even when one has a brand that is technically superior, but whose superiority is the result of highly technical and difficult-to-understand features, it is frequently more efficient to develop a simple, fraudulent claim or demonstration than to demonstrate the difficult truth.

In all these cases, the primary criterion for advertising honesty is not the honesty or dishonesty of the advertising but its imputed selling efficiency.

So far as one can tell, advertising men do not object to telling these "necessary" lies. In fact, when the necessary lie is a creative one, they take great pride in their ability to overcome the deficiencies of the product. Some indications of malaise, however, are found in the ironical ways in which they will recount their creative escapades. Ironical pride may indicate that, if they could not tell the truth, they at least did a good job of lying. Thus, virtuosity in fraud becomes a virtue. For the most part, however, even the desire to commit fraud is limited to that which is necessary to sell the brand.

Quite frequently, advertisers will be more interested in truth telling than agency people, especially copywriters. First of all, since advertisers are not copywriters, they do not get the aesthetic satisfaction, except vicariously, from producing the creative lie. Second, the client suffers more than an individual copywriter from being the object of a governmental cease-and-desist order. Such an order may be worth millions of dollars of negative advertising for a brand. To avoid such problems, a crew of high-priced agency, client, and media lawyers inspect all copy and certify its probable legality before finished advertisements are prepared. Such precautions are necessary. The creative man, if given full freedom, will at times generate such patently fraudulent advertising that only a lawyer can stop him. Such creativity, however, is relatively infrequent. Most copywriters are aware of the legal limitations and, if they are not sure of them, will consult the lawyers in advance.

Nevertheless, a few copywriters do get the reputation of being moral lepers. They love fraud for fraud's sake. Such individuals rejoice in the complicated, tricky, aesthetically satisfying lie even when the truth might be a powerful selling proposition. The moral leper is spotted almost as soon as he joins the agency. His fantastic lies (both in copywriting and in personal relations) are told and retold by all others. He is a source of humor to those not directly involved in working with him, a source of danger and chagrin to all others. He is a source of danger because, in risking legal action, he endangers the account. Moreover, everyone connected with the moral leper (and technically he is a psychopath) must attempt to avoid or repair the harm he does to the agency and to others. He therefore causes more work than he accomplishes. However, a psychopath can be a good copywriter if he is controlled. There are few limits to his fancy, his imagination, or his ability to beg, borrow, or steal ideas that may be useful.

But the moral leper is the deviant that defines the important, operative ethical norms for advertising. He establishes the boundaries that must not be crossed. If one does pass over, one receives moral disapprobation. In relation to the public, this norm is as follows: "*Don't tell an unnecessary lie.*" Necessary lies are acceptable because they are essential to fulfill the economic function of the agency. What is more, all advertising men tend to be conscious of the pressures that all other men work under. They are sympathetic to the individual who suffers from moral and ethical lapses in response to these pressures. They are totally unsympathetic to the individual who enjoys lying or to the person who lies beyond what is structurally necessary. Thus, in a genuine sense, most advertising men are profoundly moral.

Ethics in Dealing with Clients

The client is the advertising man's sole source of bread and butter. In addition to being well aware of this dependency, the advertising man has other images of the client. These include the following:

> 1. Most clients are stupid. If they weren't, they'd be working in agencies where they'd get paid more.
>
> 2. Most clients are technically incompetent.
>
> 3. Most clients are sadistic or are resentful of the agency man because of the latter's ability and salary.
>
> 4. Most clients are unreasonable and overdemanding. They also stick their noses into business they are not equipped to handle.
>
> 5. Most clients are hungry, thirsty, and vain. They need constant attention, flattery, and fake deference.
>
> 6. Most clients are ingrates. They will switch accounts for petty reasons, especially after the agency has done a superhuman job.
>
> 7. Most clients want the credit for work well done and will blame the agency for their own mistakes.
>
> 8. Some clients are gullible fools, but these are nice people.

Not all of these images are applied to all clients. In fact, each agency has one or more clients whose personal qualities, business acumen, and administrative ability set so high a standard that all other clients look feeble in comparison.

These images set the stage for the discussion of client-focused ethics. The fundamental strategy of the agency is to make convincing its claim for distinctive agency superiority and indispensability in meeting the client's needs. Once one acquires an account, the initial argument plus its proof must be continuously demonstrated, even in the face of falling sales ("They could, under other circumstances, fall even faster").

Ethics in relationship to the client are based on the norm, "*Don't ever tell a direct lie to the client.*" This may not even be an ethical norm, since it is based on the assumption that without the client's trust in one's basic honesty, no enduring client-agency relationship is possible. The norm is thus a pragmatic device to keep the account.

If we consider the rule as an ethical norm, however, another set of normative propositions follows. While one does not tell a lie to the client, one does not always have to tell the total truth. The agency's fundamental business requirement is to keep profitable accounts. Therefore, agency communications to the client tend to conceal negative aspects of agency operations—inefficiency, indecision, or lack of attention to the client's account because major attention has been given to other accounts. It is assumed that clients are big boys and that it is their problem to discover the negative aspects of the client-agency relationship, not the duty of the agency to inform on itself.

When an account is secure, however, the agency may criticize its own advertising. It may volunteer research results that are negative or otherwise criticize its own operation, especially if the agency is immediately prepared to take protective action. Such self-criticism builds trust and forestalls client-originated criticism.

The deviant individuals in client-agency ethics are of two types: The *schlemiel* [bungler—Ed.], who reveals agency difficulties to the client (either by accident or as an attempt to curry favor), is a menace who cannot be kept around. The moral leper, on the other hand, who tells the client lies that are too big, risks creating a basic mistrust by allowing himself and the agency to be exposed as "defrauding" the client. He is the worse menace. Between these two extremes are the tough realists who know how and when to tell the truth.

The "tough realist" client is respected but feared because there is less need to manipulate him and less danger of a sudden disenchantment. The tough realist expects more and less of the agency at the same time. He does not ask for miracles, but he does ask for hard, creative work. A good agency can provide this without the necessity for deception.

The Ethics of Interpersonal Relationships

There are a few general norms that apply to all people in an agency, a great many that apply to specific types of social relationships. The general ones are considered first.

An overall rule is, "*Don't lie, cheat, steal unnecessarily.*" This is the same rule as applied to the public, but now it is applied as a norm for interpersonal relations. Again, the same general limits apply. A great many otherwise unacceptable actions are viewed as tolerable (except to the injured party) because all are aware of the pressure that causes individuals to act in ways that are outside the Judeo-Christian ethical framework. The individual whose ethical lapses are due only to a desire for personal advantage or for "joy through crime" is viewed as a moral leper. If one lies to avoid endangering the agency or to avoid losing one's job, then the lie is necessary.

Another norm involves keeping one's promises. The rule is, "*Don't make empty promises; but when you make a promise, keep it.*" This is a general application of the norm of not lying to the client. The individual must establish himself as being trustworthy. To do so, he must keep his personal promises. However, he should not place himself in embarrassing situations by giving promises he cannot meet. Personal honor, in this sense, is one of the most valued qualities in a man. Word keeping indicates "character" and helps a man to gain the reputation of being "responsible"—an indispensable quality for mobility to "business-oriented" positions.

The demand for word keeping is nevertheless not so stringent as it may first appear. If there is a choice between keeping one's word to a client or a superior and keeping it to a peer or an inferior, the choice is always made in favor of the former. This is excusable if the promise was made in good faith and if the conflict in promises was unavoidable. Again, all parties recognize the pressures involved. The moral leper makes indiscriminate promises that he has no intention of fulfilling or that he fails to fulfill simply because of inconvenience.

A third general rule involves one's private life. The agency makes no demands on the individual's private morals, ethics, or character, as long as they do not impinge upon the conduct of business or agency-client relationships. An individual can be a homosexual, a lecher, a drunk, or a psychopath as long as he is discreet. He should not display his vices in the office, nor should he get his name in the papers. The client, in short, should think of an agency man as a pillar of the community unless, of course, the client is a lecher or a semialcoholic himself. In such a case, the agency man may assist the client in assuaging his vicious needs. But in every case, the obligation is to keep one's ill-fame out of the newspapers.

As for their personal standards of judgment, agency men appear to be tolerant of others' idiosyncrasies as long as they are not obtrusive or threatening. One does not impose one's personal taste on others.

A final rule, more a job requirement than an ethical norm, is, "*Never lose your temper, no matter what the provocation.*" Losing one's temper causes the individual to say things, or expose things, that are best left unsaid or unexposed. Personal control is a means of avoiding "spilling the beans." And spilling the beans is one of the most serious violations of agency norms. Being a vicious gossip, whether in anger or not, is almost automatic grounds for firing.

Ethics for Bosses with Respect to their Subordinates

A boss is expected to give credit to juniors for work they have done. He should not "hog" the glory. It is assumed that since most work in an agency is collective work, it is not necessary for one man to have all the credit. Moreover, since the boss recruits, hires, trains, and supervises the work of his subordinates, credit for a subordinate's outstanding work automatically belongs to the boss. Since this is true, the boss gets the credit, even if he graciously renounces it in favor of his subordinates. The boss who "hogs the glory," then, takes the credit he would get anyway, but takes it by denying it unnecessarily to others. He gets the reputation of being a moral leper, and subordinates seek to transfer from his jurisdiction, if necessary to another agency. They may even attempt to keep their ideas secret, announcing them only in public meetings in which their bosses' peers or superiors (including representatives of the client) are present.

Similarly, a boss is expected to take the blame for a subordinate's mistake, even though the boss is not responsible for the mistake. He is viewed as responsible for hiring the miscreant and for supervising his work. If a mistake reaches that point where it can be publicly called a mistake, the boss has failed. If he is a "man," he will take the blame in public and settle with the subordinate in private.

This norm is again limited by the reality of pressure. If the boss is endangered personally by the mistake of the subordinate, it is "understood" when he allows the subordinate to take the blame. If he does so when there is no pressure, he approaches moral leprosy. When he allows a subordinate to take the blame gratuitously for his—that is, the boss's—mistakes, he is a moral leper.

Additionally, the boss is expected to try to get higher salaries and stock for his subordinates and to fight for them when they are criticized by the personnel of other departments. He does so because his subordinates are extensions of himself. He asserts his self-esteem by fighting for his "children." Not infrequently, though, the boss may think that there is a "fixed pool" of money available for raises in his department or a fixed amount of stock available for such disposition. He can thus conceive of himself in competition with his subordinates. To get a larger share for himself, he denies benefits to his subordinates. Subordinates, if they discover this, will conceive of the boss as a leper and act accordingly.

A boss is allowed the pleasure of inventing "exercises" for his subordinates—hard, senseless work that keeps them on their toes and reminds them of who is boss. However, this right is limited. The boss should rotate his "favors" among subordinates. Picking on one man is regarded as a sign of weakness rather than strength. Causing a subordinate to break down because of unnecessary exercises or pressure is a stigma of moral leprosy. In short, no matter how great the pressures placed on him, the boss is obligated not to increase the pressures on his subordinates just to make someone suffer as much as he does. This norm is more honored in its breach than in its acceptance. The boss who does honor the norm is viewed somewhat as a saint in Ivy League clothes.

Ethics for Subordinates with Respect to their Bosses

The ethical norms for this situation come close to being work rules. Since the boss has means of enforcing the norms, the individual may comply simply in recognition of the power differentials involved. Yet advertising men do recognize some as ethical norms. Briefly:

> 1. Never denigrate your boss, even in situations where he has no chance of hearing about it.
>
> 2. Never take credit for your own work unless the boss has publicly acknowledged your contribution. After he has done so, one should modestly acknowledge the help, encouragement, and contribution of the boss.
>
> 3. Take the blame for the boss's mistakes if it won't get you fired.
>
> 4. Never go over the boss's head; don't squeal on him to *his* boss.
>
> 5. If you know that your boss disagrees with his boss or with the client but is afraid to express his disagreement, express the boss's arguments for him, even if you don't agree, so long as it doesn't get you fired.
>
> 6. Always show deference and respect for the boss in public situations.
>
> 7. In short, loyalty, deference, trustworthiness, and reliability are all indispensable characteristics of the good subordinate.

Ethical Norms Applying to Peer Relationships

The norms that govern relationships between equals, or between individuals who are not in a super-subordinate relationship, are essentially norms that define and regulate unfair competition.

The paramount norm of this order is, "*Don't squeal to the boss about the derelictions of your peers.*" The individual who squeals is a moral leper not only to the injured party but also to the boss and to anyone who discovers the talebearing. The reason is obvious. An individual who squeals against a peer is capable of squealing against a boss to the boss's boss, or against the agency to the client. Squealing is thus evidence of untrustworthiness. It is also indicative of an inability to handle oneself in competition. Only the man who is incapable of taking care of himself "runs to Papa." Squealing thus indicates lack of manliness, lack of toughness, and lack of nerve.

The boss may encourage a subordinate who squeals to him. But if the subordinate does squeal, the boss may punish the party squealed against and distrust the "spy" who squealed. He is likely to inform the victim of the name of the informer and perhaps encourage the growth of counterinforming. The boss who encourages subordinates to inform against one another is also considered to be morally leprous.

The norm against squealing is likely to cause a great deal of personal conflict and anxiety on the part of an individual who is aware of malfeasances committed by his peers. If he squeals, he is considered untrustworthy. If he does not, the malefactor can endanger himself, the account, the boss, or the agency. The individual must learn techniques whereby malfeasances can be brought to light without resort to squealing. He must arrange for the boss to discover the "crime" before it is too late. In the case of "too lateness," he must pretend not to have known about the crime because, had he known, he could have helped prevent it at the cost of acquiring the stigma of being an informer.

The ethical norms against squealing and against losing one's temper substantially limit the techniques of interpersonal competition and rivalry. Advertising men are frequently in serious competition with all whom they work for and with, even though they are dependent upon those with whom they compete. The forms of competition are further circumscribed by norms against squealing, loss of temper, and direct appeals to authority. The solution to this problem is simple in theory and difficult in practice.

If there is to be competition, rivalry, and conflict between individuals, the norms "require" that all competitive activity be expressed in terms of the objective, stated, and public business of the agency. In appearance, this means doing a better job than a peer or attempting to prove on objective grounds that the job one does is so good that all other jobs must, by implication, suffer in comparison.

One waits for or arranges an issue where one is diametrically opposed to the rival on objective grounds. One marshals one's facts, arguments, and supporters to one's offense or defense after the rival has committed himself irretrievably to his position. One impersonally, objectively, and without anger demolishes the rival's arguments and does this so conclusively that his nerve fails. If he concedes defeat, loses his temper, or is publicly embarrassed over a major issue, he may be forced to resign. The ultimate argument is that the rival's policy would result in the loss of an account, the inability to secure business, or the embarrassment of the agency before the client.

If the rival adopts this same line of attack against an individual, the latter can respond in a number of ways. He can refuse to become committed irretrievably to a position, and thus remain inaccessible to attack. Or he can have his defense, arguments, and facts all prepared to meet the issue whenever it is pressed. The "likable fellow" attempts to avoid attack by never placing himself irretrievably in any position. He may succeed for a long time. He may take a position only after a stronger person, a "tough realist," has affirmed the same position. No individual can avoid taking a position indefinitely. This is the weakness of the "likable fellow." By not taking a position, he can be accused of neglecting his responsibility to the client. The client demands the best policy for his brand; having no policy is having a bad policy. If the "likable fellow" hides behind a "tough realist," he condemns himself to a subaltern's role. What is more, he is likely to be considered as not quite a "man," someone whom one does not have to reckon with. Moreover, a "tough realist" can reverse himself suddenly, leaving the sycophant high and dry. When this happens, the "likable fellow" may find himself committed to an irretrievable issue.

The "tough realist" is a man who can recognize when an irretrievable issue is being raised, can foresee when to decline or accept the issue and can carry his position through to a successful conclusion when he does accept such an issue. Fortunately for all parties concerned, such irretrievable issues do not occur frequently, and, when they do, they can often be avoided.

Another ethical norm governs the ethics or perhaps the aesthetics of defeat. If one has been publicly humiliated, has lost one's nerve, or has been revealed as a "dangerous" person in a semipublic situation, one is done for. A person knows he is done for when other agency personnel begin to avoid him, when subordinates become less deferential or even argumentative or insolent, when peers begin to disagree with his most innocuous, agreeable statements, and when bosses begin to give him a continuous series of exercises or no work at all. The ethical thing to do in such a situation is to look for another job or, if necessary, to resign. By hanging around after having outlived one's usefulness, one reminds others that it could happen to them. One tempts others to self-destructive sympathy. One evokes guilt in the party who "necessarily" caused the defeat. One becomes an open sore in an organization that needs healthy defenses to stand the day-to-day pressures of work. Agencies are likely to give such a person plenty of time to find another job so that he does not have to appear unemployed while looking for it. What is unethical in this situation is to force one's boss to fire one. When one does so, one forces the boss personally and falsely to bear the guilt of firing a man, when that act is actually due to the remorseless operation of the system.

One final ethical norm regulates the relationship between peers. This is related to the stealing of ideas. Ideas, plans, proposals, slogans, and strategies are the basis of an agency's existence. Being fruitful is a major way toward success in an agency. It might therefore be expected that stealing ideas would be a major violation of advertising ethics. Yet stealing ideas is at most a minor vice. If an idea has been successfully stolen, it has been useful to the boss, the agency, or the client. No one complains about a useless idea that has been stolen. Thus the boss, agency, executive, or client that accepts a stolen idea is pleased (at the moment of acceptance) with the idea. He is less concerned with the origins of the idea than with its utility. Moreover, the thief of an idea, to be successful, must first be able to "sell" the idea. The idea becomes an objective reality when it is "sold." Thus, originating an idea is less important than selling it. The originator is to be pitied only if he allowed someone else to steal and sell his idea. The thief is not to be blamed.

The originator may have a sense of personal injury toward the thief, but the sense of loss is not transferred to higher levels so long as the agency gets credit for serving the client. When a man gets the reputation of stealing all his ideas, either from peers or outsiders, he is *not* considered to be a moral leper so long as he steals "good" ideas and sells them successfully. But he earns disapprobation on other grounds. A man who is forced to steal ideas obviously cannot create them. Stealing ideas thus is proof of lack of creativity, talent, and imagination. Such an evaluation of a man is made not on ethical grounds but on grounds of lack of ability. It is made primarily by his peers and not by his superiors. Superiors are concerned with results. A successful idea is a successful idea no matter where it originates, and one should perhaps not inquire too closely concerning sources.

Conclusion

The image we present of advertising is not a pleasant one. In some sense, we have overdrawn the picture. Certainly, the norms of not losing one's temper and of competing in terms of public, objective, and functional purpose mean that the public life of the agency does not appear unhealthy. Moreover, the relatively quick resignation of the "open sores" keeps the "unhealthy looking" man from beclouding the sunny, optimistic, and constructive atmosphere of the agency.

In addition, it is difficult to be overly critical of advertising because it is not so very different from most areas of upper-middle-class life. We have noted that advertising is different from other "executive suite" life only insofar as it distills and concentrates the essence of the executive suite. Advertising pays the same material rewards that are central to the American dream. The rewards are greater than can usually be found in other businesses and are available to more individuals. It is perhaps only just that the risks—personal, professional, and psychological—are greater in advertising than in most other professions. If one wants to play for big stakes, one must be prepared to suffer big losses.

Moreover, simply because of the pressures, difficulties, and irrationalities that are central to its structure, advertising recruits, selects, and rewards those individuals who are psychologically attuned to its environment. In addition to material rewards, it offers deep-seated, psychological rewards, a feeling of narcissistic well-being, to those who can meet the demands imposed on them by the nature of the work itself. It is unfortunate that many men discover only after having devoted half a career to advertising that they are not equipped to work in the field. This belated discovery occurs only because the demands and pressure placed upon a man increase with length of service and with responsibility. Moreover, failure in advertising is often more final than in other professions.

One way to evaluate advertising as a career or a profession is to ask the questions "Would you recommend advertising as a career to the son of a dear friend?" and "Under what conditions would you recommend it?"

The answer that this author would make constitutes his summary of this essay. If the son has genuine talent or creative ability in any field, advertising is the last place for him to be. A truly autonomous, creative person will find the pressures of committee politics and decision making destructive of his creative talent. If he accepts his new assignments, he must experience guilt for having betrayed his original talent.

If the friend's son is kind, gentle, ethical, or religious, and believes in spontaneous social relationships, advertising would be an incompatible profession. Advertising requires strong defenses, toughness, nerve, the willingness to exploit oneself and others. Our young man might crack under the pressure or, worse, develop these characteristics necessary for occupational survival.

There are individuals for whom one could recommend advertising as a profession. If a young man had no great creative talent, but was a good technician in an applicable field, he might be a prospect one could recommend. If he was fairly bright but had no talents, he might also be a prospect. In addition, he would need a healthy constitution, "nerve" but no nerves, and the capacity for hard but not necessarily meaningful work. He would have to have the capacity for handling himself, tact, and the ability to enjoy superficial social relationships. He should be something of a show-off who could control the need to show off and, in doing so, be able to enjoy showing off to himself.

If he had all these qualities, and if monetary success or the sense of power was a sufficient motivation for his actions, he could be a successful and, perhaps, well-adjusted advertising man.

Obviously, advertising does attract the kind of men it needs to do a reasonably effective job of selling its clients' wares. In doing so, advertising as an industry fulfills the requirements placed upon it by other segments of the economy. Because it does so, it is difficult to say that advertising is better or worse than the society for which it is a cynosure. If advertising is to be condemned, much of our society is also to be condemned. But, as a place of work, advertising leaves much to be desired. All work, but especially advertising, demands that the worker give much of his total personality, his total self, to the job. The very creative sources of a man are involved in what he gives to others through his work and what he receives from others by virtue of his work. The quality of one's work shapes, channels, and gives expression to one's creative energy. If the job demands the ability to exploit and manipulate others, both in personal and in impersonal relationships, the very self that provides the basic energy for these actions must of necessity be corroded by these actions. If one attempts to build walls against one's own exploitation and against attempted exploitation by others, a great deal of one's psychic energy is invested merely in self-protection. It is no wonder that the field is populated by would-be artists, novelists, scholars, and poets who rarely manage to fulfill the promise that gave meaning to their youth.

It is perhaps not demanding too much to ask of people to give to their work that which they value most highly in themselves—in abstract terms: love, creativity, and authenticity. But these demands cannot be made of the vast majority of employed persons in our essentially materialistic society, since the demands made by their work are somewhat less than individuals at their best can give and, more often, are somewhat perverted versions of what individuals at their best have to offer.

Advertising simply accepts the world as it is, and then makes it even more so.

Notes

1. Value added to the cost of raw materials.

2. Average salaries in a large advertising agency in 1967:

Account Supervisor	$30,000-$40,000
Account Executive	$15,000-$25,000
Asst. Account Executive	$6,000-$12,000
Merchandising Director	$25,000-$35,000
Asst. Merchandising Director	$15,000-$20,000
Market Research Director	$20,000-$40,000
Media Director	$20,000-$40,000
Media Buyer	$10,000-$15,000
Junior Media Buyer	$5,200-$6,500
Creative Director	$25,000-$60,000
Copy Chief	$35,000-$45,000
Copy Supervisor	$25,000-$35,000
Copy Group Head	$18,000-$30,000
Copywriter	$8,000-$18,000
Head Art Director	$30,000-$45,000
Group Head Art Director	$20,000-$25,000
Art Director	$12,000-$20,000
Art Director (Board)	$10,000-$15,000

TV Art Director	$15,000-$25,000
TV Story Board Artist	$8,000-$12,000
Production Manager	$12,000-$18,000

3. In his famous "Television and the Public Interest" speech to the National Association of Broadcasters on May 9, 1961, Minow condemned American commercial television programming as a "vast wasteland." He especially excoriated the endless commercials that sustain television programming.

7

Ethics and Social Structure

Joseph Bensman

Our studies of the work worlds of advertising, the academy, anti-poverty programs, and social work, suggest that the conditions under which people work and their behavior at work do not make for self-realization, satisfaction, or even elementary psychological well-being. This impression may be due in part to the nature of these particular occupations. Certainly, they do not constitute a cross section of all occupations. The advertising man is not representative of all businessmen in general, especially not skilled professionals in business like engineers, chemists, and accountants, whose work is related to producing a tangible product by using techniques that produce objectively measurable results. Instead, advertising represents an extreme form of a business-oriented occupation. Its high-risk and high-reward potential and the impracticability of objectively measuring individual or group contributions are characteristic of much work in the middle and upper reaches in business and government organizations. But only in a few areas—perhaps politics, the theater, and the mass media—do these conditions obtain to the same degree.

Published originally in a slightly different form in Joseph Bensman, *Dollars and Sense: Ideology, Ethics, and the Meaning of Work in Profit and Nonprofit Organizations* (New York: Macmillan, 1967), 183-208. Republished by permission from Marilyn Bensman.

Nonprofit work may also be atypical. Certainly, antipoverty programs represent an extreme case of the creation of an entirely new occupation and, as such, may be revealing. The academic occupations represent an institution unique in Western society, comparable in the past only to the ministry in the halo of ideological legitimacy they enjoy. Academia is a world that celebrates creativity and protects its celebrants. Yet it is substantially different from the arts, which offer less financial protection to the creator and more risk of failure and which reward the creator only for work done, if at all. The new atmosphere of grants, philanthropic support, government subsidies, and academic positions for creative artists makes artistic work increasingly similar to academic work, especially as the latter becomes subject to the same influences. And yet the painter, the independent writer, and the performing musician all live in worlds different from that of the academicians. Social work is similar in many ways to much civil service work, in which an ideology of service combines with the bureaucratic organization of work. Yet because of its high ideals and the confrontation of those ideals with the most intractable realities, social work is different from much civil service work, where the "office" rather than the field is the focus of work.

The analysis here does not cover such professions as medicine, the law, and those others whose practitioners may be largely self-employed or, even when not so, enjoy vast opportunities for identification with their profession because their success and self-esteem stem principally from their own work, instead of from identification with a bureaucracy that they might serve. And we have overlooked the work of the farmer, skilled and unskilled laborers, small businessmen, and the low-skilled and semiskilled service occupations. These are the limitations of our study.

Yet our study points to a number of general problems characteristic of most occupations in our society. Some of these problems relate to (1) the nature, locus, and level of ethics within an occupation and the focus of those ethics on the behavior of individuals as members of an in-group or on their relationship with outsiders or the society at large; (2) the role of ideologies in the formulation of occupational ethics and in providing meanings for work; (3) the level of autonomy and bureaucratization of work and its effect on the meaningfulness of work; and (4) the relationship of work to deeper levels of the personality of the individual. The wide range of fields covered provides a framework for studying a variety of other occupations.

Comparative Ethics

Occupational ethics are norms that govern relationships, first, among the members of an occupation and, second, between the members of the occupation and outsiders. Looking at advertising, the academy, antipoverty officials, and social workers, we find a vast range of behavior in both of these categories.

Advertising

In advertising, there are highly defined ethical norms that operate internally. This code sometimes goes so far as to include the client. Thus, needless exploitation, deceit, and manipulation are frowned upon, and in blatant forms evoke disgust. At the same time, the rule "caveat emptor" is the principle governing relations with the public. So far as I know, there is no level of deceit, misinformation, or manipulation that advertising men would not employ to help sell their clients' products. Although a few agencies decline to accept liquor or cigarette advertising, they do so more often on economic grounds than on ethical ones. This does not mean that all advertising is dishonest and deceitful. At times, honesty pays. A totally fraudulent claim may be disproved in such an obvious way that exposure reflects negatively on sales. A Federal Trade Commission (FTC) cease-and-desist order may likewise produce "negative advertising." As a result, advertising agencies, under protest, will often produce copy that literally complies with the requirements of the FTC and will attempt to develop products whose advertising reflects the requirements of the Pure Food and Drug acts and the Department of Agriculture. They will carefully write copy that suggests a vast range of benefits without ever claiming benefits that are not demonstrable. Thus, it is governmental rulings and public opinion that make advertising as honest as it is. Ethics are irrelevant in this area. Law replaces personal ethics as a guarantee of minimally decent behavior. Only a few manufacturers and their agencies are willing to take a chance on obviously illegal advertising or obviously illegal products, in the hope of not being caught or in the hope that sufficient profits will justify the fraud before governmental action suspends the illegal marketing. Companies that do so are usually small companies that have little to lose and much to gain by fraud. Larger companies, with vast capital investments, heavy costs, and expensive, established "public images" are less likely to risk the losses that may result from bad publicity. When the criteria for legally acceptable advertising are clear-cut, agencies and their clients attempt to comply. They may attempt to overstate their products' claims as much as possible, risking a cease-and-desist order, when the criteria are vague. Thus, it is more the uncertainty of legal prohibitions than their severity that poses a problem for the advertiser and the agency. This, of course, does not prevent copywriters, agency officials, and advertisers from complaining about the "dictators" in Washington, especially if sales of an inferior product are declining. Yet, with all of this, it is law, not ethics, that governs these external relations, and a well-administered but severe law will work to protect the public, despite the lack of ethics of the advertising man.

There are relatively strong and high standards of interpersonal ethics in advertising because of the absence of any other means of justifying one's actions except personal acceptance of the informal norms of the occupation. Advertising has no strong ideology that allows the individual to sacrifice everyone else for the cause. Moreover, the pressures in advertising are so intense that the agency could easily become much worse than it is—that is, could destroy itself—as a result of personal and clique warfare, a phenomenon that occasionally occurs. Thus, personal ethics appear to be a response to the dangers of overaccepting the pressures and opportunities in the field. By limiting one's own exploitation of others to those actions that are necessary for survival, the members of the agency assure one another that an occupational life is possible despite the pressures. Advertising men are constantly aware of pressures. In recognizing them, they attempt to limit them. The limitations become the basis of ethics. In short, advertising men enact a "social contract" to let one another live and thus guarantee the possibility of their own occupational existence. Since this is done in the absence of strong ideologies, it represents a minimal but naturalistic basis for social life. It is a genuine social contract.

Academic Ethics

If advertising represents a field with high levels of internal ethics and low levels of external ethics, then academia represents the opposite. The traditions of the past, the ideology of the disinterested search for truth, and the educational, intellectual, and cultural improvement of society are continuously reinforced by the public relations of the university and of the scholar, as well as by the scholar's trade associations or professional societies. His claims are reinforced by a vast output of books, articles, speeches, and scientific discoveries that frequently astound the lay public. Moreover, the sheer appearance of knowledge and erudition, of scientific and technological complexity, serves to keep even the intelligent and educated nonspecialist from looking too closely at the institutions of academia and discovering what lies behind the public facade. The difficulty in comprehending scientific phenomena creates the possibility of a fraud. Indeed, in view of the possibilities inherent in modern science, it is a wonder that frauds are not commonplace.

An amazingly large number of academicians are genuinely disinterested. They support the eternal verities, beauty, truth, art, culture, and liberal, humanitarian causes. In this respect, they represent a reservoir of talent supporting the higher ideals and aspirations of our society. Some of these ideals and aspirations are based on purely professional concerns. For example, a professor of painting is expected to like and appreciate art. Yet many professors, perhaps the vast majority, enter their respective fields knowing that they could earn much more in other professions.

At the same time, the "science and knowledge explosion" has suddenly brought the marketplace into the academy. Vast opportunities now exist for the application of knowledge and techniques that previously bestowed only honorific benefits. As a result, the academicians are increasingly "interested" and concerned with "mundane," "practical," and "more lowly" affairs. Increasingly, they sell themselves to the highest bidders, though it is still considered preferable to sell oneself to a government agency, a foundation, or a union than to a lowly commercial, profit-making organization. As yet, the new applied sciences have not completely penetrated the university. Some universities are "backward"; others respect their past traditions. And the full understanding of the commercial talent available in the university has not reached all would-be purchasers of such talent. The ideology of science and the disinterested search for truth remains the most important selling point for the university professor who wishes to cash in on his talents.

While recognizing all these weaknesses, we must also acknowledge that the university provides the possibility of a life where ideals can be advanced and where much of the best elements of our culture are carefully preserved. There are many devoted, honorable, idealistic, and truly uncorrupted men on the campus.

All of this does not alter the fact that, in terms of personal ethics, the university all too frequently resembles a cesspool. The universities have the highest ethical standards and are among the lowest in performance of all the professions that I have studied. Many individuals are ethically and morally superior. But these are deviants from the operative standards of their environment. Why this is true is indeed an intriguing question. I think that it is primarily because of personal failure that individuals become ethically and morally corroded. A university post offers the professor the greatest opportunities for professional and personal self-realization. All that is required for self-realization is that he do in a disciplined, organized, and creative manner the work that he trained himself for. He is given the time, the opportunity, and sufficient salary to prove to himself his capability. Failure under such conditions is corrosive because under these conditions it is difficult to blame the external environment, the cruel Philistines, or the corrupting Maecenases for one's failure. There is no one to blame but oneself, but, one cannot resist trying. The deflated narcissism, the sense of boredom, and the necessity for self-vindication, all result in the creation of obstacles that justify failure. Thus, the vendetta is a major way out, as are investments of inordinate amounts of time in teaching and make-work administration. Living the role of the prophet or the perennial youth leader also serves to make life meaningful. Contract research provides opportunities to do work that is requested and defined by others. It provides an external rhythm for an intense life, while teaching or self-directed research might not.

Such forms of self-dramatism and narcissism are supported by the absence of genuine, independent criteria for the value of work done. As a result, even in comparison with the advertising man, the academic man is not subject to external discipline or standards. The choices he makes are his own, and he has more alternatives in selecting his brand of poison than does any other professional. If he develops and lives up to his own high standards, none of the worst of academic culture need be relevant to him. If he fails, the absence of standards allows him to wallow in a wide range of behavior much of which violates his own ideological, work, or ethical standards.

The Ethics of the Poverty Official

The poverty official is different from both the advertising man and the academician. He inherits the worst of both worlds. There were neither internal nor external ethics in the antipoverty program I studied. There *is* recognition in our society that poverty is evil and that poverty based on discrimination, segregation, and exploitation is evil. But opposition to the evils does not by itself constitute the basis for ethics. For an ethical system to be operative, it must include some set of self-limitations that are principled rather than expedient.

The poverty program had limits imposed on it only from outside, limits created by other people's budgets, competition, and the desire to own and control a jurisdictional area, a valuable property called "poverty." Instead of ethics, there were ideologies. Each ideology served to justify whatever program and action that the individual ideologist adhered to. But the ideologies did not serve to act as limits on action. They served only to justify claims, attacks, and presumed rights. They did not include a sense of responsibility to the program.

There was no ethical responsibility in actions addressed to the "white power structure." The city and various federal departments constituted both obstacles and sources of opportunity to the program. The "power structure" had both the money and the power to grant or withhold it and to control the conditions for the expenditures of funds by the project. Project executives responded in minimal ways to the power of these "masters" but did all they could to undermine these masters when expedient. It was perfectly appropriate to mislead, deceive, flatter, and be servile to these masters when useful and to attack, insult, and abuse them for their imputed racism when they asked embarrassing questions. The extremists in the organization tended to feel even less restraint than others in dealing with the white power structure. They regarded it as the enemy and were reasonably open in doing so.

The attitude of poverty officials toward the "community," the black ghetto itself, is much more complicated. Many of the board of directors, the representatives of the community, did not live in the community. Neither did the executive directors. Both executive directors were disdainful of the "community" as being totally disorganized and lacking sufficient leadership to be called a community. However, as the project began to fight city hall, the second executive director "organized" the community as a political instrument. As a result, the term *community* began to take on a new meaning. The project spoke of "representing the community" and "expressing its needs and aspirations." The term became a master symbol in conflicts with the outside "power structure," a designation that elected officials understood in terms of votes. Of course, rival and competitive organizations also claimed to represent the community.

For political purposes, it was necessary to involve and perhaps create a community—that is, a viable body of public opinion. On specific issues, there were temporary agreements among those community members who participated in public events. However, the numbers involved were relatively small. But throughout the entire length of the planning and summer phases of the project, the rival groups in the community were utterly fragmented and deadlocked over basic issues. In this sense, the community did not exist. The project's success in getting funded created a community of sorts, insofar as the leaders of the project could speak with the authority of their budgets, and others were forced to listen to them because of the budgets.

But the issue here is, did the idea of a "community" set any restraints on the project or did it serve only as a propaganda device? All the ideologists defended their programs or lack of them in terms of ideas of the "community." But all attempted to impose their personal or outside organizational vision upon the community. The community was only raw material for propaganda or manipulation; since the ideologists were concerned primarily with their own message, they did not modify their views to take into account the probable response of the community. The project-oriented professionals also attempted to manipulate the community. Since they were concerned with success, they modified their aspirations to take into account the possibility of getting sufficient support to overcome their "enemies" in and outside the community. In this sense, they became responsive to the community. It was not clear whether the community ever became more than a propaganda or organizational device for the community leaders or project professionals. Certainly, I was never aware of any genuine response by the community. Nevertheless, even these developments represented an improvement over the total apathy and withdrawal into the ghetto that preceded the project.

The internal ethics of the project, as we have indicated, were nonexistent. Ideologies served as excuses both for nonperformance so far as work and duties were concerned and for the frequent occurrence of behavior that in all other organizations would be regarded as morally leprous. The highest ideals appear to justify the shabbiest behavior both in academia and in the ghetto, but in the ghetto the absence of standards is more striking than the violation of standards.

The absence of ethical standards can be explained not only by the belief in absolute ideologies, but also by the growth of vast new opportunities in comparison to past opportunities. In this sense, the great opportunities for success or failure, as in advertising, place pressures upon individuals to operate in ways that in other settings would be considered unethical.

A new organization in a new area, in the process of being organized, in a short time, by an inexperienced staff, under conditions of pressure, stress, and conflict, is not likely to start with high ethical standards. The process of bureaucratization, with the firing of incompetents, "boat rockers," and undisciplined ideologists, necessarily leads to the creation of norms of work and ethics. In this sense, the money invested in poverty programs may not have been wasted.

The Ethics of Social Work

Social workers attempt to operate within the range of external and internal ethics. This does not mean that there are no violations of their ethical standards. But the violations are viewed *as violations*; they evoke negative reactions and serve as controls over moral leprosy.

The insistence on ethical standards comes from the fact that most social workers take the idea of service seriously. Moreover, their jobs force them to see what ignorance, poverty, disease, and destitution can do. They are forced to deal with social reality at its worst. As a result, the easy dodges and pat solutions that serve as an escape and retreat from these realities are not readily available. Numerous professional and nonprofessional social workers do attempt to develop these forms of evasion, but the structure of their work makes this more difficult than in other occupational areas.

The word *ideology* of course must be qualified. Social workers have two types of ideology: one, the ideology of service to the client is heir to all the ideals of Judeo-Christian philanthropy and benevolence; the other, the ideology of social work *as a profession* rests on claims to the peculiar professional training and qualifications to do a job that no other profession or amateur can do. In part, the professional claim is a claim to monopolize jobs for those who have undergone a prescribed course of graduate training. The ideology of social service, whether it comes from social work schools or not, is reinforced by the clients, who obviously need the service. Thus, welfare workers and social workers tend to identify with their clients simply because their clients are so dependent on their services. By identifying with their clients (and sometimes overidentifying with them), they come to oppose their own bureaucracies, whose rules and procedures are often designed to limit the services they can offer their clients.

Their ethical codes are geared primarily to serving the clients and are thus external in orientation. As professionals, they lobby for the extension of social and psychological services for their clients. Since the needs are so great, they argue for more than an increase of the number of jobs and the size of social service budgets. They become, to some degree, a conscience for society. Some will argue for changes in the structure of society in order to modify the conditions that force their clients to seek help. But here, too, the vision of the unique individual in immediate need tends to restrict their revolutionary fervor. They find it difficult to neglect their clients while advocating overall reform of the society. Since they are forced by the structure of their jobs to live with the results of their advocacy, they are likely to be responsible in formulating the solutions they advocate. They differ from ideologists, who are free to advocate extreme and radical solutions because they know these solutions are not likely to be adopted and, if adopted, would become someone else's responsibility. They are thus more "conservative" than ideologists.

Of course, those welfare and social workers who become identified primarily with their professional and occupational bureaucracy are less likely to insist on other standards than those of professional service per se. "Careerist" professionals will identify, at times, with the restrictive rules of their own bureaucracies and with the professional aspiration of their trade. In part, as must be expected, the needs of the social and welfare worker become more central than those of the client. This is the case of professionalism and careerism everywhere and is not distinctive to social work. However, the increasing professionalization of social work is likely to result in an increased care for the welfare of the social workers and less care for the client.

The internal ethics of social service work are based primarily on identification with the client against the supervisor and the social service organization. It is antibureaucratic. Thus, the breaking of work rules is ethical from the point of view of the field worker if it is in the client's interest, but it is unethical from the standpoint of the organization. The result is a double set of ethical norms, one from the worker's point of view and the other from an organizational point of view. The clash between these two systems of ethics is mediated by a secret language that permits illegality without involving the supervisor in the illegality. Both the supervisor and worker are able to cooperate in order to get necessary work done without allowing their differences to prevent action. Each can preserve his primary identification, and both can do their respective jobs. Such a system is always required when individuals who differ are forced by their work or social situation to cooperate. But this system results in a complicated pattern of doublethink, which is often more desirable than the open expression of differences. It does, however, create many surrealistic situations in which each party to a social relationship is forced to protect his enemy so that his enemy can protect him, a situation not unlike that of invoking the social contract in advertising. In the community action program, where ideological differences were "openly and honestly" expressed, the ideological conflicts that ensued resulted in organization paralysis. A feeling of responsibility, then, necessarily results in some "dishonesty." In this sense, all organizations produce a necessary minimal amount of fraud. Many, of course, go beyond the minimum.

The Bureaucratization of Work

All four of the occupational fields we have described are at least partially bureaucratized; that is, they operate on the basis of standardized procedures that constitute part of their work norms.

However, they are bureaucratized to different degrees. The academician, as a teacher, is freed, while in the classroom, from the direct supervision of a supervisor. Since the professor is regarded as a specialist in his own field, there is little that his boss can tell him about the substance of his teaching. In his own scholarly research, he is subject to no rules or regulations other than those he chooses. Contract research, of course, is subject to the rules either of research organizations or of the contractors.

Advertising agencies are bureaucratic and authoritarian in nature. Only if the agency is small or is imperfectly organized is it free from the rules of bureaucratic organization.

Most social work agencies are more or less bureaucratically organized, depending on their size; and poverty programs, at this writing, are not bureaucratically organized only because haste and confusion in organization have prevented them from achieving their legally defined forms.

The advertising man's response to bureaucracy is entirely different from that of professionals in these other fields. Despite the fact that work in an advertising agency is subject to infinitely greater stresses, anxiety, insecurity, and pressures, those who do not break take pride in overcoming the pressures. To be able to handle pressure and to surmount it is the greatest virtue among advertising men. The capacity to accept the heightened pressure and a bureaucratic framework is due in part to the lack of an ideology. The advertising man has no independent ideology that enables him to stand apart and judge his organization. He must operate within the framework and goals of his organization (which are not ideologically determined) because he lacks these independent standards. His goals become psychological and material in nature. Strength, finesse, capacity for work and dissimulation, control of impulse, and pride in skill replace the immanent values of the work itself. For the social worker, academician, and poverty worker, there are ideologies that are independent of the organization. The disinterested pursuit of science, knowledge, and culture and the rescuing of individuals from the depths of misery, poverty, ignorance, and disease or other forms of degradation are independent of any particular organization. The organization is only a means to achieve these ultimate ends. Since it is only a means, it is subject to criticisms of even the lowliest staff members who have independently internalized these ends. If, as in advertising, there are no highly ideologized ultimate ends in the organization, the individual does not have the moral and ideological basis for criticizing or feeling superior to the organization. He is on the same moral plane as his bosses.

As a result, in all nonprofit work areas, it is extremely difficult for the top officials to discipline, organize, and control the lower ranks.

The lower ranks set up their own goals for the organization and attempt, in violation of their bureaucratic obligations and positions, to move the entire organization along a path they have predetermined. Ideologists, from the standpoint of their bureaucratic bosses, thus become irresponsible, undisciplined, and disloyal officials. Wherever possible, high-level bureaucrats purge the ideologists. They do this primarily not out of ideological concerns, but only to develop a responsive, disciplined, loyal, and technically competent staff. At the same time, the bureaucratic elites will use existing ideologies relative to their field as means of advancing their respective organizations. Thus, to bureaucratic elites, the only acceptable ideologists among their staffs are those that support the organizational purposes at any given time. As a result, the bureaucracy as a form attacks all independent ideologies and replaces them by forms of ideological expediency. In addition, it worships competence, discipline, self-control and self-management, technical virtuosity, nerve, and an achievement motivation that is detached from the end or the values that the organization is set up to serve.

The bureaucratic ideology tends to replace all other ideologies as bureaucratic forms of organization begin to predominate in business, government, universities, philanthropy, and other occupational areas. The bureaucratic attack on independent ideologies takes the form of not hiring ideologists, firing them, retraining personnel to accept the bureaucratic ethos, and promoting those who do accept it. It takes the form of doing these same things at the level of graduate and undergraduate education so that, if successful, the system operates to preselect only those who can conform.

Sooner or later, potential bureaucrats (bureaucratic employment is the largest source of professional and white collar work in our society) must see the light if they wish to succeed with or without trying. They are forced to make themselves over to meet the requirements for success in bureaucratic society. They have plenty of help in this re-creation.

In this sense, we can talk of "the end of ideology." Bureaucracy needs very little independent ideology. As bureaucracy grows, all other forms of ideology are depressed because the occupational and economic rewards of nonideological commitment are made more attractive. The capable, competent, technically trained, disciplined, ideological, and morally neutral individual becomes the cynosure of a bureaucratic world. The other-oriented, organizational man is simply the domesticated bureaucrat.

These processes are implicit in the range of occupations discussed here. In the community action program, a totally new area, the presence of ideology was a predominant feature, resulting in the inability of the executive directors to control their staffs. After wholesale firings and forced resignations, a new breed of black bourgeois became the predominant staff official, a caricature of the bureaucrat. There is little doubt that, after the passage of time, the caricature will become the real thing. In social work and in the academic trades, the conflict between ideological and organizational commitment dominates the culture of the organization. Because both sets of commitment in these fields are strong, the conflict is likely to be a lasting one. However, the tremendous resources and organizational efficiency of bureaucracy result in an ever-increasing bureaucratization of work and the reduction or control by bureaucratic elites of its ideological content. Advertising has totally achieved this control, and, as a result, psychological values replace ideological ones.

Bureaucracy and the Rhythm of Work

Bureaucratic organization takes the form of a strict, mechanical delineation of tasks in an ordered sequence of operations to meet the needs of the overall operation of an organization as defined by bureaucratic or superbureaucratic elites. The individual must adjust his needs, work rhythms, and psychological states and moods to the requirements of an organization. The opposite of bureaucratic organization in this respect might be that of the painter or independent writer who can, if he is productive and prosperous (either through work or an independent income), lie fallow for extended periods and make up the time lost in periods of intense, feverish creativity. He can work at night or at odd hours and appear to be an idle man when others are working.

The advertising man, in adjusting his work rhythm to the requirements of "senseless" work pressures, represses any personal rhythm that he might have. Regardless of any need to "lie fallow," to relax, or to take it easy, he disciplines his inner urges to the demands of the bureaucratic machine. In fact, the advertising man, after developing such discipline, is frequently unable to respond to a relaxation of work pressures. He invents pressures for himself and for others in order to allow for the release of narcissistic energy that accumulates as a result of his job.

A poverty program, at least in its early phases, is similar to advertising. Continual crises, in part self-engendered, create an emotional intensity in work. This intensity allows for dramatic victories and defeats, self-dramatization, overwork, and elation and enthusiasm in demonstrating one's mastery over crises. Poverty programs, however, because of their youth, tend to have all the crises of advertising with none of its discipline or routine.

Social work in established agencies tends to have a more stabilized routine of work whose rhythm is objective—that is, externally imposed. While most social workers are overworked, the sense of crisis is not a normal feature of work. The major problem of work rhythm for the social worker is how to "goof-off" successfully and still meet his minimal or self-imposed obligations.

This is a problem that most academicians have solved. The external work rhythm for the professor is embodied in the requirement that he meet his classes at fixed times and places for six, nine, twelve, or fifteen hours a week, that he grade exams and papers in a predetermined time period, and that he take on a number of committee assignments. All other forms of discipline and work rhythm are determined by himself. Since the external discipline and work rhythms are so slight, the academician can, to all intents and purposes, achieve the autonomy to determine his own pace and tasks. But the vast majority of professors fail to use this structurally determined autonomy for the purposes embodied in their obligations to their colleges, their students, or themselves. Instead they invent vastly complicated social, psychological, and organizational devices that enable them to avoid the responsibilities explicit and implicit in their positions. The vendetta, politicizing, the ritualization of teaching, "school services," and endless administration are all devices of this order, not unlike the self-engendered crises in advertising and poverty programs. Even contract research can be viewed as an attempt to submit to an external discipline and rhythm of work.

For the academician, this avoidance of autonomy is particularly self-destructive. The ideology of the academic world and the personal appeal of an academic career glorify autonomous creativity and productivity. The structure of work permits it. Thus, the academician who fails to use his opportunities has no one to blame but himself. And this is the most intolerable situation. For as long as he can blame the system, the bosses, the crass, vulgar public, or some other external obstacle to self-fulfillment, he can preserve his pride and sense of injured manhood despite failure to achieve his ideals. When there is no one to blame but oneself, self-hatred and despair are the likely results. It is thus not difficult to see why it is necessary to invent obstacles where none exist. Most of what one sees on the academic scene represents the invention of obstacles—pseudodisciplines, pseudorhythms, and pseudocrises that prevent self-realization.

But this analysis does not explain why, in the light of the opportunities for creativity and productivity, so many academicians fail. It would be easy to suggest that academicians as a group are an inferior breed who develop false notions of what they can do and then find that, in reality, they are incapable of realizing these goals. There is a germ of truth in the argument. Academicians, at least in their youth, are exposed to the works of the greatest minds in the world. They identify with the beauty and clarity of thought of such men as Einstein, Freud, Keynes, Weber, Newton, and others. Among their own professors, there may be several who seem to embody the quintessence of achievement. But when the academician graduates from the role of student—that is, consumer—to that of producer, he may find that it is not enough to appreciate or identify with beauty, truth, or genius. The realization may be crushing.

Another possible explanation might be that the process of graduate education rewards the insensitive, the persistent plodder, and the sycophant. As a result, the successful doctoral candidate is well equipped to work under somebody else's direction, but is unequipped to be autonomous.

Both of these explanations might explain the high rate of failure among academicians, but neither explains the vast amount of time and energy used by the failures to invent objective conditions that make success impossible. Moreover, they do not account for the fact that the vast majority of academicians, whether productive or creative or not, are extremely bright and intelligent as well as energetic. Their brightness, intelligence, and energy are simply invested in self-destructive activities.

Here is a speculative explanation. Every individual has at his core vast amounts of energy at his disposal, even at birth. The energy so available is more than he can channel, use, and direct, either in socially approved or in disapproved goals. The process of socialization uses some of this energy to block the release of other energy. Thus, in developing defenses and means of repressing his own uncontrolled energy, the individual weakens the driving force that can be the source of either the greatest productivity or the greatest destructiveness in an individual. Most of the rituals and ceremonies of society, including the endless distractions of mass communications, are devices that sponge up the energy that, if uncontrolled, might be destructive. The synthetic violence in television and in sports allows for the dissipation of aggressiveness that might, without such release, result in direct physical violence. Organized leisure and aggression, turned against the self or dissipated in countless small feuds, serve to keep the energies of the individual from exploding in one particular direction.

Occasionally, the entire energy output of an individual becomes focused and released in one direction. Then the individual who is so fortunate can discover that he has the strength of ten. There is no amount of work too great for him, nothing he cannot accomplish. Nothing is impossible.

An analysis of the great creative geniuses would, I am convinced, indicate that equal to their talent is the ability to organize, focus, and direct a vast amount of energy into the field that becomes the medium of their genius. Art, science, scholarship, statecraft, warfare, almost any occupational field, can be the medium by which such energy is released and directed. If the individual finds such a medium and can focus all his energy into it, he can accomplish phenomenal things.

The problem here is to account for (1) the release of energy, and (2) the failure or success in finding a medium.

The release of energy is probably accounted for by a loving, warm, responsive treatment in infancy, with minimal threats, repression, and frigidity in treatment accorded the child. Warm and loving parents or parental surrogates give the infant a chance to develop psychological strength through identification. At later dates (from a year on), the parental figures must repress and inhibit the child if he is to become human. The repression simply means that he is forced to control his own behavior, appetites, and demands and to mold them into styles and forms that evoke parental approval or at least avoid disapproval. Overrepression can result in guilt, inability to express one's primal energy, or hostility against the parent even at the expense of achieving one's own goals. Overrepression can result in overconformity. If the repression is mild and given in a loving context, the child will still resent the parent's attempts to deny him his own instinctual needs. The child will reject, in part, the world as presented by the parent and create his own imaginary, private world, one that is partially antiparental and more comfortable than that which he is being forced into. When this process takes an extreme form, the child-created world may replace the world he lives in; that is, he may become psychotic. In the normal process, this secondary world is a world of imagination, of creativity, or art and fancy. It is a world that allows the child to express his own unique image of the world and to create and re-create it along lines that give him aesthetic satisfaction. If the "demands" of reality are too strong, the child will neglect this secondary world and comfort himself with "ordinary" problems in ordinary terms. To do so, he must repress even a mild fantasy world, thereby using up a substantial amount of energy necessary for such repression and control. Remaining in the here-and-now is as costly as departing from it.

If the child discovers by accident an aspect of the "real world" that corresponds to his secondary fantasy world and if he is encouraged to expand, discipline, and stylize his fantasies, the original energy invested in rebellion becomes a source of creativity. The child links the medium of literature, art, music, science, or the accumulation of knowledge to his fundamental sources of energy. The fantasy becomes a form of reality that projects the individual into the world instead of, as in the case of a psychosis, isolating him from it. This discovery of a link between one's private form of rebellion and a positive medium of culture is usually accomplished by the availability of a parent or adult figure who embodies, exemplifies, and encourages development into the field which previously had been, to him, only a fantasy. The uncle, a parent, a teacher who exemplifies the field reinforces the individual in developing systematic, stylized, and technically realized forms of his original vision. If the ideal does not become repressive, and if the parental figure does not smother the child with overagreement and thereby steal the private world from the child, the parental figure confirms the child's development in an autonomous direction. When vast amounts of energy are invested in the medium, vast amounts of accomplishment are possible. If the child can transcend each parental model made available to him and can replace it with more able ones, he is capable of almost unlimited growth. Obstacles, if they are not insuperably repressive, may harden the determination of the individual as he moves onward. The threat of the withdrawal of love and affection by parents who do not approve of a child's drive to goals that do not appear to be practical can be dangerous, almost as dangerous as parental approval that is exploitative in nature. Appreciation of a child for "childish enthusiasm" followed by disapproval of the child for the same activities at a latter age because they are "childish" is likely to result in an attitude of conformance, of looking to others for goals, discipline, and work rhythms. Allowing the child to develop his own goals, discipline, and approval, while providing noninterfering and nonexploitative love is a most difficult task for a parent. It requires maturity, confidence, and health, all scarce products in any society.

If all these factors are operative, the child has a chance. As he develops his own talents, he may discover that the only models he needs are those provided by his own inner demons. He can pursue them without dependence upon others. If he does so, he has at his disposal unlimited energy, a set of goals, a medium by which he expresses them, and the skill and technique to express them.

Quite frequently, only a part of the process is achieved. The child or young man is able to release his energy without developing the medium for disciplining the energy so released. If this happens at a very early age, before the child learns any social controls, he may become a monster, a psychopath. All the energies of a near genius can be used to gratify purely hedonistic, antisocial needs. The individual becomes a menace who may well end up with his name in the papers. If the explosion occurs after the basic socialization of the child has been achieved, the child will look for modes of activity in the "real world" that allow him to express his energy. Unrepressed energy is a source of danger to its bearer, since it leaves him with turbulent, unsettled, and unrelieved feelings of internal pressure unless he moves, works, acts, or plays. The organized life of a society allows the individual to use its patterns of organization as a medium for releasing this energy. If the work or social organization permits only a slow, even unhurried pace, the energized individual may become a disruptive force, upsetting the pace of others in order to live by his own internal rhythm. If he can control himself, however, he can become a dynamic mover in such an organization. He can use his energy to become a pyramid climber. As such, he may be a constructive force. He may, however, be fortunate enough to find another organization whose demands upon him are such that his total energy can be absorbed by the external demands of the organization. If he is so fortunate, one can be sure that others who are either autonomous or whose rate of energy release is lower than his may be out of phase with the external rhythm and discipline of the organization.

Advertising thus allows for, in fact requires, the release of high volumes of energy by individuals who submit to the demands of the agency in releasing their energy as required. An ideology also allows for the release of vast amounts of energy in the name of a cause or the organization that embodies the cause. It allows for the release of energy by those who find no other way in a society for expressing, directly or truly, energy that is hard to contain.

The academic environment is based upon the assumption that individuals have at their disposal vast amounts of energy, that their chosen field is its medium, and that they have developed the discipline, autonomy, and technique to direct it in their own work. The failure of the vast majority of academicians to achieve the promise of their field undoubtedly rests upon the partial achievement of autonomy. The majority of academics, through a favorable social environment, have achieved the ability to release vast amounts of energy. They have acquired the techniques and the media of their respective fields. What they lack is the ability to define their own problems or the ability to discipline themselves to an autonomous work rhythm that would result in fulfilling their occupationally defined tasks. Failure to achieve this form of autonomy is destructive since the energy to do so has been released but, owing to the lack of an operative medium, has no constructive way of being expressed. All the forms of compensatory or substitute behavior are attempts to discharge this energy without directing it into the medium for which it was originally released.

In such situations, having the energy available may well be worse than not having contained the energy at a more primary or elementary level. For without a disciplined medium for being autonomous, the energy shakes, rocks, and rattles the individual. At times, even the greatest discipline will not control the released energy. Van Gogh, Modigliani, Toulouse-Lautrec, Gauguin, Berlioz, Wagner, Balzac, Jack London—all are examples of an individual whose undoubted genius could not contain his energy. Cézanne, Freud, Haydn, Einstein, Henry James, and J. S. Bach are individuals who achieved some serenity despite a vast amount of energy. Others—Hugo Wolf, Beethoven, and William James, for example—alternated between fits of tormented depression and constriction and the periodic release of vast energy.

In part, such risks are necessary to the freeing of vast amounts of energy. If the inspiration, health, or discipline fails to go with the energy, depression and withdrawal can result.

The academic world produces, perhaps at lower levels of genius, sufficient numbers of individuals who achieve some level of serenity. It produces also anguished creative individuals who are tormented either by periods of depression, fallowness, and sterility or by an excess of energy. But it produces, most of all, individuals who have everything but the self-discipline and autonomy necessary for them to live with either themselves or their occupational responsibilities. Advertising achieves perhaps a better blend between occupational demands and psychological response. It does so by eliminating those who do not "fit." In the university, those who do not fit are the vast majority.

The Senselessness of Work

The fundamental philosophical problem throughout the ages is how to deal with the "senselessness" of the world. The world is experienced as senseless because history, nature, and man's experience contradict all of his theories and preconceptions. "The best laid schemes o' mice an' men / Gang aft agley." War, death, revolution, disease, and misfortune strike with little relationship to the worthiness of those so afflicted, and good fortune often falls to those who are deemed to be unworthy.

In some way, all individuals at all times suffer from the experience of the senselessness of the world. They attempt either to understand the world, to render it "meaningful" by developing a theory that explains its "senselessness" or to control the world or one another by science or magic. So far, men and women have failed in these attempts. The more professional and complicated our theories become, the more they are removed from the ordinary experience we wish them to explain. Moreover, we are increasingly able to develop the critical abilities to discover the fallacies in our own theories. Finally, so far, science has not enabled us to deal with the irrationality of war and total destruction. And, taking the world as a whole, the problems of poverty, misery, disease, and starvation are multiplying faster than the solutions to them. One might argue that man as an experiment is a failure.

Each of the various occupational fields considered here confronts the problem of senselessness in its own way.

The social worker attempts to repair the damage by providing services to his clients. He most often feels he is bailing out a leaky boat with a sieve. Despite this, he attempts to help in his own way, realizing that at best he will help repair some damage after it has occurred, while still more damage is being done. The ideologist attempts to make the world "sensible" by remaking it. He must avoid facing the fact that, all too frequently, while he opposes the bureaucratization of present society, he will, if successful, be the advance agent for even more destructive forms of the bureaucratization of society. In the meantime, he is likely to be destructive in his occupational world, if only to prove his own sincerity and commitment to higher values.

The academician as social philosopher and humanist attempts to understand the world, and the scientist attempts to help control it.

He does not know who will yield this control or for what purposes. In the meantime, many sell their services to the highest bidder. Most, despite their high ideals, either "goof-off" or create a personal and institutional culture that gives the lie to their aspirations.

The advertising man confronts the senselessness of the world in a unique and modern way. Instead of talking about it or attempting to correct it, he lives it. Mastering the senselessness of the world by living it, results in an ethic of self-mastery, pride, and a definition of virtues that makes personal survival in a senseless world the greatest of all virtues. The Philistine (in our age, the bureaucrat) who accepts, without questioning, the opportunities inherent in any given situation is equally a modern man, adjusted to whatever form modern society takes. But Philistines have always existed; only the form changes with the passage of time.

Beyond this, the continuous attempt to pierce the "senselessness of the world," even if unsuccessful, results in the most sublime works of art, literature, music, science, philosophy, and the social sciences. The creation and enjoyment of these modes of science, knowledge, and sensibility represent the highest achievements of man. As long as man continues to attempt to solve the puzzle of the senselessness of the world, his experiment cannot be judged a failure. Failure consists only in surrender.

PART III

Leadership and Legitimacy

8

The Crisis of Confidence in Modern Politics

Joseph Bensman

In contemporary society, we increasingly hear complaints of the "crisis of confidence" in society, its leadership, its prestigious classes and professions, and indeed in society itself. President Carter bemoaned this crisis of confidence and faith in democracy. And the "neoconservatives" of contemporary society define the crisis of confidence as the failure of legitimacy. They ascribe that failure to our society's inability to develop a system of beliefs that produce confidence in the political and economic systems of the society. This failure may be due to the inability of intellectuals to develop ideas that embrace current realities and the disarticulation of political ideas from realities. It may also be due to the apparent disarticulation of realities themselves. In regard to the latter, in fact, the institutions of modern society have become so complex that individuals suffer anomie because no unified image of society is accessible to them. The lack of "ideological" unity produces a failure in belief.

One of the most obvious hypothetical reasons for the failure of belief in society and its leaders and its institutions is that modern political audiences, the public, have perceived too often that they are the objects of lies, deceit, and fraud, of unfulfilled and unfulfillable

---

Previously unpublished. Originally presented in a slightly different form at the Conference on the Legitimacy Crisis, Bridgeport, Connecticut, April 1975.

promises, rip-offs, and postelection neglect. This has been called the "crisis of credibility."

During the Senate Watergate Hearings (1973-1974), for instance, the public was exposed to the deliberate, cynical planning of lies and deceit, stonewalling, and to the obscene contempt that President Nixon and his lieutenants had for the public. They have also been exposed to the incompetence of Nixon's successors and have come to recognize that brilliant campaigning and promises do not necessarily mean good government.

In other arenas, the public has been exposed to the incompetence of physicians and hospital staff as suggested by rising malpractice suits, the venality of Medicare and Medicaid prosecutions, and reports of substantial fee splitting and unnecessary surgery by medical practitioners. Moreover, the press routinely reports the suborning of justice by corrupt judges and district attorneys and, of course, the ever-recurrent exposes of scandals involving police, whether bribery, featherbedding, or outright participation in crime.

Both giant business corporations and small businesses are also routinely reported as suborning legislatures, regulating commissions, and government purchasing agents by payoffs and political contributions. Periodically, legislators, civil servants, and political leaders are indicted and often convicted of accepting bribes and illegal contributions.

If one wanted to construct a theory of the "crisis of confidence," one could base that theory on the crime and corruption that seems endemic to public life and professions in America. Yet such a theory would be too simple. Malaise about the sense of incompetence and drift in modern society and the inability of our leaders to solve the major domestic problems of modern society—inflation, unemployment, environmental pollution, and both street and corporate crime, to name a few—is not necessarily related to perceptions of pervasive venal behavior or crime in public affairs. Worries about our domestic troubles are compounded by the profound international tensions we experience today that stem largely from the failure of the United States to maintain its dominance in international affairs in the post-Vietnam-War era. Today, American leadership is routinely rejected by both allies and client states. This loss of national prestige has increased Americans' anxieties about our nation's direction and future, even as it produces a sense of American nationalism and patriotism during moments of crisis. But more strongly pronounced is the long-term sense of the loss of national purpose and the failure of American leadership that permits this.

In this paper, we are concerned with "structural" factors that account for the loss of credibility, the "failure of legitimacy," and the crisis of confidence. We focus on the expectations that citizens place upon their leadership and institutions, how these expectations are aroused, and how citizens respond to the failure of expectations. Finally, we examine how leaders arouse and deal with both of these expectancies.

The New Demands

In ancient China, the emperor was thought of as being the son of heaven. Heaven was the source of his legitimacy. If heaven smiled upon the Emperor and his kingdom, then all went well. If heaven withdrew its favor, famine, flood, plague, and defeat in war ensued. When the Emperor had lost the favor of heaven, his subjects were entitled to rebel. Yet, in this case and in similar cases, the fault was not the emperor's. That belonged to "the stars."

So long as men believed in God, ultimate responsibility for human destiny was in the hands of God or the gods. The gods could be humanly "irrational," full of lust, greed, and vanity as were the Greek Gods, or totally mysterious and inscrutable as was the God of

Calvin. In some cases, leadership consisted of consulting the oracles and divining the omens in order to read God's intentions accurately. In other cases, leadership meant proper propitiation of the gods. With an ethical God, it meant obedience to God's commandments and proper ethical or ritual behavior. In all these cases, the ultimate source of worldly leadership was God's will or the acceptance of that will.

Even when God was replaced by a divinely ordained natural law, or by the dialectic—that is, the "laws of history"—the task of leadership was that of correctly reading transcendental plans and following those courses of action consistent with these higher designs. The failures of political leaders were still attributable to an incapacity to fulfill some kind of transcendental will.

The rise of secularism (whether or not formally acknowledged as atheism) produced our inability to blame God for human failure. Men, our political and institutional leaders, are required to justify themselves and their policies on the basis of their wisdom and judgment, personal and institutional competence, knowledge and foresight, that is—by their personal success as leaders. We no longer trust the gods, nor can we blame them for our failures.

In addition, the rise of secularism has coincided with a half-millennium of rising expectations. Since God, or his equivalent, can no longer be blamed for poverty, misery, injustice, and inequality, men now bear this burden. And the deprived can no longer accept inequalities in privileges previously thought to be based on God's will or the "nature" of things. If equality, rights, and privileges are of man's making, not God's, then all men are entitled to these social rights. Secularism was both a product of demands for change stemming from revolutions in rising expectations and, at the same time, the cause of the rising expectations. In the former case, it was the rise of the bourgeoisie and the proletariat that caused a new worldliness.

In the latter, the new worldliness caused the rejection of inequalities attributed to God.

A new secular dispensation, originally based on natural rights, caused a demand for "responsible" leadership, a demand that leaders cannot reject, at least verbally, if they want to enjoy the benefits and responsibilities of leadership—whether material or ideal, money, power, prestige, the sense of excitement, or the ability to implement their own values.

Yet responsibility, unlike the market, does not create the supply to fulfill the demand or the demand to use up the supply. The failure of responsibility that evokes the crisis of leadership and legitimacy is the product of structural factors that make responsible leadership a virtual impossibility. Let us examine three sources of structural constraints on leadership.

Jurisdictional Problems

The rise of modern society has meant the rise of problems of national and international scope. These problems are larger than the political and administrative jurisdictions of any set of leaders.

The rise of the national state and international global politics, international economies, worldwide competition, multinational corporations, world wars, and worldwide struggles for power have produced arenas of conflict and competition that exceed the power of any one leader or jurisdiction. During World War II, at least for a short period of time, Stalin, Churchill, Roosevelt, and Chiang Kai-shek, had the illusion that they collectively could control the world. Yet they were unable to agree, and the agreements they achieved were short-lived. The era of the cold war was, at most, an attempt by the leaders of the United States and the Soviet Union to limit their conflict in order to avert nuclear war, an attempt that was successful, though it produced a series of limited wars, uprisings, and mutual interventions in their respective client states. Moreover, neither major power was able to control fully its own clients. Splits and defections occurred in the East, among others, in Yugoslavia, China, Indonesia, Romania, and Ghana. And in the West, Charles de Gaulle and the British trade-union leader, Ernest Bevin, among many others, were often "anti-American," while other American allies demanded policies favorable to their countries or regimes and instituted economic warfare against the United States.

The United States could not prevent military or diplomatic defeats in Korea, Thailand, Vietnam, Cuba, Angola, Iran, India, and later Pakistan. Nor could Russia or China, then competing with each other, prevent defeat in the Congo, Indonesia, North Korea, or Eritrea.

The Third World rebelled against the United States, even as Third World countries came to exert great influence in the United Nations, which is largely sustained by United States moneys. Syria, Iran, and Iraq rebelled against American influence. And many countries rebelled against the Soviet Union's dominance.

The polycentered world of the postwar era, regardless of détente, resists the claims of the leaders of the world powers to exercise responsible leadership over world affairs. Yet American leaders after World War II had tried to exercise that claim, as did England in the nineteenth century on a worldwide basis between 1814-1914, with the help of Bismarck in Europe.

Gunboat diplomacy worked intermittently only for half a century between the 1870s and 1920. Moreover, it did not work well. Nor were the victors of World War I able to control their own and the world's destiny, as evidenced by the Great Depression and the rise of Hitler.

If leadership is to be responsible, and if responsibility is measured by success in coping with the problems of a society, then all leaders have failed. Their jurisdictional limits are smaller than the problems they face, yet to achieve positions of leadership they must promise and claim ability to handle problems that are outside the limits of their jurisdiction. Because of the size of the problem, it is frequently impossible to assess the ability of leaders who claim to be leaders. In times of "normalcy," mediocre leaders may appear to succeed or, at least, avoid the appearance of failure; and in times of crisis, leaders who are imputed to be great may fail. Others may "rise to the occasion," but these post hoc evaluations are reassessed over time.

Our previous illustrations, based upon international relations and war, understate the cases. In the realm of economics, business, and labor, the same strictures apply at more immediate levels. The heads of corporations, domestic and multinational, trade unions and nonprofit agencies all base their leadership on promises of successful performance within a matrix of political and economic institutions they do not wholly control. A major depression, unexpected technological changes, changes in the political climate or in public law, styles, and fashion all undermine "sound leadership practice." Leaders of institutions may at times be able, in the short run, to predict, profit from, or anticipate the negative impact of change, but various institutions, because of their characteristics of history, may be particularly vulnerable to negative external changes (others are in opposite, fortunate positions) and more subject to blame for failure to respond to uncontrollable and often unpredictable but favorable events.

Yet economic and institutional disasters result in a crisis of confidence for those leaders who fail, regardless of the jurisdictional cause of failure. And if the failure is worldwide or nationwide, all leaders (except the peculiarly prudent or circumstantially lucky) get the blame. This blame can be called a crisis in legitimacy either of the system, the institution, or the leaders.

Yet the demand for responsibility and the crisis of legitimacy and confidence are due not only to the fact that the jurisdictions of leadership, their *spheres of competence* to use a Weberian term, are smaller than the jurisdictional limits necessary to fulfill the promises implicit in their leadership positions and in their claims for leadership. They are also due to the lack of technical competence of virtually all leaders.

Technical Competence

It is by now a truism to speak of the vast technical complexity of science and modern technology and of the opaqueness of science and technology to the layman and even to those scientists who are not specialists in a given narrow area of decision. The technical complexity of science is even a barrier to the specialist. They themselves often do not know in advance how their experimental work will come out, nor do they know even more often than not the technological, economic, or social implications of their own work.

For at least two hundred years (perhaps four hundred years in the case of printing and gun power), political and other institutional leaders have had to base their policies upon the existence of technology and science that they do not understand and whose implications are unknown. They are forced to rely on "experts" whose expertise they are often unable to evaluate. Moreover, experts often disagree, and there are no clear ways to settle objectively the disagreements between experts. Expertise may be evaluated relatively easily in fields where the science and technology is clearly understood and where their applications have been long-established. But science, technology, and social and economic policy are clearly most problematic when that understanding is absent, when experts are not experienced in social and economic outcomes, and when the outcome of alternative policies is unknown. And these conditions are exactly the conditions of any emerging field of knowledge.

Yet leaders have to make major decisions based upon the operation of a science and technology they cannot know in detail. Thus, the United States won World War II in Japan based on an application of a nuclear science that did not exist at the beginning of the war. President Roosevelt had to rely on experts' knowledge of physics in the absence of personal knowledge, and Truman's decisions to drop the A-bombs on Hiroshima and Nagasaki have been open to question ever since.

Adolf Hitler, with a head start in nuclear science, did not press for work in this area until, fortunately, it was too late. Instead, he developed guided missiles, too little and too late even from his point of view, and lost the war.

The United States and the other major countries in the world have developed atomic energy on the assumption that such energy is safe and economically feasible. But in neither case is the verdict in. Nuclear power is still the most expensive form of energy available, still subject to vast conflicts over safety. The same problems exist in the development of fusion-based energy, uncertainties that cost hundreds of billions of dollars to test without any assurance of success or economic feasibility.

The uncertainties over science and technology are intrinsic problems for leadership. If the leader fails to adopt an unproven technology, he may be left out in the cold and be blamed for lacking foresight, as was the case of the Chrysler Corporation before Lee Iacocca became its president. But, if like the makers of the Mazda automobile, a leader adopts the innovation (pistonless engines) and it fails (or some other technology works better), he is blamed for ineffective leadership.

The Hazards of Long-Term Planning

The third dimension of leadership is effectiveness in long-term planning. John Kenneth Galbraith has emphasized the importance of lead time in the development of the automobile and Daniel Bell the importance of long-term planning in general. For Galbraith, the lead time in producing an automobile was eight years; for Bell, it was twenty-five years and up for producing new versions of airplanes.

Yet both estimates emphasize the necessity for leaders to predict the future. This includes predictions of:

> a. Technological and scientific development, including unexpected breakthroughs.
>
> b. The level of the economy at the end point and at various intervening points in the planning cycle. Included are predictions of the level of economic activity, production, and gross national resources; energy and labor within the world and within the effective jurisdictions of their authority; the state of public opinion and law; and worldwide international economic conditions and relations.

Such predictions are extremely difficult. We have infinite conflicts among experts concerning the reserves of natural gas and petroleum in the world. The economic experts, despite a century of work, are unable to agree on the state of economic activity three months in advance. Longer-range predictions are, of course, more difficult, but less pressing.

Scientific prediction is essentially different from long-range forecasting in politics or in economics, and even from the prediction of scientific and technological development. In scientific prediction the parameters within which the prediction is made are specified and accepted as given. *Ceteris paribus* or *pari passu* are its watchwords. Yet even scientific prediction may be difficult, especially when scientific prediction rests within a framework of contingencies—that is, alternative sets of conditions—and when a series of predictions are made based on each set of alternative conditions. It may be nearly impossible to predict the occurrence of the conditions on which scientific prediction rests.

Thus, in the early fifties, the leaders of American industry and government took a series of actions based upon short- and long-term predictions on their immediate interests. Bigger automobiles were built that consumed gas in large quantities; highway construction was subsidized, electric utilities switched to gas and oil as did home and industrial heating. The coal mining and the railroad industries suffered in consequence; and American domestic oil industries, highway construction and the automobile industries were in fact subsidized by tax exemptions and budget subsidies. Nuclear energy plants were also subsidized.

Thirty years later, we have discovered that the policies that underwrote much of the prosperity of the 1950s and 1960s were mistaken. They were based on assumptions of continued low-cost energy and our confidence in our ability to control the oil-producing nations and multinational petroleum companies, and at the same time placate environmentalists. They were also based on pleasing the consumer in the short run. Moreover, these policies subsidized the "golden years" of the 1950s and 1960s.

By now, we know that these policies were wrong, or at least we lament their consequences. Most of the individual leaders such as Robert Moses of highway construction fame and others who were the innovators and advocates of these policies are dead. It is difficult to blame them. Only those companies slow to recognize and adjust to shifting realities are presently available for blame. These include the oil companies whose corporate lifespan and personification makes them immortal in their culpability. Some corporations and older northeastern cities suffered the blame for not having moved fast enough or for being residual legatees of universal incompetence.

Yet, at another level, the worldwide failure of leadership—that is, the failure to solve the major existential problems of ordinary citizens—inflation, unemployment, poverty and misery, international tension, and the denial of individual human rights—produces a sense of disenchantment with all leaders, East and West, who, because of their leadership roles, are expected to provide the policies and the economic and political frameworks within which satisfactory and rising standards of life can be realized.

In short, the crisis of confidence, the delegitimization of both political and economic institutions and their leaders, is a fact of contemporary world society.

The Role of Leaders

Yet our social institutions continue to operate with the appearance of effectiveness. Leaders continue to exercise their functions and authority and, of course, gain the rewards thereof, despite the general crisis of leadership and the concomitant lack of moral authority, credibility, respect, and inability to avert crises or control organized opposition. The problem under such conditions is, How do leaders operate despite the necessary lack of jurisdictions, technical expertise, and ability to undertake effective long-term planning?

The range of available leadership tactics is broad. Moreover, failure in using one tactic does not necessarily mean total failure. Let us bypass the myriad university and institute programs that purport to trade in "leadership skills." Here are just some of the major patterns of actual leadership tactics under the "new" conditions of indeterminacy that are readily observable in the actions of public leaders. These reveal a logic of leadership whether that logic is explicitly stated or not.

The first, and most obvious, tactic is to lie. Lying, of course, includes more than the big lie of Hitler or even the avoidance of the explicit, direct lies of the legal profession ("as best as I can remember"). It includes vast patterns of deceit, misdirection, the withholding of information, and the projecting of information, ideologies, public relations, and propaganda known to be untrue (disinformation).

Thus, almost every institutional leader knows how his organizational subordinates regard him. He knows the disagreements among his staff and among the several interest groups connected to his organization. He knows the uncertainties and difficulties in resolving these conflicts. He becomes aware of the incompetence of some of his subordinates and the weaknesses of some divisions of his organization. He knows the hopes for and uncertainties of science and technology. He may not know all of his organization's weaknesses, confusions, and failures, since his jurisdictions are large. Yet he must evaluate his organization, personnel, competence, and policies in order to pursue the mission that he and his close colleagues define for the organization. Some leaders may be more perceptive in these tasks than others. Some may blind themselves to weaknesses. Yet the very operation of an organization yields to its insiders a measure of the uncertainties, confusion, incompetence, lack of effective power, and internal conflict that are ever present in modern organizations.

In dealing with the public, clients, outsiders, the heads of other organizations, and internal constituencies, the leader must exude confidence, competence, optimism, and a sense of his ability to address any problems his organization faces. In ordinary situations, he must minimize or cover up the indecision, uncertainty, division, and incompetence in his organization—his own and that of others—or accept responsibility for mismanagement.

The lies and deceit thus take two forms. Precisely because the leader knows the unresolved problems and uncertainties of his organization, he is always engaged in public cover-up, the withholding of negative information, insider secrecy, and the quiet dismissal of embarrassing personnel and the problems they cause. All the while, his public face must always be sunny, projecting a can-do, serene optimism. In switching his attention from internal to external concerns, the leader reverses the focus and evaluation of his mission and policies. He thus is forced to lie, in the sense that we have defined lying. He may, of course, psych himself up to believe what he is saying at the necessary moment, perhaps to be able to lie more effectively and to avoid the knowledge that he is lying. But if he consistently believes his own lies, he will be unable to monitor his organization—that is, to be aware of and eliminate incompetence, indecision, and confusion and to referee between contending interests, groups, and experts.

The solution, of course, is doublethink, to lie with conviction when necessary, but to be able to do so without being taken in by one's own lies. Through doublethink, Orwell tells us, the liar at no time has to be aware of his lying. Because he is not self-conscious of his lying, he can lie more effectively. He needn't be a hypocrite because he is unaware at any given moment of his lying. When the situation that requires lying is past, he may be able to recognize the manifest truth he lied about in the past, even as he prepares new doublethink lies in the present for the future.

Lying assumes a different quality when, after the exposure of incompetence, fraud, mismanagement, and deceit, the leader faces direct attacks on his credibility. Here, direct, conscious lying may be necessary and must be planned with the aid of experts, public relations practitioners, lawyers, media specialists, speechwriters, and other kinds of ideologists. In a legal situation, the problem is one of avoiding the direct lie, or the traceable lie, the falsifiable statement, the "smoking gun." The tricks of memory, euphemisms, implicit understandings that underlie manifest meanings are substitutes for more direct but nonreflective doublethink. Stonewalling may be a way of avoiding lying, but stonewalling may also be a form of lying: one tells the small, less culpable lie to avoid the culpability of the big, direct lie.

Yet lying is only one form of public presentation in the cover-up of personal and structural incompetence.

A more prosaic technique is the issuance of new promises to remedy past "mismanagement." This technique obviously applies to candidates for leadership positions, individuals not encumbered by the "mistakes" of the past and specific knowledge of the structural limitations on leadership in any given situation. Such aspirants' very lack of responsibility allows them to make new promises along with claims to competence, expertise, and foresight that cannot be disproved by examining their past experiences. This works especially well when an aspiring leader seeks higher levels of leadership than he has occupied in the past. And, if he is fortunate and able, he will have concealed his handling or mishandling of structurally irresolvable problems as well as his own venality and incompetence. He can conceal these by public relations, by avoidance of a track record, or by thwarting the release of any records that do exist.

Yet he may be subject to the cry: Would you buy a used car from this man? Would you let this man have his hand on the button? Or, is he mature enough to overcome a history of undergraduate cheating, sexual immorality, or substance abuse? Finally, one can say, "After all, he was only indicted, not convicted." Or, "He confessed his past crimes, didn't he?"

But in the main, new promises and claims, when done well with the aid of speechwriters, opinion polling, makeup, and the right media support, can assure the public that the failures of the past will not continue. Seeming personal honesty and competence, even when based on the complete lack of a record, will usually trump verifiable accomplishments. And even when some members of the public, presumably those who are more sophisticated or decadent as the case may be, are skeptical of hard-charging, ambitious young men and women, they still respect the abilities of neophytes who exhibit virtuosity in lying and making clear-eyed innocent claims and promises precisely because public presentation is at the core of modern leadership. Skeptics can identify with the fresh-faced artful deception and the ability to project images of skill that candidates for leadership must possess if they are to achieve their aspirations.

The kind of systematic lying under discussion here does not stem from personal morality. Institutionalized lying is a structural problem, based on incompetence of leadership, lack of effective jurisdiction and control, lack of determinate knowledge, and lack of ability at prediction or long-range forecasting. On achieving office, new leaders assume responsibility, and they must confront continuously emerging problems. The reality of these problems, and leaders' own incompetence or inevitably limited competence to deal with them, become the theater of decision making, replacing the assertion of claims, promises, and even virtuosity in public relations.

Yet the changes of administration in both the private and public sectors—with new faces, new hopes, new deals, square deals, new frontiers, new freedoms, and new crusades—have the effect of a turnover of lies, new lies for old, and the opportunity to refurbish illusions. They allow the public to feel that the mistakes, errors, mismanagement of the past are over; a new start can be made. This honeymoon, however, is usually short-lived. The promises and claims become clichés, and the new administration becomes entrapped in structural incompetence. This usually leads to increased public cynicism, disenchantment, and a renewed crisis of confidence and legitimacy, especially when successive regimes fail dramatically to avoid scandal or when they provide public demonstrations of incompetence to avert or to solve political, economic, or technological crises.

One characteristic way that these crises are resolved, in the political realm at least, is by fomenting external crises that clearly do not appear to be the fault of the leadership. Precipitating a war is a classic device, though usually this involves rigging events in such a way that another power is led to declare war and appears to be the aggressor. Unity created by war or the threat of war may temporarily suspend criticism of a regime and of its failure to solve the problems that constitute the source of its impending "illegitimacy."

All these devices have the effect of "rolling over" the claims that a population understandably makes on a regime as a result of the promises made by leaders to justify their leadership and officeholding.

The successive changes in regimes may maintain the total political order; that is, changes in leadership may preserve the order as new promises replace old ones. For any one regime to accomplish the same goal, it may, to repeat, continuously revise its programs, policies, strategies and slogans, hoping that new promises replace old failures. For this to happen, however, dramatic evidence of incompetence, corruption, and abuse of power must be kept from the public. This is done positively by public relations, news management, and by exploitation of the desires of the public that their leaders are not crooks. This is the charisma of office, which is unconnected to the personal gifts of particular officeholders. On the negative side, it is done by the use of censorship, official or unofficial, by the ideology of professional or bureaucratic secrecy, by belief in professional or collegial loyalty, and by daring the opposition to prove its case in the face of legal and dramatic standards of proof (where's the smoking gun?). In the latter case, the very complexity of the administrative state and bureaucratic organization makes hard proof of incompetence and corruption extremely difficult to achieve and even more difficult to dramatize. The unproven, but rumored, suspicion of incompetence or criminality thus remains as a constant specter questioning legitimacy and a source of public skepticism, distrust, and cynicism that is neither allayed nor resolved. It produces a generalized malaise, a suspicion of illegitimacy.

In undemocratic—that is, authoritarian—societies, the knowledge of bureaucratic, political, and economic crime and incompetence becomes the inside knowledge of those near to the centers of power. It also diffuses in wider and wider circles to the outlying populations, where it results in deep-seated attitudes of distrust, apathy, and noncooperation. But such knowledge is not likely to produce organized attacks on the regime. Instead, it produces a withdrawal of efficiency, a lack of productivity, and minimal cooperation with established organizations, because there is no point in working hard for crooks or exploiters.

In democratic societies, the exposure of scandals of incompetence and crime of the regime is usually left to the press, to opposition parties, to "back benchers," or to ambitious members of the party in power. Exposure, however, rests on the invulnerability of the opposition to counterexposure. Since most leaders of opposition institutions are themselves subject to charges of structural incompetence, as are all incumbents, their weaknesses limit their power of exposure. Moreover, since the incumbents control the agencies of law enforcement and the means of publicity, the opposition must step with caution. The opposition, however, being out of power or not in a position to risk major mistakes or criminal action, still has the advantage of irresponsibility. And this facilitates the possibility of exposure.

Yet, overall, leaders have a mutual respect for other leaders, including their opposition, because all organizational leaders face similar structural problems. Thus, the leaders of dominant institutions are unlikely to "blow the whistle" on each other. The implicit collusion between different leadership corps limits the possibility of exposure of structural incompetence and fraud, except when one leadership group, struggling to survive, tries to blame another leadership corps for past or present dramatic failure.

Another "technique of neutralization" of the blame for structural incompetence is patriotism and nationalism. Images of the distant enemy or the hidden internal enemy, such as communists, Jews, the running dogs of capitalism, fascists, and Hitler (to Eastern Europeans) are preserved and presented as threats to the system. Mistakes, incompetence, and inducements to crime can be blamed on these enemies, without having to blame one's own incumbent leadership. It is in this sense that nationalism and patriotism are the last refuge of scoundrels.

In Russia today, the love of Mother Russia and memory of the death and destruction hurled upon her by Hitler and Germany is the most exploited theme in Soviet society. It is a national religion casting Hitler as the devil, Lenin as God, and Stalin as Cain. But nationalism and patriotism allow the regime to inflict constant exploitation on its masses. The religion of the state along with endless repression of those who resist exploitation and the isolation of the masses from information and alternative means of collective expression results in a political stability that resists erosion by high-level structural incompetence and political criminality. Yet such patriotism does not induce deep levels of commitment to work, efficiency, and personal responsibility by the masses, despite the second major secular religion of the Soviet Union, the celebration of heroes of productivity.

In repressive societies, cynicism, apathy, and inefficiency—that is, sabotage and the withdrawal of efficiency—are the true indicators of illegitimacy, despite attempts at creating the secular religion of the state and nation.

Long-Term Forecasting and Planning

The strategy of "rolling over" claims and promises is consistent with the need for long-term forecasting and planning. This is due to the lack of congruity between terms of office and planning needs. In most democratic societies, the term of political office is four years or less and is then subject to renewal by election. In other institutions, the achievement of top positions comes relatively late in life and is terminable by death or retirement. Long-term planning may require eight years in the case of the automobile industry, thirty to forty years in the case of the construction of power plants, and generations in terms of long-term military and national economic, political, and security planning.

Any leadership corps or regime, if driven not by illusions of immortality or historical eminence, but rather by the necessities of continuation in office despite structural incompetence, can solve the problems of planning simply by being dead, out of office, or retired when the necessary or culpable failures are revealed. Practically, in "open" societies, this means delays in revealing the inadequacy of planning, failures to foresee problems, lack of correct, expert assessment of the potentialities, outcomes, or costs of scientific development or of the consequences of planning.

This may not be too difficult. First, unanticipated developments may be favorable as well as unfavorable; a mistake in intended technology, planning or forecasting may be compensated for by unforeseeable but favorable changes in the external structure of events. We may be victorious for the wrong reasons. We build a small automobile because we lack the capital to build a large one, and subsequently the oil crisis makes us wise.

Second, it may happen that no crisis occurs to test leaders' plans until after they are dead or out of office. Thus, it is said, time and again, that political assassinations make heroes of incompetents (or the mildly incompetent) because the hero does not have to face the consequences of his own planning and actions. This seems to hold as long as the hero did not invite the assassination.

Third, the long-term planner can postpone problems until after he leaves office. This is possible because of the technological complexities involved in the assessment of the operation and consequence of plans, the lack of clear criteria of success, and the shift in the salience of issues over time. Control of information, misdirection, and the creation of new issues, crusades, and causes may also serve to misdirect attention from the failure of planning. When dramatic crises occur, and when attention—that is, culpability—is sought for failures, the original leaders may be long gone, and the assignment of blame to the initiators of a policy may be a ritual act to serve those currently in power. We especially blame our predecessors if they came from the party of the opposition.

The incumbents have as part of their function the responsibility for reevaluating plans and policies established by previous regimes. But such reevaluations are concurrent with learning the operation of establishing control over the vast operating organizations of government. When there are failures in the new regime's operations, they reveal, usually too late, the need for reevaluation of their predecessors. From the standpoint of incumbents, the issue can be resolved by blaming one's predecessors (the stab in the back) and by hoping that the failure of reevaluation will go unnoticed.

The Aesthetics of Lying

As noted, a regime in power has vast resources to address attacks on its legitimacy in the face of its own structural incompetence. Most of these highly developed techniques are well known to leaders, though they are not necessarily codified. But, in any event, they become available, discoverable and re-createable by a regime once it ascends into power. Such necessary responses to structural incompetence may become even more than responses.

These techniques have an autonomy of their own, once they become known and available and worked out with high levels of competence and technological know-how. The mastery of these techniques confers prestige, positive value, and opportunity. Propaganda, public relations, and outright lying may become a reflexive action, practiced both as a prerequisite for gaining office and as a means of demonstrating leadership. At times, some members of a distant public may even identify with the public relations ability of a leadership group, admiring the poise, skill, presumable charisma, knowledgeability, facility, smoothness, and even the daring of the artful dodger in the propaganda wars. These members of a public imagine that everyone is deceived but themselves and therefore they are coconspirators in the lies, deceits, and frauds of their leaders. It is not difficult to understand how Hitler could announce the "big lie" as an instrument of policy and receive acceptance. Nor is it difficult to understand how confessions of past deceit—for instance, Richard Nixon's Checkers speech or Ted Kennedy's admission of youthful indiscretions—get interpreted as indicators of growing maturity and candor. In many cases, our capacities to forgive the sins of the past invite future betrayals.

Virtuosity in fraud becomes important only because it is autonomous; that is, it goes beyond the levels required by structural incompetence. Yet autonomous lies, deceit, and cover-ups add to a greater sense of disenchantment after a crisis reveals the fraud as well as the particular form of incompetence in question. Then the public that was knowingly charmed, seduced, and identified with the cleverness in propaganda of their leaders feels betrayed when they discover that they, not others, are the victims. The search for villains and devils then becomes a major escape in order to avoid self-inculpation by both leaders and followers. Only the labeling is different. The leader becomes the devil and his coconspirators by identification now become the blameless victims.

While crises in legitimacy may be sporadic, these processes reveal that each crisis provides opportunities for the personification of illegitimacy—scapegoats—and for the transfer or redistribution of images of legitimacy and illegitimacy between various leaders and groups and between leaders and followers.

If these transfers are made easily, illegitimacy may be "psychologized," attributed to persons, and the system thereby saved. Yet the consequence is always an increase in the level of cynicism as exemplified by the question, How is it that crooks, murderers, incompetents, liars, and thieves can become leaders of the system? Additionally, one can ask, How many of their aides, coconspirators, and protégés, still remain in leadership positions? These questions, though "natural," tend to limit the eradication of "crimes against the people."

If these compromises in the restitution of legitimacy occur together with public recognition at some levels of the public's own complicity in the fraud and deceit by legitimate leaders, then the crises in legitimacy are never fully overcome. Cynicism reigns, and the major problems of leadership and legitimacy persist even without the recognition of structural incompetence as a source of the crisis of legitimacy.

Yet because of the transferability and redistribution of attribution of legitimacy and illegitimacy, crises in legitimacy and illegitimacy do not necessarily lead to the collapse of the system. A particular crisis leads to such collapses only when the entire political, economic, and constitutional machinery also collapses. Major defeats in war, deep economic depression, unemployment, and the failure of the machinery of repression are additional preconditions for a genuine, revolutionary shift in the basis for legitimacy. Though such shifts do, of course, occur frequently in individual countries throughout the world, crises in legitimacy typically result only in the loss of credibility, institutional malaise, some withdrawal from the symbols of legitimacy, apathy, cynicism, and inefficiency in particular countries.

Prospects and Conclusions

Modern society is characterized by increasing demands for responsible leadership. These demands are the product of a secularism that does not allow fate, destiny, God, or the gods to be seen as the source of failure in leadership. At the same time, and for some of the same reasons, modern society has seen a long-term revolution of rising expectations that demands that leaders justify themselves to large masses of subjects by performance, by providing better life conditions, material and ideal opportunities, better standards of living, peace, security, health, and the possibility of social and personal development. Leaders are compelled to and want to promise these benefits, and these become the basis for modern forms of legitimacy.

Jurisdictional limitations, scientific technological complexity and uncertainty, and the problems inherent in long-term planning, all limit the possibility of leaders fulfilling the promises they make and satisfying the claims that followers make on them.

Yet the failure of leadership to solve the basic claims of the populace does not in itself inhibit leadership or social development; the rewards of leadership are either a challenge or the anticipation of great rewards. The institutions of the world do not lack claimants for leadership.

The leaders, however, all inevitably have to become aware of the problems that lead to "structural incompetence," and they have to act within the framework of these problems. It is difficult for them to deny their structural incompetence, since they sought leadership on the basis of their ability to solve societal or institutional problems. The profession of modesty, self-limitation, or lack of expertise or judgment is unbecoming to leaders, except in the experience of major defeats immediately after an election, and never before one.

In leaders' inability to admit structural incompetence even as they grapple with unsolvable problems, leaders must necessarily develop a vast number of techniques of leadership that generate public confidence in their regimes. These include public relations, propaganda, lies and deceit, misdirection, secrecy and cover-up, mystification, delay, and the "roll-over" of promises. They include the deflection of criticism to enemies of the state, appeals to nationalism, patriotism,scapegoating and blaming one's predecessors. In totalitarian societies, all of the above are involved, but they also include greater degrees of repression of any potential opposition and the press, the total control of information, and the isolation of the population from images of the good life in order to keep expectations low.

None of these techniques work fully. As a result, even in the modern world, the legitimacy of social and economic and political systems has come under attack. The form of attack can become outright assaults on the total system, attacks on regimes, and upon individual leaders. Dissatisfaction can also be manifested in increased cynicism, generalized malaise, withdrawal of efficiency, apathy, and the privatization of life.

The major form of reestablishing legitimacy in the face of structural incompetence is the rotation of leadership—that is, the transfer or redistribution of legitimacy and illegitimacy among leadership groups. This preserves the legitimacy of the system, while allowing structural incompetence to become treated as a personal rather than structural problem. Such attribution is usually partly correct, since leaders are inevitably personally drawn into the deceit that makes leadership possible.

Yet this method of treating leaders as sacrificial victims to structural incompetence is effective. It preserves the system. Moreover, some leaders thought to be personally incompetent in their own time, become elevated to virtually national heroes or deities as successive generations of leaders appear to be even worse. Abraham Lincoln, Franklin Roosevelt, and General Eisenhower are prime examples in the United States. And even Richard Nixon might rise in stature, having no other direction to go, except into oblivion.

The crisis of the whole system appears to be more than a problem in structural incompetence. In the modern world, the decline in legitimacy of a system is likely to be the result of a total collapse of a society under the impact of the loss of a war or depression. In the ancient world, such factors were accompanied by famine, plague, and the inability to repress charismatic warlords. In the modern world, an additional factor is present—that is, the inability of repressive regimes (for instance, Batista's Cuba) to maintain total repression of its population.

In other, less repressive regimes the crisis of legitimacy is a natural consequence of the contradictions within secular society. Here its forms are not as severe. They include cynicism, apathy, and the privatization of life, along with extreme inefficiency in production.

Cynicism, privatization, and substantial apathy seem to be permanent conditions of modern, complex societies. Yet a major existential reality of the modern world is structural incompetence, the technical problems of which are not solved by romantic pseudocharisma. Moreover, the political conditions imposed by successful revolutionary romanticism can be worse than the incompetence and lies of philistine political leaders. After all, neither Hitler nor Stalin was a Philistine. They were in their own ways true believers.

The problems of political malaise are also a major existential reality. The public would be less disenchanted by exposed lies and deceit if it had no expectations of secular salvation and if leaders felt they did not have to lie and use the techniques of misdirection necessary to attain and retain leadership. Yet the public will make claims for a better life, and leaders will promise unrealizable goals in order to achieve leadership positions. The autonomous greed, venality, exploitation, deceit, and fraud that occur within the ranks of all elites and leadership groups invite constant vigilance. But the exposure of one gang of charlatans only invites another gang to try its hand at leadership under the same existential conditions.

9

Charisma and Modernity

Joseph Bensman with Michael Givant

From time to time, a relatively esoteric academic field and/or its concepts becomes highly popular among lay audiences, and its vocabulary enters the common language. Thus, the concepts of physics associated with the atom bomb, at least at the level of vocabulary—for example, *fission*, *fusion*—are part of the ordinary speech of millions of people. Psychology, especially Freudian psychology, has enriched or, according to some, helped to debase everyday language. Sociology has produced or reintroduced such terms as *serendipity*, *alienation*, *anomie*, and a wide variety of other terms usually deemed barbaric by defenders of literate English. In this essay, we are concerned with the term *charisma*, which by now is not only the name of a perfume and the title of a pop tune, the name of a laundry and a shirt brand, but also widely applied to virtually every situation in which the popularity of a political or any public personality is involved. In a famous article, Edward Shils similarly notes the vulgarization of the term: "Charisma has come to be widely used in current high and middle-brow speech, in sociological and political analyses, and in the superior ladies' magazines."[1]

Published originally in a slightly different form in *Social Research* 42 (Winter 1975), 570-614. Republished by permission from *Social Research*.

The transformation or migration of meaning of such terms is always of interest. As a term gains currency, some of the specific original meaning may be lost and new meanings added. In addition, once the new meanings are added, readers who take the new meanings as given read into the earlier discussions meanings that were not intended and that do violence to the original literature and to the historical context to which they refer. *Charisma* is such a term. Moreover, we contend that Shils, in his own way, contributes to the contemporary shift in the meaning of charisma.

Weber's Concept of Charisma

The term *charisma* was originally coined by Rudolf Sohm in his *Kirchenrecht* to refer to the gift of grace, the possession of *pneuma*, breath or spirit, by a religiously inspired individual. Sohm's term was adopted by Max Weber and became an important part of his sociology of religion and of his political sociology. In adopting the term, Weber placed great emphasis not on the possession of grace itself (as in Sohm) but on the *belief* by the followers of such a religious leader and by the leader himself of such possession. The belief of possession of divine inspiration (or mana in the case of military charisma) was critical for Weber:

> The term *charisma* will be applied to a certain quality of an individual personality by virtue of which he is considered extraordinary and treated as endowed with supernatural, superhuman, or at least specifically exceptional powers or qualities. These are such as are not accessible to the ordinary person, but are regarded as of divine origin or as exemplary, and on the basis of them the individual concerned is treated as a "leader." In primitive circumstances this peculiar kind of quality is thought of as resting on magical powers, whether of prophets, persons with

> a reputation for therapeutic or legal wisdom, leaders in the hunt, or heroes in war. . . . What is alone important is how the individual is actually regarded by those subject to charismatic authority, by his "followers" or "disciples."[2]

The link between the charismatic hero and his followers is direct. It is not mediated by established institutions, organizations, doctrines, or rituals. The charismatic hero occupies no office within established religions or military organizations.[3] If he occupies an office, the attribution of charisma is not based upon his office:

> The charismatic hero does not deduce his authority from codes and statutes, as is the case with the jurisdiction of office; nor does he deduce his authority from traditional custom or feudal vows of faith, as is the case of patrimonial power.
>
> The charismatic leader gains and maintains authority solely by proving his strength in life. If he wants to be a prophet, he must perform miracles; if he wants to be a war lord, he must perform heroic deeds.[4]

He invokes his claim to leadership not on the basis of office, but rather upon belief in the direct and unmediated possession of the gift and grace:

> The prophet, unlike ordinary pathologically ecstatic men, had no vision, dreamed no dreams, and heard no mysterious voices. Rather he attained clarity and assurance through a corporeal divine voice of what Yahwe had meant by these day-dreams, or the vision, or the ecstatic excitement, and what Yahwe had commanded him to say in communicable words . . . Always . . . the prophet's calling came directly from Yahwe, and the classical prophets among them told us of their visionary or auditory "call."

> None of them used any intoxicants, the use of which they cursed on every occasion, as idolatry.[5]

Weber makes the same point with reference to Jesus's charisma:

> It must not be forgotten for an instant that the entire basis of Jesus' own legitimation, as well as his claim that he and only he knew the Father and that the way to God led through faith in him alone, was the magical charisma he felt within himself. It was doubtless this consciousness of power, more than anything else, that enabled him to traverse the road of the prophets.[6]

The nature and conditions of a society or group governing the assumption of charisma establishes much of the subsequent characteristics of charisma. First, charismatic leadership, according to Weber, usually arises in times of crisis in which the basic values, institutions, and legitimacy of the society are in question. War, revolution, military defeat, foreign domination, natural disaster, or unexplained natural phenomena all shake the faith in the legitimacy of the established order and established belief systems. The religious, political, and social hierarchies that sustain and are identified with these belief systems are similarly questioned.

This crisis in faith, and thus in the legitimacy of previously accepted leaders and leadership groups, provides opportunities for unmediated claims for power by would-be charismatic leaders. In some cases of primitive military charisma, the charismatic leader arises periodically even in the absence of crises of the social order. Charismatic leadership is the normal but intermittent way by which a warrior assumes, at least temporarily, the leadership of a band. The potential leader (military or religious) often isolates himself from his peers and from all others, undergoes rites of purification and mortification in the attempt to induce possession by mystical, psychic states, visions, dreams, and signs that he has been visited, possessed, or seized by mana, a god or the powers of god. If, after he returns to tribe and peers, he can provide evidence of such possession and power, he may recruit a band of followers who believe that his possession of powers will grant success to their joint enterprise. The continuance of his leadership depends on his demonstrating charismatic qualities as evidenced by success in raids, warfare, and the hunt:

> Where war and the big hunt are absent, the charismatic chieftain—the "war lord" as we wish to call him, in contrast to the chieftain of peace—is absent as well. In peacetime, especially if elemental calamities, particularly drought and diseases, are frequent, a charismatic sorcerer may have an essentially similar power in his hands. He is a priestly lord. The charisma of the war lord may or may not be unstable in nature according to whether or not he proves himself and whether or not there is any need for a war lord He becomes a permanent figure when warfare becomes a chronic state of affairs.[7]

Failure in such activities is evidence to his followers that he no longer possesses charisma. Thus, while primitive societies institutionalize charisma, charismatic leaders appear intermittently. Such leadership is of uncertain duration and reappears only after the failure of earlier institutional charismatic leadership:

> Even the old Germanic kings were sometimes rejected with scorn. Similar phenomena are very common among so-called primitive peoples. In China the charismatic quality of the monarch, which was transmitted unchanged by heredity, was upheld so rigidly that any misfortune whatever, not only defeats in war, but drought, floods, or astronomical phenomena which were considered

> unlucky, forced him to do public penance and might even force his abdication. If such things occurred, it was a sign that he did not possess the requisite charismatic virtue and was thus not a legitimate "Son of Heaven."[8]

Moreover, the charismatic military leader is drawn from no particular hereditary leadership group, nor is he elected by any regularly and routinely operative machinery of election or co-optation. Rather, the charismatic military leader "selects" himself, and achieves "selection" if he can evoke and direct an immediate belief among a band of followers that he possesses divine power or mana.

In all these cases, the evocation of charisma and charismatic leadership always leads away from the world of everyday life. It rejects the routine life of traditional societies, the purely hierocratic elements of religions, and the bureaucratic and machine operation of political organizations. And it rejects as undignified the methodical, rational pursuit of money or wealth. It occurs in times of crises.

Thus, pure charisma not only claims extraordinary powers but occurs in extraordinary situations and leads, at least temporarily, to actions, movements, events, and organizations that are extraordinary, not routine, and outside the sphere of everyday life.

It is important to note—and, as we shall see, it is almost always overlooked—that pure charismatic leadership (with the exception of primitive military charisma) is revolutionary. It is a means by which established institutions and organizations become fully delegitimated. It thus conflicts with the established order. The concept of pure charisma is also a means, in Weber's overall philosophy of history, by which traditional and rationally organized power structures and their bases of legitimacy become replaced by new and discontinuous forms of order, which are subsequently justified with new bases of legitimacy.

Weber may well have overemphasized the importance of charismatic leadership in introducing indeterminacy to the historical process. Equally important, if not more important, according to Weber, is the intellectual process of rationalizing the world. Ideas, driven by the dynamic of interest, determine the course of history.[9] Thus, Luther's and Calvin's ideas, leading to the Protestant Ethic, arose primarily from an autonomous intellectual development, the process of rationalizing existing ideas to make them more consistent and accurate. But in the process, new ideas emerged, which were selected and reinterpreted by existing and emerging classes and status groups to meet their economic, political, religious, and ideological needs (real and ideal interests). Once harnessed to these interests, these ideas helped to transform the world, in virtually all dimensions of human existence.

Pure or genuine charisma is personal, direct, radical, revolutionary, and extraordinary. But when the charismatic *movement* is successful, charisma becomes ordinary. Its leadership becomes routinized, depersonalized, and de-radicalized. Thus, Weber writes, "Every charisma is on the road from a turbulently emotional life that knows no economic rationality to a slow death by suffocation under the weight of material interests: every hour of its existence brings it nearer to this end."[10] Charisma may become attached to an office;[11] that is, the gift of grace becomes attached to the person who occupies the office. In so becoming, it is depersonalized; but more important, in being attached to an office in an established political, religious, or military order, it is no longer radical. In such circumstances, the magic or grace of charisma can become the basis for the legitimacy of the order itself. Thus, Weber develops subtypes of routinized,[12] depersonalized, and "legitimate" charisma. These include charisma of office (as defined above), lineage charisma,[13] where a whole clan or kin group may claim unusual power and privileges on the basis of descent from a charismatic hero, and hereditary charisma,[14] in which a prince, king, or emperor may justify his rule by descent from a charismatic hero.

A special form of the concept of charisma of office is used by Weber in the attribution of magical qualities to Chinese emperors and mandarins. The emperors (and offices) are invested with a special magic despite the fact that their accession to office is routinized (and in the case of officials is the result of passing examinations). But the emperor (or the governor of a province) receives the divine grace of heaven in the exercise of his function. If war, natural calamity, or disaster occurs, it is because heaven has withdrawn its grace. The emperor, or official, loses his charisma and can be removed.

But all of these cases are the opposite of pure charisma. The pure charismatic leader most often opposes or attacks the various kinds of routinized, established, or depersonalized regimes that often descend from earlier pure charismatic leaders.

In these later contexts, Weber uses the term *charisma* almost as a synonym for legitimacy, as the basis for faith or belief in an established order, institutional leader, or leadership group. In almost all other contexts, Weber differentiates between pure charisma (which is revolutionary, direct, and unmediated, as well as outside all institutional organization) and the charisma of office, which is, though legitimate, the opposite of pure charisma in each aforementioned respect and different from primitive military charisma, which is not revolutionary—that is, which is institutionally permitted but not prescribed or routinized.

In pure charisma, the claim to obedience is personal. It is based on the ability of the charismatic cult leader to evoke the sense of faith, loyalty, and obedience of a group of personal followers to the message that the charismatic leader has derived from his unmediated communication with supernatural power:

> The personal call is the decisive element distinguishing the prophet from the priest. The latter lays claim to authority by virtue of his service in a sacred tradition, while the prophet's claim is based on personal revelation and charisma. It is no accident that almost no prophets have emerged from the priestly class. . . .
>
> But the prophet, like the magician, exerts his power simply by virtue of his personal gifts. Unlike the magician, however, the prophet claims definite revelations, and the core of his mission is doctrine or commandment, not magic.[15]

However, the charismatic man becomes a leader only if there are followers:

> Charisma is self-determined and sets its own limits. Its bearer seizes the task for which he is destined and demands that others obey and follow him by virtue of his mission. If those to whom he feels sent do not recognize him, his claim collapses; if they recognize it, he is their master as long as he "proves himself."[16]

Thus, Weber uses the prophetic phrase, "It is written but I say unto you." The legitimacy of charismatic leadership in the sociological sense, as Weber uses it, is an attribute of the *belief of the followers* and not of the quality of the leader. The leader is important because he can evoke this sense of belief and thereby can demand obedience. "However, he does not derive his claims from the will of his followers, in the manner of an election; rather, it is their *duty* to recognize his charisma."[17] Potential charismatic leaders do not passively await recognition by their followers:

> The genuine prophet, like the genuine military leader and every true leader in this sense, preaches, creates, or

> demands, *new* obligations—most typically, by virtue of revelation, oracle, inspiration, or of his own will, which are recognized by the members of the religious, military, or party group because they come from such a source. Recognition is a duty.[18]

Finally, charismatic leadership is not rational in the sense that it is based on rational argumentation, presentation, and defense. It is based primarily on the faith of the followers and the leader that the leader has access to the divine and therefore has unquestionable authority. The charismatic leader thus does not attempt in principle to argue logically the validity of his message, though he does attempt to claim for his message the authenticity of its divine source. He validates his claim by success or, rather, the faith in the success of his possession of charisma based upon the results of his prophecy or action. Thus, rationality, in the sense that it implies a formal logic, is not relevant to charismatic leadership:

> Since it is "extra-ordinary," charismatic authority is sharply opposed to rational, and particularly bureaucratic, authority, and to traditional authority, whether in its patriarchal, patrimonial, or estate variants, all of which are everyday forms of domination; while the charismatic type is the direct antithesis of this. Bureaucratic authority is specifically rational in the sense of being bound to intellectually analyzable rules; while charismatic authority is specifically irrational in the sense of being foreign to all rules. Traditional authority is bound to the precedents handed down from the past and to this extent is also oriented to rules.[19]

Weber points, in addition, to the conflict between charisma and rational-legal norms: "Hence, its attitude is revolutionary and transvalues everything; it makes a sovereign break with all traditional or rational norms: 'It is written, but I say unto you.'"[20] He stresses the contrast between bureaucratic rationalism with respect to modes of "proving" their claims to legitimacy:

> The power of charisma rests upon the belief in revelation and heroes, upon the conviction that certain manifestations—whether they be of religious, ethical, artistic, scientific, political or other kind—are important and valuable; it rests upon "heroism" of an ascetic, military, judicial, magical or whichever kind. Charismatic belief revolutionizes men "from within" and shapes material and social conditions according to its revolutionary will.[21]

However, to the extent that validity or authenticity is measured by "success," there is an experiential test of charisma. The unsuccessful leader loses his charisma:

> By its very nature, the existence of charismatic authority is specifically unstable. The holder may forego his charisma; he may feel "forsaken by his God," as Jesus did on the cross; he may prove to his followers that "virtue is gone out of him." It is then that his mission is extinguished, and hope waits and searches for a new holder of charisma. The charismatic holder is deserted by his following, however, (only) because pure charisma does not know any "legitimacy" other than that flowing from personal strength, that is, one which is constantly being proved.[22]

Proof of success, to some extent, lies in the hands of the followers of the charismatic man:

> If proof and success elude the leader for long, if he appears deserted by his god or his magical or heroic powers, above all, if his leadership fails to benefit his followers, it is likely that his charismatic authority will disappear.[23]

In almost all the historical cases of pure charisma, the routinization of charisma did not occur within the lifetime of the charismatic leader. Therefore, the radical nature of the religious rejection of the existential world was maintained during the lifetime of the leader. As previously noted, when a charismatically led movement is successful, the nature of charisma becomes modified in the process of routinization, and charisma is attributed to office, lineage, or clan. Charisma is no longer pure charisma in the original sense as discussed above, but the routinization of charisma provides the basis and the legitimacy for newly established traditional or rational-legal hierarchies and systems of domination, which, in the process of routinization, become conservative. The radical nature of charisma disappears with routinization.

Current Revisions of the Weberian Concept

In this discussion, we have argued that Weber used the concept of charisma in precise ways. When he referred to a specific aspect of *charisma*, he tended to qualify the term, indicating the specific aspect of the meaning he intended. Thus, "pure" charisma, charisma of the office and/or "genuine," lineage, and hereditary charisma are all precise and differentiated specifications of meaning. We have also noted that in some cases Weber used the term in an undifferentiated way, suggesting in these cases a meaning that comes close to that meant by the term *legitimacy*. However, in these cases, primarily in ancient China, the legitimacy so indicated is the legitimacy of princely power. Apart from these latter contradictions, Weber's delimitation of the various subtypes of charisma indicates that each subtype may have opposite and contradictory social consequences and functions: some types of charisma are revolutionary, innovative, and delegitimizing, while other types are "institutionalizing," conservative, and legitimating of established regimes and societal orders. Thus, an unspecified or unqualified concept of charisma would overlook the specific social functions of charisma and would ignore the specific meanings and theoretical problems posed by Weber with his use of the term.

The new and popular usage of *charisma* among lay audiences contains such unspecified or unqualified usages. It selects only one aspect of all the various meanings of the term and treats that aspect as its only (or major) meaning. The selected and emphasized quality is the quality of the extraordinary character of the charismatic hero. Extraordinariness is treated in two senses. One sense is unusual psychological qualities and "presence." The other is an unusual ability to embody the central values of society.

The focus of these aspects of charisma leads one to ignore what is central to Weber's analysis: the revolutionary qualities, the irrationality, and the discontinuity in social structures accounted for by the emergence of pure charisma and by the subsequent institutionalization of charisma. In short, Weber is interested in charisma as a process accounting for changes in fundamental social structures.

Edward Shils attempts to refocus the discussion of charisma, claiming, in part, that Weber's concept needs such refocusing.[24] In so doing, Shils emphasizes the elements in charisma that link it to established orders. Thus, charisma becomes, for all intents and purposes, legitimacy. The major qualities that to Shils are relevant for these legitimacy-conferring aspects of charisma are the "awe and reverence" evoked by charisma. The charismatic hero is the extraordinary man. The qualities that are extraordinary beyond personal presence are the fact that the charismatic hero personifies and embodies the central or core values of man's existence, man's life, and the cosmos, together with an intensity of presence that makes it extraordinary: "The centrality is constituted by its formative power in initiating, creating, governing, transforming, maintaining, or destroying what is vital in man's life."[25]

Charisma, as thus related to man's existence, man's life, and the cosmos, is difficult to define, since such centralities have different meanings in different societies and at different times and social locations within a society. Specifically, the social results of charisma—in forming, initiating, creating, and preserving, or, on the other hand, transforming and even destroying institutions—can only be known empirically after the fact.

Charisma's "maintaining and governing" powers can be posited by definition or taken in a metaphysical sense as referring to man's ultimate life and existence and the cosmos. But they are known only as related to a given, existing social order, society, or set of legitimating values and are therefore historically specific. The idea of centrality can and does refer either to the central values of an ongoing society or to the "essential" values of that society. Referring to central value systems, Shils defines *charisma* as follows:

> That central power has often, in the course of man's existence, been conceived of as God, the ruling power or creator of the universe, or some divine or other transcendent power controlling or markedly influencing human life and the cosmos within which it exists.[26]

But charisma, according to Shils, is also related to specific social orders, in addition to being the creator of a generic order:

> The generator or author of order arouses the charismatic responsiveness. Whether it be God's law or natural law or scientific law or positive law or the society as a whole, or even a particular corporate body or institution like an army, whatever embodies, expresses, or symbolizes the essence of an ordered cosmos or any significant sector thereof awakens the disposition of awe and reverence, the charismatic disposition.[27]

Charisma is therefore anything in the order of society that produces a sense of awe and wonder among the populace. It includes transcendental values and the order conferring powers on corporate and political bodies and the wielders of power, the older and dominant classes, status groups, elites, and occupational groups.

In the original Weberian sense of the term, neither set of meanings of centrality is relevant. The charismatic hero, in the sense of pure charisma, is a deviant, radical, or revolutionary figure. The values that he espouses are not necessarily central to the ongoing central order—except when the charismatic hero can refer to values that have been discarded by the established political, economic, legal, or religious orders. To the extent that the pure charismatic hero bases his prophecy on values that have been central to the past, those values in order to be radical or revolutionary must be deviant or, at least, not central to ongoing established institutions. To the extent that its values become central to a society, they become central—that is, established—after charisma loses its radical and revolutionary quality and becomes a specialized form of charisma different from and opposed to pure charisma. It is this latter, specialized form of charisma that Shils treats as the generalized quality of charisma. Shils thus is manifestly concerned with the diffusion of charisma throughout a society—its embodiment not in a charismatic hero, nor in the charisma of an office, but in the entire institutional structure of a society, in the society itself, in its elites, in its central values, in its population, and in groups that have high prestige.[28]

In these illustrations and in all other references to charisma except those that directly summarize Weber's work, Shils's use of the concept does not, in contrast to Weber, refer to a charismatic hero, prophet, officeholder, lineage, or king. Instead, it refers to the general quality of charisma, an inherent element that evokes awe and reverence, wherever that quality may appear. It thus has no specific institutional base, nor any specific attributes. It is a free floating attribute that can attach itself to anything, including individuals. It is a metaphysical entity.

However, charisma is, according to Shils, included as a component in every act of voluntary obedience to established authority.[29] Thus, charisma is legitimacy, as that concept is usually defined.

It is difficult to argue against such a broad definition of *charisma*, since it includes the legitimation of everything that is established. The very broadness of Shils's usage inhibits the making of specific distinctions and does not allow the principle of falsifiability to operate. Thus, Shils is concerned with the diffusion of charisma throughout an established order and its adhesion to all established institutions, classes, and elites in a social order. Shils attempts to ground this generalized adhesion of charisma to established orders by locating it in what he conceives to be a metaphysical need for order. It is a metaphysic in the sense that the need for order is taken as a given, beyond explanation or beyond reduction to simpler elements. Thus, Shils states:

> I do not know why this need for order exists. It is not simply a need for an instrumentally manageable environment, though that is a part of it. It is more like the need for a rationally intelligible cognitive map, but it obviously is more than cognitive. There is a need for moral order—for things to be fit into a pattern which is just as well as predictable.[30]

The individuals in any society do need to have conceptions of the social world, or cosmologies, and relationships to others that are meaningful. The quality of providing meaning can be conceived of as rendering intellectual, theological, emotional, and psychological order.[31] The function of the charismatic hero in the past and charisma in the present—that is, in less personified terms—is, according to Shils, to provide systems of meaning and systems of order:

> The central power might be a fundamental principle or principles, a law or laws governing the universe, the underlying and driving force of the universe. It might be thought to reside in the ultimate principles of law which should govern man's conduct, arising from or derived from the nature of the universe and essential to human existence, discerned or elucidated by the exercise of man's most fundamental rational and expressive powers. Scientific discovery, ethical promulgation, artistic creativity, political and organizational authority (auctoritatem, auctor, authorship), and in fact all forms of genius, in the original sense of the word as permeation by the "spirit," are as much instances of the category of charismatic things as is religious prophecy.[32]

Shils explains the individual's metaphysical need for charisma and charismatic "others" as follows:

> Most human beings, because their endowment is inferior or because they lack opportunities to develop relevant capacities, do not attain that intensity of contact. But most of those who are unable to attain it themselves are, at least intermittently, responsive to its manifestations in the words, actions and products of others who have done so. They are capable of such appreciation and occasionally feel a need for it. Through the culture they acquire and through their interaction with and perception of those more "closely connected" with the cosmically and socially central, their own weaker responsiveness is fortified and heightened.[33]

Thus, in embodying central values, as Shils defines the term, *charisma* makes systems of meaning and order available to society. He gives to the concept of charisma all the qualities that Weber attributes to the process of intellectual rationalization and to rational systems for the diffusion of intellectually rationalized thought. These are not and never before have been thought of as charismatic. All of these, according to Shils, are charismatic functions. In this sense, any institution may have charisma if it also has power even though there were no charismatic elements in that institution's past:

> The charisma of an institution or of a corporate body does not depend on its foundation by a charismatic person (although it might well be true that only charismatic persons can command the authority and resources to create a new and very powerful institution or corporate body). Corporate bodies—secular, economic, governmental, military, and political—come to possess charismatic qualities simply by virtue of the *tremendous* power concentrated in them.[34]

To the extent that a system of thought or the promise or claims of a charismatic hero may have order and coherence (and that coherence may exist at a logical, psychological, emotional or aesthetic plane), any system of thought, of course, has order. But one should *not*, as Shils apparently does, equate the order of a system of thought with an "order" of society. For Shils, charisma produces this linkage. Thus, Shils states:

> The disposition to attribute charisma is intimately related to the need for order. The attribution of charismatic qualities occurs in the presence of order-creating, order-disclosing, order-discovering power as such; it is a response to great ordering power. The effectiveness or successful exercise of power on a large scale, on a macro-social scale,

> evokes a legitimating attitude. Every legitimation of effective large-scale power contains a charismatic element.[35]

Pure charisma, in the Weberian sense, may have order to the extent that it has coherence, but pure charisma inevitably and, by definition, attacks the "order" of a society. Therefore, pure charisma is always opposed to the existing social order until it is institutionalized in the newly established and ongoing order. It is important to note that political or social order as embodied in the structure of society need not be logical or coherent. To prove that political orders are also logical or meaningful is, in any empirical situation, a major task. Shils attempts to reconcile the various meanings of the term *order* by indicating the order-conferring functions of power; that is, simply because power is centralized, the institutions and groups that have power in a society evoke charismatic attachment. They accomplish this because they are salient and because they confer intellectual order on the society as a whole:

> This is "institutional" charisma; it is not a charisma deduced from the creativity of the charismatic individual. It is inherent in the massive organization of authority. The institutional charismatic legitimation of a command emanating from an incumbent of a role in a corporate body derives from *membership in the body as such, apart from any allocated, specific powers.*[36]

Because these institutions "order" and organize the society as a whole, they evoke the awe and reverence of the populace. They answer the metaphysical need for order that is apparently necessary to social man.

Again, Shils proves too much. Pure charisma, according to Weber, arises in opposition to centralized power, the order embodied in and provided by powerful institutions. If awe and reverence are functions of centralized power, then new forms of charisma, pure charisma, could not come into existence. One can rescue Shils's position, however, by arguing with some degree of plausibility that new forms of charisma—that is, forms of pure charisma, come into existence with the failure of a political order to provide or sustain its power. This, of course, appears to be tautological in the sense that Shils is arguing that when a system of power loses authority it loses its authority. It does so because *legitimacy* is equated solely with *authority* in Shils's sense of that term. If charisma means legitimacy and legitimacy means the acceptance of authority, then the failure of legitimacy is the failure of authority; substituting terms, the failure of authority is the failure of authority.

In addition, the equating of power with charisma does not explain the fact that some relatively powerful groups or institutions in a society do not appear to have much charisma: some gigantic corporations are relatively unknown and thus appear to have relatively little charisma. On the other hand, some relatively powerless individuals who have "presence," personality, and public appeal appear to have much more charisma. Thus, one of the most persistent problems in the fields of advertising and public relations is how to make the corporation known to a wider public. The economic and institutional power that a corporation has does not by itself confer charisma and legitimacy. Special techniques and processes of diffusion are required. The personalities that we and Shils have identified with the vulgarization of the term *charisma* are not necessarily powerful persons.

Shils, however, reverses himself and argues that tremendous centralized power, the awe and reverence inspired by powerful institutions, are not enough to confer legitimacy on a society, its government institutions, other central institutions, its class and status system, elites, occupational groups, and on the society itself. The power, awe, and reverence caused by power and the need for order *must* be moralized—that is, equated with moral order.[37] Thus, priests, religions, intellectuals, and scientists, as well as symbolic leaders, create symbolic systems, ideologies that confer moral order and consistency on the political power that, by itself, confers legitimacy—that is, charisma—to the system.

But society is stratified with respect to distance from the central sources of power and hence charisma. Distant groups and emergent groups do not have as much charisma as those close to the centralized power and institutions in society. Older ideologists are closer to the moral order of the society.[33] These newer ascendant groups, as well as some distant groups, attempt to appropriate charisma for their own purposes by denying deference to charisma-monopolizing groups, by developing ambivalence to established definitions of charisma, to its exponents, and to the political order itself. In extreme cases, such distant groups can reject the established order and its established forms of charisma.[39]

But if charisma is power, legitimacy, awe, and wonder and resides in the central values, institutions, and collectivities of the society itself, then this summary of Shils's argument states that charisma also resides in the opposition to each of the major central dimensions that contain it. A theory or concept that explains equally a phenomenon and its opposite explains nothing.

Shils makes the concept of charisma general and diffuse in equating it with centralized power and with legitimacy. In equating charisma with legitimacy, Shils apparently follows Parsons, who says, in *The Structure of Social Action*:

> The distinction between legitimacy and charisma can be stated in general terms as follows: Legitimacy is the narrower concept in that it is a quality imputed only to the norms of an order, not to persons, things or "imaginary" entities, and its reference is to the regulation of

> action, predominantly in its intrinsic aspects. Legitimacy is thus the *institutional* application or embodiment of charisma.[40]

If, however, *legitimacy* is, by definition, institutionalized *charisma*, then all voluntary obedience is by definition charismatic. Given the definition, there is no need to prove one is related to the other or to use both terms. By using both terms and the definition, Parsons, like Shils, is simply being tautological.

Shils also destroys whatever specific utility the concept may originally have had. In defining the concept specifically, in limiting it, and in specifying subtypes of charisma, Weber was able to apply specific concepts of charisma to particular historical and organizational contexts. He was thus able to treat the various concepts of charisma as independent factors to be counterpoised in analysis against concepts of power and authority in relationship to revolutionary and conservative movements in history. The concepts he used permitted a resolution of the problems he posed in historical and empirical research. The problems were not resolved by definition, nor were their solutions contained in his statement of the problems.

Finally, Shils, in his argument, suggests the diffusion of charisma throughout the society and through all of a society's major components. But he does not articulate the specific mechanisms by which such diffusion takes place. One can conclude only that, given the metaphysical need for intellectual order and the availability of political order, the supply generates its own demand by unknown metaphysical processes and that the demand in time elicits the supply. But since individuals and groups are differentially placed socially, economically, politically, and with reference to the available supply of transcendental and institutional charisma, these individuals and groups modify and manufacture their own charisma. But Shils does not specify these institutional processes.[41] Charisma appears to be a universal phenomenon, metaphysically available at all times and places, but one that adheres to all established, central, and powerful institutions of society, as well as to those individuals and movements that ultimately become powerful.

Charisma as a Psychological Concept

The psychologizing of the concept of charisma is self-consciously attempted and carried through most thoroughly and brilliantly by Donald McIntosh."[42] McIntosh is aware of the divergences between a sociological and psychological point of view. He is aware of Weber's rejection of the psychological point of view and is further aware of those aspects of Weber's work, especially in his treatment of charisma, that are amendable to psychoanalytic development. Yet he, in violation of Weber's caveats, chooses quite explicitly to make such extensions. In principle, one cannot be opposed to such extensions of an idea into another field, if such work helps to promote clarification. There is danger, however, that the stretching of the concept, in this case of charisma, obscures the problem that evoked the original concept and obfuscates the central issues that are the focus of analysis in the original field.

McIntosh emphasizes the idea of the extraordinary quality of charisma and locates this extraordinariness in magic, the belief in the power of magic as embodied in primitive religions. He emphasizes that attitudes toward the supernatural are the source of all charisma, whether magical or prophetic, and states—incorrectly, we believe, but somewhat like Shils—the idea that "the legitimacy of all authority rests on attitudes toward the supernatural."[43] In doing so, he does not, however, discuss Weber's concepts of warrior charisma, primitive military charisma, or political charisma as exhibited in ancient China. He does not mention hereditary or lineage charisma, nor does he mention the charisma of office. The revolutionary nature of charisma is briefly mentioned but then dropped. Charisma thus becomes virtually a pure psychological state. Thus, McIntosh states, "The outstanding quality of charisma is its enormous power, resting on the intensity and strength of the forces that lie unconscious in every human psyche," and "Charisma is an unconscious force which has been displaced outward."[44] The bulk of McIntosh's work is thus an effort to demonstrate the basic psychological components and dimensions of charisma.

Again, if one were to accept the notion that charisma is purely a psychological state, the definition of its components would be perfectly acceptable. McIntosh, however, goes beyond this construction of a psychological phenomenology of charisma. He finds, like Shils, charismatic components in traditional and rational forms of domination; in each form, he finds the psychological correspondences of charisma in that form of domination. Because he does not distinguish between the various types and subtypes of charisma, he does not distinguish between the differing functions and forms of charisma for each system of domination. Nor does he deal with the tensions between the forms of charisma and the various forms of order. Thus, he argues, like Shils, that charisma "for Weber is the legitimating principle behind all authority."[45] We find no evidence for this statement in the corpus of Weber's work. Such a notion would invalidate Weber's entire work on bureaucracy and on the rational-legal form of legitimacy. To be sure, traditionalism may have charismatic components; that is, the traditional leader may be a descendant of a charismatic hero whose charisma has become routinized. However, the basis for the legitimacy of traditionalism is not charisma but the sanctification of usage. Legal authority is a major basis of legitimacy and produces a charismatic element—the charisma of office. Legal authority, according to Weber, is not, however, based upon charisma.

But the converse is true: charisma of office is possible only because it rests on legal and traditional authority. McIntosh thus makes essentially the same error as Shils: he treats charisma as an undifferentiated trait (for McIntosh, a psychological trait), universalizes it by ignoring its specific forms, and then posits the generic psychological form as the basis for completely different kinds of institutions, potential orders, and forms of legitimacy. Thus, McIntosh says, not unlike Shils, that "charisma is a universal human experience,"[46] an idea that we find nowhere in Weber. Such a statement, whether or not found in Weber, would lead us to expect all social actions, institutions, social movements, and forms of legitimacy are deeply imbued with charisma. Such an argument would force us to ignore all noncharismatic types of action. Moreover, it would conclusively prove that the extraordinariness of charisma is ordinary. Because of this remarkable inversion, the universalization of the extraordinary, all elements in society must be imbued with the extraordinary. This again is similar to Shils's equating of legitimacy with charisma and to his contention that all forms of authority, elites, dominant institutions, upper-level prestige groups, the nation, the state, and the "people" are charismatic.

Yet the foregoing arguments are only preliminary to McIntosh's major argument. That contention is:

> On Weber's account, when authority has a religious justification, the leader himself may or may not possess charisma. What is crucial is that his authority is backed or validated by a divinity. Secularization must thus involve more than a change in vocabulary and imagery through which the charisma of the leader is described and understood. In addition, the secular equivalent of a legitimating divinity must appear.[47]

and:

> But once it is grasped that the modern state is legitimated by a secular charisma fully as powerful and effective as the previous religious charisma, and entirely compatible with the new institutional forms, the Weberian opposition between charisma and reason appears to disappear.[48]

To us, it would not seem difficult to accept the notion that secularization would require a different, nonreligious kind of charisma. Weber himself was aware that secular, political charisma could exist in the modern, secular state:

> In times of great public excitement, charismatic leaders may emerge even in solidly bureaucratized parties, as was demonstrated by Roosevelt's campaign in 1912. If there is a "hero," he will endeavor to break the technician's hold over the party by imposing plebiscitary designation and possibly by changing the whole machinery of nomination. Such an eruption of charisma, of course, always faces the resistance of the normally predominant pros, especially of the bosses who control and finance the party and maintain its routine operations, whose tools the candidates usually are.[49]

Weber discusses the necessity of monetary contributors and sponsors. He then states:

> The regular manager and political professional, the boss or the party secretary, can expect their financial support only if he firmly controls the party machine. Hence every eruption of charisma is also a financial threat to the regular organization. It happens quite frequently that the warring bosses or other managers of the competing parties combine in defense of their common economic interests to prevent the rise of charismatic leaders, who would be independent of the regular party apparatus. As a rule, the

> party organization easily succeeds in this castration of charisma. This will also remain true of the United States, even in the face of the plebiscitary presidential primaries, since in the long run the continuity of professional operations is tactically superior to emotional worship. Only extraordinary conditions can bring about the triumph of charisma over the organization.[50]

In addition, Weber attributed charisma to Gladstone,[51] a special form to Kurt Eisner,[52] and to modern business Maecenases.[53]

Carl Friedrich has objected to the application of the term *charisma* to any phenomenon other than a religious one. He bases his objection on the first use of the term *charisma* in the New Testament. He argues that to broaden the term would be to combine such "genuine" leaders as Jesus, Calvin, Buddha, and Luther with such profane leaders as Lenin, Mussolini, and Hitler.[54]

While such a combination might be grotesque to a religious person, Weber recognized the possibility. He argued that his use of the term implied neither a metaphysical validity in the attribution of charisma nor approval or disapproval of such attribution. All that mattered was that followers accepted the claim of unusual powers, gifts, mana, of a charismatic leader.

The Application of the Concept to Modern Politics

A number of scholars, using this Weberian notion of acceptance of charismatic claims, have found it easy to find modern charismatic leaders.[55] We are less willing to make such designations without first attempting to reformulate the concept of charisma as it applies to the modern world.

Certainly modern "charismatic" leaders have claimed universal power because they have allegedly embodied the genius of the "race," have concentrated in themselves the spirit or essence of an earlier, more glorious period in a nation's history, or have claimed to be uniquely qualified to understand the dialectic or the laws of history and thus to bring the future into being. But secular charisma as an abstract, generalized, universal quality has exactly the same conceptual weaknesses as the conception of an undifferentiated religious charisma. Some secular charisma is revolutionary, some is conservative. Some secular charisma can be based upon personal qualities, and some on particular roles in organizations. Some may appear to be irrational; others while appearing to be irrational are based upon rational calculation, bureaucratic organization, and organized staff work. But McIntosh, somewhat like Shils, only deals with those forms of charisma that are attached to the state, corporate bodies, and established institutions or highly organized social movements. While the whole burden of his essay suggests the "irrational" psychological bases of the attribution of charisma by followers, he does not examine, though he implies through his illustrations, that charisma is evoked by rational bureaucracies and the staffs of political and economic elites. While the charismatic followers may see substitutes for personal relationships (paternal or maternal ego identification), the surrogate personal relationships are offered on an impersonal basis by centralized, bureaucratic, rational staffs and elites.

McIntosh makes an important criticism of the application of Weber's sociology of religion to the modern world. He argues, as we have noted, that the secularization of religion means that religious charisma is no longer important in a world that is no longer religious and that a secular charisma replaces the older religious charisma.[56]

Weber was at least partly aware of these phenomena. He argued in all his late works[57] that the process of intellectual and formal rationalization and the "disenchantment of the world" increasingly made the world seem senseless, and this senselessness led to a quest for the irrational, for "experience," and for sterile excitation. However, Weber did not argue, except in the previously cited references, that such senselessness led to charisma.

In making this criticism, McIntosh neglects to make a more serious criticism of the applicability of charisma to the modern world. That criticism rests upon the manipulation of charisma by rational, impersonal, established groups. McIntosh seems partially aware of this point when he argues:

> This point may also be made with respect to other institutions besides the modern state. The business corporation has reached the most advanced form of rational organization in the United States. Precisely those firms in the forefront of this process have sought, more or less successfully, to legitimate their role among the members of the firm by fostering ties of identification and loyalty similar to those which legitimate the nation-state. We seem to be dealing here also with a secularized charisma.[58]

One can agree that modern corporations attempt to legitimate themselves in the eyes of their employees and foster ties of identification and loyalty. Whether this is charisma is a separate question. Modern corporations may or may not claim extraordinary powers in the specific sense denoted by the term *charisma*. Very few are radical in the sense of pure charisma, and the evocation of charisma is rational, planned, and due to the operation of a bureaucratic staff.

Ultimately, McIntosh sees secular charisma in social groups as "ego identifications among the members and superego identifications of the members with a leader . . . or, we would add, a personalized institution."[59] Given this definition, one could argue then, as he does, that all successful group socialization is charisma. He concludes:

> This formulation suggests the position adopted here: that in general a stable order within a social group must

> depend on sentiments of legitimacy springing from superego identifications. On this view, a stable non-legitimate order would be possible only when imposed coercively by one group over another, or for a group which operates inside the framework of a larger legitimate order. If the possibilities of identification with an institution are taken into account, non-legitimate denomination may be rarer than Weber thought.[60]

McIntosh, unlike Shils, concludes that legitimacy is achieved when an elite group or would-be elite group succeeds in causing a subordinate group to identify with and accept its dominators. Whether this type of legitimacy is charisma is the crucial question. McIntosh appears to be using Weber's definition of *legitimacy*, but he, like Shils, seems to equate all legitimacy with all charisma.

The only process of legitimation specified by McIntosh, apart from "fostering," is that of identification. The psychological process of identification with the master by the subordinate is, of course, important in understanding the psychology and sociology of secular charisma; but processes of identification, as social processes, are equally important when organized, ordered, conceived, and planned by noncharismatic leadership. Thus, the processes of identification are broader than the processes of charisma or of the routinization of charisma.

In a specifically secular, modern world composed of large-scale states, business organizations, political parties, and mass media, all operating over vast social and psychological distances, the processes leading to identification, legitimacy, and charisma are somewhat more differentiated, specific, and complicated than can be subsumed in any one term or concept. The broadening of each term, as done by Shils and McIntosh, so that each subsumes the others, leads neither to clarity nor to understanding of the modern world. Rather, the breakdown of conceptual distinctions leads only to a theoretical circularity wherein each term dissolves into each other, with little reference to what occurs in the empirical world.

Modern Charisma

Of all the recent popular definitions of *charisma*, perhaps the best one is *political presence.*[61] Some political leaders seem to have the ability to project themselves directly, clearly, and immediately through the mass media in images that seem larger than life. They can dramatize issues, project sincerity, induce suspension of disbelief, and attract personal followers and distant supporters. They can become the objects of intense admiration.

In the theater, cinema, and television, such qualities have been called stage presence or star quality. At various times, the embodiment of these qualities in an individual has been called sex appeal or personal magnetism. Such personal qualities refer not only to the ability to project oneself over larger distances than are usually encompassed by the physical presence of the actor but, in so doing, to project a larger, more powerful image than mere physical presence suggests.[62] Professional athletes, too, due to the massive televising of sports, can become "charismatic" heroes in the warrior image—especially with the aid of movie, television, or commercial merchandising exposure.

Such presence has been an object of self-rationalization in the development of "personal magnetism" in salesmanship, in institutional leadership, and in interpersonal relationships. But it is not charisma, as we hope to demonstrate in the following pages.

The concept of charisma as used by Weber appears to be historically limited and far removed from popular or political stage presence. It appears to be limited primarily, but not exclusively, to discussions of ancient civilizations.

The broadening and generalization of the concept of charisma in modern society is not inaccurate, in and of itself, since language derives its meaning by usage and convention, and terms and concepts change meaning over time. However, the changes in meaning sometimes obscure specific theoretical problems, the answers to which might be useful in the analysis of the worlds referred to by such language and concepts. The dimensions of the concept of charisma that are obscured by the broadening of the concept are fundamental. These, as we have noted perhaps too often, are: (1) the personal nature of charisma, (2) its radical (or revolutionary) nature, (3) and its irrationality. Ultimately, the modern usage of the term *charisma* refers to an ability to project an image of a direct, warm, or exciting and sincere, engaging, personal, or unofficial "human" persona. The very term *project* implies, in the modern world, that these qualities are presented from a distance. The personality projected is a personality that can be projected despite the existence of the vast social, physical, and psychological distances that prevail in modern mass and bureaucratic societies. Modern mass communication uses charisma to overcome these distances. Modern charisma entails the ability, whether planned or unplanned, to use or be used by the mass media in such a way as to convey a sense of immediacy that appears to negate the very media that require its uses.

Karl Loewenstein and Reinhard Bendix have specifically recognized the importance of the mass media in modern "charismatic" politics. Bendix writes:

> Modern means of publicity can give such leadership all the appearance of charisma: the singular gifts of the leader and the unquestioning devotion of his followers. But such appearances can be misleading.[63]

Loewenstein states:

> In a closed and authority-directed society, in which the organs of propaganda are controlled by the supposed holder of charisma and his subservient following, the mass media can produce a reinforcement and deepening of an originally spurious but artificially promoted charisma attributed to the ruler.[64]

Loewenstein thus argues that "in earlier times" charisma had to be genuine to have lasting effects and that in modern times it is spurious and artificial. He argues, as does Bendix, that genuine charisma in modern times may be a rare event.

We agree entirely with Loewenstein that the "genuine" charisma of the ancient (pre-Cartesian) world rarely exists in the modern era. We also have indicated that Weber was aware of the existence of spurious or, in his words, "demagogic charisma" (in the case of Kurt Eisner). Because of changes in the mass media and in social and political structures covered by politics, the distinctly modern form of charisma is spurious charisma.

While we call this modern form pseudocharisma, we recognize that genuine charisma may be possible in the modern world, but that the most frequent form of modern charisma is not *charisma* in the original Weberian sense of the term. When Bendix uses the phrase "the appearance of charisma," he properly suggests that much of modern charisma is not genuine.[65] Karl Loewenstein makes this point even more strongly:

> No one familiar with the mechanism of his [de Gaulle's] plebiscites will have much doubt that what zealous legend-builders may represent as charisma is actually the result of extremely skillful manipulation of propaganda techniques.[66]

Loewenstein goes on to argue that radio intensified the personal magnetism of Franklin D. Roosevelt because of the special quality of his voice and oratory. However, he argues that daily presentation of the would-be charismatic leader via mass media in an open society disenchants the public.[67]

Modern charisma imparts to *social relations*, to use Merton's term, a form of pseudo-*Gemeinschaft*[68] that, by the very nature of the media and the social order that frame it, makes genuine *Gemeinschaft* impossible. *Charismatic leadership* in the classic sense of the term meant direct, immediate social relations; it was not conveyed by indirect, mediating, or intervening agencies.

Thus, *charisma* as used in the modern, undifferentiated sense of the term takes for granted the existence of a large-scale mass society and psychological distances that are both created and appear to be overcome by highly organized networks of communication and by social and economic organizations that are themselves part of the very structure of mass bureaucratic societies.

David Apter, in his study of political leadership in Ghana,[69] attempts to retain the notion of personal leadership by suggesting a two-stage process of leadership. Thus, Nkrumah as a political leader had a small personal cult of followers, who, Apter claims, stood between him and a mass following. The entire study suggests the use of conscious cultivation of an image of personality by Nkrumah and his staff. Stuart Schram[70] similarly suggests the conscious manipulation of a cult of personality in the creation of Mao as a charismatic leader.

Robert Tucker[71] presents a convincing image of Lenin as a powerful personality, but does not inquire into the mechanics or techniques by which Lenin achieved his effects. Richard Fagan[72] advances Fidel Castro as a charismatic hero, but again does not inquire into the mechanics, the media and stage effects by which such results are achieved. Ann Ruth and Dorothy Willner[73] detail some of the psychological and personal methods used by modern charismatic political figures, but do not emphasize the organizational and media devices.

Charisma adds a veneer of personality to the impersonal relations that govern urban, market, bureaucratic, and mass technological societies. To the extent that such a veneer is the result of planned, rationally calculated programs, and to the extent that such a veneer is what is vulgarly referred to as charisma, the personal elements projected in modern charisma may be viewed as fraudulent. The concept of genuine charisma, as used by Weber, referred to actual personal relationships between a leader and his followers. The mass media substitute symbolic social relationships for actual ones.[74] To the extent that the evocation of charisma is the result of rational calculation, and that planning may create the image of a warm, sincere, emotional or "genuine" personality, it violates the original criterion that charisma is irrational or nonrational.

Every study of modern charisma but two suggests the rational planning and calculation of the appearance of charisma. The two exceptions are Fagan's and Tucker's, which, as we have indicated, do not inquire into the central issue. The case of Nkrumah is especially enlightening. Some theorists (for example, Apter) argue that Nkrumah was a charismatic leader who lost his charisma when he tried to shift to parliamentary tactics. Others argue that Nkrumah was a genuine charismatic leader who simply lost his charisma, and still others (like Runciman[75]) claim that Nkrumah never had genuine charisma. Charisma would seem, according to Runciman, to reside in Nkrumah's political party, not in Nkrumah.

Apter, as we have indicated, provides sufficient data in his own study to demonstrate the rationality, impersonality, and institutionalized aspects of Nkrumah's regime. He also provides evidence that Nkrumah was personally appealing and popular and that some followers might have regarded him with the awe and reverence that might have led to his characterization as a charismatic leader. Once it is clear that modern charisma is not necessarily genuine or pure *charisma*, in Weber's sense of the term, then these contradictions disappear. Nkrumah achieved the *effects* of charisma partly by rationally calculated means. He succeeded in some cases in creating a charismatic response, while simultaneously achieving mere popularity and negative responses. The fact that he was not successful in maintaining his charisma may be due less to the failure of charisma than to the failure of his policies, strategy, and planning.

Modern charismatic leaders may rationally select irrational themes, motifs, and values to personify those themes and values and a sense of pseudo-*Gemeinschaft* to distant publics. The managers of large-scale political parties, bureaucracies, advertising and media agencies will often select an individual who seems peculiarly able to project the desirable qualities to a "target population." The selection of a leader who embodies these desired qualities is thus the result of rational decision making by formally rational bureaucratic or political staffs whose very existence precludes the spontaneous self-selective nature and self-discovery of charisma. In addition, the development of the qualities that project personality images through the mass media is a result of product planning, of rational and systematic media strategies, of political market research, and of the training of voice, gestures, drama, and makeup.[76]

The development of modern "scientific" politics includes the rational, planned search for a star—that is, a "charismatic" leader. Public opinion research, audience testing, and pretesting of issues, themes, symbols, and slogans for their salience and valence, as well as the ability of various potential charismatic leaders to embody or project the selected themes, are by now standard political methodology.

Thus, to a large extent, the modern "charismatic" leader is given speech and dramatic lessons and is surrounded by elaborately planned ceremonies and rites. Parades are presented in settings likely to induce the sense of excitement or warmth and to emphasize personality. A sense of awe and mystery is evoked by the use of emblems and symbols—the swastika, the fasces, the red star, the hammer and sickle, the enlarged portrait. Some "charismatic" leaders will, after achieving a degree of prominence, demonstrate their larger-than-life humanity by showing themselves in carefully arranged situations to be human and personable. Others will emphasize the awe and mystery by maintaining distance and an attitude of formality toward their followers. Lighting, camera angles, makeup, distance, and camera focus as well as, at times, face-lifting and other cosmetic and illusion-producing stagecraft help to produce "charisma."

The procedures employed are no different from those used in the creation of movie, theatrical, or television stars. The image of the movie star is enhanced by public relations, press releases, planted personal anecdotes, managed television interviews, and photographic posters. But a central characteristic of all these techniques is that they are planned and thus represent formal rationality. For our purpose, it matters little whether the modern charismatic leader makes himself over, thus using himself as the medium for image projection, or the political planners select and use a leader for such purposes. The important element, as related to the concept of pure charisma, is that rational planning is involved rather than the direct imputation of supernatural power or the divine gift of grace by followers without the planned intervention of rational political managers and staff. In the Weberian sense, the pure charismatic leader does not worry about his image, for his image is, to him, his reality. That reality is an attribute of God or of a power beyond himself. He need not calculate the effect of his imagery on his actions, because the outcome of his actions are not the result of his own efforts but rather the effect of the power that possesses him. Failure is not the result of his conscious decision making but the effect of his failure to retain the power that possesses him.

Modern charisma, in addition, rests upon the conscious selection of themes, appeals, slogans, and imagery that is based upon the systematic study of audiences, target populations, constituencies, and strategic publics. Such planning of appeals may be a result of a political outlook that convinces a leader or leadership group that they possess knowledge of the secrets of political practice or the techniques of measuring the importance and range of political appeals. Theoretical rationality in the practice of political arts is a distinctly modern phenomenon, emerging with Machiavelli and achieving full application with the French Revolution and the study of the Revolution by Marx, early Marxists, and Lenin. American public relations and advertising based on Freudian and behaviorist psychology give scientific rigor to such efforts, as does the science of public opinion polling.[77]

This, of course, does not mean that charismatic leadership is equivalent to popularity. Even pseudocharisma attempts to produce an attitude of awe and wonder or extraordinariness. Some modern fascist political leaders, basing much of their theory on Marxian teaching, carried out the rational exploration of irrationality to previously unheard-of limits. But, by now, the principles of the employment of personality and pseudo-*Gemeinschaft* in politics are so general that it is extremely difficult to conceive of a modern political or social movement, democratic or totalitarian, without a "charismatic leader" to personify it.

Not all political leaders are charismatic or even attempt to present charismatic images (excluding, of course, the charisma of office). The decision to attempt to project a charismatic image by a political leader may rest on his or his staff's estimate of the leader's personal resources, his potential following, other resources, his milieu, or the political situation.

In the underdeveloped world, highly sophisticated, European-trained political leaders adopt the masks of charismatic leadership in order to create a national consciousness among a populace that under colonial administration had been fragmented by localism, tribalism, and the absence of tradition of citizenship and a viable public opinion or of a national political or moral community. Such charisma becomes a device by which the charismatic leader attempts not only to construct the idea of a nation for his followers, but also a national bureaucracy and state machinery as well as the foundations for a political tradition and a nationwide public opinion. Thus, the appearance of charisma is often a screen for the construction of national political forms used by leaders who often have to create the appearance of irrationality in societies where personal, irrational forms and symbols are the only meaningful styles of communication.[78] This, however, is not too different from what takes place in advanced Western societies in which, from time to time, the response to impersonality, rationality, incomprehensibility, and crises force national political leaders to adopt various styles of irrationality as a screen behind which highly sophisticated, rational political programs are presented.

In modern bureaucratic government and politics, an image of charisma may be evoked—using all the aforementioned techniques—in which the images of bureaucratic impersonality, dehumanization, economic exploitation, political corruption, etc., are raised as counterimages to justify a claim to power by a reformer or aspirant to power. In such cases, the reformer may project all the characteristics of personality, anti-institutionalism, or radicalism, but he aspires to a position in the establishment and usually seeks it by using the established machinery of election or selection. He does so with a political or elective apparatus that is part of the ongoing institutional machinery of the society. Beyond this, such evocations of charisma are usually rationally planned and calculated, despite the appearance of spontaneity and personality that is projected as the manifest content of the political message.

Finally, such reformers usually do not seek to reconstitute radically the political order or even the bases for legitimacy of a political order. They usually seek to restore, reform, or implement the original institutional or normative forms of an established order. Nevertheless, many, if not most, reform movements attempt to use charismatic leaders, persons who symbolize youth, honesty, energy, and incorruptibility as counterimages to the political machines they seek to destroy, reform, or replace.

The employment of such charismatic leadership by political and bureaucratic organizations implies another contradiction between the concept of pure charisma and the reality of modern charismatic leadership. As indicated, pure charisma is revolutionary in its political stance. Modern rational charisma becomes a set of techniques and devices used by rational leaders and planners to both transcend and to veil the use of rationality in political action. *Charisma* in such a context means the use of selected techniques regardless of ultimate goals or political values. Modern charismatic leadership can be revolutionary or nonrevolutionary. It can be instrumental to liberal, conservative, or reactionary traditions and goals. Modern charisma is no longer connected to the original radical, deinstitutionalizing forces attributed to it by Weber.

Another key issue in the contemporary application of the concept of charisma to modern society is the conditions under which charisma may arise. Blau has argued that Weber did not adequately specify the conditions under which charisma occurs. He states that Weber's theory of charisma

> encompasses only the historical processes that lead from charismatic movements to increasing rationalization

> and does not include an analysis of the historical conditions that give rise to charismatic eruptions in the social structure.[79]

This argument has been repeated by a number of scholars. David Apter cites the following conditions under which charisma develops:

> It is likely to arise where there exists an attenuated normative situation which, although it may not challenge pre-existing norms directly, allows new combinations, where behavioral situations show a more random basis for the selection of normative alternatives than is presupposed by an institutionalized acceptance of any one particular set, traditional or modern.[80]

Weber made essentially the same point when he argued that charisma arises in times of crisis:

> The "natural" leaders—in times of psychic, physical, economic, ethical, religious, political distress—have been neither office holders nor incumbents of an "occupation" in the present sense of the word, that is, men who have acquired expert knowledge and who serve for remuneration. The natural leaders in distress have been holders of specific gifts of the body and spirit; and these gifts have been believed to be supernatural, not accessible to everybody. The concept of the "charisma" is here used in a completely "value-neutral" sense.[81]

Conclusions

We have sought to demonstrate that the concept of charismatic leadership as developed by Weber is of little use to the analysis of modern political and social movements. This is not because the modern movements are secular and the older ones were religious. The Weberian concept was originally applied to highly personal social movements that were not only personal but were revolutionary and irrational. The modern world, at least at the political level, is based upon political machinery that is geared to mass-scale operation. Impersonality, formal rationality, and bureaucracy are central to the very operation of contemporary society. The scale of mass politics involves the participation in politics by millions. These millions are not always socialized to stable political traditions and to institutions that have become routinized and legalized. The very size, impersonality, and fragility of mass society produces crises and stresses that can be exploited on a mass scale by means of the rational use of the forms and styles of irrationality by leaders who are rational, at least in their decision to employ such devices of irrationality. This is a possibility that Weber did not fully foresee. Weber saw mass democracy only as related to the occasional irrationality of coffeehouse intellectuals and the quest for irrational experience by youth who could not cope with the extremes of rationality, impersonality, and disenchantment that a fully rationalized image of the world entailed. He also saw, as indicated above, the use of pseudocharisma by reformers of caesaropapists and machine demagogues in mass-political democracies.[82] But he did not foresee the systematic use of the appearances of charisma as a continuous, rationally calculated strategy by the staffs and agencies of bureaucratic and political machines and elites in large-scale mass bureaucratic societies.

In short, he failed to foresee the "rational" political movements based on the systematic exploitation of irrationality. He did, however, see that the quest for a deeper, meaningful, and irrational emotional and spiritual existence could lead to new forms of totalitarianism.

While Weber's original concept of pure charisma may not be applicable to most modern political movements, the recent correction of this deficiency in Weber's work may be even more inadequate, for treating charisma as a free-floating universal element or as purely personal or psychological attribute—almost as a form of dramatic presence—beclouds or minimizes the very contradictions between pure charisma and the modern world that make the original concept inadequate to the modern world.

It is the contradiction between the impersonality of social relations in the modern world and the use of images of personality that is central to the political processes of the modern world. Similarly, it is the rational exploitation of irrationality that has been a major theme in political and social movements in the modern world since the French Revolution and possibly even the earlier Counter-Reformation. Finally, it is increasingly true that modern establishments, regardless of political orientation, use revolutionary symbolism, slogans, and appeals whether or not the employment of such devices is aimed at radical social change. Thus, a concept that focuses attention on the tension between political means and ends, motives and practices is of particular usefulness in the analysis of modern political and social movements.

If the concept of pure charisma is irrelevant to the exploration of these tensions, the use of charisma as a personality trait avoids focusing on critical modern political processes. It also avoids focusing attention on those substantive issues, interests, ideologies, and interest and ideological groups, classes, and elites that are hidden or hide behind the personality screens of charisma. Treating charisma as a universal, and thus abstracting it from its particular historical, social, and economic context, diverts attention from the use of charisma as a screen for specific ideological or material interests by relevant interest groups. In addition, the reduction of particular historic forms to their alleged metaphysical essence automatically bestows a kind of universalism to those forms. Thus, the fraudulent becomes the real, and the use of the concept can help to bestow legitimacy to groups that would claim power on the basis of their rational manipulation of symbols of charisma.

To avoid these reifications, we propose the term *pseudocharisma* in much the same manner that Merton has used pseudo-*Gemeinschaft.*[83] *Pseudocharisma* simply means the employment of the means, the imagery, the appearance of charismatic leadership as a rational device by which rationally calculating leadership groups attempt to achieve or maintain power. A major strategy is the selection or creation of a leader who appears to possess the forms and styles of an extraordinary man. Such selection and assumptions, however, are rationally induced. Appeals are made to ultimate and irrational values that the leader purportedly symbolizes. But the leader, in addition, conveys or is made to appear to convey a direct, personal contact that transcends the distance between himself and his followers. The concept of pseudocharisma suggests that charisma is a series of devices that serve other goals, purposes, and interests. In pointing out the manufactured appearances in pseudocharisma, the concept focuses upon the motives, interests, and rationality or irrationality that may lie behind these devices and underscores the extent to which the symbols and images are consciously fabricated. It would focus then on the means of fabrication and the ends for which they are fabricated.

The focus on the fabrication of charisma as a means of concealing or obscuring other, hidden ends by an interest group leads—in fact, forces—the analyst to consider the nature of the underlying interests, goals, and ends that are the latent content of the pseudocharismatic message. It necessitates probing into the relationship between various levels of meanings, latent and manifest, and motivations contained in modern pseudocharismatic leadership. It entails the analysis of the policy implications of messages that apparently have little direct relevance to policy.

Such a program does not necessarily preclude the possibility that pure charisma might exist. But one can only establish whether in fact pure charisma does exist by inquiring into the means and the intentions that govern the attribution of charisma by followers, leaders, sponsors, and supporters. Beyond this, the explanation of the indicated ends and means allows one to ascertain the specific content of pseudocharismatic leadership movements at specific times and places and their relationships to ongoing historical social structures.

Nor does such a program preclude the possibility that genuine or spurious charismatic leaders are capable of inducing a sense of awe and reverence in a given population. But when this occurs, the research should focus on more than the aforementioned techniques of evocation of charisma. It should focus on the qualities of followers who attribute charisma to a real or pseudocharismatic leader. Specifically, what are their class and status positions? What sense of crises, tensions, and alienation do they respond to? What specific social, economic, or political conditions give rise to charisma both as leadership and response? What aspects of a charismatic message are salient and attractive? Finally, what specific needs does charisma meet among those who accept specific charismatic leadership?

Notes

1. Edward Shils, "Charisma, Order, and Status," *American Sociological Review* 30 (April 1965), 199-313, at 201.

2. Max Weber, *Economy and Society: An Outline of Interpretive Sociology*, eds. Guenther Roth and Claus Wittich, 3 vols. (New York: Bedminster Press, 1968), 241-42.

3. *Economy and Society,* 1112-13.

4. Max Weber, "The Sociology of Charismatic Authority," in *From Max Weber: Essays in Sociology,* eds. and trans. Hans H. Gerth and C. Wright Mills (New York: Oxford University Press, 1946), 248-49.

5. Max Weber, *Ancient Judaism*, eds. and trans. Hans Gerth and Don Martindale (New York: Free Press, 1952), 290-91.

6. *Economy and Society,* 440.

7. Max Weber, "The Sociology of Charismatic Authority," in *From Max Weber,* 251-52.

8. *Economy and Society,* 242-43.

9. The complete statement referred to here is perhaps Weber's most general expression of his approach to the sociology of knowledge. It is: "Not ideas, but material and ideal interests, directly govern men's conduct. Yet very frequently the 'world images' that have been created by 'ideas' have, like switchmen, determined the tracks along which action has been pushed by the dynamic of interest." (Max Weber, "The Social Psychology of the World Religions," in *From Max Weber,* 280).

10. *Economy and Society,* 1120.

11. *Economy and Society*, 248-49; 1139.

12. Weber, "The Social Psychology of the World Religions," in *From Max Weber*, 297; *Economy and Society*, 246-54; 1121-24.

13. *Economy and Society*, 1136.

14. *Economy and Society*, 248.

15. *Economy and Society*, 440.

16. *Economy and Society*, 1112-13.

17. *Economy and Society*, 1113.

18. *Economy and Society*, 243-44.

19. *Economy and Society*, 244.

20. Max Weber, "The Sociology of Charismatic Authority," in *From Max Weber*, 250.

21. *Economy and Society*, 1116.

22. Weber, "The Sociology of Charismatic Authority," in *From Max Weber*, 248.

23. *Economy and Society*, 242.

24. Edward Shils states that Weber's "historicist concern to delineate the unique features of 'modern society' hindered his perception of the deeper and more permanent features of all societies." Shils, at 203. He further states at 213 that charisma is more "complicated" and more "protean" in the modern industrial society. Concerning Weber, Shils comments, "He did not consider the more widely dispersed, unintense operation of the charismatic element in corporate

bodies governed by the rational-legal type of authority. . . . Weber had a pronounced tendency to segregate the object of attributed charisma, to see it almost exclusively in its most concentrated and intense forms, and to disregard the possibility of its dispersed and attenuated existence. He tended indeed to deny the possibility that charisma can become an integral element in the process of secular institutionalization. (This might well be part of Weber's more general tendency to see the modern world as *entzaubert,* as devoid of any belief in the possibility of genuine charisma.)" Shils, at 202. A major premise for Shils is that "institutionalized" charisma exists in the modern world.

25. Shils, 201.

26. *Ibid.*

27. *Ibid.*, 205.

28. *Ibid.*, 204-13.

29. *Ibid.*, 206.

30. *Ibid.*, 203, n. 7.

31. *Ibid.*, 203-04.

32. *Ibid.*, 201.

33. *Ibid.*, 202.

34. *Ibid.*, 207.

35. *Ibid.*, 204.

36. *Ibid.*, 206.

37. *Ibid.*, 207.

38. *Ibid.*, 210.

39. *Ibid.*, 210, 212.

40. Talcott Parsons, *The Structure of Social Action* (New York: Free Press, 1968), 669.

41. Claude Ake makes this criticism of the concept of charisma as used by Weber, Shils, Wallerstein, and Apter: "One will have to insist on an explanation of the process by which the masses identify with a particular leader in an atmosphere in which parochial loyalties largely determine the leader with whom the individual identifies. Unfortunately the theory of charismatic legitimation says little about this process and this is why it is so difficult to relate it to phenomenal experience." And he concludes, "Our critique has aimed to show that the theory of charismatic legitimation is still too incoherent to merit serious consideration as a realistic response to the problem of political integration." Claude Ake, "Charismatic Legitimation and Political Integration," *Comparative Studies of Society and History* 9 (October 1966), 8, 12.

42. "Weber and Freud: On the Nature and Sources of Authority," *American Sociological Review* 35 (October 1970), 901-11.

43. McIntosh, 902.

44. *Ibid.*, 902, 903.

45. *Ibid.*, 909.

46. *Ibid.*

47. *Ibid.*

48. *Ibid.*, 910.

49. *Economy and Society*, 1132.

50. *Ibid.*

51. *Economy and Society*, 1132-33.

52. *Economy and Society*, 242.

53. Max Weber, "The Protestant Sects and the Spirit of Capitalism," in *From Max Weber*, 309.

54. Carl Friedrich, "Political Leadership and the Problem of the Charismatic Power," *Journal of Politics* 23 (February 1961), 15.

55. David Apter, "Nkrumah, Charisma, and the Coup," *Daedalus* 97 (Summer 1968), 757-92; Reinhard Bendix and Guenther Roth, *Scholarship and Partisanship: Essays on Max Weber* (Berkeley: University of California Press, 1971), ch. 9; Richard Fagan, "Charismatic Authority and the Leadership of Fidel Castro," *Western Political Quarterly* 18 (June 1965), 275-84; W. G. Runciman, "Charismatic Legitimacy and One-Party Rule in Ghana," *Archives Europennes de Sociologie* 4 (1963), 148-65; Stuart Schram, "Mao Tse-tung as a Charismatic Leader," *Asian Survey* 2 (June 1967), 383-88; Robert Tucker, "The Theory of Charismatic Leadership," *Daedalus* 97 (Summer 1968), 731-56; Ann Ruth Willner and Dorothy Willner, "The Rise and Role of Charismatic Leaders," *Annals of the American Academy of Political and Social Science* 358 (March 1965), 77-89.

56. McIntosh, 910.

57. We interpret this argument as being the major thrust of his "Social Psychology of the World Religions," "Religious Rejections of

the World and Their Directions," "Science as a Vocation," and "Politics as a Vocation," in *From Max Weber.*

58. McIntosh, 910.

59. *Ibid.*, 911. A similar emphasis on identification and the need for transcendence with much less emphasis on the psychological dynamics (Freudian) is presented in John Marcus, "Transcendence and Charisma," *Western Political Quarterly* 14 (June 1961), 236-41. Marcus tends to combine Shils's emphasis on transcendence from the immediate and ordinary with Freudian psychological process.

60. McIntosh, 911.

61. Anthony Lewis, "A Strayed Candidate," *New York Times*, September 16, 1972, 29.

62. Edgar Morin, *The Stars* (New York: Grove Press, 1960).

63. Bendix and Roth, 172.

64. Karl Loewenstein, *Max Weber's Political Ideas in the Perspective of Our Time* (Amherst: University of Massachusetts Press, 1966), 86.

65. Bendix and Roth, 172.

66. Loewenstein, 84.

67. *Ibid.*, 85-86.

68. Robert Merton, Marjorie Fiske, and Alberta Curtis, *Mass Persuasion* (New York: Harper, 1946).

69. Apter, "Nkrumah, Charisma, and the Coup."

70. Schram, "Mao Tse-tung as a Charismatic Leader."

71. Tucker, "The Theory of Charismatic Leadership."

72. Fagan, "Charismatic Authority and the Leadership of Fidel Castro."

73. Ann Ruth Willner and Dorothy Willner, "The Rise and Role of Charismatic Leaders."

74. For a discussion of symbolic leaders and symbolic leadership, see Orinn Klapp, *Symbolic Leaders* (Chicago: Aldine, 1964).

75. Runciman, "Charismatic Legitimacy and One-Party Rule in Ghana."

76. Joe McGinniss, *The Selling of the President 1968* (New York: Pocket Books, 1968); Daniel Boorstin, *The Image* (New York: Atheneum, 1962), 41-42, 249.

77. For an extended treatment of these themes, see Joseph Bensman and Robert Lilienfeld, *Craft and Consciousness* (New York: John Wiley & Sons, 1973), ch. 12.

78. David Apter, *The Gold Coast in Transition* (Princeton: Princeton University Press, 1955), 292-97; K. J. Ratnam, "Charisma and Political Leadership," *Political Studies* 12 (1964), 352.

79. Peter Blau, "Critical Remarks on Weber's Theory of Authority," *American Political Science Review* 57 (June 1963), 309.

80. Apter, "Nkrumah, Charisma, and the Coup," 766.

81. Max Weber, "The Sociology of Charismatic Authority," in *From Max Weber*, 245.

82. Weber, "Politics as a Vocation," in *From Max Weber*, 106; Max Weber, "Capitalism and Rural Society in Germany," in *From Max Weber*, 370.

83. In "Political Leadership and the Problem of Charismatic Power" at 24, Carl Friedrich actually uses the term *pseudocharisma*, but he uses it to reject the suitability of the concept of charisma in all but a religious context. We agree with Friedrich's—and, for different reasons, with Bendix's and Loewenstein's—notion that *pure* charisma is extremely rare in the modern world. But pseudocharisma, as we have defined it, is very common. Instead of using the term *pseudocharisma* to reject Weberian notions of charisma, we would use it to extend those notions, which we have repeatedly pointed out were foreshadowed by Weber himself. This essay represents an attempt to extend the Weberian concept.

10

Max Weber's Concept of Legitimacy

Joseph Bensman

Max Weber's concept of legitimacy is perhaps the most widely accepted of all his many contributions to political science, sociology, and the social and historical sciences in general. The thesis of the Protestant Ethic has produced interminable conflict, and his theory of bureaucracy has generated numerous revisions and modifications. His theory of charisma has aroused fierce opposition, as have—on entirely different grounds—his methodology, the concept of *verstehen*, the ideal type—and less so—his comparative historical method. Curiously, while his essay "Class, Status and Party" has received almost universal acceptance (and has been widely reprinted in anthologies), his substantive studies of social stratification have rarely been examined, either on their merits or in relation to his general theory of social stratification.

Similarly, Weber's theory of legitimacy has been largely accepted, especially in terms of his major, overall definition; but the extremely complex and often contradictory ideas and concepts that serve as the problematics for his substantive research have been virtually ignored.

Published originally in a slightly different form in Arthur J. Vidich and Ronald Glassman, eds., *Conflict and Control: Challenges to Legitimacy of Modern Governments* (Beverly Hills: Sage Publications, 1979), 17-48. Republished by permission from Ronald Glassman and Joseph Vidich.

In this chapter, we shall attempt to explore Weber's basic concept of legitimacy and the use he made of it. We shall do so in order to assess whether in fact the concept is usable (that is, operational) in contemporary political theory and political sociology, especially with reference to current concerns with the concept of *delegitimation.*[1] We will focus on Weber's use of the concept as a basis for voluntaristic, consensual theories of political systems. We contend that the concept of legitimacy as developed by Weber is so multifaceted and so oriented to particular theoretical and research problems that it does not (nor was it intended to) constitute a general theory of legitimacy. Moreover, Weber's particular formulations of the theory involve contradictions that are not surprising given his purposes, but they make his account of limited use as general theory. We shall attempt to show that Weber rarely used the concept as he defined it. Our purpose here is not to denigrate Weber's work but to specify its contemporary value within the problematics of a field that largely was defined by Weber himself.

The term *legitimacy* was coined by Prince Talleyrand and used in the slogan "Restoration, Legitimacy and Compensation" for the Congress of Vienna. The slogan emphasized that the regimes instituted by the French Revolution and Napoleonic domination were illegitimate, based upon the seizure of power and not on legal descent, lineage, and tradition. Chateaubriand, the French historian and premier, used the concept in order to justify the constitutional monarchy of Louis-Philippe.

Weber, in adapting and defining the concept and making it central to much of his political sociology, focused on the voluntaristic elements in legitimacy. He comes close to defining *legitimacy* in his first use of the term under the concept of legitimate order in *Economy and Society*:

> Action, especially social action which involves a social relationship, may be guided by the existence of a legitimate order. The probability that action will actually be so governed will be called the "validity" of the order in question.
>
> The validity of the order means more than the mere existence of a uniformity of social action determined by custom or self-interest. . . . When a civil servant appears in his office daily at a fixed time, he does not only act on the basis of custom or self-interest which he could disregard if he wanted to, as a rule, his action is determined by the validity of an order (viz., the civil service rules), which he fulfills partly because disobedience would be disadvantageous to him, but also because its *violation would be abhorrent to his sense of duty (of course, in varying degrees).*[2] (emphasis added)

The *validity* of a set of legitimate norms (traditional charismatic, rational-legal) rests on the *voluntary obedience* of a follower, a disciple, or official to a leader, tradition, or legal code. While legitimacy may exist to support a system of domination or political order, others' motives, pure expediency, or responses to naked coercion may also sustain that order. But to the extent that legitimacy is a factor responsible for compliance, the validity of the order rests upon voluntary obedience

Legitimacy as Claimed

While the "validity" of a legitimate order is ultimately based on the consent or voluntary obedience of followers, it is necessary to note that legitimacy is always *claimed* by a political, military, or religious leader or his staff.[3] Weber, again, used the term *claim* in almost every discussion of legitimate domination:

> Experience shows that in no instance does domination voluntarily limit itself to the appeal to material or effectual or ideal interests as a basis for its continuance. In addition every such system *attempts to cultivate the belief in its* legitimacy. But according to the kind of *legitimacy which is claimed*, the type of obedience, the kind of administrative staff, and the mode of exercising authority will differ fundamentally. Equally fundamental is variation in effect. Hence, it is useful to classify the types of domination *according to the claim to legitimacy typically made by each.*[4]

If we take the two separate concepts of legitimacy used by Weber (as in the above quotations), *legitimacy as claimed* and *legitimacy as believed*, we begin to perceive the beginnings of the Weberian "system of thought" in this area. In almost every theoretical discussion of legitimacy, Weber used the concept of the *claim for legitimacy*—charismatic, rational-legal, or traditional—or he used a synonym for the term. He used such terms as *expected*, *duly to recognize a claim*, *compliance*, *demands*, *must obey*, *obedience is expected*, *conduct is conditioned* or *habituated to compliance and obedience*, *the governed must submit*, and *submission to authority*. The point here is that in each statement a demand by those who claim authority is imposed upon subordinates who are expected to submit voluntarily. Typical statements are:

> Every such system (of domination) attempts to establish and cultivate belief in its legitimacy . . . according to the kind of legitimacy *claimed.*[5] He [the charismatic leader] does not derive his claims from the will of the followers in the manner of election: rather *it is their duty to recognize his charisma.* . . . The genuine prophet like the genuine military leader and every true leader in this sense creates or demands new obligations.[6] (emphasis added)

> If the state is to exist, the dominated *must obey* the authority *claimed* by the powers that be.[7] (emphasis added)

> Finally there is the dominance by virtue of belief in the validity of the legal statute and functional competence based on rationally created rules. In this case *obedience is expected* in discharging statutory obligations.[8] (emphasis added)

> Organized domination which calls for continuous administration *requires* that human conduct be conditioned to masters who *claim* to be bearers of legitimate power.[9] (emphasis added)

> To begin with, in principle, there are three inner justifications, hence basic legitimations of domination.

> First is the authority of the "eternal" yesterday, i.e., the mores sanctified through *unimaginably ancient recognition and habituation* to conform.[10] (emphasis added)

Legitimacy as Acceptance of Claims

If the above listed sample of quotations suggests the basis of the expectations that make up the claim for legitimacy in various types of legitimate order, they do not in themselves constitute the "validity" of the order. The validity is achieved only when followers accept, believe in, or grant the claims for legitimacy. Weber used a wide variety of terms to describe this acceptance. They include *emotional surrender,*[11] *belief,*[12] *emotional faith,*[13] *rational faith deduced from an absolute,*[14] *what is believed to be,*[15] *derives from voluntary obedience,*[16] *is held to be legitimate,*[17] *acceptance,*[18] *established belief in the sanctity of tradition,*[19] *devotion to exceptional sanctity . . . of a heroic person and compliance to rationally determined rules,*[20] and *habituation to conform.*[21]

The Process of Claiming and Granting Legitimacy

If we consider both the process of claiming legitimacy and the acceptance or granting of the claim, we are then able to pose an underlying theoretical problematic: What are the conditions for and the processes of the granting or denying of legitimacy to a regime, and what are the conditions for and processes of delegitimation?

The tautological answer is that legitimacy is achieved when the claims for legitimacy are believed, or when the dominant group successfully habituates its followers to the claim, or induces belief, faith, devotion, or rational belief deduced or derived from agreed-upon principles. Weber states this tautology as follows:

> Only then will a legitimate order be called "valid"—if the orientation toward (determinable) maxims occurs, among other reasons, also because it is in some appreciable way regarded by the actor as in some ways obligatory or exemplary for him.[22] What is important is the fact that in a given case the particular claim to legitimacy is to a significant degree treated as "valid"; that this fact confirms the position of the persons claiming authority.[23]

Yet domination does not rest exclusively on legitimacy.[24] Some staff members of a dominant group may adhere to their power positions because they enjoy the benefits thereof and from the fear of loss of positions and privileges; others submit because of coercion, and still others because they are caught in an inexorable machine from which they cannot escape. Some individuals may reject a given norm accepted by others, but find that they must conform simply because everyone else accepts it. Others may orient some of their actions to two contradictory systems of legitimate order and even the same action to different systems of order.[25]

Weber recognized that acceptance of the claims does not have to be universal to create a legitimate order:

> For so far as the agreement underlying the order is not unanimous, as in the past has often been held necessary for complete legitimacy, the order is actually imposed upon the minority; in this frequent case the order in a given group depends on the acquiescence of those who hold different opinions. On the other hand, it is very common for minorities, by force or by use of more ruthless and far-sighted methods, to impose an order which in the course of time comes to be regarded as legitimate by those who originally resisted it.[26]

Moreover, at any given time and place, two or more competing, contradictory, or alternative systems for claiming legitimacy may coexist. These overlapping systems may exist in the transition from the dominance of one system to another, or their coexistence may be a relatively stable feature of a social order. Weber says with reference to legitimate order:

> Thus for sociological purposes there does not exist as there does for the law, a rigid alternative between the validity and lack of validity of a given order. On the contrary, there is a gradual transition between the two extremes; and it is also possible, as has been pointed out, for contradictory systems of order to exist at the same time. In that case each is valid to the extent that there is a probability that action will be oriented to it.[27]

Yet these qualifications and limitations suggest that legitimacy is not the only basis for domination. Legitimacy does not have to be consensual or universal. All subjects of a system do not have to believe in the ideas that justify it. In fact, legitimacy can be imposed upon a society from without by converting a minority claim to a majority one, with acceptance emerging only after forceful domination.

Legitimacy as Justification

At times, the concept of legitimacy was defined by Weber as justification of domination—that is, the term *legitimacy* was a synonym for *justification*. At other times, legitimacy was not the equivalent of justification, but was the *means* of justifying domination:

> When and why do men obey? Under what inner justifications and upon what external means does this domination rest?
>
> To begin with, in principle *there are three inner justifications, hence basic legitimations* of domination.[28] (emphasis added)
>
> Indeed the continued exercise of every domination always has the strongest need for self-justification appealing to the principles of its legitimation.[29]
>
> We have encountered the problem of legitimacy in our discussion in the *legal order.* Now we shall have to indicate its broader significance. For a domination, this kind of *justification of its legitimacy* is much more than a matter of theoretical or philosophical speculation; it constitutes the basis of very real differences in the empirical structure of domination.[30] (emphasis added)

Yet even if legitimacy is understood as justification for achieved power or for as yet unrealized claims for power, that idea does not answer the question "When is an order 'legitimated'?" "When enough people believe in it" is a circular answer. We do not know how much is enough, nor the social characteristics of those who "believe," nor do we know how much is *not* enough—not enough to cause delegitimation.

We must thus ask further questions of Weber's work: (1) When and how and under what conditions does a new form of legitimacy arise and gain acceptance? (2) Under what condition does an old legitimate order lose its legitimacy?

In seeking the answers to both questions, we are concerned with *legitimacy as belief*, acceptance as "granted" and as "valid" in terms that are "sociological," and not in *legitimacy as claimed*. That is, one can recognize that many claims are made, but the knowledge of the conditions under which the claims are accepted or rejected requires a different set of questions and answers.

These questions *were not* consistently asked or answered by Weber. In part, Weber's "failure" to ask and answer such questions was intentional. Weber stressed in his methodological writings the necessity for the construction of concepts and definitions in such formal terms as the probability that a plurality of actors will act in a given situation in a given way with a given typical set of meanings or motivations. The concrete substantive descriptions of actions so indicated by the definition or concept were to be derived only by historical or substantive research. Thus, the definitions, in principle, do not a priori establish the substantive empirical truth of a formal proposition; only empirical research can do that. The answer to the questions we have raised could only be discerned from Weber's specific substantive work. Yet even here, Weber did not answer our questions at our hoped-for level of generality. In principle, given Weber's extremely general concepts and his extremely specific answers, no *general* answer is possible. For Weber, sociology was scientific history, aimed at providing specific answers to general questions. It does not produce general, essential, or universal answers.

Yet the methodological impasse is not as bleak as these formulations suggest. In his methodological writings, Weber used historical illustrations that posed and answered the questions that, in principle, he did not allow himself to ask. In his late essays—"Religious Rejections of the World and their Directions," "The Social Psychology of World Religions," "Politics as a Vocation," "Science as a Vocation," "On Socialism,"—and in *The City*, and *The General Economic History*, as well as in his political journalism, Weber raised and answered questions in terms of a philosophy of history and metaphysics that entirely contradicted his avowed epistemology. He answered substantive and historical questions in general terms, even when denying the possibility of a metaphysical philosophy of history and the desirability of a metaphysical foundation to social science.

Because Weber did not follow his own methodological prescriptions, it is possible to ascertain partial answers to the questions we have raised. These answers, we note, are not systematic or complete, nor do they in this area constitute a philosophy of history or a general theory of legitimacy. In extracting these answers, we thus risk converting Weber's limited and restricted answers into a general theory. If we do so (and to the extent we do so), we risk "reifying" Weber. We may extend his work beyond the limits he allowed to himself and cite Weberian authority for our reconstruction or we may create a general theory out of the deliberately restricted fragments created by Weber and use the legitimacy of Weber's scholarship to substantiate our own creation. In extending Weber's work in the following pages, we will attempt to distinguish Weber's work from our own speculations and extensions.

Delegitimation and New Claims for Legitimacy

The general concepts cited above serve only as an introduction to Weber's discussion of his three major types of legitimacy and legitimate orders: charismatic, traditional, and rational-legal.[31] But his discussion of charismatic leadership allows us to make some statements on conditions favorable to "delegitimation" in the sense that charisma always involves a revolutionary transvaluation of existing systems of legitimacy. The rise of charismatic leadership is always a product of extraordinary events, and usually—but not always—these extraordinary events are of a negative nature, "moments of distress" caused by the failure of an existing legitimate order to meet the expectations it generates:

> Every event transcending the routines of everyday life releases charismatic forces, and every extraordinary ability creates charismatic beliefs, which are subsequently weakened again by everyday life.
>
> However, the charisma of the hero or the magician is immediately activated whenever an extraordinary event occurs—a major expedition, a drought, or some other danger precipitated by the wrath of the demons, especially military threat. *When wars become chronic and technological development necessitates the systematic training and recruitment of all able-bodied men, the charismatic war hero becomes a king.*[32] (emphasis added)
>
> All extraordinary needs, i.e., those which *transcend* the sphere of everyday economic routines, have always been satisfied on a *charismatic* basis. The further we go in history, the more strongly does this statement hold. It means the following: the "natural" leaders in moments of distress—whether psychic, physical, economic, ethical, religious, or political—were . . . the bearers of specific gifts of body and mind that were considered "supernatural"—in the sense that not everybody could have access to them.[33] (emphasis added)

Charisma emerges when the established, legitimate order, whether traditional, rational-legal, or patriarchical, produces, allows, or fails to avoid distress, be it economic, political, psychic, religious, or military. The same "criteria" apply to charismatic leadership:

> If proof of success eludes the leader for long, if he appears deserted by his god or his magical or heroic powers, above all if his leadership fails to benefit his followers, it is likely that his charismatic authority will disappear.[34]
>
> Even the old Germanic kings were sometimes rejected with scorn. Similar phenomena are very common among so-called primitive people. In China the charismatic quality of the monarch which was transmitted unchanged by heredity, was upheld so rigidly that any misfortune whatever, not only defeats in war, but droughts, floods, or astronomical phenomena—which were considered unlucky, forced him to do public penance, and might even force his abdication. If such things occurred, it was a sign that he did not possess the requisite charismatic virtue and thus was not a legitimate son of heaven.[35]

Legitimacy as Promise

Thus, it appears that charismatic leadership implies a promise, or is understood by the followers to imply a promise, to relieve distress, win wars, and solve problems of drought, famine, plague, and so on. The failure to solve these problems is ground for rejecting the claims of the charismatic hero, or for the growth of disbelief in the hero's charisma, and hence the destruction of the "validity" of charisma.

While this process of "delegitimating" charisma is well developed in Weber's work, it is not as well developed with respect to the other forms of legitimacy. Yet Weber made similar points with respect to traditional and rational-legal orders. Thus, Weber argued that loss of wars by a monarchy or "striking victories" by a republic may produce charismatically led revolutions:

> In general, it should be kept clearly in mind that the basis of every authority, and correspondingly of every kind of willingness to obey, is a belief, a belief by virtue of which persons exercising authority are lent prestige. The composition of this belief is seldom altogether simple. In the case of "legal authority," it is never purely legal. The belief in legality comes to be established and habitual, and this means it is partly traditional. Violation of the tradition may be fatal to it. Furthermore, it has a charismatic element, at least in the negative sense that persistent and striking lack of success may be sufficient to ruin any government, to undermine its prestige, and to prepare the way for charismatic revolution. For monarchies, hence, it is dangerous to lose wars since it makes it appear that their charisma is no longer genuine. For republics, on the other hand, striking victories may be dangerous in that they put the victorious general in a favorable position for making charismatic claims.[36]

> The history of the dissolution of the old system of domination legitimate in Germany up until 1918 is instructive in this connection. The War, on the one hand, went far to break down the authority of tradition; and the German defeat involved a tremendous loss of prestige for the government. These factors combined with a systematic habituation to illegal behavior, undermined the amenability to discipline both in the army and in industry and thus prepared the way for the overthrow of the older authority.[37]

Traditional and rational-legal orders are thus subject to some of the same dynamics as are charismatic orders. The very existence of such orders is an implied *promise* to relieve distress. Traditional and rational-legal orders promise implicitly to routinize everyday life.

When such orders fail to do so, they appear to violate their promise. They invite—that is, provide opportunities for—new, ersatz, pseudocharismatic heroes. Napoleon, Kurt Eisner, Theodore Roosevelt, and Gladstone are examples that Weber cited for the modern era.

Thus, there is in Weber's work, an implicit notion of the *promises* implied in a claim for legitimacy. While Weber *did not* use the term *promise*, we infer the concept of promises from his specific discussions of the conditions under which claims for legitimacy are rejected or from situations in which established orders lose their legitimacy.

Weber did use the concept of promises explicitly in his sociology of religion, but not in his political sociology. In "The Social Psychology of the World Religions," Weber used that concept with reference to charisma:

> The prestige of particular magicians, and of those spirits or divinities in whose name they have performed their miracles, has brought them favorable patronage, irrespective of local or tribal affiliation. Under favorable conditions this had led to the formation of a religious "community," which has been independent of ethnic associations. Some, though not all, mysteries have taken this course. They *have promised* the salvation of individuals *qua* individuals from sickness, poverty, and from all sorts of distress and danger. Thus the magician has transformed himself into a mystagogue; that is, hereditary dynasties of mystagogues or organizations of trained personnel under a head determined in accordance with some set of rules developed. The head has either been recognized as the incarnation of a superhuman being or merely a prophet, that is, the mouthpiece and agent of his god.
>
> The annunciation and the *promise* of religion has been addressed to the masses in need of salvation.

> Among people under political pressure, like the Israelites, the title of "savior" (Moshuach name) was originally attached to saviors from political distress, as transmitted by hero sagas (Gideon, Jephthah). The "messianic" promises were determined by these sagas.
>
> The *promises* of the religions of salvation at first remained tied to ritualist rather than ethical preconditions.
>
> Whenever the *promises* of the prophet or the redeemer have not sufficiently met the needs of the socially less-favored strata, a secondary salvation religion of the masses has regularly developed beneath the official doctrine.[38] (emphasis added)

The emphasis given to the idea of *promises* here not only parallels Weber's concepts of claims and beliefs used in his political sociology, but also is related to the same historical data that he dealt with in his political sociology—prophetic charisma.

The process of legitimation and "delegitimation" as described by Weber and inferred from his work involves more than making promises or imposing claims upon a population of would-be believers, and more than fulfilling those claims or gaining belief in the promise of claims. Other processes are involved, only they must be identified in order to avoid oversimplifying the theory we attribute to Weber.

"Delegitimation" can be a result of the process of intellectual rationalization. The development of rational intellectual thought can undermine the belief in magic or the sacredness of traditions that are the grounds, respectively, for charismatic or traditional legitimacy. The process of intellectual rationalization need not be sudden or disastrous in its immediate effects, but in the long run, it undermines established orders of legitimacy by undermining the capacity of the follower of an order to believe in that order.

In the short run, the "delegitimation" of charisma follows either from the failure of the charismatic hero to "prove" his charismatic quality through miracles, victories, or other successes—that is, "through the welfare of the governed,"[39] or through the death and succession of the charismatic leader. The routinization of charisma can follow many paths. It can lead to traditional or rational-legal systems of legitimacy. It can lead to patriarchal and patrimonial bureaucracy and from these forms to "pure" bureaucracy. If it leads to bureaucracy, the dominant form of legitimacy becomes rational-legal. If it leads to patrimonialism or patriarchy, the dominant form of legitimacy becomes traditionalistic, based upon hereditary charisma, lineage charisma, or charisma of clan or family. Bureaucratic forms of organizations, whether patrimonial or pure, stress charisma of office.

The form of legitimacy that follows the routinization (and delegitimation) of pure charisma is determined in the process of succession, by the nature of the personal staff of the charismatic leader, and by the form of remuneration offered to and received by these staffs and by the ways their "rights" are expropriated and transmitted.

When succession institutionalizes patrimonial and, later, "pure" bureaucracy, the new claimants to legitimacy tend to argue their case in terms of the order they represent. Rational jurists emerge and articulate systems of law and legitimacy based on abstract, general, and—usually—functional principles, on the rights and duties attached to legally defined offices, and on the demand that obedience and discipline be based on the right of officials to exercise command by virtue of the legality of their office and their right to occupy that office.

In a few cases, Weber points out, bureaucratic officials seized control but legitimated themselves in the name of the king and the traditionalism upon which the monarchy was based. This results in constitutional monarchy in which the king becomes an emblem of authority. Bureaucrats rarely legitimate themselves in their own name.[40]

However, charismatic leaders do seize authority over a bureaucracy in the name of the people—that is, plebiscitary democracy—or in the name of values and ideals that underlie the bureaucracy. But they usually reject the formalism that constitutes a basis for rational-legal legitimacy.

Weber's discussions of these forms of legitimation (and delegitimation) are subsumed under specific discussions of a wide variety of particular forms of domination. Yet one general point emerges relative to our interest in the "functions" and meaning of legitimacy. This is *legitimacy as self-justification.*

Legitimacy as Self-Justification

Legitimacy can be analyzed as belief in, claims for, and the promises of a system of domination or of a social or political order. It is also the justification of a political or social order or system of domination. But it is more than that; it is the need for *self-justification* by those who obtain privilege, power, and "good fortune" in a social order:

> We must now go back to those economic motives mentioned above that largely account for the routinization of charisma: the needs of privileged strata to legitimize their social and economic conditions, that is, to transform them from mere resultants of power relationships into acquired rights, and hence to sanctify them. *But after its routinization its very quality as an extraordinary supernatural and divine force makes it a suitable source of legitimate authority for the successors of the charismatic hero*; moreover, in this form it is advantageous to all those whose power and property are guaranteed by this authority, that is, dependent upon its perpetuation.[41] (emphasis added)

> His [the war lord's] existence depends solely upon a chronic state of war and upon a comprehensive organization set for warfare. On the other hand, the development of kingship into a regular royal administration does emerge only at the stage when a following of royal professional warriors rules over the working or paying masses, at least, that is often the case. . . . Internal class stratification may bring about the very same social differentiation: the charismatic following of warriors develops into a ruling caste. *But in every case, princely power and those groups having interests vested in it—that is, the war lord's following—strive for legitimacy as soon as the rule has become stable.*[42] (emphasis added)
>
> The fates of human beings are not equal. Men differ in their states of health or wealth or social status or what not. *Simple observation shows that in every such situation he who is more favored feels the never ceasing need to look upon his position as in some way "legitimate," upon his advantage as "deserved," and the other's disadvantage as being brought about by the latter's "fault."* That the purely accidental causes of the difference may be ever so obvious makes no difference.
>
> This same need makes itself felt in the relation between positively and negatively privileged groups of human beings. Every highly privileged group develops the myth of its natural, especially its blood, superiority. Under conditions of stable distribution of power and, consequently, of status order, that myth is accepted by the negatively privileged strata.[43] (emphasis added)

This "need" for self-justification by those who acquire the "good fortune" of power is at the heart of all claims for legitimacy, except those made by the charismatic hero. The latter's claim is based on a direct mission from a god, gods, or spirit. But the self-justification that is the motivating drive for legitimacy is a particular expression of what for Weber was a deep, metaphysical need: the need for a rational meaning of the cosmos, the world, and for man's place in it. It includes a need for an ethical interpretation of the world. This need emerges once the process of intellectual rationalization takes place:

> The need for an ethical interpretation of the "meaning" of the distribution of fortunes among men increased with the growing rationality of conceptions of the world. As the religious and ethical reflections upon the world were increasingly rationalized and primitive and magical notions were eliminated, the theodicy of suffering encountered increasing difficulties. Individually "undeserved" woe was all too frequent; not "good" but "bad" men succeeded—even when "good" and "bad" were measured by the yardstick of the master stratum and not by that of a "slave morality."[44]

This "need" for an ethical reinterpretation of the world to justify the differential distribution of good and bad fortune applies to the favored classes and the unfavored, to the powerful and powerless, and to the rulers and the ruled. It is the basis of all rationalized religion:

> In treating suffering as a symptom of odiousness in the eyes of the gods and as a sign of secret guilt, religion has psychologically met a very general need. The fortunate is seldom satisfied with the fact of being fortunate. Beyond this, he needs to know that he has a *right* to his good fortune. He wants to be convinced that he "deserves" it, and above all, that he deserves it in comparison with others. He wishes to be allowed the belief that the less fortunate

> also merely experience his due. Good fortune thus wants to be "legitimate" fortune.[45]

The last two quotations are taken from Weber's "Social Psychology of the World Religions" in a discussion of intellectual rationalization. They include a statement of the need of the fortunate for "legitimate" fortune. But they are totally consistent in form, content, and language with Weber's discussion of the various forms of political legitimacy in *Economy and Society.* Thus, the need for self-justification is as important to the ruling strata as their "need" to justify the dominant political and social order to the dominated strata.

The Various Meanings of Legitimacy

Thus, we see in Weber's work five different meanings of legitimacy. These are:

1. The *belief* in a political or social order.

2. A *claim* for the right to rule over a political and social order.

3. A *justification* for an existing form of political domination.

4. The *promises* (actual or implied) that a given order of political domination will contribute to the well-being (political, religious, economic, material, or psychic) of the underlying population.

5. The *self-justification* by the ruling strata for its "good fortune" in securing or monopolizing an unequal share of favored values, rights, privileges, and opportunities in a society.

The concepts and meanings underlying the quest for legitimacy are not, of course, the only basis of support for a system of domination. They are intermixed with direct material rewards and opportunities based on expedience and with coercion inspired by fear and habituation based on powerlessness and a long-term lack of intellectual, political, and material resources.[46] All of these factors contribute to the maintenance of a system of political domination.

Given these meanings of legitimacy and its "function" as a support for an ongoing or new system of domination, we can now state and assess Weber's "theory of legitimacy." We recognize that such a theory of legitimacy is stated only fragmentarily in Weber's work. His interest in legitimacy was in determining how specific claims for legitimacy helped to determine or limit emerging systems of domination.[47] In pulling together Weber's various discussions of the topic and treating them as if they constitute a general theory, we have gone beyond Weber's manifest task and perhaps subjected him to illegitimate criticism. This can be justified only because our purpose is to explicate and evaluate the concept of legitimacy as a general theory.

The basic substantive theorem in the entire theory of legitimacy is the following idea: legitimacy is a claim for power that is made "valid" to the extent that its claimants can induce *belief* in its tenets. The idea that legitimacy is an implied or actual promise is perhaps a more specific and extreme statement of the idea of *legitimacy as claim*, but *legitimacy as promise* suggests the parallel idea of legitimacy as validated by the fulfillment of promises. The idea of *legitimacy as justification* of a system of domination also raises the question of fulfillment. The idea of *legitimacy as self-justification* is not of the same order. It does not have the same external referents as do the other senses of the concept. Legitimacy as self-justification is only validated inwardly. We can restate Weber's "theory" paradigmatically by considering each meaning as an idea communicated and received. Thus, each concept has two meanings, as follows:

Meaning communicated as	*Received as*
Claim	belief
Promise	delivery
Justification	delivery
Self-justification	inner certainty

Yet if the inferred conversion of communicated messages to internalized validations is the basis for the achievements of legitimacy, then Weber's theory is curiously opaque. In this discussion of pure charisma, where charisma is presumably based on belief, Weber emphasized that the charismatic hero has to deliver miracles, booty, victories, and so on. Weber, in this context, made explicit the relationship between input and output of a system of promise and delivery. But, in almost all other discussions of legitimacy, Weber did not stress legitimacy as received communication, as belief. To be sure, he emphasized the need for followers of a charismatic hero to monopolize offices, benefices, fees, and other opportunities, but these are claims, not beliefs, and they are based upon rational expediency. He emphasized the need of the Emperor in classical China as well as the needs of ancient Germanic kings to maintain the well-being of their subjects against war, famine, flood, pestilence, and other external and internal crises. He pointed out the dangers to monarchies of losing wars and to republics of winning them too easily.[48] Moreover, he suggested the dangers during times of crisis in plebiscitary democracies of claims for substantive rationality wielded by a charismatic leader who ignores formal rationality in the name of immediate results.[49]

Yet all of these citations add up to nothing more than a statement of exceptions. While Weber ultimately defined legitimacy in terms of *the capacity of a populace to believe in or accept* claims, promises, and justifications, virtually his entire work in this area (the exceptions cited above) is concentrated on the presentation of claims, promises, and justifications, and not on their acceptance. If Weber had applied his original concept of the validity of legitimacy as the *belief or acceptance of* claims, that application would have required an analysis of the populations to which the claims, promises, and justifications were addressed. Instead, Weber concentrated his work on the formal presentation of claims, promises, and justifications as presented but not received. This focus made it virtually impossible to raise the question, with the exceptions noted, of the conditions for the fulfillment of communicated claims.

In his sociology of religion, as distinct from his political sociology, Weber did concentrate a great deal of attention on the social psychology of the underlying populations. He examined the religious "needs" of virtually every class, occupation, or status group in terms of their economic, social, and historical predispositions (elective affinities) to theology and theodicy at each crucial step in their economic, social, psychological, and historical development. He did so in order to understand the *acceptance* of religious claims and the way in which followers reinterpret the content of religious doctrine. A similarly detailed analysis of the various publics and constituencies is absent in Weber's political work, except in those cases where his sociology of religion and political sociology overlap in the discussion of charisma.

But one also sees a more serious difficulty in Weber's work in this area. If legitimacy is based on claims, promises, and justifications that are accepted or believed in, then one would expect Weber to give a great deal of attention to the substance and content of the theories used as vehicles for the claims for legitimacy.[50] These theories in the language of other political theories are the political myths, ideologies, ruling formulae, or idols of the city. Yet, in all of Weber's political sociology, there is virtually no discussion of the manifest *content* of political theory as a basis for legitimacy. In these terms, Weber has a few sentences on natural law and some very important summary paragraphs on the nature of the political and social theories of universal churches, but no detailed treatment of the specific content of these theories.[51]

In the comparable treatment of religion, Weber dealt extensively with the substantive theology of Protestant Christianity, ancient Judaism, Confucianism, Mencian and Taoist doctrine, Hinduism, and to a lesser extent Pauline and other Catholic religious doctrines. But in the area of politics, Weber eschewed intellectual history.

How do we account for this "oversight," if indeed it is an oversight? We have indicated that Weber's neo-Kantian methodology concentrated on the concept of *social action* in formal terms. The categories of meaning that he focused upon were those appropriate only to his understanding of the particular social action under discussion. This forced him to treat as minimal and secondary ideas that are conceived as systems of thought, as "cultural" or "structural" systems. In dealing with the sociology of religion and in late essays, Weber abandoned this methodological position in order to deal with ideas as the basis for the intellectual rationalization and disenchantment of the world. In doing so, he articulated an implicit metaphysical system based on the "need" for an intellectually rationalized image of the world in the face of a reality that made such a task impossible.

Weber's reliance on a formal theory of social actions made it virtually impossible for him to pose problems and achieve answers that identify the conditions under which legitimacy is achieved and secured. His answer—that is, that legitimacy is valid in the sociological sense to the extent that it is believed in, is a necessarily tautological or circular thesis, so long as it is not accompanied by an investigation of the belief patterns of the appropriate underlying populations. To the extent that Weber provided fragmentary answers, these were the products of specific historical research or they were illustrations or inferences that, if treated as generalizations, violate his formal methodology.

We know from Weber that a political order can be sustained by expedience, the delivery of material rewards, and terror and coercion, as well as by the need for self-justification of a ruling strata. We know from Weber that it can be sustained by sheer routine (habituation) and by the lack of transparency of a system of exploitation. It can be sustained by the privatization of the underlying population, its apathy, and the quest for personal joy and salvation. Given all these alternatives to *legitimacy as belief*, how does one explain the dominance of a given legitimate order of domination? How many "believers" are necessary to legitimate a system of political domination, and of what characteristics? Weber did not and, we believe, could not answer this question. Nor did he "prove" that legitimacy is "necessary" to a system of domination. He "proved" only that ruling strata *need* to feel that their positions are legitimate.

One must also remember that Weber argued that, in any empirical situation, more than one system of legitimacy may coexist, and an individual may believe in elements of more than one system, and may not believe in any (though he must recognize that others do believe, including others with power to reward or control scarce values).

In such a situation, Weber recognized that a universal consensus does not exist. Such consensus may in fact be a virtual impossibility. The *claims* for legitimacy may be minimally accepted so long as no other claimants offer alternative claims in strongly supported political movements that challenge the dominance of the strongest incumbent claimants for monopolies over political institutions and values. In the absence of such challenges, routine, tradition, and inertia support the "legitimacy" of the dominant strata, even if those strata base their claims on rational-legal grounds.

In this sense, *traditionalism* means inertia, the "acceptance" of things as they are, not because of positive belief, but either because no other possibilities suggest themselves to a population on organized, ideological, political grounds or because the sense of powerlessness is so great that passive acceptance is the only possibility. This kind of acceptance—passive, hopeless, resigned—can become habitual, so deeply ingrained by the fact of powerlessness that it is no longer a political attitude. It is a form of depoliticization that allows no self-conscious articulation. Yet such attitudes may, because of the absence of direct opposition to a regime, support a regime.

In these societies where a relatively small politicized ruling class governs by authoritarian or totalitarian means, a vast majority of the population may "accept" the regime because of their depoliticization and the lack of alternatives. And the ruling classes may support the regime because of either their material interests in the regime or their "need" for self-legitimation. Yet none of these bases for *legitimacy* are what is usually meant by the term.

Crises that produce charismatic heroes and adventurers in a society have many possible consequences. Such crises may destroy the routines on which apathy and resignation are based, routines that establish a daily life to which a population may be habituated even under conditions of minimal survival. Such crises may expose or "make transparent the causes and consequences of the class situation."[52] Weber states this specifically with reference to legitimating myths:

> Every highly privileged group develops the myth of its natural, especially its blood, superiority. Under conditions of stable distribution of power and, consequently of status order, that myth is accepted by the negatively

> privileged strata. Such a situation exists as long as the masses continue in that natural state of theirs in which thought about the order of domination remains but little developed, which means as long as no urgent needs render the state of affairs "problematical." But in times in which the class situation has become unambiguously and openly visible to everyone as the factor determining every man's individual fate, that very myth of the highly privileged about everyone having deserved his particular lot has often become one of the most passionately hated objects of attack.[53]

A crisis may provide opportunities for would-be charismatic leaders to articulate expressions of disenchantment against the system and possible alternatives; indeed, it may result in the actual appearance of political alternatives. It thus may politicize the underlying population either in active opposition to the regime or in support of individuals and movements who attack the legitimacy of the regime and attempt to create the basis for a new legitimacy.

But if this is true, then the concept of legitimacy is important only during periods of crisis—for example, in the creation of a new regime or in the attempts of those who gain power after a political crisis to "legitimate" themselves—that is, to justify their seizure of power, their new privileges, and status monopolies.

But such speculations do not answer the questions: How much legitimacy is necessary? Or even, is belief, as distinct from support, even necessary?

One can only answer these questions *after the fact*. An order has become illegitimate, or delegitimated, when it has lost the support necessary either to defend itself against attacks or to gain ascendancy. As *a predictive* concept it is no more valuable than the concept of "revolutionary situation." Identification of a revolutionary situation during periods of crisis is a question subject to endless debate among would-be revolutionaries. The answer is usually determined *after* the attempt to seize power has succeeded or failed. But even here the existence or nonexistence of that situation is beclouded by postmortems concerning the appropriateness of tactics, strategies, timing, and the amount of preparation made to take advantage of the postulated revolutionary situation.

In the same sense, the existence or nonexistence of "legitimacy," illegitimacy, and the growth of delegitimation can only be determined *after the fact* of failure or success. The concept and theory do not provide the specific theoretical criteria for invalidating it, nor do they provide a basis for anything other than retrospective evaluations. The methodological tautology in Weber's definition of the concept remains: a political order is legitimate when enough people believe in it or accept it sufficiently to keep it in power, and a political movement is legitimate when and to the extent that enough people believe in it to maintain it as a movement.

The Utility of the Concept of Legitimacy

Does this mean that Weber's theory of legitimacy as explicated here is useless? Or does it have other uses that make it worthwhile despite its tautological character? What is the possible utility of a formal theory of legitimacy?

It is necessary to summarize what can and cannot be established by a Weberian theory of legitimacy. It is relatively easy to establish empirically that claims, promises, and justifications are made for or against an existing or potential political order. It is also relatively easy to establish or infer that many of these claims, promises, and justifications are self-justifications. It is possible in principle, though somewhat more difficult in practice, to establish that some or all of these claims are in whole or in part believed or accepted, though it may be difficult to establish at what level of depth the claims are believed. It is also relatively easy to establish, in principle, that regimes are supported by considerations of expediency and by fear of actual or anticipated coercion. But it may, in coercive systems, be difficult to separate expressions of belief from cynical opportunism or from defensive conformity, even while recognizing that all organized societies are at least minimally coercive.

What cannot be established, except as a tautology, is that *belief* in claims, promises, and justifications make a structure of domination legitimate. More importantly, there is no way to establish empirically the amount and character of belief or believers necessary to sustain a legitimate system of domination.

Yet the concept of legitimacy may have other uses.

As a *heuristic* theory, as a set of questions and not as a deductive system, the concept of legitimacy enables one to ask: Who are (and what are the characteristics of) the supporters of a political order? On what grounds do leaders claim support? Who believes or accepts the respective claims? And with what degrees of enthusiasm, passivity, or resignation? As a heuristic system, the theory enables one to ask: Who are the competing individual or group claimants for political ascendancy in a society, and on what grounds do they compete? Who do the competing claims and claimants attract or antagonize, and who do they neutralize by rendering them passive, depoliticized, or without hope?

To the extent that such questions stemming from or embodied in the concept of legitimacy may be answered empirically, the use of the concept may facilitate specific empirical research that may yield specific empirical answers in historical terms. But the same questions as the basis for deductive theory cannot yield general, deduced answers implicit in the very notion of deductive, systematic theory. To the extent that the purpose of theory is to facilitate specific empirical research, one cannot find fault with such a methodological program. To repeat, it is precisely this program that animates much of Weber's formal methodological writings, especially *Economy and Society*. Yet it is precisely this program that Weber at times ignored and transcended in much of his work.

The theory of legitimacy as used by Weber was particularly important in the analysis of the directions of routinization of charisma. The various claims for legitimacy by the disciples and staffs of a charismatic leader become, according to Weber, the basis for power struggles that, when resolved, determine (along with other factors) the institutional character of the ensuing structure of domination. The use of the concept of legitimacy in these terms focuses on legitimacy as claim and as self-justification, and on theories of power (as combined with claims), but does not focus on legitimacy as belief (except in the tautological sense). The idea that the particular resolution of conflicting claims among potential claimants of power determines the institutional character of the evolution of a society is the major way that Weber did in fact use the concept of legitimacy.

Beyond this, the Weberian theory of legitimacy, as extended here and that is implicit and partially explicit in scattered fragments of Weber's work, suggests other possibilities for useful questions and hypotheses. Here are some of these possibilities.

As already noted in Weber's work, any established political order may embody elements of more than one system of legitimacy, and an individual may subscribe to, acknowledge as binding, or believe elements of more than one system of claims. Yet, at any one time, there is likely to be a dominant order—dominant in the empirical sense that it is supported by the law, the state, political and economic institutions, and the like. The dominant form of legitimacy takes many forms of expression and has many objects. Thus, depending on the type of legitimacy, the object of legitimation may be an individual or his immediate followers (the charismatic hero and disciples or staff or the charismatic community, the *Gemeinde*). It may be a lineage, kingship, or a family in traditional charisma. It may be an office, a bureaucracy, an entire system of administration, a regime, a state, or an entire political order. Legitimacy may justify law, whether natural law, codified law, Kadi justice, or the common law. It can be attached to, or be expressed in terms of, a class or caste system, a property system or a kind of property holding, ethnic superiority, or a particular interpretation of a social order or even a cosmos, including a god.

Thus, both the objects of legitimation and the theories that legitimate these "objects" are, in a given "system" of legitimacy, interlaced at different levels of generality. It is not possible to understand the legitimacy of bureaucratic office without reference to the legitimacy of bureaucratic law, the bureaucratic state, even though these principles, when dominant, may be taken for granted.

This differential specificity and hierarchy of the principles of legitimacy are of prime importance in understanding "systems" of legitimate order. Thus, the behavior of an individual bureaucrat is judged to be legitimate or illegitimate in terms of principles embodied in administrative laws and codes that in their own terms are accepted or enforced by the standards of a more general theory of legitimacy. The behavior of a president may be judged illegitimate (and he may be impeached) because he has been considered to have violated the principles of legitimacy embodied in the construction. A particular regime may be discarded for violating, exceeding, or failing to fulfill the legitimating promises of its state system.

In these terms, every specific judgment of illegitimacy is an affirmation of principles of legitimacy that are accepted at a broader and presumably deeper level of generality. It is for this reason that the exposure of violations of principles of legitimacy is at the same time affirmation of the larger systems within which the violations occur.

In fact, it is through the prosecution of specific violations that the more general system is affirmed. Without violations and their prosecution, the more general system becomes taken for granted, and its parameters become or remain undefined. It is substantially on this ground that Durkheim argued that crime and its punishment reaffirm the constitutive law of society and society itself. It is on these grounds that the impeachment and resignation of Richard Nixon for illegitimate behavior in office can be celebrated as a triumph for the legitimacy of the American constitutional system as a whole.

In this sense, the legitimacy of a political order and its legal framework has to be understood as a highly articulated "system" of different levels of specificity and generality. It may be embodied in "cases," as in the common law, or in tradition, custom, and usage, as in traditional legitimate orders. But whatever the order (pure charisma excepted), the accepted and enforced system of legitimacy operates as constraint upon the behavior of all those who accept or are forced to accept the system of legitimacy embodied in the established legal framework. Thus, the legitimate order, to the extent that it is accepted and enforced, has a binding, obligatory character and makes an organized society possible. This is the major "function" of legitimacy. Its "validity," however, rests upon its acceptance and enforcement, regardless of the amount and character of *belief* in its tenets. It is, in part, for this reason that Weber attacks Stammler for "reifying" legal systems—that is, for giving them an absolute, universal character.

A system of legitimacy provides an *internal* standard for judging the legitimacy of specific actions, institutions, rights, and duties within the system. But the legitimacy of the system as a whole is not itself capable of validation by any means other than on external standards, combinations of faith, expediency, and force. And it is in these terms that we have argued that it is not possible to ascertain on theoretical grounds the thresholds of the legitimacy of a total system.

In these terms, how can we define *delegitimation*? Delegitimation is the process of making explicit, self-conscious rejections of a social order on the ultimate grounds on which that order's legitimacy is predicated. It is the explicit, theoretical rejection or defiance of a philosophical, legal, property and/or state system that legitimates specific actions and codes. Prosecution of illegitimacy thus affirms the principles of a system by punishing its violation. Delegitimacy attacks the system and usually attempts to assert the fundamentally opposed axioms of an alternative or substitute political order.

The extent to which claims, promises, and beliefs are essential to a system of legitimacy is thus their efficacy in averting attacks on a political order, whether or not these claims, promises, or justifications are fulfilled or redeemed.

But legitimacy has other important uses. Legitimacy not only serves as a means of justifying for the fortunate both the claims to and enjoyment of good fortune, but also justifies the distribution of "bad" fortune to the unfortunate. It provides grounds for obedience by the powerless and justification for the fact that they enjoy less than a proportionate share of goods of this world. It gives warrant for the exploitation of the larger masses by dominant elites. It makes opaque and thus helps to sustain the economic, political, and administrative arrangements that make good and ill fortune accepted facts of political life. It is for this reason that rapid social change and crises "make transparent" the systems of domination and exploitation that govern social and political life. And it is for this reason that the transparency of class and status domination threatens the legitimacy of established political orders; that is, it provides the opportunity for delegitimation by claimants for new systems of legitimacy.

In the absence of the transparency of social relations and of direct attacks on the legitimating systems, legitimacy thus contributes to a system of social controls that lowers the economic and military costs of domination. To the extent that an underlying population can be induced to accept or believe in the claims, promises, and justifications of a system of legitimacy, the dominant classes can reduce the cost of coercion. Yet every state rests ultimately on a legitimate monopoly of the means of violence.

The balance between naked coercion, legitimate violence, and pure legitimacy is thus decisive for the concept of legitimacy. "Pure legitimacy,"—that is, legitimacy based on belief—cannot even be approached if a state system rests preponderantly on organized violence, coercion, terror, and the isolation and depoliticization of its underlying population. Legitimacy in such a situation is too transparent a contradiction in terms.

Yet every state and every ruling class or strata claim legitimacy; that is, they attempt to construct a political myth, ideology, or political formula that justifies their political and social status. This is easily understood as *self-justification*, but cannot be understood as legitimacy of belief. However, if no feasible alternative appears to challenge such domination, a "legitimacy of force" based on apathy, privacy, and hopelessness emerges.

The concept of *legitimacy as belief* thus implies a democratic principle in which the legitimacy of claims, promises, and justifications can be tested in the absence of extreme coercion and by the presence of voluntary compliance. Such compliance can only be ascertained when certain crucial political freedoms exist, even though the existence of a state requires a monopoly of the legitimate means of violence.

Another function of legitimacy is implied in the foregoing analysis. Force, terror, coercion, and rational expediency, the alternatives to legitimacy as belief, all—in the long run—either diminish the motivation to work and the productivity of the labor force or raise the material costs of inducing work and productivity. To the extent that ruling strata rely on force, coercion, and violence, they reduce the productivity of the societies they rule over; if rational expediency is the prime means of control, it increases costs. Both means may be conceived as minimizing efficiency. A society that succeeds in producing legitimacy as belief can increase, to that extent, its motivation, productivity, and efficiency, while reducing the costs of control.

It is for this reason, among others, that long before "human relations in industry" became a science, the advocates of dominant regimes developed theories of natural law, divine right, nationalism, morale, "blood," religion, and other bases for legitimacy addressed to publics who were not the primary material benefactors of the order justified by these respective legitimating ideas. It is for this reason, too, that many claims, justifications, and promises (but not self-justifications, coercion, and rational expediency) may be advanced. But to the extent that such claims and justifications (and their supporting myths, ideologies, and ruling formulae) imply promises, the failure to grant the promises necessitates rational expedience and state-supported violence and coercion. And to the extent that a regime relies primarily on the latter, it can neither fulfill its claims nor produce the productivity that would fulfill at least its material promises. A society based exclusively or predominantly on force thus can be neither legitimate (as belief) nor efficient. A low standard of well-being is thus the cost of exploitative, totalitarian societies.

A final "function" of legitimacy needs to be mentioned. We have noted that unchallenged power appears to confer legitimacy of force. Opposition is silenced, alternatives disappear, but—after the initial enthusiasm of victory— "acceptance" becomes minimal and passive. Yet, when we consider the relationship between states, an "illegitimate state" such as the First Republic of France, the Soviet Union, or Communist China (illegitimate in the eyes of its enemies) must be dealt with as a reality whether approved of or not. Recognition of such "illegitimate" regimes does not usually mean approval or acceptance of claims for legitimacy. It only recognizes their existence and the fact that an unfriendly regime can or must deal with that existence.

Yet, to the leaders of a regime striving for legitimacy, diplomatic recognition may be interpreted as recognition and "proof" of its proffered claims for legitimacy that they then broadcast to their underlying population in their attempts to justify themselves. Such recognition provides the ruling class of an "illegitimate" regime a basis for self-justification because it gives them the prestige of recognition from those who already have that quality. This kind of legitimacy need not be based on any other belief than the belief that the regime has power and is likely to endure.

Conclusions

This analysis of Weber's work on legitimacy and the implications of that work allow us to suggest a number of conclusions.

Weber uses the *concept* of legitimacy in at least five different ways, or—to state it differently—with five different meanings. These are:

1. legitimacy as a *claim* to power;

2. legitimacy as the *justification* of a regime;

3. legitimacy as the *promise* of a regime;

4. legitimacy as *self-justification* by the fortunate;

5. legitimacy as *belief* in the claims, promises, and justifications of the aspirants to, or holders, of power.

The first three of these meanings refer to legitimacy as *communicated* primarily to outsiders; the fourth as communicated to the self; and the fifth as communication *received* by the underlying population.

A sixth meaning is implicit in Weber's work: legitimacy as a by-product of power, the *legitimacy of force.* In this meaning, the very appearance of a stable, perhaps monolithic concentration of power grants a regime an acceptance based on the mere fact of power, on the absence of alternatives, and the hopelessness of challenges to the regime. This acceptance is minimal, passive, and may even become habitual (that is, not based on conscious acceptance of a regime or the awareness of the possibility of alternatives).

Established regimes are based on—in addition to legitimacy—rational expediency, their ability to provide material benefits, jobs, and positions of wealth, power, and prestige that are unrelated in "belief." But to the extent that they create such positions of good fortune, they create the need for legitimacy as self-justification. Established regimes can also be sustained by force, coercion, and the ability to terrorize, depoliticize, and privatize an underlying population and to render obedience into habitual behavior. These coercive aspects of power may result in the "legitimacy of force."

But because every legitimate political order, other than those based on pure charisma, rests on some amount of force and because all are based upon some amount of rational expediency, a regime based exclusively on "pure legitimacy," *legitimacy as belief,* cannot exist. This is to say that the *theory* of legitimacy is unprovable. That theory ultimately asserts that government rests on the *belief* in its underlying principles. This does not mean that some segments of a population do not believe in the principles of legitimacy of a government or that governments do not make claims, promises, or justifications. But it does mean that there is no way to ascertain, before the fact, how much belief or positive acceptance is necessary from how many members of a regime's underlying population (and of what characteristics) in order to justify the regime's legitimacy via belief. Ultimately, it is not possible to separate "believers" from self-justifiers, expedient supporters, passive accepters, or the apathetic, the hopeless, and the apolitical, whose support is purchased by the gratification of material or ideal interests other than that of belief, or by "legitimacy of force" per se.

Thus, governments are not "required" to redeem their claims, fulfill their promises, or justify their existence. To exist, they are "required" only to maintain sufficient positive and passive support on any basis whatever—including belief—to prevent parties and movements based upon other principles of legitimacy from becoming dominant.

Since the *theory of legitimacy* is untestable in the absence of empirical situations of pure voluntarism, the attribution of legitimacy as *belief* to an empirical political order is indeterminable.

Another criticism that we have made of Weber's use of the *concept* of legitimacy is that any system of legitimacy implies a political theory, an ideology, a political myth, or formulae, a theoretical system that gives substantive content and consistency to its particular claims, promises, or justifications. In his formal political sociology, Weber barely mentioned these theoretical underpinnings to legitimate political orders. From time to time, he referred to "myths," "maxims," even "ideologies," but he did not develop in any detail those concepts concerning the relationship of legitimating theory to "the legitimacy of social action." His central focus in *Economy and Society* was on social action and control, and not on the history of ideas. In his sociology of religion, Weber concentrated on precisely those underlying "rationales," theodicy and theology, as providing the theoretical background for religious action and organization. In his sociology of religion, he dealt with those aspects of charismatic religious movements that he avoided when dealing with the same topics in his political sociology. We may conclude that Weber may have neglected legitimating political theory because his work in political sociology was much less developed than was his work on the sociology of religion, or we may speculate that his political sociology was much more formal than his sociology of religion.

Regardless of these speculations, one can infer that the study of political legitimation, if it is useful at all, would require much greater emphasis on legitimating theory than Weber suggested in his work. But the fact that Weber's general theory of legitimation is not falsifiable does not mean the concepts of legitimacy and its various subtypes or the theory of legitimacy itself are useless for a variety of purposes.

At a heuristic level, the specific concepts and theory of legitimacy point to attempts of regimes and claimants to political power to justify their claims and to attain or maintain support from critical groups in a population. The content of these claims and their communication and reception among critical groups, along with other techniques of achieving and retaining power, are of critical importance in posing basic questions in political sociology. The answers to these questions in specific empirical work are indispensable. But the theory per se does not provide at a theoretical level the answers to the questions posed, nor does it provide clear-cut criteria for the resolution of the problems it raises in research—especially the inability to separate legitimacy as belief from other kinds of legitimacy and from other kinds of "support" for a regime. The absence of these theoretical criteria means that the results of research on legitimacy have to be evaluated after the fact of research and must be based upon criteria and evidence that emerge in the process of the research. Since this is Weber's ultimate evaluation of the importance of theory in research, criticism of Weber's work on this ground would have to be made from methodological perspectives other than his own.

Weber used the concept of legitimacy primarily to focus on the emergence of rational-legal orders of domination, particularly bureaucracy, and on rational systems of law emerging out of traditional (especially patrimonial) and charismatic regimes. His emphasis was on how claims for legitimacy influence the way legitimate orders were fashioned or evolved. He was less interested in, and rarely studied, the element of *belief* in the claims for legitimacy. Instead, he concentrated on the consequences of claims for the ensuing legal, administrative, and political orders of a society. Again, it would be difficult to argue against such a position if Weber had not stressed legitimacy as belief.

Another basic idea of Weber's is involved in his conception of rational law and rational-legal legitimacy. He reasoned that once a legitimate order becomes dominant—whether based upon belief, expediency, or coercion—the principles used to claim legitimacy and the promises and justifications of its theory or myth become, in principle, binding on all those who advance or in some way accept the claims of the system, to the extent that they accept or are forced to accept its claims. We have indicated that Weber suggests different levels of generality and "jurisdiction" of a given set of "maxims" deriving from a theory or system of legitimacy. Thus, once a system is accepted and institutionalized, power holders and those who accept or are forced to accept the system at *any level of belief* (except, by definition, charismatic leaders) are constrained by the system of legitimacy and become subject to its sanctions, legal or conventional, for violation of principles of legitimacy.

The prosecution of violations of the dominant principles of legitimacy, when enforced, define legitimacy as precedent in traditional or common law or, when spelled out in detail, become the basis for rational-legal codes.

Thus, within the area of their acceptance and implementation, a system of legitimacy has a degree of objectivity and "validity" that makes it something other than a chimera or phantasmagoria. But that objectivity and validity are not based on natural law or natural right.

Legitimacy is thus minimally based upon formal acceptance and implementation of a state's or ruler's claims, promises, and justifications. Within that framework of acceptance, the state can provide the basis for specific legal and quasi-legal extensions and applications (either rational or traditional).

Illegitimacy is thus a means for defining legitimacy. Prosecution of illegitimacy defines (and is defined within) the framework of accepted or extended principles of legitimacy. Delegitimation is of an entirely different order. Delegitimation can only be understood as the overt outright, self-conscious attack on the very principles on which a political order ultimately makes its claims, justifies itself, or makes its promises.

The relationship between legitimacy and delegitimation is not linear. Delegitimation—that is, attacks on the legitimacy of a political order—may be evoked by a crisis in a legitimate order that reveals suddenly and dramatically the extent to which the legitimate order has failed to justify its claims or, minimally, to keep its promises. But such "delegitimation" is likely to occur only when the legitimate order is unable to squelch opposition or to keep it from growing. Legitimacy is thus attained by a balance of terror.

Yet such an argument—that legitimacy does not exist—is extreme. In extreme situations, even the appearance of legitimacy is likely to be sacrificed to the necessity for maintaining political power, usually, however, under the banner of legitimating slogans. In less extreme situations, the need for self-justification by the *fortunate* facilitates a minimally voluntaristic acceptance of the claims for legitimacy. Any regime that even pretends to claim legitimacy thus must put its claims to a test, the test of voluntarism. If a regime practices total coercion, terrorism, and depoliticization and renders its population passive, apathetic, or privatized, it cannot base its claims even on the appearance of belief by its subjects. The existence of totalitarianism is prima facie evidence of illegitimacy. The absence of totalitarianism, however, as previously indicated, is not evidence of *legitimacy as belief.*

Systems of legitimacy have three other functions. First, to the extent that a regime can establish some degree of acceptance by *belief or expediency*, it can minimize the cost of repression, surveillance, and police work. Second, to the extent that a regime can gain acceptance by either belief or rational expediency, it can motivate its populace to work and to increase productivity. Legitimacy produces moral, willing obedience, work, and productivity. This function of legitimacy may well have stimulated modern totalitarian states to seek less terroristic means of securing obedience than they have in the past. But, if legitimacy is to be based on voluntary acceptance rather than on organized terror, then the political activation involved may result in rising expectations, with new, politically conscious masses becoming aware of transparencies in the systems of exploitation that have governed them in the past. Stable patterns of legitimacy based on relatively voluntaristic acceptance are difficult to attain.

A final function of legitimacy is the ability of a regime to trade off its internal power for international recognition and to use its international recognition as a justification for its power within its domestic society. While such trade-offs occur, and are the basis for a great deal of international politics, they are only as stable as the regimes themselves. They are necessities of the moment and revisable with each turn in internal and international politics. Yet they constitute an additional basis for "legitimacy of power."

Thus, the concept of legitimacy may have a variety of meanings and "functions" of which "pure" legitimacy, understood as legitimacy as belief, may be empirically one of the least important meanings. This does not mean that the term *legitimacy* must be abandoned. It does mean that extreme care must be used in applying the term; one must recognize the various specific dimensions of meaning involved in concrete, historical situations and not theorize from an "essential" definition.

Notes

1. Weber did not use the term, but, in the following discussion, we will use that term when its use is implied in the context.

2. Max Weber, *Economy and Society: An Outline of Interpretive Sociology*, eds. Guenther Roth and Claus Wittich, 3 vols. (New York: Bedminster Press, 1968), 31.

3. One may add that this notion of a process of claiming access and monopolization over social, sacred, and political values is one of the most general social processes in Weber's work. "The development of status is essentially a question of stratification resting on usurpation." See Max Weber, *From Max Weber: Essays in Sociology*, eds. and trans. Hans H. Gerth and C. Wright Mills (New York: Oxford University Press, 1946), 189. And "For all practical purposes, stratification by status goes hand in hand with the monopolization of ideal and material goods and opportunities in a manner we come to know as typical." See *From Max Weber*, 190. Weber uses the concept of claims, monopolization, and closure with respect to all values, politics, honor, salvation, occupational and professional preferment, citizenship, eligibility for salvation, and so on. *Economy and Society*, 43-47, 341-48.

4. *Economy and Society*, 213.

5. *Ibid.*

6. *Ibid.*, 113.

7. *From Max Weber*, 78-79.

8. *Ibid.*, 79.

9. *Ibid.*, 80.

10. *Ibid.*, 78-79.

11. *Economy and Society*, 35.

12. *Ibid.*

13. *Ibid.*, 36.

14. *Ibid.*

15. *Ibid.*

16. *Ibid.*

17. *Ibid.*

18. *Ibid.*, 217.

19. *Ibid.*, 215.

20. *Ibid.*, 117.

21. *From Max Weber*, 7.

22. *Economy and Society*, 31.

23. *Ibid.*, 214.

24. *Ibid.*, 31.

25. *Ibid.*, 32.

26. *Ibid.*, 37.

27. *Ibid.*, 32.

28. *From Max Weber,* 78.

29. *Economy and Society,* 954.

30. *Ibid.,* 953.

31. *Ibid.,* 935

32. *Ibid.,* 1134.

33. *Ibid.,* 112.

34. *Ibid.,* 242.

35. *Ibid.,* 243.

36. *Ibid.,* 263.

37. *Ibid.,* 265.

38. *Ibid.,* 272-74.

39. *From Max Weber,* 296.

40. *Economy and Society,* 266.

41. *Ibid.,* 1146-47.

42. *From Max Weber,* 252.

43. *Economy and Society,* 953.

44. *From Max Weber,* 275.

45. *Ibid.,* 271.

46. For Weber, the relative weight of voluntaristic factors such as belief or rational decision, of material factors, and of pure political

power is determined by specific historical research and not by a priori theoretical formulae.

47. *Economy and Society*, 953.

48. *Ibid.*, 263.

49. *Ibid.*, 268.

50. Here we are concerned only with the analysis and description of ideas as theoretical systems or structures, not with their "truth" or their consequences.

51. *From Max Weber*, 337, 340.

52. *Ibid.*, 184.

53. *Economy and Society*, 953.

PART IV
Expertise

11

Toward a Sociology of Expertness

Joseph Bensman with Israel Gerver

In all societies, the quality of expertness (virtuosity in the application of institutionalized skills) is highly valued and eagerly sought. Objectively, expertness is the quality of those who possess highly developed skills and techniques in any given field of activity. Such skills and techniques are consciously known and can be transmitted to others. As a social phenomenon, this objective aspect of expertness is only a point of departure for the sociological analysis of expertness and experts. Objective expertness is given social recognition that taxes the forms of prestige and esteem valuations and income possibilities. In part, the social rewards for expertness are related to the operations of social institutions and, in part, these rewards are related to the claims to expertness put forth by diverse groups.

The relationships between *objective* and *socially recognized* expertness are not simple ones. For example, groups receiving high status may retain such status even in periods where the institutional bases for their skills have disappeared.[1] Conversely, groups of experts may have objectively ascertainable skills but lack social recognition. To further complicate the picture, spurious expertness—for example, groups lacking skills but claiming social recognition—is another possibility.[2]

Published originally in a slightly different form in *Social Forces* 32 (March 1954), 226-35. Republished by permission from Oxford University Press.

Expert status is granted or denied by public acceptance or rejection of claims. In a society where ascriptive criteria are emphasized, the public designation of experts is fairly easy. In an open class society, the public selection of experts and the criteria of expertness are more difficult. The difficulties arise because vast segments of the population are unfamiliar with objective expert skills and with the operations of major social institutions and, therefore, unable to evaluate and select experts and criteria of expertness with reference to the requirements of institutional operations.

Thus, in complex societies the term *expert* includes a range of real experts, pseudoexperts, socially recognized and unrecognized experts, and various combinations of these. Such a heterogeneous mixture implies confusion by the public between the objective and socially recognized expertness. It is this public confusion that provides the basis for the following analysis. That is to say, it is on the "commonsense" level, paradoxical in that as knowledge is ordered and reduced to objectively known techniques, techniques become more developed and inaccessible to the public at large.

Elaboration of Concepts

Historically, the rise of the expert as someone tending to monopolize skills is associated with the development of intricate techniques in a society within which experts have demonstrated socially valuable results of their efforts.[3] Experts do not arrive in a society spontaneously, but are the result of a complex process of institutional development, claims for recognition as experts, and the granting of social recognition by strategic groups.

A significant element in this granting of recognition is the *social visibility* of those claiming expertness and the *social distance* of the conferring groups from the alleged experts.[4] The more distant groups—that is, those least technically qualified—grant recognition that is based not on a knowledge of expert procedures, methods, and information, but instead on the imputed consequences of expert action. Thus, recognition of expertness carries with it the conferring of prestige. The procedures and methods of the expert are viewed by the distant lay person as a form of magic. The imputed results of expert action are the results that *appear* to be observable to the distant lay person. The results *actually* observed at a more intimate level—that is, by other experts—would be assigned to other factors by the particular experts in question. Among peers, the expert is granted recognition as expert less because of results but more with reference to scientific, technical, and procedural competence. Such esteem is not, of course, necessarily congruent with the prestige accruing from out-group evaluation.

The recognition of expertness, then, will vary with the social distance of conferring groups, and their criteria of recognition.[5] When these elements are analyzed, it can be seen that experts are socially recognized in terms of four different possibilities that can be viewed as aspects of expertness found in large-scale organizations.[6] (See table 1.)

Substantive Aspect. This aspect, deriving from the dual relationship of a relevant in-group and their criteria of judging expert peers, implies technical virtuosity per se. This means that the substantive aspect of the expert is known fully only to those who possess the requisite knowledge and, thus, are in a sufficiently close position to evaluate the operations of others with reference to their possession of techniques and theoretical and empirical knowledge for any given specialized field.

Administrative Aspect. This refers to the judgments of the in-group with reference to their selection and evaluation of others, who are not practicing or substantive experts. However, those viewed under this aspect can communicate with substantive experts, possibly because the administrator may have been trained as a substantive expert. A typical example of what we have in mind in distinguishing the administrative and substantive aspects would be the hospital administrator who is also an MD. The administrative aspect refers to those experts who coordinate, facilitate, recruit, and arrange the activities of other experts in a formal association in order to execute agreed-upon policies.

Table 1. Aspects of Expertness

Conferring groups	Criteria of recognition	
	Technical knowledge	Non-technical knowledge
In-group	Substantive	Administrative
Out-group	Interpretive	Symbolic

Interpretive Aspect. This expert viewed in this manner performs the procedures of negotiating, communicating, translating, and making comprehensible the mysteries of substantive knowledge to the distant and lay public. His expert stature is granted by the laymen, whereas the substantive experts devalue him as a popularizer at best and a vulgarizer at worst. He may be attached to an organization or be in a semiautonomous position. He is usually not a practicing substantive expert for reasons that will be apparent in a later section of this paper.[7]

Symbolic Aspect. Here we deal with those individuals or groups who personify and symbolize expertness in any given complex field for the uninitiated public. However, symbolic experts may personify complexities not only for the distant public, but also for insiders under conditions that are sufficiently complex so that these complexities cannot be understood exclusively and immediately in terms of direct participant experience. For example, an Einstein will symbolize the expert physicist to all in- and out-group members, except perhaps to those who are his peers. However, Einstein is not merely a *self-selected* symbol of expertise. He is a practicing substantive expert. In many fields of endeavor, the symbolic expert is not actually a substantive expert but appears to be one. The symbolic expert is not necessarily a particular living person but may be a complex of traditional evaluations and definitions that become personified. The history of artistic taste provides numerous examples, such as the evaluations at later times of Rembrandt, Beethoven, Bach, and Van Gogh. In science, the names of Copernicus and Galileo exemplify the strength of nonliving symbols.

These four aspects represent a formulation of the ever-present dilemma of all mass organizations—namely, the problem of simultaneously presenting a favorable image to the public in response to its demands and maintaining the integrity and coherence of the organization. The successful large-scale organization expresses both objectives by orienting the substantive and administrative aspects toward the internal organizational structure, while the symbolic and interpretive aspects are directed toward the rest of the society.

Perspectives of Experts

In large-scale organizations, these aspects of expertness become recognized and embodied in tables of formal organization.[8] One result of this formal recognition is the segmentation of expert aspects and a tendency toward polarization into expert role types—that is, *the administrator, the researcher.* While polarization is never actually complete, the assumption that it is complete becomes a heuristic device for the analysis of tensions resulting from differential perspectives of the corresponding expert types. These tensions not only affect particular experts within a given organization, but also have consequences for the total organization.

This means that different expert types become preoccupied with different types of problems—that is, pure research, dealing with the outside public, coordinating formal divisions within an organization, and so on. Out of these different problems, each type of expert develops different perspectives corresponding to the peculiarities of his preoccupations. The discussion at this point will concentrate on divergences of other types from the perspectives of the substantive expert.

The substantive expert is interested most typically in increasing and enlarging the scope of the available knowledge in his field. This means that he is also interested in developing techniques, procedures, and means of making his conceptual schema more explicit and verifiable.[9] In the role of substantive expert, his strategic public consists of other substantive experts, and his communications are directed to them. He is not primarily interested in communicating with the general public and indeed may become increasingly removed from nonexperts. Thus, his field of substantive knowledge will appear to distant lay persons increasingly mysterious and incomprehensible as he pursues his demons.[10]

Costs and organizational arrangements interest the substantive expert only insofar as they impinge upon or interfere with his major preoccupations. He is only peripherally interested in the consequences of his results for nonexperts and for the administrative, symbolic, and interpretive types of experts within his own organization. The results expected by others from the practice of his expertness in his job do, however, provide an opportunity for him to develop basic substantive additions to his knowledge.

In contradistinction, the administrative expert aims for efficient means of obtaining organizationally defined practical results. He is interested in minimizing costs, stabilizing and routinizing the flow of operations, and coordinating diverse types of substantive expert activity with the activities of nonexperts. The primary concerns of the administrative type are of secondary concern and are even irritations to the substantive expert, and vice versa. However, the administrative type may provide favorable protective strata for the substantive expert and relieve him of extraneous problems of organizational routine. From the viewpoint of the substantive expert, the best administrator is one who takes control of organizational tasks—for example, equipment, supplies, and budgetary appropriations—and does not press for results or interfere in the substantive expert's major activities.

Similarly, the interpretive and symbolic experts focus on results—that is, visible results. The *pure* symbolic type, one who is not a substantive expert as well, is interested in the results but not primarily in the procedures for obtaining them. He symbolizes these results in his role of public representative of a large-scale organization. The interpretive expert who is attached to the organization publicizes the results and creates and maintains the symbolic expert. Both emphasize the magic of scientific technique to the public at large. Both are likely to pressure the substantive experts for publicly demonstrable results and are more likely to announce these results before the substantive expert would do so.[11] Such a tendency may be checked by the administrative and substantive experts. The substantive experts tend to be ambivalent toward the symbolic and interpretive types. They can raise the prestige level of expert fields, but may do so by means that are viewed as unwarranted and occasionally reprehensible. Generally, the substantive expert views the symbolic and interpretive group as amateurs in the grossest sense.

Typically, one can find divisions and conflicts within organizations on the bases of these differing perspectives, but, given these differences, some degree of conflict is intrinsic to complex organizations. To the uninitiated, this situation is viewed with surprise and alarm. However, conflicts do become real problems when they threaten the effective operation of the organization or imperil the status holders within it.

These differences in perspective not only can account for periodic organizational disruptions but also can lead to interesting consequences for the substantive expert as he incorporates the views of others into his own perspective.[12]

No *actual* substantive expert *completely* corresponds to the model previously drawn. As an individual dealing with nonexperts, he becomes a symbol of the field for them and is expected to act as a symbol of his profession. In his relationships with administrators, institutionalized symbols, and communicators, the substantive expert is expected to respond to their definitions of his role. To complicate matters further, he also may act in terms of a prior self-image of scientist, professional, and scholar.

Given this plurality of expectations of others and his own occupational standards, the substantive expert may view these expectations as a series of alternative choices. Actually, his responses are further limited by his set of personal value preferences that makes the rewards of alternative choices meaningful.[13] In his responses to nonscientific expectations, he may (1) reject behavior that is inconsistent with his image of the scientist; (2) compartmentalize his behavioral responses into work and nonwork spheres or public and private patterns, thereby rendering unto Caesar what is Caesar's; or (3) define the situation in its immediacy and act accordingly, thereby responding to the strongest pressures. In this case, his behavior does not reflect any particular perspective. Psychologically, the long-run cost of such segmental behavior is very great. In this case, he ceases to be exclusively a substantive expert and acts as if he were a calculating opportunist. He may even become an unwitting instrumentality for achieving the goals of others. In order to minimize conflicts resulting from divergences between his perspective and external demands, the substantive expert has to respond in the long run to that set of external demands that is most consistent with his own core values and occupational ethos. The rewards for such selective behavior partially determine the pattern of his mobility.

Divergent Perspectives and Career Mobility

In modern large-scale industry, expertise becomes the basis of mobility for the substantive expert into nonsubstantive positions. Expertise can be an entry point or a necessary requirement for a large number of status positions. Mobility involves the possession of skills of high order and shifts in type of expert perspectives. If these changes are either great or rapid, psychological tensions may result.[14] Tensions among those who shift perspectives or who simultaneously adhere to different perspectives are normal psychological concomitants of institutionalized mobility patterns.[15]

Keeping in mind the roughly drawn differences in perspectives of our four types of expert, we can now focus on the consequences of a shifting career; that is, what can and does occur when, for example, the substantive expert in his mobile career turns into one of the other types?

The substantive expert, when he moves to another position in an organization, is forced to some extent to abandon his original perspective. The requirements of an administrative position, for example, demand a refocusing and reorientation of the canons of the disinterested seeker after truth.[16] At the same time, the substantive expert retains in part a perspective that has been basic to his professional training and development. There exists in such situations a potential conflict within the mobile expert. Mobility is made difficult by the existence within an expert of these divergent perspectives. If the mobile expert persists in retaining completely the initial substantive ethos, he will be hampered in his administrative duties. If he adopts the administrative expert's perspective, he may feel guilty of abandoning what to him and his formerly significant public is a primary ethos. This can further result in insecurity in his relationships with those experts who still practice their professions. This is especially true because substantive experts viewing the organization from their special standards are apt to see other expert types as derivative, incompetent, or restrictive agents who take credit for substantive work, which they both hinder and misunderstand. Thus, in all bureaucracies, there is a myth that incompetence leads to advancement. See, for example, the use of terms like *kicked upstairs* and other, usually unprintable, terms in common usage.

Similarly, such conflicts may arise within the substantive expert who becomes a symbolic or interpretive expert by his own choice. To justify his new symbolic position, the self-selected symbolic expert must increasingly abandon his own ethos and replace it with a symbolic perspective that is congruent with the public's image of his new role. This does not apply of course to the *other-selected* symbolic expert who still is a practicing substantive expert—for example, Einstein, Toscanini, or, in his own time, Darwin. Conspicuous examples of self-selected symbolic experts who abandoned their substantive roles are numerous. Hindenberg and Petsin might be conceived of in this way; in music, Giacomo Rossini; in literature, Alexander Dumas père: in painting, Salvador Dali. In the latter instance, Dali, while still producing, has selected himself to symbolize surrealism. He secures his expert stature not only by virtue of his accumulated technical perfection, but also by behavior that is admitted charlatanry. Dali exemplified a case of charlatanry that has become a field of expertness. Thus, Dali is also a self-selected and self-admitted symbol of charlatanry.[17] Contemporary examples of the self-selected symbolic expert moving from substantive stature can be found in almost all large-scale business, educational, and political institutions.

In order to appeal to the public image, the symbolic expert as head of an operating organization continuously demands "visible results" from substantive experts and claims these results easily in order to legitimize securely his new position. The substantive expert who becomes an interpretive expert may experience similar tensions if he relinquishes his substantive role entirely.

Institutional Determinants of Expertness

The responses to mobility situations, the discrepancies between public and self-images of experts and expertise, the proliferation and divergency of expert perspectives, are not only significant in and of themselves; they attain a broader meaning when viewed in a context of institutional changes. Indeed, the dynamics of expertness can also be fruitfully viewed as indicators of changes in the larger society.

The following institutional elements are postulated as conditions for the existence of differentiated expertise: (1) the development of scientific technology with a history of demonstrable results requiring (2) an ever-increasing social division of labor and (3) an ever-increasing segmentation of work tasks occurring as part of (4) the rise of bureaucratic organization based on a rational and "firmly ordered system of super- and subordination," resulting in (5) the physical and social alienation of individuals from others in organizations and from organizations as entities.[18] The significance of points one through five rests upon the technical superiority of bureaucratic organization over other forms and from the resultant absorption of the working force and the rest of society into bureaucratic procedures.[19]

This dominance of society by bureaucracies is not a smooth process and produces resistance; when *scientific technology* (that is, substantive expertness) becomes ordered by *scientific organization* (that is, administrative expertness), conflicts between the two become the basis for ideological conflicts. This "silent warfare" of opposing myths has not the spectacular pyrotechnic of "the class struggle," but it is probably as basic in bureaucratic societies. This is not a case of ideology and utopia but rather the frequently overlooked conflict between two conservative vested interest groups.[20]

Expertness and Legitimacy

Historically, substantive experts have received and taken credit for additions to knowledge and demonstrated practical results. They have also received a high degree of prestige resulting, as previously noted, from achievements not thoroughly understood by the outgroup but nevertheless recognized as valuable achievements. Thus, substantive experts in our society, especially in fields of work clearly recognized as part of science, are traditionally legitimized. Other groups aspiring to the heights of expertise borrow the halo of science—for example, scientific salesmanship, advertising, social welfare, scientifically designed toothpaste, breakfast cereals; indeed, the whole paraphernalia of science—terminology, equipment, and furnishings—are all used to capitalize on the prestige of scientific expertness. This is apparent even in fields where scientific concepts and techniques are either primitive or nonexistent.[21]

Given this halo of science, the administrative expert who controls the organizational structures employing the substantive expert is in an anomalous position. He is confronted with the stupendous monopolization of accrued legitimacy by science and at the same time is forced to pay homage to science. The administrator's problem in view of his *dominant* position as an official of a bureaucracy is to achieve legitimacy for his position. His problem is especially complicated because the established legitimacy of his subordinates is a barrier to his own. Three possibilities exist, the first of which—the rejection of science—can be usually ruled out.

An outright rejection of science would be tantamount to occupational suicide by the administrator. Nonadministrative groups, for example, the *literati,* may in effect reject science by a romantic affirmation of a nonexistent past. The administrator can, however, attack a particular version of science as being an erroneous distortion of true science. If he is successful, he can substitute his preferred version of science.

The second possibility is to borrow the halo of science and confer it on administration. One way of doing this and gaining public consent is to equate scientific and administrative aspects of an organization and present the total organization to the public as a *scientific organization.*[22] Administrative aspects are easily concealed from the public because of social distance and the complexity of the phenomena. The bureaucratic ethos and ethic[23] is one of concealing internal administration and political arrangements from the public.[24] Both symbolic and attached interpretive experts are instruments for his transvaluation of an organization.[25]

The third method of achieving legitimacy is to create and present administration as a science in its own right—thus, the vogues of scientific management, business, and public administration found in contemporary university curricula and in some of the intellectually oriented business organizations. The literature on the application of science to all types of administration has reached monumental proportions and constitutes a growing portion of the behavioral sciences. A quasi-scientific undergraduate education is assumed to be a requirement for those aspiring to administrative positions. This development has been fostered by the schools and supported by both businessmen and public administrators.

Both the development of administration as a science and the equating of science and administration within organizations are neither mutually exclusive nor contradictory. The latter is practiced by the hard-boiled and nontheoretical working administrator, while the former is the concern of university business schools and intellectuals in business and politics.

Expertness and Organizational Power[26]

Through time, experts increasingly develop prestige and legitimacy. However, the power and prestige of an individual expert worker (apart from the symbolic personalities) decrease. As any substantive field of expertise increases in prestige, larger numbers of workers are attracted to the field. This growth of an occupational population decreases the indispensability of any *particular* member of that segment of the labor force, making the individual worker more replaceable and interchangeable.[27]

The consequences of the inconsistency between the legitimacy and power of administrators in bureaucratic societies are equally important for the substantive experts. As the substantive field expands in knowledge, concepts, and techniques, specialized fields emerge. As specialists flood into these newer branches, the generalized type of substantive expert tends to disappear from the occupation and can possibly remain as a symbol of the general field. At the work level, only a bureaucracy has the apparatus to handle rationally this proliferation of substantive expertise. The specialists develop narrower perspectives that hamper them in attaining positions within the substantive framework that would permit them to comprehend the larger field of knowledge, work, and organizational context as a totality.[28]

The specialized substantive expert confronted with the omnipresence of bureaucracy is not in a position to deal with it as a totality.

Only the higher administrative expert and some of the self-selected symbolic experts can approach such comprehension. Since the substantive specialist cannot deal with organizations as a totality, he is relatively powerless.[29]

The affiliation of the specialized expert with a substantive field that has publicly recognized legitimacy intensifies this quixotic position. The attainment of power for the individual specialist in a bureaucratic setting is made difficult because he is now a specialist and more isolated than the older-style substantive expert; he is devalued because he is more subject to manipulation by nonsubstantive experts. His vulnerability to manipulation is therefore a dual function of his overspecialization and his interchangeability.[30]

Viewed then in the larger historical sense, expertise increasingly develops prestige and legitimacy, but the power and prestige of the individual working expert decrease.

In a bureaucracy, the substantive "specialist" expert consequently becomes resentful because his power position is not consistent with his traditional legitimacy. When, in addition, administrative and symbolic experts borrow his prestige halo and identify it with the organization generally and themselves in particular, moral indignation then achieves its highest level. All the frustrations and resentments developing in fragmented perspectives, isolation, mobility, and powerlessness reach their zenith.

The Independent Professional[31]

The major trends in the development of bureaucratized expertise become pointed in the contemporary difference between the employed and free professional. The special characteristic of the substantive expert who is not employed in a bureaucracy is that he is simultaneously a substantive expert, an administrative expert, and a symbolic figure. Because he is in direct and continuous contact with large numbers of clients, he is viewed as a symbol of the profession and is likely to accept this role and adopt a symbolic perspective. This means that he might exaggerate and emphasize the mystery and magic of his expertness before the uninitiated. As an interpreter, he is likely to mix this aspect with his symbolic role. He is also an administrator, though relatively little administration is required.

In contradistinction to the bureaucratized expert, the free professional is therefore not oriented toward administrative goals, is not isolated from the public, and is not merely a functionnaire. Instead, all of the separate aspects of the bureaucratized types of experts are integrated into a series of interlocking roles expressed by one person.[32]

What is central to the development of bureaucratized expertness is the separation of roles. Hierarchical and functional integration is emphasized at an organizational level rather than at a personal one. Complexity in social relations is introduced. The public becomes increasingly distant from the administrative and substantive aspects of work and is presented with symbols of organization especially manufactured by interpretive and symbolic experts. Thus, a halo of science, efficiency, service, and results is associated with bureaucratic organization for the purposes of those who control it. In common parlance, this is known as "public relations" both in its broadest and narrowest sense.

The Collapse of Socially Objective Reality

Because of the alienation of all groups from the actual technical workings of bureaucracy, no single group can judge it from first-hand experience.[33] This is especially true of the distant public. Given increasing role segmentation, any particular person's experience is relatively valueless as a guide to the comprehension of the experiences of a differentiated complex society. In other words, personal experience does not provide sufficient reference points for the understanding of public affairs.[34]

In addition, these synthetic substitutes have little coherency. One reason is the existence of pluralities of vested interest groups and concomitantly a plurality of competing symbol manufacturers. Thus, there is no single, integrated, coherent symbolic system that can organize experience. One consequence of this situation is public apathy.[35] Apathy, however, alternates with a rejection of one's own personal experience and a romanticizing of either the past or some not-too-far-distant utopia.[36]

The fragmentation of expertise represents the fragmentation of social experience in an incomprehensible society.[37]

The social scientist is in a unique position in confronting the problems posed here. The very nature of his expertness enables him to go beyond the symbols and analyze the experiential basis of social existence. At the same time, his technical virtuosity enables him, if he wishes, to assist in the manufacture and manipulation of symbols or in preparing the ground for symbol manufacturers and manipulation.[38] In a bureaucratic world, power holders can grant him prestige, employability, income, and the illusion of power and authority if he can demonstrate results. If the latter course is followed, social science can assist in the collapse of reality and the devaluation of experience.[39]

Conclusions

One relationship between objectively defined expertness and socially claimed and recognized expertness is generally understood by expert groups. In a society where symbolic expressions of reality are emphasized and the underlying experiential reality is devalued, the achievements of experts who manipulate symbols—that is, the interpretive type and the achievements of those who personify and symbolize a field—transcend the objective skills and techniques associated with an occupation. The attainment of expert status thereby becomes equated with successful public relations. The measure of expertness then is increasingly the extent to which publicizing "leads" to social acceptance.

In bureaucratic settings, experts can rarely publicize themselves. As already noted, substantive expertness is often co-opted and publicly presented as an organizational attribute. The net effect, though not necessarily the intention, is that the individual substantive expert in such a situation can usually only publicize the bureaucracy.[40]

Notes

1. Arthur J. Vidich, *Social Structure of Palau* (PhD Dissertation in the Department of Social Relations, Harvard University, 1953), later published as *The Political Impact of Colonial Administration* (New York: Arno Press, 1980).

2. Grete De Francesco, *The Power of the Charlatan*, trans. Miriam Beard (New Haven: Yale University Press, 1939).

3. Talcott Parsons, "The Professions and Social Structure," in *Essays in Sociological Theory, Pure and Applied* (Glencoe, IL: Free Press, 1949), 189: "This professional authority has a peculiar sociological structure. It is not as such based on generally superior status. . . . It is rather based on the superior 'technical competence' of the professional man. . . . A professional man is held to be 'an authority' only in his own field."

4. Walter Lippmann, *The Phantom Public* (New York: Harcourt, Brace and Company, 1925), 42: "Modern society is not visible to anybody, nor intelligible continuously and as a whole. One section is visible to another section, one series of acts is intelligible to this group and another to that."

5. Lippmann, 144: "The specific, technical, intimate criteria required in the handling of a question are not for the public. The public's criteria are generalized for many problems: they turn essentially on procedure and the overt, external forms of behavior."

6. Lippmann, 150: "The fundamental difference which matters is that between insiders and outsiders. Their relations to a problem are radically different. Only the insider can make decisions, not because he is inherently a better man, but because he is so placed that he can

understand and can act. The outsider is necessarily ignorant, usually irrelevant and often meddlesome, because he is trying to navigate the ship from dry land."

7. Alfred M. Lee, "Public Relations Counseling as Institutional Psychiatry," *Psychiatry* 6 (August 1943), 272 (quoting J. P. Jones and D. McL. Church, *At the Bar of Public Opinion: A Brief for Public Relations* [New York: Inter-River Press, 1939]). See this article also for Lee's analysis of public relations counselors as scientific reformers, and psychiatrists catering to institutional problems. For an analysis of the composition and ideology of the interpretive expert, see Lelia A. Sussman, "The Personnel and Ideology of Public Relations," *Public Opinion Quarterly* 12 (Winter 1948-49), 697-708. For the most recent appraisal of the role of public relations, see William H. Whyte Jr., *Is Anybody Listening?* (New York: Simon and Schuster, 1952).

8. Robin M. Williams Jr., "Application of Research to Practice: Sociological Research and Intergroup Relations" (paper presented before the American Sociological Society, September 3, 1952), 3-6.

9. Max Weber, *From Max Weber: Essays in Sociology*, eds. and trans. Hans H. Gerth and C. Wright Mills (New York: Oxford University Press, 1946), 138.

10. The substantive type is deliberately overdrawn. No persons who are practicing experts exclusively adopt this role in *all* their social behavior. The consequences of multiple role involvements are discussed below.

11. Robin M. Williams Jr., 6: "The social scientist is confronted with the further fact that the practitioners tend to be heavily committed to 'action rather than talk': there is a pragmatic emphasis upon 'getting things done,' either because of intense value commitments

and ideological convictions, or because of pressures (from relevant publics, sponsors, administrative superiors, and so forth) to 'show results.'"

12. Robert K. Merton, "Role of the Intellectual in Public Bureaucracy," in his *Social Theory and Social Structure* (Glencoe: Free Press, 1949), 163-72.

13. See Max Weber, *The Theory of Social and Economic Organization*, trans. Talcott Parsons (New York: Oxford University Press, 1947), 88-124, for a discussion of social action as action involving subjective meanings to actor. See also Talcott Parsons and Edward. A. Shils, eds., *Toward a General Theory of Action* (Cambridge, MA: Harvard University Press, 1951), 309, for Tolman's statement on the importance of including the actor himself as part of the action situation.

14. William Miller, *Men in Business* (Cambridge, MA: Harvard University Press, 1952), 293.

15. Merton, 177-78. See his list of frustrations from conflicts of values between intellectuals and policy makers and from the bureaucratic type of organization itself.

16. Miller, 298-99 (quoting Chester Barnard, *The Functions of the Executive* [Cambridge, MA: Harvard University Press, 1933], 224); "The Thirty Thousand Managers," *Fortune*, February 1940, 62; and David Riesman, "The Saving Remnant: A Study of Character," in John W. Chase, ed., *Years of the Modern* (New York: Longmans, Green, 1949), 31. See also Merton, 165.

17. De Francesco, *The Power of the Charlatan*; Salvador Dali, *The Private Life of Salvador Dali* (New York: Dial Press, 1942).

18. Miller, 291-92.

19. Seymour Martin Lipset and Reinhard Bendix, "Social Mobility and Occupational Career Patterns, II: Social Mobility," *American Journal of Sociology* 57 (March 1952), 497; and Kermit Eby, "The Expert in the Labor Movement," *American Journal of Sociology* 57 (July 1951), 32.

20. *From Max Weber,* 243: "Behind all present discussions of the foundations of the educational system, the struggle of the 'specialist type of man' against the older type of 'cultivated man' is hidden at some decisive point. This fight is determined by the irresistibly expanding bureaucratization of all public and private relations of authority and by the ever-increasing importance of expert and specialized knowledge. This fight intrudes into all intimate cultural questions."

21. Whyte, *passim.*

22. Reinhard Bendix and L. R. Fisher, "The Perspectives of Elton Mayo," *Review of Economies and Statistics* 31 (November 1915), 312-19, especially 316-19.

23. *Ethos* refers to a universal principle of bureaucracy, while *ethic* refers to a personal code of honor—that is, an internalization of the ethos.

24. *From Max Weber,* 233: "Every bureaucracy seeks to increase the superiority of the professionally informed by keeping their knowledge and intentions secret. Bureaucratic administration always tends to be an administration of 'secret sessions'; insofar as it can, it hides its knowledge and action from criticism."

25. Miller, 288.

26. *From Max Weber,* 232-39.

27. Karl Mannheim, *Man and Society in an Age of Reconstruction* (New York: Harcourt, Brace and Company, 1940), 100: "The glut of intellectuals decreases the value of the intellectuals and of intellectual culture itself."

28. At a nonoccupational level, learned societies attempt to provide a forum for such comprehension.

29. Mannheim, 47.

30. Shepard Mead, *How to Succeed in Business Without Really Trying* (New York: Simon and Schuster, 1952), 4-5: "*Don't Be a Specialist.* If you have a special knack, such as drawing or writing, forget it. You may receive more at the very start for special abilities, but don't forget the *long haul.* You don't want to wind up behind a filing case or writing! It is the ability to Get Along, to Make Decisions, and to Get Contacts that will drive you ahead. Be an 'all around' man of no special ability and you will rise to the top." See also Wilbert Moore, *Industrial Relations and the Social Order* (New York: Macmillan, 1947), 124: "The higher the position a person occupies in a line of authority, the more general must his abilities be."

31. The independent professional is not here regarded as, for example, Laski, Carr-Saunders, Wilson, and Parsons regard him. The emphasis here is rather on those aspects of "free professions" that point up the phenomenon of bureaucratized expertness. Thus, such aspects of professionalism as fees, ethical codes, professional societies, journals, etc., are not treated here.

32. Alfred M. Lee, "The Social Dynamics of the Physician's Status," *Psychiatry* 7 (November 1944), 371-77.

33. Mannheim, 59.

34. C. Wright Mills, *White Collar* (New York: Oxford University Press, 1953), 347-48: "The issues of politics, it is often said, are now so technical and intricate that the individual cannot be expected to understand them or be alert to their consequences. . . . The idea that the issues are too intricate for a people's decision is a curious blend of bureaucratic perspectives (which would equal the public with the executive organs of the government, rather than with effective intervention in general decisions of general consequence)." See also Lippman, 13-14: "Yet these public affairs are in no convincing way his affairs. They are for the most part invisible. They are managed, if they are managed at all, at distant centers, from behind the scenes, by unnamed powers. As a private person he does not know for certain what is going on, or who is doing it, or where he is being carried. No newspaper reports his environment so that he can grasp it; no school has taught him how to imagine it; his ideals, often, do not fit with it; listening to speeches, uttering opinions, do not, he finds, enable him to govern it. He lives in a world which he cannot see, does not understand and is unable to direct."

35. Mills, 339.

36. Karl Mannheim, *Ideology and Utopia* (New York: Harcourt, Brace and Company, 1936), *passim.*

37. *From Max Weber*, 356-57: "Viewed in this way, all 'culture' appears as man's emancipation from the organically prescribed life cycle of natural life. For this very reason culture's every step forward seems condemned to lead to an ever more devastating senselessness. This advancement of cultural values, however, seems to become a senseless hustle in the service of worthless, moreover self-contradictory, and mutually antagonistic ends."

38. Merton, 171.

39. Merton, ch. 13, especially 323-24 on "Specialization and the Professional Ethic."

40. One exception to this may be found in the occupational society that cuts across specific organizations employing experts. In the professional and learned societies, the expert may achieve recognition as an individual apart from recognition deriving from his bureaucratic membership. This can work in two ways. Individual recognition may be limited to recognition by peer experts. Concomitantly, professional and learned societies can function to cut across specifically bureaucratically oriented jobs and permit substantive experts to play out their substantive expert roles apart from their occupationally derived role patterns. Even here, however, the substantive contribution of a particular expert results in the conferring of his peer-granted prestige to the organization that employs him. In university life, as Logan Wilson has searchingly noted, this becomes an important element in institutions' rating of staff.

12

The Springdale Case

Joseph Bensman with Arthur J. Vidich

Since the advent of large-scale research and large-scale financing of research, the community study has come to be thought of as a "project" for which it is necessary to have a systematic statement of problem, a staff, legitimate sponsorship, and a budget. One of the first steps in setting up a research project is making application for the research grant, a procedure requiring a formal statement of the problem, an explicit theory, and a specific methodology that will be used as the operational procedure in conducting the research. The dignity of scientific enterprise is attached to the whole of the project structure.

In this essay, we report on the consequences of carrying out a community research study that ignored all the procedures of the scientific project research. The community study that we reported in *Small Town in Mass Society*[1] was unintentionally unplanned, had no budget, no a priori theory, no staff, no research stages or phases, and was not conceived as a study or a project until it was almost over.

Published originally in a slightly different form as "The Springdale Case: Academic Bureaucrats and Sensitive Townspeople," in Arthur J. Vidich, Joseph Bensman, and Maurice Stein, eds., *Reflections on Community Studies* (New York: John Wiley and Sons, 1964), 313–49. Republished with permission of Marilyn Bensman and Joseph Vidich.

Although the research and writing that resulted in *Small Town in Mass Society* were informal and unprogrammed, the work was actually carried out within the formal structure of an organized and programmed research project known as Cornell Studies in Social Growth, sponsored by the Department of Child Development and Family Relationships of the College of Home Economics, School of Agriculture, Cornell University. We must note that our study could not have been done except as a by-product of this formalized and organized research structure.

Our study of Springdale was related to the Cornell Studies in Social Growth project by the accident that one of the collaborators was hired as a resident field director (Arthur J. Vidich) to observe and participate in the life of the community, to maintain liaison between the community and the research organization, to administer and supervise mass surveys, and to provide background social structural data for the project's formal study of modes and qualities of community participation and leadership.[2]

The responsibility of the field director was to collect the data necessary to the formal study with a minimum of embarrassment to all parties concerned while not compromising the quality of the data. For this reason, all research activities in the town were highly calculated and restricted to those areas of investigation and community personnel that had a direct bearing on the project design at the time each specific field operation was being carried out.

Administratively, the field director was a temporary employee of an annually renewable, long-range research project housed in and "supported" by Cornell University. The job requirement was that the field director live in Ithaca for several months until he could become familiar with the project and that he then move with his family to Springdale where he would live as if he were a resident of the town working for the university that was doing a study of the town. This was thought to be a reasonable approach to the town because other Cornell employees, including a professor, a graduate assistant, and extension agents already lived in the town, thus giving the role some legitimation. These administrative and residence arrangements had a number of implications pertinent to nonprogrammed research.

Simply by being present in the town and by being interested in the day-to-day nonresearch life of the community residents, a great deal of material that was not encompassed by the Cornell Studies in Social Growth study design inevitably came to the attention of the field director. In some instances, highly personal information was acquired from personal friends in the town, and this information remains as part of the personal experience of the field director. In other instances, the field director was advised or directed to join organizations and activities for purposes that were not directly related to the project design. For example, it was a joint staff decision that the field director should go to church, but be given a personal option on teaching Sunday school. Although the project was almost exclusively interested in the participational structure of church life, the field director, by participating in the church himself, became familiar with at least some dimensions of all aspects of church life.

Theoretically, the project research design allowed for all levels of information, but only on the grounds that anything and everything that could be known might be relevant. This was why the field director was put into the town. Practically, however, there was a project tendency to regard as data only the information that found its way into a formal protocol or an interview schedule, so that even within the framework of the official research, the material that came to the attention of the field director exceeded the limits of the formal study. By being in the town, it was difficult not to see more than could be contained in field reports. The general, informal experience resulting from continuous exposure left an image of the town that was never quite summed up in staff and field reports. As a result of these differences in the quality of information possessed by different researchers on the staff, different images of the town were held by researchers who occupied different positions in the research organization.

These differences in imagery were further complicated by the difference in intellectual starting points of the different members of the research staff. Data became relevant to the field director simply because he had previous theoretical interests and field experiences in "primitive" and other rural communities that were independent of the research design. For example, the field director's earlier field experiences left him with the impression that Springdale was as much a "colony" as Palau in the Western Carolines and as deeply penetrated by central bureaucracy as Kropa in Yugoslavia.[3] So compelling were the similarities among Palau, Kropa, and Springdale that all points at which Springdale had a relationship to the rest of American society began to stand out as especially salient data. This orientation resulted in semisystematic observation and collection of data on a number of peripheral issues that seemingly had no relationship to any formal design or, least of all, to the project design. At this stage of the informal research, the continuity and structure of these observations were provided by the personal life history of the field director.

Both of the authors had been interested in some of these peripheral issues from previous collaborative work, and out of this mutual interest and a continuing personal friendship came discussions of some of the implications of these early observations. The project had no interest in the ideas that evolved from these observations because, from the project's point of view, these ideas were peripheral. As a result, we explored the ideas as a personal project that we conducted informally in the form of conversation.

After we had explored what seemed to us to be all the implications of Springdale's relationship to the external world, we discovered that certain dimensions of the class and status structure of the town could not be explained by external factors. The social and economic position of prosperous farmers, for example, could only be explained partially by subsidy programs and price supports. Part of their status in the community rested on the productive mystique of agriculture for other members of the community. This and other leads forced us to look into the internal dynamics of the community in a way that otherwise would not have been accessible to our consciousness. It was at this point that the field director secured permission from the project director to conduct twenty special interviews focusing on the social structure of the town. These interviews (conducted with Jones, Flint, Lee, Peabody, several merchants, ethnic leaders, religious leaders, and industrial workers) were specifically aimed at discovering some of the internal dimensions of community life as seen by the individuals interviewed. Though it is apparent from the selection of informants that the interviews focused on special themes, at that time there was no notion of doing a study, a project, or a book independent of the formal project.

As the informal work progressed, a number of ad hoc memoranda, outlines, and analyses of specific problem areas were submitted to the project as relevant theoretical themes implicit in the situation of the small town. We thought these analyses had a direct importance for the theoretical foundations of the project's research design and offered a basis for its conceptual reformulation in a way that accounted for the total situation of the small town in the modern world. The leaders of the project were interested in these formulations, but did not feel they were of crucial importance to its central study design. The authors continued to work on these problems simply because they were fascinating to us.

After two more years of continued informal work, a series of other areas had been explored on an ad hoc basis, and it was only then that it occurred to the authors that they were actually doing a community study that not only had a unified theoretical focus, but that could actually become the object of an extended and integrated monograph. At this point, which coincided with the field director's termination of his employment with the project, we asked for and received permission to do an independent study with the understanding that our work be submitted to the directors of the project as it was being written and revised so that it would be available to the project staff while its members were making their analysis of the formal survey data.

Programmed Versus Unprogrammed Project Administration[4]

It was our experience that by and large the logic of a problem has its own internal dynamic, which means that once one has embarked on the pursuit of the problem and is willing to follow its logic, the researchers must *administer* in terms of where the problem leads and not in terms of prearranged schedules.

It is in the structure of project organization that termination points must be set, deadlines must be met, production schedules must be set, annual reports must be made, production functions must be distributed among staff members, and so on. Bureaucratic structure and staff organization in and of themselves impose on project research a flow whose direction is not easily redirected. Staff and organization become significant functions of research in programmed studies.

In the Springdale research, we observed a variety of tensions arising from the conflict between research functions and bureaucratic functions:

> 1. Staff distribution of field functions leaves each staff functionary with a uniquely specialized view

of individual informants and of the dimensions of community life. There are as many images of the community in circulation as there are staff functions in the research organization. This means that staff conferees are continuously involved in discussions the major latent function of which is to reduce the community to a single bureaucratically acceptable image. In other words, for the project research purposes, a major objective of the committee process is to reach a mutually acceptable fictional definition of the community that all staff members can work with while playing their project roles.

2. Since each interview is a source of standardized as well as subliminal information, all standardization of observational or interview procedures necessitated by quality control requirements arising from the uneven distribution of skills and interests among the staff has the effect of destroying all but formal information.

3. Staff execution of research, which must necessarily be guided in part by time and logistic factors relevant to other organizational and personal responsibilities (teaching, committee meetings, staff discussions, travel, vacations, family, etc.), prohibits continuity of contact between informants and researchers. That is, the informants meet a variety of researchers, and the researchers infrequently meet their informants in depth. Under this system, the simple building up of personality profiles and sketches involves vast amounts of filing and collecting of information by

> clerks whose final product is always less than the cumulative impression that is acquired by the continuous observation by one person or another over a period of time.
>
> 4. Once the research machinery is committed to securing a certain type or level of information, it is difficult for the research organization to accept, absorb, or acknowledge data that might threaten to undermine that commitment. In accepting a "fixed" statement of the project problem, it is both psychologically and bureaucratically risky to move in directions that might deviate from the last agreed-upon plan.

In the Springdale research, the project was committed to finding solutions to what makes for constructive, positive, community functioning. The project thus directed itself to a study of creative activity and to the locating of leadership and participator types of local citizens who could exemplify constructive activity.

Because it was assumed that there was creative activity in the community, it was psychologically difficult for those committed to the research design to acknowledge the absence of creativity where, at first glance, it might have appeared to exist. Thus, the case of the telephone company's expansion program, which was to have been a major illustration of community creativity, was simply abandoned as an illustration when it was found that the modernization program had nothing to do with the local town except insofar as the local town was a front for the state telephone company.[5]

In the same manner, the research organization made a major commitment to the local community club as a creative community activity. When it was found that the community club involved only a few hundred persons and that nine-tenths of the community was excluded from participation in spite of the club slogan that all were invited even if they did not pay dues, the research project continued its commitment to the club for research reasons. Even after the practical limitations of the club's role in community affairs were acknowledged by all research personnel, it was not possible to ignore the club because ignoring it would have been a violation of the previous commitments to the club.

The community club represented a handful of activists and a shifting number of aspirants. It excluded all shack people, the marginal middle classes, and major portions of all other classes, including the middle class. In short, the community club represented the minor segment of the middle class that was most attuned to social affairs and the outside world. The inspiration for the founding of the club was initially provided by community organizers and extension specialists hired by the same institution and the same college as those who were studying it as a creative community activity. Acknowledgment of these observations would have constituted a major embarrassment for the project since it would have meant in effect a reformulation of the study design. Instead, a number of defenses were invoked that allowed prior commitments to be upheld. The defenses were:

1. A blindness to the existence of all community groups except the middle class and an equating of creative activity with middle-class activities.

2. Failure to see any relationship between social club activity leaders and the community's economic and political structure.

3. The necessity to see the town only in terms of itself and without reference to anything located outside it,

> especially Cornell University and the research project itself.
>
> 4. The unwillingness to acknowledge all critical groups in the town and especially the refusal to listen to other outside experts who were the project's counterparts in the town. Thus, the 4-H agent became the enemy of the project because he was a concrete counterimage of what the project "expected" of the town even though the original idea for a community club had come from the 4-H agent.

The foregoing illustrations indicate a fundamental tension between research as a bureaucratic enterprise and the perceptual freedom that nonbureaucratic research usually involves. As a bureaucratic employee, the functionary has the responsibility of following those problems that are bureaucratically defined by authority as the purpose of the project. The project directors are obliged to stay with the problem for which they received money. The problems must be approached with the previously specified methods, and, moreover, official interpretations of what constitutes a finding come to pervade the entire project structure. Individual discoveries may be expressed as long as this is done with due caution and within the previously agreed-upon framework.

The research perspective of an individual who is independently pursuing knowledge is quite different from the one that prevails in bureaucratic settings. The perspective of independent investigation is based on whatever concatenation of theoretical background and experience the researcher brings to the field and on his discovery of problems while he is in the midst of the field experience. He devises means to follow those insights that appear to him to be appropriate to the insights that emerge out of his data; he tends to push his explorations to their logical conclusion (whether they result in failure or success) to the point where he is satisfied he has made all efforts possible in examining the problems that stimulated inquiry.

The existence of external and formalized bureaucratic constraints may:

> 1. Deflect the worker from seeing the problem except perhaps as a minor deviation from a central plan, since the preordained design acts to funnel his vision. Thus, there is always the possibility of a number of leads that were not followed up that then constitute the fund of anecdotes about the project.
>
> 2. Force the investigator systematically to avoid pursuit of such insights even if they are central to his own theoretical and perceptual apparatus. To accomplish this form of avoidance involves complicated intellectual self-manipulation.
>
> 3. Make it necessary to find ways of reporting findings that are not relevant to the agreed-upon research design, even though such findings are actually acknowledged by the investigators to each other.
>
> 4. Force the investigator to find devices such as Aesopian language to sneak in the point in the report.

The result of all of this for the bureaucratic researcher is that he must build up a complicated apparatus to justify the neglect of the perceived issue when he feels that bureaucratic loyalty is more important than the issues that he himself thinks are more important. The pressures "to play ball" are enormous, and ways are found.

Most of the issues developed in *Small Town in Mass Society* did not fit the formal design of the Cornell project. The issues we saw were:

1. The relationship of the community to the society at large

2. The analysis of social and economic class as central to the community

3. The analysis of power and politics

4. The inclusion of economic data as relevant to the design

5. Reporting on the actions of individual institutional leaders in the exercise of their institutional roles

6. Reporting on "negative" or not affirmative aspects of community life[6] as necessary to an examination of the social and psychological basis of community participation.

Our pursuit of these issues that were personally interesting to us could be carried out without conflict or tension within project administration so long as our work was not made public. As we shall later note more fully, however, it is difficult for programmed project administration to tolerate public discussion or publication of non-programmed issues. Under ordinary circumstances, the structure of project administration, with its hierarchy of control, committee meetings, and other forms of maintaining discipline, prevents the individual from developing an independent perspective. This has a number of consequences for both the intellectual development of the individual and for the project bureaucracy.

In the extreme case, the inability on the part of an individual to find a way of developing his theoretical perspective or of pursuing what he regards as valid insights results in doublethink, wherein language publicly sanctioned by research officials defines "research realities" as opposed to "normal" realities. In other instances, it results in forms of research and nonresearch language, ironic detachment from one's own work, or compliant work as a "team man" who moves intellectually in phase with project policy changes. The net result of all this for the individual is various forms of conscious or subliminal self-hatred, so that all of the categories that are found in Merton's description of bureaucratic self-hatred are found in bureaucratic research.

The failure of the foregoing techniques to function adequately leads to personnel crises, demoralization of staff, bickering, feuds, and stalemates. The measure of the failure of these techniques is the rate of labor turnover of project personnel. The unsuccessful project never quite succeeds in repressing intellectual individuality and is thus fraught with tensions and impasses, whereas the successful project succeeds in achieving organizational stability, regulated production schedules, and so on, at the cost of repressing the individual idea.[7]

In the face of these dynamics, a large part of such a research project becomes the reconciling of differences of viewpoints and insights and arriving at formulas of consensus that are quite similar to those described for village politics in Springdale. Issues disappear, problems lose their sharpness, and talking and memo writing define the dominant ethos of the research enterprise until no individual insight embarrasses the smooth functioning of the organization of the project. In terms of organizational operations, this means:

1. When there are differences of opinion between researchers, especially between subordinates, supervisors, or project heads, endless meetings ensue.

2. If the differences are fundamental and irreconcilable, there may be a suppression and postponement of an accumulating pile of differences.

3. Self-imposed conscious and begrudging suppression of differences of opinion and hostility, especially on the part of subordinates, and the development of factions and private gossip groups build up around stylized forms of suppression.

4. Diplomatic styles of language and other linguistic formulas develop that allow different views to be expressed in the same sentences, paragraphs, or chapters.

5. Long, drawn-out feuds and political factionalization of the research organization build up, all of which is usually covered over on public occasions and always concealed from the view of the financial backers of the research.

6. The factions and feuds embellish the research with various forms of bureaucratic chicanery.

7. A continuous possibility for the occurrence of shifts in the direction of the project problem and in the research design exists as different individuals become predominant in the organizational structure over the course of the history of the project. As a result, a project can have dozens of false starts,

none of which is pursued because no one individual or faction ever achieves a clear victory.

8. There is always the chance for publication of multiple reports, a solution that, in our opinion, is the best method of resolving differences.

Retrospectively, only two things can be concluded from all this. First, it seems that the best bureaucratic research is achieved when one man is able to set himself up as an absolute dictator, almost no matter on what basis he gains his power. Then at least *his* point of view comes through in the work, thus giving the project a focus, even if this denies "democracy" to the other participating academicians. Second, it appears that the primary qualities necessary to doing bureaucratic research lie in the fields of statecraft, diplomacy, and group work techniques by which consensus can be engineered.

From the perspective of the individual researcher, all group and bureaucratic research is a form of torture.

Project Foreign Affairs and Their Effect on Research

Just as a community exists in a social matrix larger than itself, so any formal research project operates in an institutional context that encompasses more than itself. This fact may or may not determine the direction of research. The individual researcher who lacks plan and design and who has no staff or budget can ignore almost all problems of "foreign affairs" if he has the time and resources to pursue his demons wherever they lead. Programmed research finds itself in a much more complicated situation. The programmed project always faces outside publics and must come to terms with them, make agreements with them, and reach an understanding on problems and issues defined by those publics. In university-connected community research, these publics include the sponsor, the community, and the university. Each of these publics is a reference group, and each poses distinctive problems for scientific research investigation.

The Sponsor as Reference Group

The first problem facing the prospective researcher is to find a project for which a potential sponsor exists. Since it is only in extreme cases that a researcher will completely phrase his problem to meet sponsorship requirements, the usual tactic is to find a sponsor who will be interested and willing to provide funds to support a study that is still in some way related to the researchers' interests.[8]

The sponsoring agency, as is clearly understandable to everyone, wishes to support research within an area or within a range of problems related to its fundamental purposes as specified in its mission statement. For a sponsoring agency to do otherwise is a breach of trust and is sometimes illegal as well. The researcher, then, begins his research by conducting research on sponsoring agencies that are likely to support his research.

Although basic research on sponsors has itself progressed to the point where directories of sponsors and synopses of their interests are published, the existence of these research tools does not solve the researchers' problems. Sponsors are suspicious of claimants, first, because there are so many of them and, second, because some of them from the sponsor's viewpoint are quacks whose ideas are inadmissible. This then leads to the necessity for finding "respectable, clean-cut, stable, responsible" directors and negotiators to meet with their foundation counterparts. The requirements for creative research are only accidentally related to the talent for negotiating with foundations. If and when the smooth, pleasant negotiator gains actual authority in the project (on the basis of his access to funds), any value of the research findings is also likely to be accidental.

In spite of all basic research on sponsors, the project researcher is still faced with:

> 1. Making contacts with the potential sponsor either through third parties, by hiring personnel because they bring the contacts with them, or by directly hiring the sponsor's personnel. The choice of technique depends on the stage of research, level of organization, and quality of connections.
>
> 2. Defining the project in terms of language, theories, and hypotheses that will be congenial to sponsors' views as indicated in their statements of purpose and as expressed by specific administrative agents of the sponsors. A higher level of complexity is introduced where multiple sponsors are involved, for this means finding linguistic and theoretical compromises that will breach the differences between sponsors and that will yet appear to leave no contradictions in the statement of the problem. A field of expertise has grown up around this function.[9]

It is part of the rhythm of the total research cycle that the sponsor recedes as an important reference group after the grant has been received and is only again reasserted as a significant other when findings are to be discovered, written, and reported. No matter what happens between the receipt of money and the completion of research operations, at the time of writing and reporting, the analyst must address himself to the original problem statement because the sponsor is still thinking in its terms in spite of the passage of time and the new experiences gained by the researcher from carrying out the research.[10] As a result, the researcher is obliged to come up with findings that in some way relate to the original problem statement as worked out with and for the sponsor. Maintaining trust with the sponsor is as important for this kind of research as the research itself because, apart from other considerations, specific projects are always part of a larger career pattern that requires future sponsors.

Faithfulness to the original statement of the problem is only one of a number of problems that arise in the later stages of project research:

> 1. A report discharging, at least at formal levels, the obligation to the grant must be delivered. The pressures at this point make the successful project director a virtuoso at putting something between two covers.
>
> 2. The production of the report may not be as simple as it appears to an outsider or even to the sponsor. Since the project's inception there have been many changes in project personnel; people who carried out crucial research operations have moved to other positions and universities, and important project officers who may have had little contact with the actual research data remain. As if this were not enough, all of the data may not bear a relationship to the stated problem since some of them at least will reflect "hunches" that were followed but did not produce the desired results—during the heat of data collection the formally stated problem sometimes loses its saliency. As a consequence of factors such as these, there is the institution known as the "rescue operation" wherein no one on the staff is willing or able to write a report, so the last man hired is hired

specifically to piece together all the bits, to create the appearance of a unified structure to the data, and to write all this in a form that can be bound, even if it is only a photocopied, heavily subsidized publication.

The salvage expert may be a junior project member who happens to have literary skills; he may be a specialized expert who moves from project to project because he can write, but lacks the organizational stature and competence to get his own grants; or he may be primarily a writer who has little specialized competence in the research field. The rescue operation has become so standardized in project research that: (1) salvage skills are a recognized professional ability; (2) men may build reputations only on the fact that they have never failed to submit a report; and (3) at times the photocopied, subsidized publication has more prestige in some circles than real books because it is understood that the photocopied report represents a large cash investment, which a book may not.

3. In final form, the report must eliminate all embarrassing findings and, more specifically, all mention of specific people and instances that might otherwise be necessary to illustrate a point. The definition of an embarrassing finding is, of course, always related to the ideology of the audience to which the report is directed, but, at a minimum, the report is written with at least one eye to the sponsor, and, at a maximum, an attempt is made to create a unified and pleasant image of the whole project. The major value

> conveyed by the report is academic and research respectability. Any "rocking the boat" becomes a major crime against the sponsor, his values, and those whose careers are identified with the project.

The Community as a Reference Group

From the inception of the first contacts with the community, the town wants to know what the research is about and how the town will be affected by it. The answers to these questions define the project and the research to the townspeople and add up to a set of future promises to the town.

As in most research, many people in the community are unenthusiastic if not suspicious about being investigated. Springdale, in upstate New York, was a Republican-dominated, conservative town, which had previous experiences, not all of them happy, with researchers from Cornell University.[11] In order to secure acceptance in the face of the community's suspiciousness, past community experiences with research, and a certain amount of hostility and resentment toward the University simply because it was a big and dominant institution in the area, the research project presented itself to the town as an upholder of rural values. Scientific investigators regularly attended meetings of the Community Club and told jokes and played games with its members in order to get in exchange their adherence to the research project.

The project was committed by the terms of its own past to studying socially creative activity, and, at the time of the Springdale phase of the research, it had elected to study this creativity in the form of socially constructive community activities. Springdale was selected for study because the directors of the project thought it was more "constructive" than other towns surveyed as possible choices. Even after the selection of the town and the hiring of a field director, it was not entirely clear what was constructive activity. This was natural enough, of course, because if it had been known in advance the research would have been unnecessary.

Nevertheless, without knowing exactly what we would be studying, we were pressed by the community to tell what the study was about, who it included, what its purpose was, and what kind of book would be written. In response to these inquiries, the project developed a line that included:

> "We are not interested in the negative features of the town because too much fruitless work on that has been done already."
>
> "A positive approach is needed."
>
> "We are interested in constructive activities because from this we feel we can help other people in other communities to live better lives. Springdale is a laboratory that may help us find important solutions."
>
> "We are especially interested in the Community Club because it is a democratic organization that brings *all the people* together and there are no restrictions on membership and no entrance fees."
>
> "We have to get back to the older values of the individual, neighboring, and the neighborhood, and Springdale seems to provide an opportune setting for this. We enlist your cooperation in helping us to solve this scientific problem."

All of these commitments were made as a way of selling the project to the townspeople at a time when no one knew what the project would be studying or where it would locate the community's constructive activities. In giving "nonexistent" answers to community inquiries when the project's methods and results are indefinite, the project, unfortunately, becomes committed to those answers.

The greatest concern of some townspeople was with how they personally would be portrayed in the "book." In some instances, this concern bordered on anxiety and, in other instances, on exhibitionism, with a desire only to appear in a favorable light. In the fieldwork, the statement, "I hope you're not going to quote me on this," seemed to demand a reassuring answer, and, again, the issue of community relations played a role in shaping policy. Let us illustrate this with an example presented in another paper:

> As the research progressed, the "assurance" of anonymity came to be equated with "doing an entirely statistical report." This happened in a curiously inadvertent way: on various occasions when the project was asked to explain its purposes in greater detail or when community suspicions had been aroused, the standard practice of some staff members was to assure members of the community that there was nothing to worry about because all individuals and specific events would get lost in the statistical analysis. At the time, these assurances were very successful in allaying the fears and anxieties of the key members of the community, and so some members of the project, particularly those who were less trained and more prone to panic, began to give such assurances whenever resistances developed. Unfortunately, some key members of the community were left with the impression that the entire report would be statistical. As this impression became more prevalent in the community, it also became more prevalent in the research project until it was understood by many persons in both groups that no other than a statistical presentation of the data was to be made.[12]

This was not an explicit policy of the project. It was an implied promise always accepted more by the town than by the project. Among the project members, it tended to receive more acceptance when they were in the town than in the central offices, but, as time progressed, it became difficult for project members themselves to think of any kind of report other than a statistical one, even though it was always also assumed that there would be an analysis of the social structure of the town.

The idea of doing only a statistical report grew out of the project's promise to the community not to identify any of its members in a recognizable way. When people asked how identities would be concealed, the easiest answer was, "It'll be all statistical." In the writing and analysis, however, the problem of identity concealment could not be handled so easily. In the writing of *Small Town in Mass Society*, we decided we would employ the solution used by community sociologists in the past—namely, the use of pseudonyms.[13] When we published our book, we were criticized in *Human Organization* and by Cornell University for following that policy. However, when the staff of Cornell Studies in Social Growth later came to write its report, it discovered the same dilemma:

> We were all very much disturbed by the reaction of our major Springdale informants to your book. The essential problem was that they had been promised in their initial contacts with us that in any report out of the research they would not be personally identifiable. This was true of the kind of report which we foresaw at the time, and I think it will be true of the *Journal of Social Issues* number. However, it is certainly not true of your book, so we were naturally asked the question: "What about this?" The line we took with the support of the college administration and the Social Science Research Center was that we had

> expected you to be bound by the same promises that were made to the Springdale people before you appeared on the scene, that we were very much disappointed by the amount and kind of information about clearly recognizable Springdale individuals, which was included in your book, but that we did not have any control over what was finally published. However, we made it clear that we disapproved of this type of publication and wished to dissociate ourselves from it as much as possible. We are now faced with the problem of producing a report that will meet the criteria laid down in the original contacts with the Springdale residents. I do not know how well we will be able to do this.[14]

In the final official project report[15] on the town, the following solution to the problem of identification was reached:

> The main problem that publication presented was, of course, the one of identifying the individual participants in the community. We became convinced that you were right in thinking that it is not possible to provide a meaningful discussion of community action without describing at least some of the principal leaders in a way that makes them readily identifiable to others in the community. Consequently, we decided to use your (Vidich and Bensman) code names in our account, at least the code names Jones, Hilton, Lee, and Flint. The other main participants centering around the repair of the mill dam were people who did not seem to us to require accurate placement in the community power structure; consequently, we used pseudonyms for these people, which, I think, would not allow them to be identified by their friends and neighbors—except, of course, those who were themselves involved in the dam project. My present interpretation

> of the basic reason for the difficulty between you and the project over the write-up of your material is that the project made promises to the people in Springdale which were compatible with the kind of report which was originally planned. . . ., but which was not compatible with a report which would deal in any realistic fashion with the social structure of the community.[16]

It is in the nature of the social structure of a community that a project can never have a relationship with it as a totality. It is necessary from the beginning to deal selectively with specific persons in order to secure and sustain some acceptance. The Springdale project worked on the theory that admission to the community would be best secured by working through the important social and organizational leaders. The logic of this action was that since leadership and social organization were the important dimensions of the study, gaining support and acceptance from these sources would both secure legitimacy quickly and efficiently and give access to a strata of important respondents. In practical field terms, this strategy was effective—the doors to the community members and organizations were opened—but, in scientific terms, the implications of this identification with the town fathers and social respectability had far-reaching implications:

> 1. Because of the organizational importance of particular individuals, these individuals came to be regarded as more valid sources of information than others. As the work progressed, it was assumed that, before starting fieldwork plans for new research, activities would be presented to the executive officers of the Community Club and then to the entire club. The club became a major sounding board for

the project, and some of its members were used as "consultants" on matters concerning project-town relations. The more the project began to depend on selected informants, the more it became committed to and dependent on their perspective of the town. An operating structure of images of the town was built up that would be violated if other informants were to be used. In practice, critics of the Community Club and community leaders were dismissed as "bad citizens."

2. The project's image of the town thus came to coincide with the image held by the town's leadership strata. This created its own problems. Since the official, dominant image of the town was not held by all members of the community, the problem arose of disposing of the unacceptable counterimages in circulation in the community. Two methods of disposition were found. Minority images could be dismissed as being irrelevant to the project because they did not fall within its purview. This was the case with the worldview of the shack people as a whole, who were not regarded as instrumental in promoting community mindedness. Or those holding counterimages of the town could be dismissed as representing a deviant or ridiculous viewpoint. The project's attitude to West, the potato and gladiola farmer, became the same as Lee's. West was laughed off the stage. Though West almost became a major innovator by his near successful political campaign to oust the town powers from office, it never occurred to anyone

> in the central research offices to consider this as creative activity or even leadership.

After three years of contact with the community, the members of the project and "The Project" as an official organization had established many personal and official contacts, commitments, friendships, and confidences. This was inevitable simply because of the duration and closeness of the contact. The problem was how these personal and official relations related to scientific reporting. In the Springdale case, the project director took the position that certain materials were questionable from the point of view of ethics and possible injury to persons:

> I have just finished reading the manuscript of you and Bensman and, in response to your request, am giving concrete examples of material which, though it may represent public knowledge, is, in our judgment, highly questionable from the point of view of professional ethics and possible injury to the persons involved. Since there are many instances of this kind, I shall confine myself to a few outstanding examples.
>
> 1. There are many references to the enmity between Flint and Lee. . . . Since, as you yourself have emphasized, these two persons will be immediately recognizable to anyone familiar with the community, assertions that Flint "has been excluded from town politics by Lee" who harbors "resentment" against him are fairly strong accusations. Moreover, the discussion of their personal antagonism is not really central to your analysis of the way in which the community operates and hence you would not lose much by omitting mention of the matter.

2. The whole discussion of Peabody, the school principal, and his relation to the community could, if it remained in its present form, do a good deal of harm and arouse justifiable resentment. For example, consider the possible impact on him and others of reading the following direct quotation attributed "to a prominent member of invisible government": "He's a little too inhuman—has never gone into anything in the town. He's good for Springdale until he gets things straightened out. Then we will have to get rid of him." Potentially equally damaging are the statements quoted from the observers' report, but these, along with all excerpts from the project files, would of course no longer appear in the manuscript.

3. In pointing out that the Polish community is controlled by political leaders through intermediaries who are willing to do their bidding in exchange for acceptance, is it necessary to point the finger so visibly at Kinserna? You do this very pointedly . . . where you go so far as to assert that the upshot of his activities is "to get the Poles to accept measures and policies which are disadvantageous to them."

4. Personality descriptions of the ministers are likewise conspicuously on the *ad hominem* side. For example, you refer to one as "awkward, condescending, and not of the people" and to another as a "cantankerous trouble-maker." Also, I wonder whether the description of the Episcopalian minister as trained in "one of the 'radical' Eastern seminaries" is not subject to misinterpretation by Springdale

> readers despite your use of quotations around the word radical. Given upstate New York's climate of opinion, such a statement may have some unfortunate consequences for the man concerned.
>
> 5. The clearly uncomplimentary remarks about Grainger . . . have especial importance for not only is he likely to read them himself, even though he is no longer living in the community, but they are also likely to be read by his colleagues and superiors in the Extension Service. It would be particularly unfair and unfortunate, especially in view of Grainger's whole-hearted cooperation with the project, if any statement made by you jeopardized Grainger's professional future. As the manuscript now stands, such a possibility is by no means out of the question.[17]

The issue here is not the specific items of censorship, but rather the assumption of protective attitudes toward specific community members on the basis of personal attractiveness, entangling commitments, respondents' earlier cooperativeness, and other nonresearch considerations. As a result of personal, social, and organizational commitments, the project finds itself in the position of writing its findings with an eye to other than research or theoretical interests and issues.

As a final step in viewing the community as a reference group, the project decided that:

> Before any manuscripts are shown to outside representatives, such as publishers or their agents, we will ask one or two persons within the college and possibly in Springdale to read the manuscripts from the point of view of public relations. Although the final responsibility for deciding what we publish will rest with the project staff, the reactions of such readers would receive serious

> consideration and we would probably rewrite and omit in accordance with their recommendations.[18]

In this instance, to avoid personal responsibility for the project's research reporting, selected nonresearch respondents would be invited to pass on manuscripts purely as a way of avoiding bad public relations, so that aspects of community life that may be theoretically relevant can be censored by local individuals on nonresearch grounds. Moreover, the local individuals to be selected would be specifically those who constituted the project's dominant reference group in the town—namely, the town's official leaders and spokesmen who represented most forcefully the stereotyped image of the positive-minded community that the project has absorbed as its own image of the town.

The identification of the project and its personnel with the town's interests and with the feelings and sentiments of individuals and groups being studied leads to a subtle adaptation of the research to the problems of the community even though those problems are not the problems of the research. In an extreme instance, this policy would lead to no point of view except the point of view of the community. Acting Dean Grisely[19] of Cornell University seems to take this position as the only viable one for social science:

> The first thing that happened with a book like this has to be taken in the context that people are not very happy to be studied. I don't know to what extent you may find yourselves, those of you who are becoming involved in the social science field, are likely to find that one of the most difficult things that you will have to do is to sell a project to a group, an organization, by getting them to permit you to come in and ask questions, observe them, write them up, interfere with their time, and in most cases for uses that they don't know or understand, and they are somewhat suspicious and concerned with this whole process.

This particular project (Cornell Studies in Social Growth) was introduced to the community through the Extension Service system of the College of Agriculture. People in the community who had confidence in the university for a variety of reasons accepted and sponsored the project and the individuals connected with it. Now Mr. Vidich, as he points out, lived in the community and was accepted in a real sense as one of the people in the community, with people making an effort to see that he was introduced to various groups and so on. Now when this book came out with some of the characterizations and implications, I think there were several kinds of reactions.

In the first place it made people mad. It made those people mad who had brought the study in, who had been responsible and had participated in it. It was in total violation of the understandings which they felt existed between the university and themselves and the community. Second, it made other people feel very bad and hurt them, some of them I'm afraid considerably because they felt that the friendships and confidences they had extended to Mr. Vidich and his family had been violated. Further, I think the distortion of the characterization of these people, many of whom were friends of his and some of whom were very good friends during the time he was in the community, created a self-consciousness of these individuals which they found very discomforting, which lasted for a time, but from which they recovered. Fourth, I think that the community itself could not particularly welcome the outside attention that it received, especially those people who were in a variety of ways related to outside activities and they found that they were being examined and cross-examined about the community by outsiders with whom they came in contact.

> There was a problem of some loss of faith and disruption of university relationships, and I suspect there is an increase in suspicion of outsiders, particularly inquisitive outsiders.[20]

At certain stages, the community may become a more important reference group for the project than is the scientific community to which the research is ostensibly addressed. In Springdale, for example, the study of constructive activities in the community gradually came to include the ideology that the project and its members assume constructive attitudes toward Springdale in all phases of work including community relations, fieldwork, participation, analysis of data, and reporting of scientific results.

The highest form of project identification with the town is when the research organization attempts to take responsibility for the actions of all its agents who act in and on the town. The Springdale fieldwork was carried out by more than one hundred people who at a variety of organizational levels participated in the work at different times over a period of three years. Simply by sending large numbers of people into a town, a large amount of public relations is required; new field operations have to be announced, results of preceding surveys must be tentatively reported, newspaper stories have to be written, apologies must be made for field workers' errors, the project's local landlord must be placated when the field director fails to cut the grass, and so on. In order to avoid public-relations errors, field personnel begin to be selected on public-relations grounds. Can you send a foreign student into an upstate New York community? In what positions is it advisable not to have a Jew? What about the Negro who is the husband of a staff member? Some members of the project are excluded from the town completely because they are too "argumentative," too "controversial," or too "unreliable" in some way as defined by the project.

When research workers in their fieldwork provoke a complaint from a community member or a local official, the complaint is sent to research headquarters, and, by the act of accepting the complaint, the project assumes responsibility for rectification either to the individual in question or to the "community as a whole." This means the project is placed in the position of apologizing for its research workers and on occasion publicly reprimanding and punishing its research staff. Punishment of staff usually takes the form of revoking privileges to enter the field; complaints from community members can jeopardize sociological careers.

Standard practice is for the project to make a scapegoat of the last man who left the project, so that all the project's ills in the community will be attributed to him; the man who is no longer there to defend himself serves the purpose of absorbing all of the free-floating resentment the town has against the project. In the same measure as the departee acts as a scapegoat, so his ideas, insights, and knowledge of the community can be safely ignored and forgotten. The project's offering of scapegoats to the town is always a concession to the ideology of the town.

As already indicated, the officials of the Springdale project were placed in the position of taking a policy stand before the opinion of the community on the existence of our book. There could be no question to anyone who had any familiarity with the town that *Small Town in Mass Society* would be a provocative experience for Springdale. So far had the project commitment to the community and its values become entrenched that, almost as a reflex response, the publication of *Small Town in Mass Society* evoked a public project apology[21] published on the front page of the Springdale *Courier* on February 6, 1958:

The Editor
Springdale *Courier*
Springdale, New York

Dear Sir:

We at Cornell have read the book by Vidich and Bensman entitled *Small Town in Mass Society* and wish to make clear that this work in no sense reflects the intentions or views of the Cornell Project. The book was written after Dr. Vidich had left our employ. Mr. Bensman, of course, never had any connection with the Cornell Project. The general orientation of the work, as well as the material with which it deals stands in direct contradiction to our policies regarding confidentiality of data and the publication of identifiable information.

Upon learning of Dr. Vidich's plans, we requested him to eliminate or, at least, modify the materials in the manuscript which we felt to be most objectionable, and received his assurances that he would do so. Accordingly, we were doubly shocked to find that much of the objectionable material had been retained.

Since Dr. Vidich entered and lived in the community as a member of our staff, we must accept some indirect responsibility for what has happened. Unfortunately, we know of no way to undo what has been done but can only express our sincere regrets.

Sincerely yours,

Project Director
Cornell Studies in Social Growth

This project apology, addressed though it is to the community at large, is clearly meant to placate those particular individuals and groups in the community who might have taken offense. First and foremost, these are the official leaders and the middle class. It must be recalled that the community is composed of individuals and groups who do not see eye to eye on all issues, and that not all community members would be equally offended or even offended at all by the publication of this book. However, it was in the logic of the project's commitment to the community—namely, that it was tied to certain individuals and groups—that it must necessarily condemn, disavow, and dissociate itself from the study of *Small Town in Mass Society*. The scientific enterprise had come to fully reflect the ideology of the rural community.

Insofar as the ideology of the community grew in salience and became the basis of project reactions, all project actions more and more came to be addressed to it. In due course, any offense against the community ideology became a risk to the project and a major crime for the project members.

Once the point was reached that an offense against the town was a crime, the project began to spend more and more time attempting to avert both the crime and the risk of the crime. This could be done only by making a major effort to control the town, the movements of research workers within it, and finally, by controlling the town's image of the project by organized public relations. Because of this, a large part of the field director's activities were devoted to maintaining project-community harmony. This same process apparently was carried out in just as intensive a form at the time of the publication of the book:

> At this point I [Dean Grisely] found myself in the interesting position of becoming a liaison between the director of the study who was greatly concerned with this thing being

> published over which he could not exercise any control really, and the community. I transmitted messages back and forth and so on. I thought you might be interested to know that I received during the process of this a lot of notes from people in the community, and one from an elderly lady who was a retired teacher. I just want to give you a sampling of this. She wrote the note to my wife and said, "I'm so glad your husband gave that Cornell report at the Community Club because now I feel better towards Cornell." I attempted to explain that this was not a Cornell study, it was not an official study, but it was a violation of the study itself.[22]

Once the cycle has reached this stage, there is little left of research except diplomacy and public relations. When project diplomacy and public relations win out, it means converting the town into a rat lab; that is, the project converts the community into so many actors for the research project, and the research investigators respond like actors to the roles they have created.

The reactions of both the town and the University to the book's publication reflected their accumulated public-relations expectations. A number of people, particularly those officials who had collaborated most closely with the project, felt that their trust had been betrayed, and they lodged complaints with the project staff and Cornell University. Since we were not participants to that scene, others will have to report that aspect of the problem. The official position of Cornell as already noted was to dissociate itself from the book and its authors and to identify with the town. At the time of publication, Vidich was privately reprimanded as follows:

> Having read your book, we, no less than the people of Springdale, are surprised and shocked. Despite your assurances that, wherever possible, you would delete

> material that we considered objectionable, you have made little more than a token effort in this direction. . . .
>
> It is yet too early to judge how serious the effects of your book will be on Springdale and Cornell. We already have indications, however, that a number of people have been badly hurt, and at least one of Cornell's programs in the area has encountered resistance and resentment directly attributable to your publication.[23]
>
> We find it difficult to believe that, in choosing to retain objectionable material, you were not well aware of what you were doing. In any event, we wish to make it absolutely clear that we regard your actions in this matter as a breach of faith and professional ethics both with ourselves, and, what is much more important, with the many people of Springdale who granted us the privilege of their hospitality and confidence.[24]

The town itself came to its own defense in reviews of the book which appeared in Springdale and in neighboring towns. For example, the *Times* in the county seat:[25]

> THE SMALL TOWN IN MASS SOCIETY – [SPRINGDALE] SAYS IT ISN'T SO
>
> *Small Town in Mass Society,* by Arthur J. Vidich and Joseph Bensman
>
> An accurate review of this book should be from the viewpoint of a professional sociologist since it is intended as a textbook for the social sciences.
>
> Lacking that point of view, our interest in the book stems from the fact that it is written by a former resident of [Springdale] and concerns itself with "class, power and religion" in [Springdale], called Springdale in the book.

Mr. Vidich is currently about as popular in [Springdale] as the author of *Peyton Place* is in her small town and for the same reason—both authors violate what Vidich calls the etiquette of gossip.

During the three years he lived here, Vidich was engaged in a research project. "Cornell Studies in Social Growth" sponsored by the New York State College of Home Economics and with the aid of funds from the National Institute of Mental Health, United Public Health Service and the Social Science Research Council.

He then proceeded to use portions of the survey material, making Cornell very unhappy, added a considerable amount of misinformation and gossip and drew certain conclusions based on the three sources.

The Cornell survey material is fairly accurate and pertains to economics and population trends. The misinformation indicates that Vidich is something less than a scientist and has either deliberately distorted facts to prove his personal conclusions or has failed to inquire into basic facts. For example, he states that the railroad running through the village has not made a stop there in years: this misstatement seems immaterial except that he uses it to bolster his conclusion that local business is at a standstill.

He discusses the failure of ecumenicalism in [Springdale], stating that Episcopal and Congregational churches failed to merge because of the opposition of powerful members of the older generation who were fearful of losing the traditions of their churches. Actually, no merger was ever contemplated and the temporary arrangement of sharing one minister ceased when his superior decided he was being overworked.

The inference is that [Springdale] is living in the past, unable to accept new ideas of mass society, and, further, that it is run by certain individuals.

The theme of control runs throughout the book. [Springdale] citizens will be amazed to discover that practically every phase of daily living is subject to the whims of one man and his cohorts. They run local government, including the school, decide church policies and influence the economic life of the community.

No attempt is made to disguise the individuals who may be readily identified by anyone having any knowledge of [Springdale]. In this field, Vidich seems to have resorted to pure gossip as his source of material.

The author is shocked by the fact people settle their differences in private rather than resorting to public argument; economy in government becomes "the psychology of scarcity;" he arrives at the conclusion people work fantastically hard to avoid coming to terms with themselves.

He finally sums up the whole picture by proclaiming that the entire population is disenchanted, has surrendered all aspirations and illusions. But, says he, Springdalers are too stupid to realize they are frustrated. To a certain extent (they) live a full and not wholly unenjoyable life. "Because they do not recognize their defeat, they are not defeated."

"Life consists in making an adjustment that is as satisfactory as possible within a world which is not often tractable to basic wishes and desires."

It should not have taken 314 pages of repetition and technical language to discover that life, as so defined, is not a problem peculiar to a small town. –CC[26]

The reactions of some of the people in the community were recorded in one part of a three-part feature story about the book that was carried by the Ithaca *Journal*. The varied reactions indicate that the town's response was not monolithic, and moreover, that not all persons had equally absorbed the public relations:

BOOK'S SALES SPIRAL IN SUBJECT VILLAGE

Here is the last of three articles about a book and its effect on the town about which it was written.

By Donald Greet

> For a book that costs $6 and is "slow" to read, "Small Town" proved to be a best-seller in [Springdale].
>
> Elmer G. Kilpatric, proprietor of a main street store, sold more than two dozen copies. He says only "Peyton Place" in a half-dollar paperback did better.
>
> Mrs. Mary Lou Van Scoy, librarian at the village library (which does not have "Peyton Place"), says two copies "have been on the move since we got it."
>
> One copy, she says, "got bitten up by a dog."
>
> There is evidence, then, that a good many people in [Springdale] have read the book and a good many more have been treated to certain salient passages by their friends.
>
> Ask a waitress in the local restaurant if she is acquainted with "Small Town" and she will say, "Oh, yes, that book."
>
> The three persons who felt the chief impact of the book are called in its pages Sim Lee, Howard Jones and John Flint.

Villagers know these men respectively as C. Arthur Beebe, C. Paul Ward and Winston S. Ives. Beebe is the retired head of the [Springdale] *Courier*, Ward is a partner in Ward & Van Scoy Feed Mills, and Ives is an attorney.

All three have been and are active in local politics. The book refers to the threesome as the "invisible government," a term that has provoked both merriment and anger in [Springdale].

All three proved real enough to give their impressions of "Small Town." Says Beebe: "People have talked over every situation in the book. They have not felt generally that the book was fair.

"It was not as objective as it was supposed to have been. It was only one man's opinion. He (author Vidich) was judging a small community by big city standards. We felt it was sneaky."

Ward comments: "The whole thing is based on gossip and is not a true study. He (Vidich) didn't find it out by any bona fide investigation."

"The book could just as well have been written from New York (City). It was not a scientific study, which is what it purports to be."

Attorney Ives is somewhat more generous: "Two-thirds of the book is probably alright but he (Vidich) got into his biggest difficulty with personalities and in dealing with certain recent events."

"My principal objection to the book is that there are unfortunately a number of factual inaccuracies which in some cases create a distinctly misleading impression."

> "Another objection is that the book suggests 'invisible government' had no motive but control. In my experience and to my knowledge leaders have been motivated to do what they thought best for the community."
>
> Others in town added their comments. The Rev. V. F. Cline, minister of the Baptist Church for 14 years, said: "It (the book) has caused a suspicion between individuals and groups."
>
> Funeral director Myron Miller puts it succinctly: "Much ado about nothing." Off-the-cuff statements, not intended for quoted publication, indicate that some portions of the book struck pretty close to home and gave [Springdalers] the chance to see themselves as others see them.
>
> Said one observer: "The book did more to allay apathy in [Springdale] than anything in a long time."
>
> Perhaps it is just coincidence, but interest in a village election this spring shot up from the usual two dozen votes to 178.
>
> The village's two fire companies, needled in the book for pursuing their separate ways over the years, recently joined forces.
>
> One thing is certain: Walk into [Springdale] and mention "Small Town" and you won't get away without a reaction. Those reactions range from horse-laughs, to polite smiles to the angry bristle of a porcupine.[27]

Later when the town held its annual Fourth of July parade, several floats were addressed to the book. It is clear from the following account of the event that the community had managed to reassert its image of itself:

[Springdale] Calls It Even

> The people of the village of [Springdale] waited quite a while to get even with Art Vidich who wrote a "Peyton Place" type book about their town recently. The featured float of the annual Fourth of July parade today followed an authentic copy of the jacket of the book *Small Town in Mass Society*, done large scale by Mrs. Beverly Robinson. Following the book cover came residents of [Springdale], riding masked in cars labeled with the fictitious names given them in the book.
>
> But the pay-off was the final scene, a manure-spreader filled with very rich barnyard fertilizer, over which was bending an effigy of "The Author."
>
> Vidich, who lived in the town and won confidence of the local citizenry over a period of two years, worked under the auspices of Cornell University to complete a survey of typical village life. The survey was made available to village planners.
>
> However, Vidich in collaboration with Joseph Bensman decided to capitalize on the material in a way that would benefit themselves financially.[28]

With this final defeat of the book in terms consistent with the psychology of the town's residents, the community was able to continue as if the book had never been published, or, more exactly, now that the book had been consigned to its proper place in the town's imagery, the community could return to its former self-image and to the project's definition of rural life.

Public relations is a form of promise to a public. All the public-relations attitudes and postures of the town will focus the report to the point of view that the town holds on the project in response to the project's prior public relations. Even if research administrators are quite conscious that they are using public relations to get the work done, they are forced into reporting their findings on the basis of past promises. At this point, all of the accumulated public relations stand as a barrier to reporting anything but the bonhomie that the project projected onto the town beforehand. The project leaders then have the choice of either making a bland, pleasant report, or of violating a trust relationship that they have purposely created to further the carrying out of the research. Since it is difficult for the researcher to see beforehand all of the ramifications of a public-relations program at the time it is instituted, he may find himself paralyzed by the task of writing a report consistent with public-relations commitments. Due to these dynamics many reports are never written.

The University as a Project Reference Group and Pressure Group

The relationship between the university and the project rests on the consideration that each has some value for the other. The university is interested in the research project because it helps in the financing of the institution. Project budgets contain standard overhead items, help to cover staff salaries, and help with the purchasing of equipment. Frequently, the project will bring to the university additional staff members who otherwise could not be brought because of lack of funds, because the number of departmental positions is limited or because salary rates are too low to attract the research stars. As a rule, research projects allow universities to grow, if not painlessly, at least easily.

Also, the project brings prestige to the university in its competition for prestige with other universities. A university without projects is regarded as not doing any research, and without projects it is not possible to get other projects. In addition to all this, there is at least the ideology that there should be a coincidence of interest between research and the idea of the university; that is, teaching, research, and knowledge are thought of as related to each other positively and as being necessary to the idea of the university.

For their parts, the individual project members and the project director receive status in the university because they bring money to it in the form of overhead write-offs, because the staff underwrites its own costs, and because the project brings additional staff to the university at little or no cost. If looked at only in the form of statistical aggregates, the student-teacher ratio is improved, and the standing of the university, with the accrediting agencies and other interested publics, is given a more solid foundation by project research.

In addition, the project brings a promise of prestige in the form of a future publication that will be linked to the name of the university. Not only is there the promise of publication as such, but the research may receive rewards from professional associations, and individual project members may be cited for the importance of their work by relevant reference groups. In its early stages, at least, almost any project is full of hoped-for gains to the university.

Personnel connected with the project receive short-range esteem within the university for different reasons. If the project is heavily financed by "respectable" money and staffed by prestigious "leaders of the field," almost all personnel connected with the project may absorb some of the surplus prestige as their own. At times, researchers may elect to be or not to be associated with a project accordingly as it possesses surpluses of prestige. Up to a point, at least within the world of projects, project reputation is personal and institutional prestige. For this reason, projects address themselves to prestige competition within the university.

To the university community at large, project personnel receive esteem because they are busy, because they publish, because they possess a whole range of anecdotes that enliven the life of the university with something different (especially something that appears to have some relevance to the "real" world), and because they can talk knowingly about research designs and the other apparatus of scientific research. An occasional trip to Washington or upper Fifth Avenue can be an added embellishment.

In the research project, there is a general evidence of activity that appears to be in the pursuit of knowledge, and this knowledge is different from the general run of routine teaching or "unreal" knowledge that otherwise appears to inhabit the university. Project members can hold their own in campus conversations, and the face they present to the campus world is that they are getting things done, not just teaching the standard stock of knowledge, but actually expanding its frontiers and producing what will later appear in the textbooks. The research project lends a certain excitement and importance to campus life.

Whoever brings a research project to the university enhances his department's prestige in relation to other departments in the university and helps to advertise his department to the outside world, especially in relation to the competition between departments in different universities. Gaining a competitive edge over competitive departments is important to the university administration because it not only helps the recruiting of students but more importantly creates a generalized image that important research is taking place that can then become a basis for recruiting other research funds. Economically speaking, the total corpus that is the university can reach the point where, if it has *enough* research, it can ideally live off itself.

Research projects tie in with the expansion of graduate training programs since they bring in funds to support graduate students who otherwise would not come to the university if it did not provide them with a livelihood while they are studying. The graduate student who is being subsidized by the research project considers himself fortunate to be able to continue his education without monetary cost to himself. At the same time as he is being subsidized, he is available to the administration as an item of display to potential sponsors of other research projects. The university must have projects, staff, and graduate students in order to get more projects, staff, and graduate students.

In exchange for allowing projects to settle in its territory, the university expects in return to place certain constraints on the way projects conduct their business. At a minimum, the project sponsor must be respectable within the terms of respectability adhered to by the administration of the university. Sometimes the size of a grant helps to establish the donor's respectability.

Since the university has an obligation to the community and to prestigious sponsors, there are a number of political obligations that must be met. Nowadays these political obligations are organized under the university Social Science Research Center, an institution which seems to be based on the model of the historic Agricultural Extension Services: the Social Science Research Center is to the bureaucratic age what the Extension Service was to the agricultural age. This is not to mention that the university president himself and second-level officials in the university bureaucracy have personal communication with the foundations, government, segments of the business world, and with the alumni who are themselves connected to these agencies and foundations.

Because of whatever complex network of interconnections exists between the university and the outside benefactors and supporters, the university places certain requirements on research. The major requirement is that specific findings should not alienate any group of benefactors or sponsors, including political figures in the town or the state. At the political level, there is a great deal of variability between the social and physical sciences and within the social sciences. Different schools may be connected to different reference groups with different ideologies and positions. The point here is that for any specific school, there will usually be some correspondence between research positions and the official line of the higher administrative officials of the school as a whole. This means for the research project that:

> 1. Specific findings should not alienate any groups of sponsors or benefactors or the general line of political commitment.
>
> 2. Pressure will always be placed by the school to see that the project is fulfilled in at least a minimal way. The report must be written in a way and in terms that are acceptable to the sponsoring foundation.
>
> There is always a point at which the report is unacceptable, and this point is discovered only when a project overreaches the prevailing line of the institution where it is located. At other stages, there are always points at which people who might cause embarrassment are either not hired or are fired. At every stage, it is embarrassing for the project to embarrass the administration.
>
> 3. At all points, the university administration maintains a public-relations-type supervision over the operation of its projects, and this supervision in the fully bureaucratic university is embodied in the University Research Center.
>
> 4. Apart from all this, even under ideal conditions, the project director must be aware of the consequences of research for the public-relations position of the university. One might go so far as to say that in the pure

> case he enacts public-relations functions without knowing it and that to the extent that the pure case prevails all research is a function of public relations.

When one adds up all of the pressures, conflicts, tensions, and contradictions that are functions of bureaucratic research, one can only ask how all of this affects the quality of the "official" research report. What does it mean in concrete terms when an analyst-writer responds to the public-relations requirements of the town, the politics of the university, and the internal contradictions of the bureaucratic research organization?

The official Springdale report, "Leadership and Participation in a Changing Rural Community,"[29] is available to us as a case illustration. This is to be criticized less for its viewpoint than for its lack of a focus or an organizing idea. When one has read this booklet, one is aware of having read six essays, each reflecting the interests of the given author or combination of authors. The lack of a central problem or, rather, the succession of different problems and theories introduced on an ad hoc basis mirrors the failure of any one project point of view to develop or prevail.

For lack of a consistent point of view or a problem, the report cannot present a consistent or integrated portrait of the community along several or even any single dimension of its institutional organization. From reading "Leadership and Participation," one is left with the impression that neither leadership nor participation has any relationship to the economic and political life of Springdale. The Community Club emerges as a central institution that exists largely outside the framework of other social realities, as if it were conditioned only by itself and by the project's conception of the neighborhood structure of the township. When specific roles and their incumbents are mentioned, they are mentioned not to describe their structural position in the town, but only to clarify their participation in an important Community Club project, specifically the repair of the dam. This is not the place to provide an analysis for why the project did not develop a consistent theory for leadership and participation. For present purposes, it is only necessary to note that the substantive limits set by the project for itself stay well within the limits of what the community and the university administrative officials expected. No one need be offended because everyone's feelings have been taken into account in advance. In short, the report achieves such a level of blandness and neutrality that after reading it any reader can go on as if nothing has happened to him. Nothing is said sharply enough to give anyone in the community a pretext for complaining to the university administration, and those who are dissatisfied because the report does not make any points do not complain because there is nothing to complain against.

One might speculate that the absence of a central problem, the absence of a central theory, and even the absence of the sense of the social structure of the community may be due to the inability of the project leaders to see and pose issues sharply in order to avoid offending significant members of the community.

The Ethos of Research

From the foregoing discussion it is apparent that there are at least three different criteria by which the fundamental values in research can be evaluated:

> 1. By the ethic of scientific inquiry—the pursuit of knowledge for the sake of knowledge regardless of its consequences.
>
> 2. By the ethic of bureaucratic inquiry that we have already outlined.

> 3. And by the ethic of Christian human relations—for the sake of helping or at least not hurting others.

Every organizational structure imposes its own set of ethics on the individuals who work in it. This is largely because ethics have largely come to be work rules. Knowing that bureaucratic research is here to stay means also that bureaucratic ethics are here to stay and that, furthermore, they will be elaborated in formal codes as part of the bureaucratic rules. All current trends in bureaucratic research point in the direction of ethical and professional codes that try to specify codes of research conduct that will be consistent with the exigencies of the bureaucratic method of research.

Much of the current concern with ethics in the social sciences is simply a working out of an attempt to resolve some of the contradictions between individual responsibility and corporate group responsibility. The general trend is toward statements of viable rules for specifying the canons of individuals working in a bureaucratic setting. Actually, this is not a new problem. It is the same problem that has been confronted by business and industry and government for the past two hundred years, since the beginning of the bureaucratic trend in all phases of life. These trends are only now beginning to emerge in the research process itself because research itself has come to occupy a unique position with a halo of its own, no matter how far behind the times it may actually be.

However, the ethic of independent and disinterested research with regard only for the creation of new theories and the discovery of new facts is much older than the modern bureaucratic ethic. At some point, almost everyone is willing to accept the ancient Greek ideal of personal integrity, especially after an individual scholar produces valuable and useful results.

Even in modern times, the advocates of bureaucratic research ethics are themselves at some point perfectly willing to accept the findings of individuals whose work was conducted in violation of the bureaucratic ethics, so that we assume that some value is still placed on independent research.

It is our opinion that the basic conflict in research ethics is not only a conflict of values but also a conflict in the very structure of the research enterprise. Therefore, if bureaucratically organized research is necessary and if it is the esteemed form for carrying out research activity, it appears that the conflict between the two ethics is a permanent part of the research scene that will never be resolved by any further explication of ethics. It would be dangerous for the freedom of inquiry if the formalized ethics of bureaucracy prevailed or predominated in all research. At the same time, it does not seem likely that bureaucratic research will disappear just because a few individual scholars dislike its methods and results. Therefore, pluralistic, conflicting research ethics are likely to exist so long as adherents to both types of research exist and so long as individuals have the spontaneity and the insight to see an unanticipated problem and pursue a new insight or hypothesis that contravenes the formal design and expectations of a whole series of administrators, sponsors, officials, respondents, politicians, and seekers for prospects for grants from foundations who are presold in another direction.

Fundamentally, then, the problem is not one of ethics, but of what type or method of social research is most likely to be productive.

Large-scale bureaucratic research has the advantage of being able to mobilize vast funds and large numbers of researchers in relatively narrow problem areas. It is weak in allowing the unplanned, unplannable, unanticipated, and unpredictable operation of insight, curiosity, creative hypothesis formulation, and pursuit of incongruous and inconvenient facts—all of which may challenge the validity of received theory or evoke the possibility of a new theory.

Only the individual scholar working alone—even in the midst of a bureaucratic setting—has the possibility to raise himself above the routine and mechanics of research. If, when, and under what circumstances this happens is not predictable in advance. Bureaucratic constraints make it all but impossible for the individual to follow the insights he otherwise would because such constraints are central to the plans and obligations that are the heart of large-scale organization.

As a result, large-scale research organizations are most effective at gathering and processing data along the lines of sharply defined hypotheses that have standardized variables, dimensions, and methods of analysis.

The work of the individual scholar, no matter where he is located, and no matter how he is financed, organized, constrained, or aided, is perhaps the sole source of creativity. The successful placing of limitations on individual scholarship under the guise of "ethics," work rules, institutional responsibility, or higher considerations forces a society to live off the intellectual capital of its independent thinkers.

Notes

1. Princeton University Press, 1958.

2. This study has been published as "Leadership and Participation in a Changing Rural Community," in *Journal of Social Issues* 16 (1960), no. 4.

3. See Arthur J. Vidich, *The Political Impact of Colonial Administration* (New York: Arno Press, 1980), a slightly revised version of his dissertation in the Department of Social Relations, Harvard University, 1953.

4. We have discussed two other dimensions of unprogrammed research—namely, undesigned fieldwork and heuristic theorizing in essays otherwise available. See the authors' "The Validity of Field Data," *Human Organization* 13 (Spring 1954), 20-27, and "Social Theory in Field Research," in *American Journal of Sociology* 65 (May 1960), 577-84.

5. See Vidich and Bensman, "Social Theory in Field Research," for a discussion of the telephone company.

6. It was the project that introduced the idea of positive as opposed to negative ways of evaluating the facts: "We agree with most of what these authors (that is, Vidich and Bensman) say about the facts of community life in Springdale, but our evaluation of these facts tends to be positive rather than negative." See "Leadership and Participation in a Changing Rural Community," 53, footnote.

7. The problem of repressing original ideas can be solved in advance by personnel recruitment policies: when only like-minded social scientists are hired, agreement is assured. It is for this reason that recruitment policies in bureaucratic research may be a decisive factor in determining the success or failure of the project.

8. The problem is more complicated than this. We have seen researchers whose interests have changed in phase with changes in sources of available funds. When a large number of individuals in a scientific community do this, we witness the phenomenon of research fads—for example, the mental health and organizational research that are popular at the present time. Available pools of money determine the dominant emphasis of the overall research enterprise. More recently, the directors of the philanthropic foundations and bureaus have come to conceive of themselves as possessing an explicit managerial function in choosing the direction of research investments. That is, a decision is made to invest in a given area, problem, or place, and proposals that fit the predefinition are supported. It is perfectly understandable that fund dispensers should try in this way to make their work interesting and creative.

9. In a fund-raising experience recently encountered by one of the authors, a team of two incompatible applicants agreed not to disagree with each other until funds could be secured from two incompatible agencies, each of which had "other" reasons for desiring to give research funds. Almost all of the negotiators to this transaction were experts who understood the fundamental contradictions between the participants, but who also realized that it was necessary not to mention these differences during the monetary negotiations.

10. Researchers who attempt to keep sponsors informed of every change in direction of the research find themselves involved in endless negotiations with sponsors and with little time for research.

11. Several years prior to our research, a division of the agricultural school had made a land classification survey, which rated all land from bad to excellent depending on various criteria of soil content. Farmers in low-rated areas remembered and resented this survey

because it had tended to set relative real estate values on land so that prospective buyers could point to Cornell's survey and argue land prices on the basis of its authority.

12. Arthur J. Vidich, "Freedom and Responsibility in Research: A Rejoinder," *Human Organization* 19 (Spring 1960), 3-4.

13. Our reasons for doing this have been stated more fully in Arthur J. Vidich and Joseph Bensman, "Freedom and Responsibility in Research," *Human Organization* 17 (Winter 1958-59), 1-7, and in Vidich, "Freedom and Responsibility in Research: A Rejoinder."

14. Personal communication from project official, January 1958.

15. "Leadership and Participation in a Changing Rural Community."

16. Personal communication from project official, July 1961.

17. Personal communication from project official, July 1956.

18. Personal letter from project director, January 1956.

19. Since the Dean is a resident of the Springdale community, we have, in accordance with past practice, invented this name in order to maintain the anonymity of our informants.

20. From a tape-recorded address delivered to a group of sociology students at Harpur College, 1962.

21. Letter to the editor of the Springdale *Courier* published as a lead article shortly after the publication of *Small Town in Mass Society.*

22. From Dean Grisely's address to the sociology group at Harpur College, 1962.

23. So far as we know, this was one of Dean Grisely's projects on small businessmen. If true, we refuse to take full responsibility for the resentment because, in terms of our analysis, the small businessman will seize on any easily available object of resentment so long as the object in question absolutely lacks defenses.

24. Personal communication from project director, February 1958.

25. We were not able to secure a copy of the issue of the Springdale *Courier* that carried the review of the book. Though we wrote to the publishers asking for copies and enclosed funds to cover costs, no one ever replied to our request. Our relations with Cornell have been so strained that we have not asked to see their files on the matter. Reviews appeared in other regional papers like the Ithaca *Journal*, but we have made no effort to collect these.

26. Owego *Times*, January 31, 1958.

27. Ithaca *Journal*, June 13, 1958.

28. Springdale *Courier* press release, July 4, 1958.

29. See note 2.

13

Who Writes What in the Bureaucratic University?

Joseph Bensman

In mass society, problems related to plagiarism and authorship can take on bizarre characteristics. Where large-scale organizations prevail, the head man is presumed to be too busy, too engaged, and too important to write his own speeches, policy papers, books, or letters to the editor. Instead, he has a staff of information specialists, aides, consultants, and public relations men who write for him. His name on the title page symbolizes his temporary acceptance of a document concocted for him. Convention requires that the nominal author be treated as the actual author—unless, after receiving an unfavorable response, the nominal author denies responsibility for "his" unfortunate statements by claiming that he has not read them.

In one highly publicized case, a university president was exposed for lifting a speech verbatim from a learned journal. He successfully defended himself by claiming that he had not written his speech. Among politicians, ghost writers are nearly universal. Special virtue attaches to a man who writes some of his own speeches (Adlai Stevenson) or edits them, like John Fitzgerald Kennedy.

Published originally in a slightly different form in *Dissent* 15 (July 1968), 347-50. Republished with permission from University of Pennsylvania Press.

The problem looks somewhat different in research organizations attached to universities. There, the "principal investigator" is usually a specialist in securing funds. He knows where the money is and how to lay his hands on a grant. He is a capable and sometimes a super-salesman who effectively promotes his proposal both to the funding agency and to his own university. He must know how to write a proposal or has to hire someone who does. Beyond this, it is desirable that he be a good administrator, able to employ competent researchers and reasonably articulate writers.

Grantsmanship is time-consuming. It leaves the academic entrepreneur with little energy for the day-to-day operations of his project. His own ignorance may be a major source of anxiety to the entrepreneur. Subordinates frequently implement policies that never have been communicated to them. These policies are often comprised of unspoken or half-forgotten understandings, not to speak of misunderstandings, between sponsors and project heads. Subordinates may consciously or unwittingly sabotage agreements to which they are not privy.

Since, however, the principal investigator is the visible director of "his" project, outsiders treat him as if he actually did the work. Protocol requires that he be sole or principal author of the final report. This is so even though the principal investigator has not written a line or is incapable of writing a line. Failure to list the principal investigator as an author may be construed by the sponsor (who has occupied all the work time of the principal investigator) as neglect of duty. As a result, the principal investigator forces himself to accept authorship of work initiated and completed by others, in an environment where to write something is to validate oneself.

Hence, it is possible for quasi illiterates to become the authors of innumerable speeches, papers, monographs, articles, and books, written by variegated specialists whose only relationship to each other is that they are financed by the same agency. The sheer volume of unrelated studies attributed to a single research broker serves best to indicate the nature of his authorship.

Nor is this ectoplasmic output necessarily condemned. To many sponsors, subliterary, incoherent (or elegant and cogent, but always ghostly) fecundity is evidence that they have a responsible administrator. He gets work done. His name on a bibliography or a title page then justifies the convention that allows it to be there.

More anxiety is in store for such an author. He knows that in an academic community authorship leads to prestige and promotion. Since he takes on authorship by usurpation, he tends to feel acutely uncomfortable in the presence of a genuine author. To maintain his social and occupational position, he must act as if he really writes—which will make him uneasy and, if he is capable of it, cause him to experience a sense of guilt. He is forced to accept the fraudulent role that would no doubt have seemed obnoxious to him when he initially embarked upon a career in research.

On top of all this, the putative author must find some device by which to convince his writers that he, not they, deserve authorship. In business and government, the employed journalist-author is used to accepting anonymity as a basis for employment. He does not mind; in fact, he derives personal pleasure (and professional recognition from his fellow writers) based on the amount of work done and the position of the nominal authors who use him.

The problem is, of course, more complicated when one conventional author has a stable of "ghosts," all contributing works, ideas, or lines to a given piece of work. In this case, the stable of writers becomes a brotherhood, with each writer competing for acceptance and praise from the patriarch.

When the conventional author writes a book that does not require the legitimacy of his official position, he can be magnanimous by including his actual author as a coauthor, usually under the designation, "as told to—" or "with the help of—." This technique has its advantages for the professional writer.

In the academic community, this situation results in greater conflict if only because the actual author needs to validate and advance himself through authorial credits. He is unsympathetic to the publicity needs of the conventional author. He has his own needs. In addition, by pressing his claims for authorship, he evokes guilt in the conventional author who thereupon feels obliged to justify his own claims. Because he is an academic, providing the money and the job is not enough.

He has to make a positive contribution. If he is able to dredge up an earlier essay written by himself or written under his name, he can insist that it be inserted in a later work the better to buttress his present pretensions. Thus, the ghosts of past authorship haunt the ghosts of contemporary authorships.

More typically, the conventional author can justify his claims to that title by becoming an editor. He receives the manuscript of the actual author and makes suggestions. If he is competent, or feels that he is, he will actually rewrite part of the material. Some of this editing is necessary. The project head may edit the work from the standpoint of its political implications.

Because the conventional author is the "outside man," he knows or thinks he knows how the work is likely to be received by sponsors. He can excise "unnecessary academic complexity." He can eliminate recommendations or evidence that implies a recommendation that might run counter to what he thinks is the sponsor's policy. Moreover, he is expected to censor copy that may offend the school or institution that "houses" the grant. The writer may unknowingly provide the evidence for a policy that suggests budgets or programs unacceptable to the institution "housing" the project.

More fundamentally, when much of the background for a study is based on tacit understandings and subliminal or implicit agreements, the principal investigator may only become aware of the nature or implications of these agreements by discovering their unwitting violation by actual authors who were not aware of these agreements since they had no part in them. In correcting these violations, the editor-author justifies his conventional authorship, even though it was his inability or failure to communicate to the actual author that made the revision necessary.

If all of these justifications fail, the conventional author sits down with blue pencil and "corrects" or otherwise alters the punctuation, grammar, and syntax. If pressed for time, he finds a professional writer to make certain corrections and simplifications. In doing so, he distributes the authorship to as many individuals as possible. With this tactic, his own claim is strengthened as the actual author's is correspondingly weakened. It is one form of distributive justice.

The actual author, unless he is a "pro," will resist such attacks on his manhood, and fight tooth and nail not only for the credit, but also for what he regards as the integrity of the manuscript. If he is intractable, he will be fired, or he will resign. In that case, the problem is solved; upon his departure, he can be assigned a junior authorship.

In most cases, the issue will be resolved by splitting authorship among a handful of coauthors, all under the senior authorship of the illiterate or nonwriting senior conventional author. But even in such cases, the problem is not resolved without bitterness. In a large-scale project, literally dozens of people will have worked on the research, some as staff members and others as consultants brought in to rescue a phase of a floundering study.

If the project manages to pull itself together and "gets out a report," convention demands that all contributors be acknowledged, yet convention also outlaws joint authorship by more than six persons. Others must be acknowledged by other means. Convention again allows for a list of acknowledgments to as many as twenty to thirty contributors, some of whom may be writers of preliminary drafts. The problem remains of discovering some means of distributing recognition between acknowledgment and authorship. In general, this problem is resolved by power, by statesmanship, by bargaining, and by occupational mobility. Those individuals who are still around at the time of completion of the manuscript are most likely to become authors. The continued need for a principal writer in subsequent research guarantees at least a junior authorship for the writer. The possibility of a scandal also serves to guarantee authorship. If the actual writer is a graduate student who needs the approval of his professor-employer for his PhD dissertation, his vulnerability weakens his bargaining position. It is understandable that graduate students see themselves as the most exploited class in America.

If there are numerous reports, the principals agree to rotate authorship. A number of names affixed to any one report is reduced, and each project member can be a principal or sole author. From the standpoint of jurisdictional disputes, this solution is the most efficient. It is even better than the solution adopted by commercial agencies that do not list authors but only names of the agencies or departments in lieu of authors.

All of these complexities are generally known and understood by the participants, by university administrators, by sponsors, and by faculty not engaged in project research. The net result is to devalue research authorship. Since no one knows who actually wrote what, conventional authorship is more an attribute of rank in an organization, which implies the ability to attract funds and to fulfill contractual requirements. The whole artifice contributes to inflation of the number of publications and to the devaluation of publication itself. In this context, good writing does not drive out bad writing; bad writing inundates good writing. For in the flood of "objectively necessary" but imminently useless paperwork, the real thing, conceived and recorded by one man or a pair of scholars, continues to be produced. Simply because there is a presumption of actual authorship in such work, it *is* valued. Moreover, where there are neither funds, staff, nor apparatus to intervene between the author and his work, this presumption is probably correct.

The book, the article, or the essay is valued over the mimeographed report or the government-sponsored monograph. As a consequence, many contract researchers are driven to get their reports or articles printed by book publishers or scientific journals.

To transform "practical" research with concrete recommendations into a "scientific" report is a delicate matter. A "theorist" and a theory are needed to "reframe" the report. Theory operates to take the particular, specific data of a report and reset it in a general "scientific" framework. It adds the dignity of footnotes, concepts, and definitions—after the fact. Thus, "theory" becomes public relations, and the theorist an indispensable aide to dignify project researchers. It is wise to have a "theorist" on the staff or, at least, to add one as a consultant. The theorist earns his keep by assisting in academic publication and by legitimizing otherwise nonrespectable research. He becomes a writer.

At the other extreme, professional writers are employed simply to make the work intelligible. Ordinarily, only a few key people read research reports. As pillars of the sponsoring agency and as readers, they are known to have sharply defined tastes. Moreover, their vocabulary is likely to consist of professional jargon. Writing for them requires a special kind of literacy, far removed from generally recognized standards of literary English. Haste in meeting deadlines and the fact that project researchers are hired for technical rather than literary skills make for more pedantic gobbledygook.

Once the professional writer goes to work, a new set of battles begins. The technical staff feels all too frequently that the professional editor is falsifying its results. The writer feels that technicians are illiterate barbarians, infatuated with their own words, stubborn, and intractable. The principal investigator who is destined to be the conventional author serves as mediator between technicians and professional writers, usually siding with the professional writer, but restraining him when his literary imagination provokes the threat of resignation or sabotage by the technical staff.

The flood of reports of contractual research then reaches the "publisher," a writer or would-be writer, who generally is forced against his better judgment to act as businessman. He must estimate the sales potential of a specific book for either a particular audience or that mysterious body, the general public. Usually, the editor is handicapped by his fondness for a well-made and well-written book that has something to say, even if it does not sell. But the number of prestigious books he can publish is severely limited.

Thus, the highly literate editor is inundated with specialized, badly written manuscripts, which have as their principal reasons for existence their conventional authors' need for publications to achieve promotions and the fact that a government agency or foundation financed the research on which a nonbook is based. In many instances, this problem is solved by subvention. The government agency or private foundation finances the cost or part of the cost of publishing the book. Some publishers or departments of publishing firms receive a substantial part of their income by such publications, and others are virtual branches of an agency or a foundation. Sometimes, they reject or accept unsubsidized manuscripts by judging whether they are compatible with their subsidized publications.

When this happens, subsidized publication comes to be a form of information control.

If the publisher accepts the project report, the editor at the publishing house is enlisted as coauthor of the conventional author and his anonymous editorial consultant. The publisher's editor increasingly resents both the illiteracy of the academician in general and that of the conventional author in particular. But, if he can succeed in making the report into an intelligible book, he takes pride in his virtual authorship.

This process reaches a culmination when the editor-publisher begins to resent the author for being inexpert in the field in which the book is written or for depriving him of credit for his own secret authorship. The editor tries to avoid competing with his own authors. His greatest pleasures in authorship, so long as he remains an editor, must be secret pleasures. If he claims credit for his authorship, the actual or conventional authors might seek a more self-effacing editor. Editorship is thus, in the world of bureaucratic writing, a thankless task. But so is authorship.

14

The Aesthetics and Politics of Footnoting

Joseph Bensman

Several years ago, I received from my publisher an anonymous evaluation of a manuscript I had submitted for publication. Although the evaluation was generally favorable, it contained a number of criticisms of my footnoting. The criticisms claimed that I was an elitist; that is, I cited only "stars"; was a male chauvinist (did not cite enough women); and, in general, did not do enough footnoting. The evaluator suggested additional sources of which almost half were from one author, presumably the evaluator. None of these suggestions demanded new evidence or offered new substantive points, nor would any result in additions or substantive modification of the ideas under discussion. This incident led me to reflect on the politics of footnoting.

This analysis of the field of footnoting takes for granted the explicit, manifest meanings and functions of footnoting. Footnotes provide evidence or location of evidence of a point being asserted. Beyond this, they aid in the attributing and allocating of acknowledgments,

---

Published originally in a slightly different form in *International Journal of Politics, Culture, and Society* 1 (Spring 1988), 443-70. Republished with permission of Springer Science+Business Media B.V.

credits, and priorities for work previously done. They may also locate current work in a tradition that makes that work meaningful.

In addition to these manifest functions, footnotes have important institutional, "political," and aesthetic functions. Since much of the sociology of science traces scholarly and scientific achievements through citations, it is assumed that being cited is proof of having made a scholarly contribution. It is, perhaps, as a result of this assumption that academic departments and academicians are often evaluated and evaluate themselves on the basis of their ratings in a citation index.

In contrast to the criteria implicit in the above distinctions, that citation is evidence of work well done, I initially assume that citation is an input into the work process of a scholarly field and a part of the "social construction of reality" undertaken by the citer. Yet, because of the range of choices available to the citer (and the ongoing structure of citing behavior), this input can determine, if only in part, the objective output, the continuously emerging structure and culture of a field, also seen as a social reality.

This discussion will initially focus on footnoting and citing practices—patterned social actions—as inputs into larger systems. Later in this essay, I will focus on some of the major implications and consequences for these larger social, technical, and cultural systems of which citation behavior and practices are but a part.

The Conspicuous Display and Consumption of Footnotes

Since the number of footnote citations in a work is considered to be evidence of erudition and scholarly attainment, one can increase the appearance of scholarship merely by increasing the number of footnote citations in one's publications. Given the inevitable awareness concerning the imputed meaning of footnotes, one can compete in erudition with real or imagined rivals in real or imagined battles of footnotes. Here, the concern is the number of times an author cites other authors and himself, rather than the number of times he is cited by others. The two concepts of citing (citing as input into system, and being cited) are interrelated, but not necessarily at a one-to-one ratio. Nevertheless, footnote competition at the citing level is likely to result in footnote inflation and the devaluation of an individual citation as it is submerged in a plethora of citations. The consequences of footnote inflation as a secular trend will be one of the emphasized themes in this essay.

Footnote Inflation

The best example of footnote inflation I know of is to be found in the writing of a distinguished sociologist, now dead, whose articles consisted of entire pages of, at times, no more than three sentences of text and the rest footnotes. To compound the matter, the text of the articles in question seem to have no point other than to justify the footnotes. In effect, the latter seem to shout "Look at me! See how smart I am!" As might be expected, the most frequently cited works were by the author himself, demonstrating one way in which writing is related to being cited.

The citation behavior revealed in this case is not unique. Its practice may well be the attempt of an author to validate his claims for scholarly erudition, while the self-citation may be an attempt to validate claims for originality and priority. Both may indicate attempts at conspicuous adornment, evidence of personal vanity perhaps, but may also be attempts to conceal the lack of originality and substance in one's work. The conspicuous adornment may thus cover up a deeper sense of a disfigured scholarly self, insecurities over the value or presence of one's own concepts and ideas and over fear of criticism. The same appearance may thus be a product of often separate and apparently widely divergent causes, though these imputed explanations may not be equally operative in apparently similar cases.

It is also possible to imagine a pure, autonomous delight in the mechanics and immediately visible fruits of scholarship, similar in nature to bibliophilia or, if one wishes, conspicuous avarice: no source is fully lost. Moreover, the reader may share in the delights of footnote collection, similar in passion to the delights of a museum aficionado: new and original footnote citations may be discovered and old familiar friends may be revisited while reading an article or book. Footnoting may thus establish a community of meaning between the author and his professional community or a particular scholarly audience. The author may thus imagine that the aesthetics of citation constitutes a raison d'être for himself and his audience. The reader of footnotes can thus be a connoisseur of the art, but connoisseurship starts at the productive, actually reproductive, level.

Footnote Connoisseurship

As opposed to merely quantitative warfare and aggression in footnoting practices, claims for recognition within a scholarly community may be based on footnote connoisseurship. Footnote connoisseurship rests on the quality of sources cited and the judicious selection of precious quotations. Thus, one tradition in citational behavior is the search for obscure sources, authors, and publications in order to be first in republication of germane, exotic, but prestigeful sources. In doing so, one establishes one's erudite image by ranging outside the familiar bypaths of standard sources. In the same sense, one can discover in the works of a prestigious author previously unknown works or quotations conventionally considered to be outside of his or her expertise. In all of this work, the "quality" of the citation, source, or quotation is considered to be more valuable than mere quantity.

In fact, emphasis on quantity may dilute the quality or at least the appearance of quality of one's sources.

Creativity in citation for purposes of competition over the quality of footnotes is, of course, filled with difficulties. The prestige deriving from such competition depends on the ability of the reader and other potential citers to recognize the value of the source cited. They may recognize and confirm that value by citing the source in their own work. Thus, a source, phrase, or quotation may achieve a chic or "in" quality by its multiple recitation. However, when citation emulation occurs, it is often hard to remember who is the original reciter of the prestigious footnote. Multiple claims for originality and priority in the rediscovery of a source then abound, but these claims may be weakened by the very popularity of a citation, source, or quotation. Frequent repetition devalues the citation by trivializing it or by rendering it a cliché. Because this inevitably happens to any highly valued citation, the endless search for prestigious sources goes on ad infinitum, and connoisseurship is a permanent, if specialized, underpinning to citation praxis.

In the long run, the same source, quotation, or citation may be rediscovered time and time again, given the time and memory lapses necessary to refresh old sources. This is especially true of sources in foreign languages, for the same term may be retranslated in different ways. Thus, *dissociation* may become *estrangement*, *alienation*, or *self-alienation* and may be attributed in each of its various lives to a different reciter, depending on scholarly fashion, changes in intellectual milieus, and the exigencies of connoisseurship and citation emulation. The rediscovery of rediscoveries is the major form of the dialectics of footnoting, though the dialectic has no ultimate resolution. The only resolution is in the ongoing and temporary flow of intellectual styles and footnote culture. At any given moment, the original rediscoverer of a valued source can reappropriate the source for himself, if he can defend himself against emulators and competitors, and thus appropriate or usurp space in the terrain of the continuing flow of footnote culture. The complexity of discerning the original rediscoverer of a valued source or quotation and of assigning credits and priorities often leads to footnote genealogy and archaeology, which becomes a field in itself, subject to all the same processes described above.

Another form of footnote inflation is akin to art collecting and museum keeping. Here, the scholar collects all possible mentions of a given theme or topic by classical sources in Latin or Greek, the Old Testament, the Talmud, Asiatic and Near Eastern classics, medieval and renaissance sources, and relevant sources outside the field being studied, as well as the virtually unlimited number of related modern studies in the natural sciences, social sciences, and humanities.

Voracious consumption and digestion of scholarly works—or, at least, their reflection in citations, bibliographies, and indexes—may not be due to ulterior motives, vanity, or conspicuous display, but they may be part of a pure delight in scholarship or in research for its own sake and in its own terms. The display of footnote erudition may thus be purely autonomous. While this kind of erudition may not lead to new discoveries (assuming that the discovery of a new source is not a discovery), it may produce for the reader an appreciation of the pure delight and the playfulness implicit in much scholarly research. Footnote research may, of course, lead to new concepts, themes, and rhetorics, but it also leads to the inflation of printing costs and the concealment or avoidance of substantive themes, which become overburdened by the very complexity and density of citation research.

Not the least of the consequences of this emphasis on citation research is its use as a means to avoid publication. An eminent scholar may find it easy to use connoisseurship and citation research as a means to avoid publication of his or her results. There are always more sources to investigate, works to be read, and footnote trails to follow, so that he or she is on a never-ending journey. As a result, the footnote ground covered may be immense; each side trip leads to another, and the task is never completed. Such scholarship may lead to the fact or reputation of being a living library. But the works in that library need never be assembled and published into a work itself. Immense citation and bibliographic scholarship may thus lead to its own negation, though the reputations they create may be justified.

Footnote Classicism

Footnote classicism results in citations and quotations that neither are promiscuous nor that stand alone in solitary splendor. An article written under the classical aesthetic may contain perhaps only a dozen to twenty citations, each of which refers to a major, well-established author in a given field, and each of which is so selected and edited that it presents the basic ideas of those authors in a clear, precise, and apt way. The quotations preclude complexity, contradiction, and confusion in the thought of the authorities in question. In effect, the selecting, editing, and emendation used in footnote classicism refine the thought in the works of the authors cited. But more importantly, the cumulative order and flow of citations and quotations lend balance, harmony, and order to the article in question and often to the entire field or subfield that is the objective of the work that exhibits the indicated citations. The article may itself become a classic because it uses classical sources in a way that classically organizes a field. The pattern of citations and the selection of quotations reveal the balance, harmony, and order among multiple and divergent perspectives, summarizing the field. It frequently appears in these classical and well-written articles that citations and quotations were so selected merely to produce this classical harmony and order. The net effect is to exorcise the disorder, confusion, conflict, and lack of direction that are often intrinsic to the very flow of work in a field, including the transition from one paradigm to another, the absence of a dominant paradigm, or the almost anomic appearance of the multiple paradigms of a field.

Conversely, an author may select his citations to indicate the confusion and disorder in a field (or in the work of an established authority), so that the citer's clarification can establish the basis for a new classicism, a new order, for his or her field. If the confusion, disorder, and bottomless complexity are so great, relatively simple and previously considered banal solutions and paradigms appear to rescue us from the abyss so vividly described in the summarizing work. In this case, footnotes are merely a means for achieving objectives or effects that go far beyond footnote practices in their own terms.

Footnote Legitimacy

Footnote connoisseurship, the conspicuous consumption and display of footnotes, and footnote classicism are all subtypes of footnote legitimacy. Footnote legitimacy is the attempt to establish one's own legitimacy as a scholar by citing prestigious and recognized sources whose very citation confirms or may confirm the status of the citer. This legitimacy may be traditional, accomplished by the citing of traditional sources or an entire lineage of sources from which one claims to descend. It may be charismatic in the sense that one rediscovers an old source that, in the recent past, has been forgotten. In this case, would-be prophets revive the old gods to produce revolutions in current footnote practices. Footnote legitimacy may be bureaucratic, if, for example, the emphasis on a new source or font of sources has already been appropriated by a scholarly journal or formal organization that claims the right to rationally organize the process of footnote validation or the benefits deriving from such validation.

Hence, authors may legitimate themselves by the use of bureaucratically standardized sources, a practice to be discussed in detail below. An ultimate consequence of footnote legitimation for an individual, group, or network may be the social transformation and reproduction of citation authority. Authority may shift from the cited to the citer. The reflector of established authority may become the authority himself. This dynamic transformation is a process of succession within the field and has other objective consequences for a field.

The quest for legitimation via footnotes and citation behavior may focus on much more than self-legitimation. The legitimacy sought may be for a theme, cause, or ideology and may be based on much more than citations alone. Of course, the citation of "venerated sources"—a Marx, Weber, or Durkheim—may help to authenticate the ideological or theoretical view one wishes to promulgate, and the use of language and quotations from these "saints" may serve as ritual incantations to meet present needs.

Still other, more serious issues surround the selection of quotations, the interpretation of documents, the ignoring of sources, and the alleged biases in selection from a larger work. Here, the issues are accuracy in the representation of sources, basic honesty, and technical competence in the use and misuse of sources. Whether a theme is proven or disproven by a self-conscious distortion of documents referred to in a text is a matter not merely of technical proficiency, but one that strikes at the heart of the entire scholarly enterprise. But judgment as to what constitutes an accurate representation of the evidence and of particular sources is itself conditioned by ideologies and ideological causes that may lie outside of scholarly proficiency and even self-conscious dishonesty. The very criteria for proficiency and honesty are based, in part, on ideology. The ideologist, regardless of his particular ideology, is likely to see and represent the facts from his own ideological perspective. He is likely to be ignorant of his biases just as his ideological and professional enemies are likely to be equally unaware of their own. Thus, the battle over footnoting, quotation, and citation practices is intrinsic to the scholarly process. Moreover, attacks on the footnote and citation practices of the citer will remain intrinsic to the process so long as value relevance, ideologies, and other forms of normative preferences underlie footnote and citation practices.

Footnote Elitism

Footnote legitimation easily leads to footnote elitism. This means that, among citers, only sources equal or higher in prestige than oneself are citable. When sources are so selected, citers and cited can constitute a self-selected or mutually selected elite or an aristocracy of reference. Inclusion in such an elite, which one anticipates by one's own citation behavior, may be a major objective of footnoting. The elite may thus constitute one's footnoting reference group, and failure to be included in such a social or reference group—that is, to cite without being cited in return—can often be a major source of depression and despair.

Because scholars can seek to establish their reputations for erudition, legitimacy, elite status, or image by being devoted to and orthodox within a group, movement, or cause (or by being radical, independent, or populist), it is, of course, necessary to recognize the existence of a plurality of ideologies, "schools," traditions, theoretical and methodological cleavages, invisible communities, and social networks that exist within a field. In addition, citers must bow to their mentors, past and present peers, the great masters, and current chic or "in" sources.

Thus, depending on one's position in academic structures and networks, "party lines" emerge in footnoting. Only some sources are deemed desirable, others are taboo, while still others are conventional or optional. Party "lines" may be built around a particular journal that emphasizes its own editorial or scholarly policy and its established authors. Sometimes, the lines reflect an ideological fashion. Still other sources of footnote lines are interest in a "school" such as behaviorism, symbolic interaction, structural functionalism, and so forth. Each school has a respectable font of sources whose citation is indispensable and, more importantly, another pool of sources whose affirmative citation would result in loss of prestige in the citer's reference groups. Some sources are thus cited negatively, being indicators of salience despite their negative valence.

In the Soviet Union, following changes in the party line, books and journals containing the works of proscribed authors had to be withdrawn, and some authors could not cite their own works when they were published in taboo publications. In the United States, some authors rework and rewrite their articles and books for new editions in order to clean up the language, political messages, and implications of their earlier work and to make them consistent with emerging trends in the political, intellectual, and academic milieus of an ever-changing present. They edit the content and footnotes of their work on the basis of criticisms made after initial publication. Thus, one famous author hires a clipping service to send him all references to his work. He may also use a research assistant to classify all these references as favorable or unfavorable as well as important and unimportant mentions. On the basis of this citation analysis, he rewrites the article and answers the criticisms by changing the content of the article or by engaging in a footnote duel. He then republishes the article in an anthology of his own works, leaving the revised article undated so that the casual reader, unaware of the revisions, may discover that earlier criticisms of the article appear to be gratuitous or foolish.

Footnote Democracy and Mass Culture

Wherever footnoting and citation practice establish legitimacy, elitism, respectability, or network or party-line loyalties, it serves to promote the vertical or horizontal stratification of a field. On the other hand, footnote democracy and egalitarianism are the result of less selective processes. An intention underlying footnote democracy may be to promote sales of a book, to facilitate aspirations to offices in professional associations, or to secure tenure or promotion. The author with one or more of these intentions must be aware of all of his possible readers and target his citations to strategic readers. In the case of textbooks, every possible teacher who can influence adoptions must be cited. In the case of a more scholarly work, all possible reviewers and critics must be treated favorably. In the case of promotions and tenure, the author may cite members of his tenure and promotions committee favorably and, of course, cites his own previous works. He must be aware of the fact that the most widely read part of a book is the index, especially the bibliography and notes, and that the absence of potentially relevant and sometimes irrelevant sources may incur sanctions. In order to avoid sanctions, standard procedure is to cite all possible sources and authors regardless of relevance or accuracy. To these are added, of course, prestigious references to the works of great authors of the past, currently popular sources and works, and citations that assist in networking and in future pyramid climbing.

Paradoxically, another source of footnote democracy is based on elitism—on condescension, co-optation, and the securing of succession by network leaders. In the latter case, a member of an elite may attempt to recruit followers, pay off footnote obligations, or establish his gatekeeping function by distributing rewards and patronage to juniors in the form of footnote citations. This practice offends no one, except perhaps the junior in a network who feels that other juniors are given too much citation credit. The academic leader may consolidate his jurisdiction over some area of scholarly terrain by creating a band of brothers who will support his (or their joint) claims to superiority. He may reward disciples and cast followers into a hierarchy based in part on footnote recognition. The effect, at least in number of citations, may be footnote democracy, but that democracy may lead to a new footnote elitism or even tyranny.

All of these processes of footnote democracy contribute to footnote inflation, and together with the other processes of overproduction and display and consumption of footnotes, result in onslaughts on footnote aristocracies. To state it differently, the favored and classical sources of the past are devalued by their inclusion in a vast pool of footnotes that minimizes their individual contribution and obscures, by sheer weight of numbers, their past contributions.

Another type of footnote democracy entails the use of one's footnotes to make personal attacks on the scholarship, translation, or erudition of another, usually elite, scholar. One can "correct" another's errors in one's own footnotes or surround a well-known source with a host of other, often even earlier sources, which devalue the contribution or originality of the source that is the object of attack. Footnote sabotage reaches its most convoluted, serpentine form when one attacks in one's footnotes the footnotes of another author. This is especially the case when the text of the article is innocent of the attack revealed in the footnotes. The attack may include allegations of incorrect citation, biased editing of quotations, or dishonest or incompetent interpretations of the cited texts. One coauthor of a book may make an attack on the other coauthor, even in the book they jointly write.

Footnote democracy may entail the deliberate omission of recognized sources, substituting for them less important, "frivolous," or earlier sources. Such footnote democracy may include the boycotting of a standard, legitimate source and even the high prestige sources involved in connoisseurship. Instead, one may cite "lower level," less prestigious sources and sources not usually recognized as professional within the hierarchy of a profession. In some cases, one may replace legitimate sources by, from the standpoint of the one's ideology or school, a whole pool of ideologically "correct" sources.

When footnote competition and conflict take on an ideological cast, citation must be recognized as a product of broader and deeper dynamics than are involved in personal motivations and aspirations or in technical standards of scholarship. Then, footnote competition and conflict may include the derogation of cited sources in terms of race, sex, religion, class, age, and other status characteristics, as well as the substitution of sources by others that reveal the citer's status, including ideological preferences. Thus, women may cite other women in an era, culture, or subculture characterized by feminism. When racial antagonisms are pronounced, members of a given race may cite other members of their own race affirmatively and ignore or cite negatively the members of another race.

When a field is primarily the creation of a given racial, ethnic, religious, or other status group, it is "natural" that members of that field cite the established sources of the field. These sources may constitute part of the taken-for-granted "culture" of a field, in which publications and status backgrounds have a high degree of coherence. Correspondingly, the sources both individually and as a pool of references have a high degree of prestige. The introduction of new sources, both on self-conscious ideological grounds and on a shift in the status base of authors and publications, results in a devaluation of sources seen both as individuals and as publications. This may be due to inevitable changes in the cultural and technical content of a field. But ideological/status competition may lead to a "requirement" in an ideological/status group both that one cites primarily one's status peers and boycotts or attacks one's status enemies.

On the other hand, as a new field emerges or an old one changes in content, the authors available for citation may change and will be inevitably drawn primarily from the status group that produced the scholarly work that must be cited. The particular culture of a field or subfield may become so rich and dense in itself that bias in citation may be unintentional. One may cite sources in only one language, nation, or "school." The sources, for some reason, may be drawn from only one tradition or cultural ambience. This may be due to ignorance of languages or isolation from competitive traditions.

In a world where the arts and sciences are increasingly international, parochialism in citation is an ever-increasing problem. And when the number of journals and publications in or related to a given field becomes so large that following them is a problem, there is a tendency to avoid sources that are outside one's immediately familiar scholarly or status ambience. This obstacle to mastery places a high premium on citation connoisseurship, on the discovery of sources that are rare and valuable from the standpoint of standard levels of ignorance of sources. The explosion of the possible number of sources usually results, as noted above, in a withdrawal into a status-bound parochial culture that is largely based on immediate personal concerns, commitments, ambiences, and networks.

Reciprocity and Mutuality in the Exchange of Citations

Footnote citations may be based on reciprocity, mutuality, and exchange: "If you footnote me, I'll footnote you" is the implicit understanding. I know of a case in which the departing members of a class of graduate students pledged in inebriated seriousness to footnote each other eternally during their emerging professional careers. A follow-up investigation of the scholars in question revealed that the pledge was not honored. It appears that, during their subsequent careers, new affiliations and connections had been made.

It has been observed that scholars, in checking up on each other's work, often look first at the index and footnotes to see if their own work is cited. If it is not, they may retaliate by boycotting the scholars who did not cite them. The awareness of this practice may determine who is cited and provides the grounds for alleging a "citation conspiracy." No explicit agreement is necessary in mutuality of footnoting. The result is an "as if" reciprocity or mutuality. The matter then becomes: "I will not ignore you if you do not ignore me." When fully applied, the logic means that the citer footnotes all scholars who could possibly cite him. Only after repeated asymmetry in footnoting does one, in such a case, drop the party who appears to be unwilling, by his actions, to enter an implicitly proffered exchange. Such exchanges, of course, entail only favorable or neutral references. If one makes an unfavorable reference, this must be done with deliberation and foresight concerning the possible consequences for one's future status and career. Serendipity in this area, the oversight or the negative reference, creates footnote enemies, which may extend to personal and professional enmities and be a source of damage to one's institutional and network aspirations.

The incidence of footnote exchange behavior should not be overestimated. What may look like a footnote exchange may be something related to it, but something entirely different. The most obvious case of the false appearance of an exchange occurs when an author distributes to his friends and peers hundreds of copies of his articles, and sometimes his books, in the apparent hope that he will be cited by them. He may not be looking for a job or a promotion but instead for the prestige of publishing and of being cited. As part of the process, he is likely to send reprints to all of these sources, and they, because of the easy accessibility of his work, are likely to cite him.

While the reprint sender may be inviting an exchange, the citation of the reprint by the receiver may reflect accessibility rather than reciprocity or mutuality.

Other appearances of exchanges may be even more deceptive. Since experts working in relatively narrow specialties or in dense footnote cultures must cite each other, their citations have the appearance of being the product of exchanges instead of being considered references to the same pool of standard sources, concepts, and ideas. Notions of mutuality, reciprocity, and exchange imply, in this context, gratuitous and ceremonial footnotes, but the question of what is ceremonial can only be resolved in particular cases with particular but strict standards. Some footnotes are instrumental to intrinsic, scholarly, and scientific work; others are expressive of the ceremonial aspects of a culture, while still others are, as noted, instrumental to functional purposes and motivations that are not related to scholarship per se.

In specialized areas and cultures, the mere fact of mutual or common citations may not indicate gratuitous citation. It may reflect the objectivity of a field's footnote culture, its collective representations. While it may, in principle, be necessary to make the distinction between instrumental, expressive, and gratuitous footnoting, in practice such distinctions may themselves be gratuitous. The empirical reality is too complex, blurred, and subject to particular personal interpretations. Thus, anyone who is competent to judge the necessity or redundancy of a citation is likely to be a member of the social circle or footnoting network he is judging and, therefore, has a personal interest in the judgment. The person whose citation behavior he is judging may be a network peer, exchange-mate, or enemy. Of necessity, the evaluator lacks the distance for detachment and objectivity. His hands are, in addition, not likely to be clean—his judgment is necessarily contaminated. But this "contamination" is no different than that which underlies both the citation he is asked to judge and his own citation behavior.

Footnotes and Plagiarism

There is substantial evidence that many writers plagiarize the footnotes (and bibliographies) of others—that is, that they copy another's footnotes without having read the works to which they refer. Whether this is plagiarism or "merely" footnote padding is an open question. Its major consequence and the evidence for such "deviant" behavior—if in fact it is *deviant* in the statistical sense of the term—lies in the fact that there may be little relationship and, worse, a negative relationship, between the source referred to and the citation made. Aesthetically and scholastically, such nonreferential footnotes lead to "listing." A listing is a vast accumulation of sources, cited in a virtual list of sources, with analysis of neither the documents referred to nor the interrelations of the contents symbolized by the sources on the "list."

Footnote plagiarism may thus manifest itself in the appearance of scholarly incompetence. A plagiarist may copy inaccurate and even nonexistent sources. Footnote plagiarism may also have other dimensions. Authors, particularly but not exclusively of textbooks, may summarize in detail entire chapters and even whole books by an author. To conceal their ignorance of an area, they will rely on one primary source, but, to conceal their dependence on that single source, they add dozens of footnotes to unread sources, obscuring their dependence on the one source. Footnoting in this case is used to obscure evidence of the plagiarism in the text. Here, the definition of *plagiarism* is not the legal one (seventeen or more words copied exactly without an attribution of the source), but a more loose, scholarly definition of *plagiarism*: the presentation of some other person's work without referring to the source or by concealing the source. The use of large numbers of unread, gratuitous sources conceals the one source in a thicket of citations, even when the "original" source is present in the thicket.

At a scholarly level, this "crime" is much more serious than the listing of sources. One can present an extended summation of another person's work, especially work in a foreign language, and imply by the very presentation that it is one's own work. The very presentation of a novel or original idea or discussion is, of course, a claim for priority in discovery. If one does this without citation to an original source, one leaves oneself exposed to charges of plagiarism if a later translation or publication of the original becomes part of current knowledge. One can cover oneself by citing the original work along with hundreds of other meaningless references, which not only conceal the original work but also add to the plagiarist's reputation for scholarship. I have known of cases where a scholar translated an entire volume merely to expose the "plagiarist" who relied on his ability to read a foreign language in order to enhance his reputation for originality. In another case, plagiarism has been exposed in the footnotes of an "antifraud" investigator. The investigator cited the derivative work together with the previously concealed original source.

It is often presumed that the plagiarist will read the footnotes of his nemesis, as do other specialists, so that all will know of the plagiarism without the appearance of a public scandal. In this way, the use of footnotes to both reveal and conceal footnote and other plagiarism allows for exposure at a civilized level, which maintains the scholarly reputation of a profession while being a potential source of social control. But all of these devices contribute to footnote inflation.

Footnote Deviance

Footnote plagiarism is an extreme example of footnote deviancy. Listing of unread sources, gratuitous citations, and distorted and biased interpretations of sources are other examples of such deviancy. The norm from which deviancy is inferred is, of course, the highest standard of scholarship and not a statistical average. All of these types of deviancy accept the standard forms of quotation, citation, and reference from which they deviate in the very process of so doing. They thus represent types of conservative crime. The criminal, in principle, accepts as his norm the very norms he violates. Otherwise, his violation would not have all the appearance of standard method and procedure.

Other forms of footnote deviancy reject the dominant standard norms of citation. They may depart from an explicit reference to an author, book or journal date, publication, page number, and exact quotation. In short, these "radical" departures from standard form are in some ways forms of footnoting by allusion, but they range in the evanescence of allusion. They may include citation of an author without mention either of his work or the standard forms of citation to describe the context and meanings referenced. The allusion may include a summary of the idea, concept, or meaning that is the intention of the allusion. Another allusive reference is a quotation or fragment of a quotation without any reference to the author, on the assumption that the reader will recognize the allusion. More allusive still is the use of a phrase or an image that originates with a particular author and that readers presumably understand. Finally, the use of given vocabulary, rhetoric, or style of presentation is designed to suggest the originators of these devices and is again based on the presumed erudition and sophistication of the reader and the connoisseurship of the one making the allusion.

Again, citation by allusion is deviant only against a norm of scholarly standards of explicit citation. Some nonacademic literary traditions make reference by allusion an essential to good writing; one does not clog up the flow of ideas by excessive interruptions or evidence of mechanical craftsmanship. In addition, in citation by allusion, the erudite author treats his readers as being equally or almost as well informed as he is. The allusions are self-explanatory to the erudite reader, and those who do not understand them do not deserve to be part of the erudite community of readers of an author.

It is obvious that citation by allusion, if it is deviancy at all, is "deviancy from above"—an expression of claims to connoisseurship and footnote elitism. But it may go beyond this. The cited authors' quotations, images, rhetorics, and vocabularies may be associated with a political, ideological, ethnic, racial, or gender group, as well as with adherence to a particular school of thought. Reference by allusion asserts the existence of loyalty to the status groups in question. It includes those who recognize the code concealed in the allusion and excludes those who are unfamiliar with it. Allusion thus establishes and maintains the boundaries of a status community. It also provides grist for the mill of the philological or linguistic analysis of the allusions in question.

A strong case for footnoting by allusion can, however, be made. In addition to eliminating academic obscurantism that clogs the flow of putative thought, footnoting by allusion may serve to indicate with brevity the parameters of the topic under discussion. It may merely define the take-off point for a subsequent discussion and allow the analyst to proceed with his or her discussion in terms of relevant research, analysis, and operations intrinsic to a clearly defined theme. This argument holds only for some types of work. If the work under discussion is historical, exegetic, polemical, or based on textual analysis, explicit citation may be necessary to the treatment of the materials under discussion.

A final source of allusive citation relates to the age and eminence of the citer. A young scholar anxious to make his reputation may feel obliged to prove himself and his scholarly erudition by making numerous and explicit scholarly citations. Having once proved himself, he may later feel that explicit references are unnecessary. He may then engage in citation by allusion, without fear of being thought of as lazy, arrogant, or undereducated. Thereafter, he concentrates only on what is necessary to advance the central themes of his lifework, a focus understood by most readers. The scholar who has proven himself is freed from much arduous toil and is now exempt from the purely mechanical craftsmanship of presentation and citation of sources. Here, too, there are some difficulties. The achievement of reputability by mature scholars is often accompanied by a failing memory. The scholar may blur or fail to remember the sources that inspired his original work or what they exactly said. He may remember his earlier interpretation of these sources rather than the sources themselves, and his eminence may give him enough confidence to cite, by allusion, his dimly recollected sources without checking their exact in situ meanings. He thus may make faulty allusions. In extreme cases, he may forget the original source but remember, however inaccurately, the point in question, and thus treat himself as the originator of the alluded-to ideas. As a result, footnoting by allusion, a faulty memory of sources and their content, and self-confidence are all sure steps on a path to creativity and to the reassignment of credits and priorities for original thought. This form of footnote deviancy, the misplaced allusion, thus goes far beyond more ordinary footnote deviancy. It may result in a form of unintentional plagiarism and, if accepted, fundamental shifts in emphases and priorities in the history of a science or scholarly discipline.

Footnote Socialization

All of the previously discussed types and subtypes of citation and footnoting behavior become the basis for both consciously learned and "unconsciously" absorbed socialization to footnoting norms. The "appropriate maxims and ratios" for footnoting become learned at relevant stages of one's footnoting career. This essay will not delineate the forms of footnoting appropriate to each stage in a footnote career. Characteristic forms and styles may vary depending on age, rank, status of occupational career (including academic versus non-academic positions and the character of one's college or university), publication history, success, and self-image, as well as such other status characteristics as sex, minority/majority status, ideology, and religion. Here, the primary concern is socialization in undergraduate and graduate schools and the consequences of such early socialization for one's "mature" behavior and for the later, self-selected paths of socialization of the mature professional.

After being unsystematically exposed to standard citation forms and practices in writing undergraduate and graduate term papers, the graduate student becomes submerged in the process of citation socialization when writing a doctoral dissertation. The requirement that the student do a review of the literature or "literature search" of sources relevant to his problem in order to demonstrate mastery of his problem area makes mastery of techniques of searching out sources and of citing them a self-conscious process and an autonomous skill. It is here that citation habits and practices are firmly established as part of the indelible character of the scholar. Only after these habits become firmly planted in the scholar are they subject to modification and change by subsequent career processes and status dynamics.

At this early stage in one's preprofessional career, standardized footnoting, most often done to excess and often clumsily, is the general rule. Subsequently, one may continue to use vast numbers of footnotes, but patterns of footnoting and citation are then usually refined. Some scholars may cut back on the number of footnotes because citation is a boring chore. All will attempt—depending on their motivation, ideology, and commitment—to link their citations to their textual treatment of the topics about which they write.

Yet there is one major, as yet undiscussed, deviancy to this process of refining footnote practice. In positivistic, experimental studies in the behavioral sciences, the heart of the work is the report of an experiment or statistical study based on an explicit hypothesis. It is often felt that such vulgar empiricism lacks scholarly dignity. As a result, usually added to the study is an introduction consisting of a review of the literature that ranges far and wide over the general area to which the hypothesis of the study is related. This review suggests affinities, parallels, and possibilities that presumably ground the hypothesis, but invariably suggests far more possibilities than can be tested empirically or are in fact tested in the study under discussion. The review usually contains far more citations than are relevant to the specific hypothesis being tested, but ends with the suggestion for testing of one specific hypothesis, the one that is described in the body of the study. The actual experiment, along with its hypothesis, is a product of specific research design aimed at pursuing one relatively narrow thread in a continuously evolving skein; this skein, the thematic development of a subfield of a science, is known to all specialists in an area. The assemblage of scholarly material or citations in the introduction to the study is usually superfluous to the report of methods used and experimental results and is rarely referred to in the summary of experimental results. The citations merely continue to express a habit of thought acquired in the doctoral dissertation—namely, that one demonstrate scholarship by citation and footnoting.

The use of computers has greatly facilitated the literature search and the entire process of footnoting not only in the introduction to experimental studies but also in the literature review of the dissertation, as well as in other scholarly articles that express the results of dissertation socialization. The computer search of the literature allows for the assemblage of a vast range and number of citable sources, including computerized annotated bibliographies. But such automated research is more likely to produce quantity than quality and to yield a lack of precision. The sheer number of possible citations in a computer printout may discourage one from reading, investigating, and denoting the exact relationship between the sources and the point they allegedly illustrate. Artificial intelligence thus replaces human intelligence as gross analogies substitute for precision in citation of relevant sources.

Adversary Citation

Legal briefs reveal alternate uses of citations. The advocate cites the case decisions, statutes, and other authorities necessary to advance his case. He operates in an adversary relationship wherein his citations are open to challenge both as to their application to the case in question and to the accuracy of his interpretation of the principles in the cases he cites. His citations are open to challenge by his legal adversary and by the questioning of judges and their clerks. The principles of citation here are not exclusively based on economy; unnecessary or aesthetic citations are unimportant. Citations are based on the advocated accuracy of the fit between enunciated legal principles and the facts of the case.

Yet this form of citation is not different in principle from other kinds of scholarly citation. The major difference is that in legal citation there is an institutional judge of the adequacy of citation, and there are specific institutional patterns of appeal when one's citation behavior is rejected. In the scholarly disciplines, the process of judgment is more diffuse. In the sciences, the ultimate validation of work is in its consequences, not its origins. But even here, as has been frequently noted, citation is often related to the assignment of credit and priorities after the original work and competitive work have been completed.

Another form of adversary citation is to be found in polemics over the interpretations of text. One may attempt to reinterpret the ideas of a great scholar against other traditional interpretations or against those of an opposed school of interpretation. Here quotation and citation of the primary work in question may be necessary to sustain an unconventional, challenged, or controversial interpretation, even though such citations may be many and dense. Similar patterns of quotation and reference may be necessary when dealing with one's adversaries in these scholarly disputations.

In scholarly polemics, there is no final judgment. The jury is one's scholarly peers, who, however, may themselves bear all the biases that are part of conventional habits of mind, trained incompetence, or occupational psychoses. History is the judge, but never makes a final judgment. Only provisional victories and defeats occur, and these are likely to be reversed in the endless process of scientific and scholarly discovery and debate. If one needs victories, one must be content with provisional ones, and any sensitivity to the endlessness of these processes may induce a sense of modesty, regardless of the material or ideal rewards achieved on the paths that lead to the evolution or supercession of discoveries.

Some Conclusions and Implications

In the preceding pages, I have posited a number of concepts and hypotheses, drawn primarily from the social sciences, that may be relevant to the structure of the footnoting and citation cultures of the various fields of knowledge and the sciences. In doing so, I am merely applying conventional concepts to fields whose footnoting cultures have not been studied. One must, in addition, recognize that footnoting and citations are derivative and can be autonomous from the main, manifest tasks of their respective fields. These include the acknowledgment of sources of one's ideas, the presentation of evidence, and the justification of one's interpretation of the texts and documents to which one refers. At another level, secondary to these, footnoting has the manifest function of assigning priorities and credits for discoveries and is thus interlaced with personal motivations in the quest for fame, which is the spur that clear spirits raise to scorn delights and live laborious days. Further, despite the fact that footnote and citing cultures are derivatives of other technical and cultural systems, and at times may have purely subjective meanings, they become the basis of autonomous "systems" that develop their own intrinsic structures apart from their manifest and purely technological, methodological functions.

I have indicated the existence of footnoting "aristocracies," elites, and networks, as well as universalistic, national, regional, and local cultures within the various manifest fields that produce and consume footnotes. Footnoting and citing cultures also include subcultural communities and ghettoes based on race, ethnicity, religion, ideology, and other formal and informal footnoting communities.

Status politics include the processes of reciprocity, mutuality, and exchange, but also elitism, patronage, and the construction of citation political machines. Connoisseurship may result in citational aristocracies and classical traditions that dominate even continuously changing technical fields.

Footnoting warfare may split a culture, resulting in footnote inflation, democracy, radicalization, or sectarianism. It may also result in footnote massification, a mass culture in footnoting. But such a mass culture may also be a result of conspicuous consumption and display of footnotes and bibliographic erudition. Footnote erudition may represent more subtle and personal aspects of footnote warfare, being related to aspirations for mobility, success in the acceptance of one's work, and sales and acceptance of one's books. Citation by others is thus a measure of academic or scholarly legitimacy.

Socialization to footnoting and citation practice in providing professional standing to novices is part of the manifest, technological functions of a field. Such socialization is a continuous ongoing process and is related to the stages of a career, including one's relative age, success, and eminence within the academic prestige and occupational hierarchies of the field and of one's status before external publics.

Footnoting behavior, self-socialization, and anticipatory socialization will vary, depending on one's position and relationship to the hierarchies and publics of a footnote-related field. Yet vestiges of prior patterns of footnoting will persist, in part because initial socialization in principle remains the norm for professional training, regardless of the excesses and abuses of standards that may occur even at the level of initial professional socialization.

Footnote and citation behavior is more than a cultural and structural phenomenon. It is deeply rooted in individual personality and social character as these become partially defined and integrated into social and cultural systems. Conversely, these personal motivations and strivings may deeply color social and cultural systems. Personal vanity may be a significant factor in the production of footnote inflation, warfare, and connoisseurship, but, again conversely, a sheer delight in scholarship that is autonomous from the manifest, instrumental functions of footnoting may have the same effects. Concern with style, convention, fad, and fashion may also have the same apparent effects. Desires for occupational mobility and acceptability in prestige and occupational structures and in social networks also express significant personal motivations.

The desire to affect sales of a textbook may be a purely economic motivation for the selection and number of references and authors cited, while printing costs may limit the quantity of citations and quotations. In addition, "party lines," whether formally laid down (as in totalitarian states) or informally constricted (as in democratic societies), constitute political and status bases for citation practices. These include the tabooing of enemies and pejorative footnoting. What is not footnoted may constitute as significant an area as "manifest" footnoting.

Footnoting practices may include invisible footnoting. As noted, footnoting by allusion may be a highly self-conscious, erudite, and mannered practice. It goes beyond the taken-for-granted acceptance of standard sources, quotations, images, and rhetorics of an age. It becomes an art form in itself, which lends magic and mystery, "taste," and the sense of belonging to an erudite, elite community. Only the cognoscenti know the allusion. The subtlety of footnoting by allusion may become so rarified, the original source so obscured, that the alluder may, over time, take himself to be the primary source; more modestly, he may accept the laurel for having rediscovered, popularized, diffused, or given life to long-lost words, images, phrases, or gem-like quotations.

Given the rewards that underlie and motivate footnote culture, footnote deviancy is not surprising. Footnote deviancy includes the plagiarism of another author's footnotes or bibliography, the misrepresentation or misinterpretation of the sources (a substantive crime), the use of irrelevant footnotes, "listing," and promiscuity in footnoting. These result not only in the inflation of footnote culture but also in its distortion.

Some of these deviancies are normal and structural, the result of perceived institutional obstructions to scarce opportunities and values. Others result from ideological, political, and status loyalties; one misrepresents one's enemies and, in the opposite direction, one's friends or allies.

Footnote revolutions also occur. A whole population of traditional, standardized sources is rejected, replaced by more politically desirable, stylish, theoretically up-to-date, chic, or value- and status-related sources. These reflect not only political changes in a field, but also the emergence and triumph of dominance of new paradigms, elites, and journals, as well as changes in the dominance over institutions and publications. Such revolutions occur relatively infrequently in a given field, but, when they do, footnote culture and aspects of a field's structure are radically reconstituted.

Normally, regular processes of succession and discovery allow for a continuous accretion of items into footnote culture. But footnote rebellions and reform, as well as new patterns of deviancy and technological change (for example, computers, abstracts, clipping and bibliographic services), introduce minor but significant discontinuities in the normal, ordinary processes of cultural growth.

It is obvious from this discussion that footnoting practices and dynamics can be viewed from the standpoint of their cultural and structural dynamics and consequences. Individual motivations and purely bureaucratic functions (for example, employment, tenure, and promotions) are necessary inputs into footnoting systems, but if one considers the major goals of footnote practice to be the advancement of knowledge and science, they are also sources (causes) of deviation, deflection, and goal displacement. From this point of view, however, even the assignment of credit for discovery and priority is a necessary but secondary function to the abstract, ultimate ideals attributed to the scholarly and academic, intellectual, and scientific enterprise.

Such deviancies as plagiarism and its concealment via footnotes, misrepresentations of the content of documents, plagiarism of footnotes, "listing" and promiscuity, irrelevant footnoting (especially of unread sources), and usurpation of credit by veiled allusion are recognized as violations of what is usually a taken-for-granted ethical code. Manifest conflict emerges over plagiarism and the misrepresentation of sources with reference to ideological conflicts and over misrepresentation and usurpation of credits and priorities. But most of the deviancies noted in the above pages are not the subject of public controversies even though professionals in a field know of hundreds of cases of footnote and citation deviance, which become part of the gossip and the intimate culture of professionals. Yet the minor deviancies and the not-officially-reported major deviancies may be much more serious (as well as frequent) than the major public scandals. They contribute to footnote inflation, the mystification and obscurantism of the central lines of development of a field, distortion and distrust of a field by relatively well-informed laymen, and the devaluation of the professional as one who says more and more about less and less. The abuse of footnoting may even make more difficult the exercise of the organizational functions that in part cause the deviancies. That is, the assignment of credits, rewards, and reputability may be assigned to those who accumulate the most important and largest numbers of footnote points rather than to those who contribute important ideas, concepts, and methods to a field.

Given the fact that there is a diffuse consensus over the norms and ethics governing footnote praxis, one might ask whether these diffuse norms should be codified to become the basis of explicit footnoting and citational ethical codes. In fact, such codification already exists, especially in the footnote standards of journals of professional associations and in publishers' manuals and journals that are not the official organs of an academic profession. Most of these agencies of segmental codification stress the purely technical aspects of citation and referencing. While all publishers are concerned with costs, this concern has, at most, merely limited footnote inflation. Beyond this, commercial publishers of textbooks are concerned with "balanced," classical footnoting so that no classical source is wholly lost and no potential adopter of a text is offended, regardless of the relevance of citations. Literary journals are likely to favor footnoting by allusion, since this contributes to an even flowing style, an aesthetic criterion in its own right.

But augmental codification does not always lead to "justice" since the editors of a journal or publisher are themselves implicated in the very process that results in footnote deviancy, distortion, and deflection. They, too, are professionals, ex-professionals, or paraprofessionals and are subject to all the positive and negative sanctions that express both the manifest and latent functions of a field in the full range of its ideals, norms, and deviancies.

Substantive evaluation of footnoting and citational practice is incidental to prepublication reviews in refereed journals and among publishers who use outside reviewers. Prepublication reviewers for refereed journals are often and ideally experts in topics of the manuscript to be reviewed. Even when the manuscripts are anonymous, it is possible that an author will be known, especially if he has a distinctive style or pool of ideas, sources, vocabulary, and images. He may be treated favorably or unfavorably depending on the evaluation of his reputation, ideology, paradigm, or other status criteria as viewed by the evaluator who, by virtue of his expertise, is a friend, enemy, competitor, ally, protégé, or master in the competitive struggles that underlie the search for knowledge. To state it differently, while judgment is necessary, in the scientific and cultural fields under discussion, few evaluators are so independent of the scientific, cultural, and personal struggles of a field to be able to render a free, independent, totally objective and unbiased judgment.

In book publishing, both commercial and noncommercial, the selection of a friendly reviewer is often "fixed" by an author and editor. In scholarly journals, the selection of a reviewer who is known to be friendly *or* unfriendly to the author or to the ideas in a manuscript provides a way in which an editor may avoid responsibility for the substantive decision he makes. Formal, objective procedures are used to adjudicate substantive and personal issues.

In legal proceedings, the judge is assumed to be independent, above the conflict, and subject to review. He is presumed to be uncontaminated by partisanship. In most situations of academic adjudication, partisanship, at least in the advancement and evaluation of a theory, its adherence to a paradigm, and its presuppositions or consequences, is intrinsic to the very scholarly enterprise.

The ideal of being influenced and constrained by the evidence is also an academic ideal, which may operate in the long run where judgment is made by consensus across decades and generations. But in the short run, disciplines that stress commitment and activism in the advocacy of particular approaches make evaluation of specific contributions exceedingly difficult. Thus, the judgment of footnote deviancy and conformity to the ideal goals of science are necessarily diffuse. There are no certified and certifiable judges.

But, even if such judges did exist, the standards that would constitute an ideal ethical code are, at most, only approximate. If we agree that some footnoting is excessive, who is to say how much is excessive; or, if it is allusive, who possesses the exact degree of cultivation to decide whether and when an allusion is adequate or plagiaristic? The proper interpretation of a text is in its very nature subject to conflict, and any "correct interpretation" may also be the result of conflicts that may span generations. If an interpretation is judged ideological, what is the correct ideology that makes judgment possible?

These are unanswerable questions in any absolute sense, but they are intrinsic to the very operation of discovery. Yet, again, we all know of cases that are outside the bounds of ethical decency. We rely on exposures, scandals, and angry debate to define the limits of decency in footnote deviancy, hoping that disgrace and scandal will limit deviancy and help to maintain some minimal approximation to ideal standards, no matter how far the departure from an ideal that is defined only by scandals. In the meantime, we know that much of footnote practices other than our own are shot full of deviancy and delinquency.

In the above pages, I have reviewed the personal motivations and structural conditions that underlie footnote practice, culture, structure, ideals, and norms as well as the violation of those norms. In doing so, I have mentioned a variety of motivations, patterns of behavior, consequences, and functions that ground footnote and citation practices. Many practices and standards are qualitatively different from each other, and still others operate at different levels of a culture or social structure. All are only incidental to the manifest operation, the main business, of a science or academic or cultural system. But footnoting and citation has become an autonomous culture in its own right. In dealing with these cultures and structures at a purely formal level, this essay oversimplifies the phenomena under discussion. A systematic, empirical survey of footnote practices in any one of the specific fields barely touched on in this essay would result in much more complex material. Further, the totality of specific judgments necessary to evaluate the footnoting behavior alluded to in this essay would be practically impossible to supply. This is especially true given the lack of common and precise standards and codifications necessary to make such judgments. Such complexities may account for quantitative measures of footnoting behavior such as citation indices and simple counting.

Yet it is precisely these objective measures that violate the necessary complexity and qualitative character of work in a field. To state it differently, while the evaluation of sources, footnotes, and references is an impossible job in the totality, each individual must make such judgments in his own work and his own area of competence. Because this is so, quantitative evaluations in a restricted specialized context are not difficult, but qualitative evaluations require making judgments that risk controversy, require a great deal of work, and may entail, at times, the declaration by the prospective evaluator that he is not competent to judge the work he is asked to evaluate. These factors may also account for quantitative evaluations. And perhaps the administrative requirements of large-scale bureaucracies require smooth and "objective" processes of decision making free from conflicts and personal judgments, yet these conflicts and judgments are intrinsic to the creative processes themselves.

The inadequacies of qualitative evaluations are also intrinsic to the sciences and humanities. We rely on exposure and scandal to reveal extreme frauds and to protect the scholarly ideals to which we all claim to adhere, on long-term processes of scholarly debate, criticism, and the erosion of time to discredit inadequate and useless theories. But we cannot be sure that one fashionable but inadequate paradigm will not replace another. In this sense, we are on an eternal treadmill. Still, the selection or dominance by any arbitrary or ultimate certifier of the ultimate standards by which footnotes, citations, and all knowledge are to be judged is a sure guarantee of intellectual oppression and an impediment to even proximate and temporary truths.

PART V
Culture and Community

15

Changing Institutions and Ideologies

Joseph Bensman with Bernard Rosenberg

The history (or evolution) of Western Man may be conceptualized around two basic ideas: the unity of society and the unity of personality.

The Unity of Society

The most familiar and serviceable models known to us to represent societal unity are the "folk society" and the "feudal society." These ideal types anatomize any society in which all key institutions are closely interrelated.

Whatever else the term *folk society* may mean, it always suggests simplicity—or extremely limited specialization. In such a society, religious and economic activity, warfare, government, the uses of leisure, family interaction, and education are all functions of the same people fulfilling their several roles. Few, if any, institutions are so specialized that they require full-time or expert personnel. Everything in the ideal-typical folk society reinforces everything else. All conduct emphasizes the maintenance of ongoing institutions.

Published originally in a slightly different form in Joseph Bensman and Bernard Rosenberg, *Mass, Class, and Bureaucracy: The Evolution of Contemporary Society* (Englewood Cliffs, NJ: Prentice-Hall, 1963), 497-536. Republished with permission from Marilyn Bensman and Deena Rosenberg Harburg.

Life is organized to sustain the individual in his compliance with ageless tradition.

The feudal society was more specialized than the folk society. From our present perspective, however, which is to say, from the perspective of modern, ultramodern, or postmodern society, feudal specialization seems very limited indeed. For instance, the feudal state could not be said to have existed as a separate entity. Governmental, religious, and economic institutions were intertwined. Much the same unity could be observed in every area of life. However, there *was* real occupational specialization within the feudal *church*—not only a religious institution, but also, at the very least, a political, economic, military, judicial, and educational complex.

Feudal society differed most from folk society in its extensive stratification. Noblemen, churchmen, and serfs were independent corporate groups; each had a rank order and a separate style of life; each group dressed and acted differently from the others. The Dutch historian J. Huizinga relates, "Every order and estate, every rank and profession, was distinguished by its costume. The great lords never moved about without a glorious display of arms and liveries, exciting fear and envy."[1] Huizinga explains that, even when these lords were to be executed for their crimes, "[t]he magistrate took care that nothing should be wanting to the effect of the spectacle: the condemned were conducted to the scaffold, dressed in the garb of their high estate."[2]

That garb could not be mistaken for anyone else's, nor could the conduct of the few who wore it. But though appearance and behavior were greatly diversified, feudal society exhibited an extraordinary unity in its sanctified belief that the estates, while different and exclusive, were also complementary. Each estate supported the others in providing equally important material or spiritual services. By their mutuality and interdependence, by the rights and obligations that they shared, estates sustained the unity of feudal society.

The Unity of Personality

"Unity of personality" is a Western concept drawn from religious sources. Certain characteristic consequences follow from postulating an omnipotent, omniscient, omnipresent, ethical, and anthropomorphic God. The Judaeo-Christian theological tradition, from which such a God emerged, put heavy stress (as a sociologist would see it) on the internalization of ethical norms. Within this tradition, the believer considers himself responsible before God for *all* his actions. A sinner does not feel less guilty if his transgressions go unobserved by others, for they are observed by God, from whom nothing can be hidden.

The Judaeo-Christian worldview did not admit of anything like the current division between public and private personality. Those who thoroughly absorbed that worldview were theoretically unable to split themselves by committing violations through one segment of the personality while leaving other segments untouched and unaffected. Guilt was pervasive. When aroused, it punished the whole self for any violation of norms that were meant to be applied with absolute fidelity.

The Unity of the Individual with Society

In "The Road Not Taken," the poet Robert Frost depicted a characteristic, complicated dilemma of modernity—the freedom and independence to choose between two unknown paths.

Frost's protagonist famously chooses the less common route.[3] Such a dilemma and such a resolution were unfamiliar to premodern man. The simplicity of premodern society was such that its members were rarely required to choose between irreconcilable norms. One seldom had to decide anything; one could appeal to tradition, and *it* would decide.

The social structure of premodern society set forth a number of rules and roles that reinforced each other, that were instilled in the individual without equivocation and were so absorbed as to become a major determinant of behavior. The ambiguities that simultaneously force us to make decisions and render them so hard to make were not present.

Since most men lived in small communities or local societies, rarely venturing far beyond them, social intercourse was confined to people who knew each other in the full range of their social activities. This general state of propinquity and intimacy fortified norms that were internalized without any great need for strong social sanctions.

Supernatural orientation—the church's influence permeated all phases of premodern society—was bolstered by a family system that facilitated the internalization of religious values and traits. The patriarchal father, whose sons worked in his shadow, stood as a psychological parallel to the image of God as a strong father. The child learned his ethics from a father who appeared, at least to his offspring while they were young, to possess god-like authority. By the time a son matured enough to know better, he had already internalized the father's values.

The husband and father enjoyed a superordinate position in his family so complete that its spirit is nowadays hard to recapture—a position that went unchallenged and unchecked until modern times. In all earlier periods, the father remained at home, where he was in direct supervision of the work, leisure, personal relations, and education of his sons. Similarly, the mother and other adult females provided a model of exemplary thought and appropriate conduct for growing girls. This kind of identification by children with their parents made it possible for one generation after another to internalize unified values and, by that normative process, to lay and relay the groundwork of a unified personality, supported at every point by the whole social structure.

The Decline of Societal Unity

Feudalism could not withstand the inroads of capitalism, urbanism, and industrialism. By itself, the development of a cash economy meant that indirect monetary relations would substantially replace the direct interpersonal relations that had prevailed for whole epochs. The cash nexus was a new and obtrusive (though, of course, not the only) bond relating men to each other. That bond could also be used to measure and evaluate others.

On top of this, urbanism placed thousands of strangers in highly limited and transitory relationships mediated by abstract symbolic styles of intercourse. Many more restricted but deeper and fuller forms of personality penetration went by the board.

In addition, when industrialism, or the factory system, took workers away from their homes, it transformed the old family into a new entity. It produced whole classes: first, the "bourgeoisie" and the "proletariat," and, more recently, the salaried new middle classes composed of white-collar employees, bureaucrats, professionals, technicians, managers, and scientists.

Beside and within these classes, modern industry created a horde of occupational specialists who took over tens of thousands of new jobs, each with its own narrow specialization and complex technology. These jobs required a long period of education and training, a special vocabulary, and a unique outlook on the world. We have by now moved so far in this direction that every large occupational group—and many a smaller one—has generated special interests and occupational ideologies, making strident claims for prestige, income, and power, based on the imputation of exclusive skill, greater knowledge, and functional irreplaceability.

The intense competition between these groups is far from abating. More than ever, they have different backgrounds, separate perspectives, special languages, independent ends, and rival interests. All this has had much to do with shattering the great unity—an offshoot of the great simplicity—extant in preindustrial societies.

The early phases of modern, capitalistic, urban, industrial, mass society produced new ideologies whose architects were motivated by two impulses: (1) to make the social arrangement that had begun to emerge meaningful and (2) to legitimate it.

The Decline of Liberalism as an Ideology

Laissez-faire capitalism gave rise to an ideology (subsequently labeled Manchester Liberalism) first enunciated by Adam Smith and perpetuated with extraordinarily little modification throughout the nineteenth and nearly half of the twentieth century. The school will probably not outlive its present spokesmen—economists like Ludwig von Mises and Frederick Hayek. These men, with remarkable intransigence, still hold to the view that their science demonstrates the existence of an invisible hand that, if untouched, automatically guarantees the maximum production of wealth at the lowest possible costs. Smith and his followers have also "proved" that any exploitation or misery attendant upon industrial growth came as an inevitable consequence of the iron law of wages. They have contended that the economic system can achieve full efficiency only if the state removes all unnecessary restrictions from enterprise, giving business almost complete freedom.

This ideology was attacked with vigor very shortly after Smith's first formulation. Supporters of feudal privilege attacked from the "Right." They argued that it was shamelessly mercenary, that it was inhumane, depriving the serf of the protection he had come to expect from his lord, and that it violated the Christian ethos and therefore undermined the spirit of man. The "Left" thundered just as much. Radicals and reformers attacked Manchester Liberalism by pointing to the obvious cruelty and privation visited by laissez-faire owners on industrial workers in general and in particular on minors, who suffered from child labor, and women, who were subject to many physical abuses in their long hours of labor. Further voice was given to criticism of the ideology by emerging trade union leaders. They felt that the absolute economic power of business over individual, and largely unorganized, workers was doubly deleterious; it not only deprived the worker of his chance to live above the subsistence level, but often deprived him of any real chance to live as a human being.

Apart from impassioned and hortatory polemics, technical questions were raised by the socialist theoreticians, notably Karl Marx, who attacked laissez-faire capitalism on its own grounds by challenging the assumption that free enterprise led to maximum productivity. Much later, John Maynard Keynes, and in our own time the Keynesians, have added their critique of what one of them, John Kenneth Galbraith, ironically calls "the conventional wisdom."[4]

The original case in favor of economic liberalism reflected an economy consisting mostly of small firms—none large enough to set prices by itself. At least theoretically, competition could be the sole determinant of prices. Not that it ever was; even Adam Smith reported evidence of monopolistic, noncompetitive price setting. But actual developments within industry provided the most effective rebuttal. The irresistible rise of giant corporations, the *oligopolies,* a "Big Three," a "Big Five," a trust that dwarfed or swallowed competitors and joined international cartels, made a caricature of the self-regulating market. Administrative agreement, price leadership, tacit understanding, or outright collusion with other firms accounted to an unheard of degree for price regularities and production controls. The large and powerful corporation cut much ground from under laissez-faire as an economic system and as an ideology.

The business cycle, with its periodic slumps and resultant unemployment, led to social and economic reforms that further limited the free competition of small and large-scale enterprise. The way was paved for massive government intervention in the economy. When war followed depression and Cold War succeeded hot war, the "public sector" of economic life in Western capitalistic countries expanded enormously. The Welfare State and the Warfare State were incompatible with old-style capitalism.

The Decline of Ideology

While the familiar system expired, new ideologies multiplied—but no one of them was persuasive enough to swing a West European or North American majority behind it. Several partly successful attempts to replace economic Liberalism for good and all are suggested by such phrases as: *the New Freedom, the Mixed Economy, the Welfare State, the New Deal, the Square Deal, the People's Capitalism, the Planned Economy,* and *the New Frontier.* For short periods, and with much wavering, the seal of legitimacy has been placed on all these ideological slogans. None of them has replaced a now-defunct economic doctrine.

That doctrine lives on mainly in the nostalgic reminiscence of extreme conservatives (for today Liberals call themselves Conservatives), to whom the majority turn a deaf ear. Abroad, in economically underdeveloped parts of the world, formal espousal of laissez-faire is sometimes required as a condition for loans made by the Western powers. As often as not, these powers then establish their own monopoly corporate control of the industries they have freshly installed.

Political Liberalism was the twin of Economic Liberalism, a product of the same situation. It offered Natural Law as an ideological basis for the Natural Rights of Man. Various versions of this philosophy were directly incorporated into the French, English, and American constitutional systems; no Western government was unaffected by them.

Natural Law and Natural Rights can no longer be considered scientifically acceptable. These days, the scientific description of social reality is more a matter of specific uniformities under given conditions than it is a manifestation of fanciful "laws" based on the allegedly immutable circumstances of nature. Those "laws," in other words, have yielded to empirical uniformities that hold only in specified situations and not in a mythical and unchanging state of nature.

Not many people put much stock any more in the philosophy of Natural Rights. But again, like laissez-faire economics, no single ideology has mustered enough general acceptance to replace it in Western society. National Socialism sought to justify itself on grounds related to Natural Law—in this case, natural biological law. And there are proponents of communism as a secular religion (which has appropriated and vulgarized the ideas of Karl Marx) who still cling to the idea of Natural Law—in this case, a priori natural historical law.

For the legitimation of democracy in our time there is no genuine ideological or theoretical consensus. Not that those rights once defined as natural have been discarded. On the contrary, in most Western countries, the belief in human rights, when stripped of scientific validity, simply became an article of faith. We hold fast to that belief, not because its foundation in theory is empirically established and logically consistent, but despite the fact that it is not.

The Growth of Secularism

A major blow to the ideological unity of Western society was delivered over an extended period of time in the religious sphere. The Protestant Reformation meant the end of "Christendom"—that is, the end of Christian unity. In each Protestant sect in nearly every country, new forms of theology and church organization gave different meanings to Christianity.

Almost all Protestant churches, however, emphasized the worldly side of religion—some soon after their founders' death, some later. The monastery and the cloister ceased to be favored way stations to eternity. Men "proved" themselves by their actions in this world, not by withdrawing from it.

More than the other sects, Calvinism, so variously decisive in our history, glorified work, science, industry, production, investment, and other activities (as well as attitudes) calculated to produce wealth. It was received with open arms by a bourgeoisie, large parts of which were already predisposed to such values.

These Protestant values held sway over certain segments of the population well into the nineteenth century. Then, by an ironic twist of history, the very interests they had done so much to generate, in wealth, science, and worldliness, shaded off into a new secularism, which robbed religion of much of its theological significance. Though still extensive, religious practice has retained very little of its old intensity. To many in this century, it is no more than a leisure-time activity that entails formal church participation, implying respectable or prestigious consumption.

This breathless review is intended to suggest that all the ideological systems of early Western industrial society have been vastly weakened, have lost their old vitality. Yet none has been swept completely away, and no strong substitutes have appeared to supplant them.

A kind of speculative exhaustion has apparently set in—such that writers like Daniel Bell may legitimately refer to the present "end of ideology."[5] It is not just the case that economic and political Liberalism fails to kindle as much fervor as other more recent ideologies. They too suffer from the debilitating effect that has plagued every belief system in our disenchanted age. Neither the radicals nor the conservatives can summon up much of their former enthusiasm.

Most of them now tend to be as self-critical as the Liberal who has wondered for some years whether his position is in "dead center" or the more "vital center." Ideologists are either filled with doubt, and for that reason incapable of determined leadership, or so confident that they provoke charges of naïveté and utopianism. They find it difficult to rally a skeptical public in England, France, or the United States, even at this apocalyptic moment in history, when these societies are challenged for their very existence.

That the ideological dynamic seems to be slipping in Soviet Russia and to have been erased in Germany (East and West) confirms a universal trend: those countries that have moved farthest in industrializing themselves leave the most ideological baggage behind them. Fervent conviction is most noticeable in economically underdeveloped areas, east or west of the Iron Curtain. There, people who are often bitterly disillusioned about the present still look with hope and faith to the future. But Western Man has seen the broad outlines of that future, and it has not made him radiant with hope and faith—qualities temporarily reserved for those who follow in his footsteps.

On the one hand, conscious commitment to past values that once gave us unity is in sharp decline. On the other, we are being molded by new institutional forms that have not as yet recreated the old unity. They have set the stage for a new (so far only partially articulate) ideology.

The Rise of Bureaucracy and the Ideology of Technical Competence

Bureaucracy is "the characteristic institution" of urban industrial society. Of course, bureaucracy means more than many large-scale *governmental* agencies. It means *all* large-scale administration, whether in economic, business, political, military, recreational, religious, or educational organizations. In contemporary society, bureaucracy dwarfs all institutions. Most city people work in bureaucracies; those who do not are still subject to their policies and programs—as they are to manipulation and persuasion by them.

Some consequences of the primacy and reach of bureaucracy are especially relevant to this discussion:

> 1. Bureaucracy separates the means from the ends of administration. Important policies are carried out by a large number of technical specialists; each does his particular job without having to consider the broader purpose of that activity—and often without being able to.
>
> 2. Therefore, much (perhaps most) work in a bureaucracy is—literally—meaningless to those who do it.
>
> 3. Mechanical efficiency in performing prescribed tasks, regardless of their overall purpose, is the only specific *ideal* present in any bureaucracy. Wherever bureaucracy becomes the dominant form of social and administrative organization, the society in which it looms so large begins to stress technical competence, efficiency, and professional capability. Indeed, these means of doing any task that may be assigned become ends dearly cherished in and of themselves.
>
> 4. If, in contemporary society, any overall ideology is taking over for the ideologies that have *ended*, it is this spoken or unspoken ideology of efficiency.
>
> 5. But "efficiency" does not easily lend itself to the traditional rhetoric of classical ideologies. They were closely argued and logically organized; they were "briefs" for a particular kind of human society.

> Always polemical, they could only be regarded as special pleading, which, if accepted, meant that one form of society and one class or subclass in society had advanced over others.
>
> 6. The ideology of efficiency, like the attenuated ideology of democracy, has been embraced on faith; it is lacking in the strong logical superstructure of classical ideology. A kind of secular skepticism grows apace, and it is caused in large part by disillusionment with earlier ideologies. This state of mind predisposes the individual to reject all ideological forms, dismissing them as Fourth of July orations, flag-waving frauds, political deceptions, clever masks artfully hiding selfish interests. For this reason, when men cleave to efficiency, they tend to accept it as a personal standard rather than as a "theory" of the world.

So shrunken an ideological base is inadequate to support the weight of a whole social system. In none of its several guises has the cult of efficiency served to dispel all ideological doubts. Not that there is any dearth of intellectuals who have risen to the occasion; they have simply been unpersuasive or insufficiently persuasive in their many attempts to formulate a new bureaucratic, managerial ideology.

Bureaucratic Ideologies

In his recent review of "neo-reformers," the radical writer Hal Draper discussed a group of ideologists groping their way toward formal legitimation of "bureaucratic collectivism." We have come to know several of the men he names, and their works, from years past: James Burnham for *The Managerial Revolution,* Peter Drucker for *The*

New Society, and Adolph Berle for *The 20th Century Capitalist Revolution*. Each in his fashion has supplied leads for other intellectuals, especially those like W. H. Ferry, Scott Buchanan, R. C. Murray, and still others who have lately engaged in joint deliberations under the auspices of the Center for the Study of Democratic Institutions, a subsidiary of the Ford Foundation.

Their common focus is the American corporation, viewed with equanimity as a source of expanded social, political, and economic power, under the rule of law according to Buchanan, who adds:

> This would mean that the corporation think of itself literally as a government, as Berle has put it often enough, and try to constitutionalize itself in some way. This doesn't necessarily mean that we should impose a democratic dogma on it. It means that the corporation, if it isn't going to be democratic, should say it is not going to be and find a mode of operation that will discharge its responsibilities and be efficient in its own operation.[6]

In another brochure, Buchanan asserts:

> The Marxist used to speak vividly, if not too accurately, about the concentration of capital and the expropriation of the worker. If the dialectic is still working, he ought now to point out the next stage or moment when the labor union applies for corporate membership in the big corporation whose directors grant annual tenure and salaries, pensions, and the power of veto on the policy of the corporation instead of the right to strike. As a result, the corporation is a government by and with the consent of the workers as well as the stockholders. As Adolph Berle puts it in *The 20th Century Capitalist Revolution*, creeping socialism has become galloping capitalism, and, we might add, corporate communism, free-world variety.[7]

Some sociologists have lent their authority to the new vista. For instance, we find Philip Selznick saying, more or less thematically, "The executive becomes a statesman as he makes the transition from administrative management to institutional leadership."[8] And Talcott Parsons, the very influential sociologist, has argued with some vehemence for a bureaucratic elite. In an effort to analyze McCarthyism as it was related to certain social strains afflicting America, Parsons wrote:

> Under American conditions, a politically leading stratum must be made up of a combination of business and non-business elements. The role of the economy in American society and of the business element in it is such that political leadership without prominent business participation is doomed to ineffectiveness and to the perpetuation of dangerous internal conflict. It is not possible to lead the American people *against* the leaders of the business world. But, at the same time, so varied now are the national elements which make a legitimate claim to be represented, the business element cannot monopolize or dominate political leadership and responsibility. Broadly, I think, a political elite in the two main aspects of "politicians" whose specialties consist in the management of public opinion, and of "administrators" in both civil and military services must be greatly strengthened. But along with such a specifically political elite there must also be close alliance with other, predominantly "cultural" elements, notably perhaps in the universities, but also in the churches.[9]

These are ideological straws in the wind—and no more. They bespeak much enthusiasm and a great sense of urgency among those who set them afloat. But to date there is no evidence that they have excited and interested any large number of individuals in American society, or even any large number of managers. Their disinclination to "ideologize" and their immunity to those who do seem more pronounced than ever. Bureaucracy is widely accepted as a fact; it will not do—so far—as an ideology.

The Predominance of Administrative Machinery

The rise of bureaucracy coincided with a special emphasis on the administrative machinery of modern life. For the paramount function of bureaucracy is to man and operate a multitude of complex, technical, financial, legal, educational, religious, fact-gathering, and policy-making positions. At every point, bureaucratic managers plan and administer operations covering only that narrow point. Since bureaucrats crop up and subdivide in different organizations having varied purposes, dealing with diverse segments of the society, there is no coordination, no comprehensive control or total planning of bureaucratic work. If there were, we would be living in a fully totalitarian society.

Generally, ideologies have hidden more than they have revealed about the way a social system actually works. When successful, they have veiled the real apparatus of society behind rhetoric specifically designed for that purpose. Conservative ideologies used to provide an abstract theoretical model of social action, a model that served as a common frame of reference for communication about society. The proponent of a conservative ideology could counterpose his logical formulations against the doctrine of Natural Rights. This is the point that Karl Mannheim made in his famous essay on conservative thought. Conservative ideologists attacked Natural Law when they "questioned the idea of a 'state of nature,' the idea of a Social Contract, the principle of popular sovereignty, and the Rights of Man." In the beginning, they substituted concepts like History, Life, or the

Nation, for Reason; later they redefined Reason to suit their own purposes. Although in the end we do not have "two static, completely developed systems of thought," we do have "the two ways of thinking, the two ways of tackling problems."[10] When one such model is pitted against another, men feel no overwhelming impulse to study the social reality itself. A dazzling ideology can cover, conceal, mask, and beautify the unseemliness underneath.

But it is just such ideology that has come to an end. With its collapse, all the subterranean techniques that have spread so rapidly in this century are exposed and apparent. In the absence of any exterior point of vantage from which to view the administrative machine, we are left to accept bureaucracy as an inescapable fact of contemporary life. It is ours to live with whether we like it or not, for there are no known alternatives to it.

In this context, as we have so often noted, bureaucratic administration, created at first to subserve some end, becomes an end in itself. To be efficient is to keep the administrative machinery running—and humming—to subserve no particular end.

The Rise of Professional Ideologies

Prestige, power, and income are claimed by and granted to those specialized groups whose spokesmen manage to convince a large number of people that they are functionally indispensable. Professional ideologies, seeking recognition and domination on the basis of skill and efficiency, have come to the fore. As specialization increases, so do professional ideologies, and the ensuing clamor is so considerable that most of their claims are drowned in noise. This leads to still greater ideological confusion, a condition but slightly alleviated by our growing capacity to hear some voices above others as they speak, say, for the communications industry, the military, or science.

"Functional indispensability" conveys the suggestion of higher efficiency, and efficiency is the ideological key to bureaucracy. But bureaucracy cannot be detached from specific organizations that play their vital parts in an institutional order. Top leaders devote a good deal of time to promoting the values of their organization. High and low, the rivalry is intense. It broadens, widens, narrows, but scarcely ever disappears. The National Association of Manufacturers must plump for Big Business, and the Chamber of Commerce for Little Business—but neither more energetically than, to take one example, the National Association of Pretzel Manufacturers for the pretzel dealers of America. To the officers of this organization, no fact of life is more important than the fate of the American pretzel. They are indefatigable in their pursuit of "data" about the consumption of their product, so that sales will increase—to the benefit of all manufacturers who belong to the Association. They have only one real commitment: to maintain and enhance the position of their members. This preoccupation encompasses the whole occupational existence—and hence the lifestyle—of such officials.

The Separation of Institutional Ends

The officials' situation is not unusual. It illustrates a general principle—namely, the vast separation of ends in urban, industrial society. Every institutional order is separated from the others; within each one, we see a refinement of ends; every order and all its subsections provide leadership for the selective and exclusive promotion of their ends. This puts institutional values into a constant state of competition.

Institutional separation produces normative separation. From all sides, beliefs, values, programs, prescriptions, and panaceas are presented to the individual. They are thrust at him with approximately equal sincerity, though with unequal impact—given the difference in resources available to a mass of promoters. We can only agree with Robert Lynd when he says, "All the functional areas of living are constantly interacting, and if one area is strongly organized and another weakly, this institutional situation invites the riding down of the weaker by the stronger. A case in point is the overbearing elaboration of the institution of war in our present world, which tends to render all the rest of our living insecure."[11] Yet it is the sheer number—and not so much the relative weight—of norms in present-day society with which we must concern ourselves.

The Disintegration of Value Hierarchies

Exposure to separate and distinct values has increased to a point where it is greater today for every man than it ever was for any man. A vast plurality of unrelated and conflicting values pours in on the individual from every side, cracks the unity of his personality, and reduces it to a many splintered thing. The old unity depended very largely on a *hierarchy* of values, whose phased and ordered internalization could be taken for granted. That hierarchy has disappeared, and the values that it used to arrange are greatly diluted as they mix with "foreign matter" from a thousand sources. Instead of the hierarchy, we have discrete promotion of institutionally separate and exclusive normative clusters.

This condition is aggravated by the decline of patriarchal family control which, when it operated at full force, afforded most children a firm basis for early identification with a strong father. When the traditional family structure disappeared, modern man breathed more freely, for a great burden had been lifted from him. Father, perhaps a pal but certainly not a dictator, could no longer be assumed to know best, especially when Father himself could no longer assume that he knew anything.

We are in a state of maximal freedom from Father Power, a state with many advantages and some serious disadvantages. It has not proved conducive to the formation of consistent, powerful, and securely internalized value systems—thus, the current alarm over our loss of autonomy, inner direction, spontaneity, and individuality. Mead's "Me" has grown fatter, while his "I" has shriveled to greater insignificance. His "Generalized Other"—a representation of all the norms in a society—on which the "Me" always battens, has come to be more "generalized," more diffuse and opaque than ever before. And every step made toward the institutional promotion of values impersonally directed at distant masses widens the separation as it promotes (literally) the *dis*integration of those values.

Personification and the Star System

This situation is most obvious in the mass media. Popular books, magazines, newspapers, and most films, as well as television and radio shows, are constructed to reach large audiences. To overcome formidable barriers in communication, messages transmitted by the mass media are simplified. They concretize material of every kind, strenuously avoiding abstraction and generalization. Their favorite technique is personification. Abstract ideas, values, and sentiments come into play, but only insofar as "characters" (a specific dramatis personae) can be made to embody them. Abstract questions go by the board when Justice is personified by the sheriff and Evil by the outlaw.

In itself, personification is not only older than formal drama, but dates back before Olympus to the primitive gods of preliterate society. Yet they were not quite the same. The "characters" of mass media are totally stripped of complexity; they embody usually no more than one central value; they can hardly help being caricatures and stereotypes.

Our form of personification is best expressed in the star system. In the contemporary firmament, a *star* is any person who, because of his background or his special ability to "project," is endowed by the mass media with greater-than-human proportions. These proportions are essential in order to make both the star and the media economically attractive to their peddlers. The star must be made attractive, his public character simplified, sold, and promoted, so that a colossal audience of exceedingly variegated individuals can be brought to identify as fully as possible with him. The act of creation in making a star is neither simple nor spontaneous; it requires devotion, ingenuity, energy, and the full-time interest of agents, promoters, impresarios, cosmeticians, teachers, coaches, admen, speech writers, photographers, columnists, and journalists.[12] Stars rise, after all the processing, to the degree that they are able to cause palpably favorable responses. This can occur only when they personify certain cherished values. But what to do when there is an incredible wealth of cherished values? Hollywood's answer is, Personify *all* of them.

The mass media oblige with stars of sexuality; athleticism; war and peace; science, politics, and government; the home, the family, and religion; prestige consumption; and early childhood and youthful adolescence. There are stars of law and order, of crime and vice.

Stars come and go. They may fall from the interstellar spaces of society suddenly or gradually as their popularity wanes; other stars will be there to fill in for them. Not only the person, but the *type* of person who is star material differs widely over time. For instance, no active military man in the United States at this moment (save perhaps an astronaut) can match the star status achieved by men like Generals Marshall, Eisenhower, Patton, and Bradley, or Admirals Nimitz and Halsey, in World War II. Nor have there been in any one period as many scientific stars as lived contemporaneously until a few years ago: Einstein, Salk, Oppenheimer (now a quondam star),

Teller, Fermi, Szilard, Waxman, and their very many, increasingly prominent coadjutors.

Stars as Symbols for Societal Values

Stars symbolize the values and ideas of a society—at any given time. Each star stands in mass culture for one basic value, but that same culture presents a total range of stars projected around every conceivable value. To encourage the widest possible identification, each star, and therefore each value, is presented attractively, separately, and exclusively. Consequently, all values in their total effect on us are a shapeless, helter-skelter, randomly assorted potpourri. A man is "free" to pick and choose in accord with his (probably blurred) self-image, often selecting values that consciously or semiconsciously square with those of appropriate stars.

The Stars and Gods

Morin and others have noted that our stars closely resemble the primitive gods. In Homeric and classical Greek society (we should not forget how many centuries there were between Homer and Plato), the gods were "human, all too human," with a full complement of passions, vices, and frailties. And each god incarnated a particular value or function. The Pantheon included gods of war, peace, love, industry, sports, and the hunt; "household" gods; gods of marriage and the family; and those of nature, as well as each of nature's known elements.

The ancient Greek, we learn from his legends, his epics, and above all from his immortal tragedies, saw himself as a pawn in the Olympian struggle between the gods—when he was not merely a plaything at their capricious disposal. Subject only to limits imposed by the Fates, who were above even the gods, men imagined that they were controlled, pushed, pulled, and coerced to do the bidding of the gods. These gods were depicted as rivals. They laid traps, fought, and schemed among themselves; they struggled with each other through their loyalties to and possession of human beings.

Once it is understood that the Greek gods represented major life values and life functions, the conflict between them can be viewed as a conflict of values *within* the human being himself. There were many separate values, each one making total demands on the individual who found himself torn between them.

Given their still-feeble grasp of abstract thought, the pre-Homeric Greeks personified these values, transformed them into gods or spirits, external and uncontrollable powers. As the great classical scholar, H. D. F. Kitto, has said:

> The primitive Greek seems to have thought about the gods much as other primitive people do. Our life is in fact subject to external powers that we cannot control—the weather, for example—and these powers are 'theoi,' gods. All we can do is to try to keep on good terms with them. These powers are quite indiscriminate; the rain falls on the just and on the unjust. Then there are other powers—or so we hope—that will protect us; gods of the tribe, clan, family, hearth. These, unseen partners in the social group, must be treated with scrupulous respect. To all the gods, sacrifice must be offered in the prescribed form; any irregularity may be irritating to them. It is not obvious that they are bound by the laws that govern human behavior; in fact, it is obvious that some of them are not. This is to say, there is no essential connection between theology and morality.[13]

Yet, even in this prehistoric "theology," the seeds of a more sophisticated conception were evident. Speaking of the early Greeks, Kitto tells us:

> In the first place, their lively, dramatic and plastic sense inevitably made them picture the 'powers' in something like human form. The gods became, one might say, sublimated Kings. In the second place, the impulse towards unity and order reduced the number of gods and combined them into a family and a family council. . . . But this impulse went further. Even though some of the powers may seem to be lawless and at times manifestly in conflict with each other, nevertheless there is a regular rhythm in the universe which they may strain but never break. In other words, there is a power which is more powerful than the gods; the gods are not omnipotent. This shadowy power was called Ananke, 'what has to be,' or Moira, 'the sharer-out.'
>
> The next stage is the combination of theology with morality. . . . Above all, the Greeks refused ultimately to distinguish between Nature and human nature. The powers therefore that rule the physical universe must also rule the moral universe. By this time the *gods* have been spiritualized; Ananke or Moira are now not the superiors of Zeus, but the expression of his will, and other divine powers, like the Furies or Erinyes who punish violence and injustice, are his loyal agents.[14]

Here we have the final stage of a purified Greek religion which, when variously blended with earlier stages, has for centuries permeated the consciousness of Western civilization. But the genius of classical Greece transcended religion and produced philosophy. The Greek capacity for abstract thought expanded; its power of analysis and criticism grew to a remarkable degree. Greek philosophy challenged if not the gods, then the gods' ability to control human destiny. The idea of freedom was born. Some men began to believe that they could order their own lives without divine intervention. Plato and Aristotle fashioned an ideal image of human existence by offering the harmonious balance of values as the summum bonum, "the greatest good." They sought such roundedness for the human personality that it would absorb many values and be possessed by no one of them.

We have undertaken this fairly extensive homily because, in a way (actually, in reverse), it illustrates the evolution of modern Judaeo-Christian values. These values began with great stress on the unity of personality, on internal control via a single ethical system. As our institutional life showed evidence of increasing specialization, it segmented the operation and the dissemination of values. The unitary ideal was badly battered. Each of a vast multitude of values came to be given separate and sometimes equal emphasis. The mass media developed new types of personification in which stars or fictional heroes stood for disparate values. They too are separate, exclusive, and sometimes equal. The stars, whose divinization is now nearly complete, are thus the functional equivalents of the gods.

Not that a perfect parallel can be drawn between early Greek religion and our own. Scholars used to liken *The Iliad* and *The Odyssey* to the Old and New Testaments, and we are entitled to compare the pre-Homeric mythology with an actual operative religion of the stars in contemporary society. But there are differences—of which the most decisive is that our devotion to a galaxy of stars derives from the mass media. This means that it emerges in a society with large reservoirs of ability for abstraction and self-scrutiny, one in which the unified personality is a traditional norm, a society infinitely more complex in its administrative and technological machinery.

The "God of Work" in Western Society

The star system does not permit us, as individuals, anything like full freedom to select our gods. By economic necessity, and with due allowance for status aspirations, most of us must genuflect before the god of work, who is, in his current incarnation, the god of *bureaucratic* work. Those who enjoy much wealth can be freed even from the work ethic, and only minimal attention need be paid it by those who hope solely for survival. (In our world, this is true at the extremes not only for individuals, but for whole nations as well.) But all the rest of us, especially those in the broad middle range of a complex, mechanical, administrative, and technological culture, are forced to worship, succor, and placate the bureaucratic god. This god is less exacting than he once was. Precisely because the demands made by bureaucracy are explicit, they are also limited. After these specific demands have been met, men are free to worship the other gods made so plentifully available to them by major institutional orders operating through various mass media. The circumscribed quality of bureaucratic work gives more people more time, as their comparatively greater affluence gives them more of a chance to cultivate a wide variety of nonwork values. Official life is severed from private life, and the growth of private life allows for that total pluralism of values that radiates from the mass media.

The Overabundance of Values

In this light, our society "suffers" not from the absence but from a glut of values. Like the early Greeks, contemporary man can choose his gods, but there are so many, all attractively presented, most of them exclusive, some incompatible in the loyalties they enjoin, each one beckoning for whole-hearted commitment. There is a conflict of the gods as real for us as it must have been for the ancient Greeks, who also had to contend with a mélange rather than a hierarchy of values.

Confronted with innumerable inducements, blandishments, role expectations, and idealized lifestyles, the citizen is less and less able to make any choice. His position is similar to that of the small child in a big toy shop: everything on display attracts him, but he lacks the resources to buy everything. Furthermore, he knows that whatever he does select will not please him for very long. The fact that whatever he sees might please him—that everything catches his fancy—signifies his indifference to anything specific.

The Struggle for a Sense of Identity

So, the citizen begins to crave not more things so much as a sense that something be important to him. He feels his lack of feeling very strongly; he is sensitive to his numbness, and he pines for identity. He says, in effect, Tell me who I am and what I want. Allen Wheelis, author of *The Quest for Identity* (a book whose title could have been contrived only in this day and age) has touched the heart of the matter in writing:

> Our grandparents had less trouble than we do in finding themselves. There were lost souls, to be sure, but no lost generation. More commonly than now a young man followed his father, in character as in vocation, and often so naturally as to be unaware of having made a choice. . . . Sooner rather than later one found his calling; and, having found it, failure did not really cause one to reconsider, but often was a goad to greater effort. The goal was achievement, not adjustment; the young were taught to work, not to socialize. Popularity was not important, but strength of character was essential. Nobody worried about rigidity of character; it was supposed to be rigid. If it were flexible, you couldn't count on it. Change of character was desirable only for the wicked. . . .
>
> Nowadays the sense of self is deficient. The questions of adolescence—"Who am I?" "Where am I going?" "What is the meaning of Life?"—receive no answers. Nor can

they be laid aside. The uncertainty persists. The period of being uncommitted is longer, the choices with which it terminates more tentative. Personal identity does not become fixed, does not, therefore, provide an unchanging vantage point from which to view experience. Man is still the measure of all things, but it is no longer the inner man that measures; it is the other man. Specifically, it is the plurality of men, the group. And what the group provides is shifting patterns, what it measures is conformity. It does not provide the hard inner core by which the value of patterns and conformity is determined. The hard inner core has in our time become diffuse, elusive, often fluid. More than ever before one is aware of the identity he happens to have, and more than ever before is dissatisfied with it. It doesn't fit; it seems alien, as though the unique course of one's life had been determined by untoward accident. Commitments of all kinds—social, vocational, marital, moral—are made more tentatively. Long term goals seem to become progressively less feasible.

Identity is a coherent sense of self. It depends on the awareness that one's endeavors and one's life make sense, that they are meaningful in the context in which life is lived. It depends also on stable values, and upon the conviction that one's values and actions are harmoniously related. It is a sense of wholeness, of integration, of knowing what is right and what is wrong and of being able to choose.

During the last fifty years there has been a change in the experienced quality of life, with the result that identity is now harder to achieve and harder to maintain. The formerly dedicated Marxist who now is unsure of everything; the Christian who loses his faith; the workman

> who comes to feel that his work is piecemeal and meaningless; the scientist who decides that science is futile, that the fate of the world will be determined by power politics—such persons are of our time, and they suffer the loss or impairment of identity.[15]

The Loss of Identity and the Decline in Ideology

The loss of, and the current quest for, identity are crucial phenomena directly linked to the many factors with which we have dealt in this book. Of these, as Wheelis implies, none is more symptomatic than the decline of ideology. We can best understand why this should be so by briefly reviewing the principal functions of ideology. When an ideology acts as an agency of legitimation, it:

- Justifies the overall institutional framework of a society.

- Justifies the distribution of wealth, power, income, and prestige.

- Provides a simple explanation of the way society works, clarifies the system, makes sense of it.

- Enables men to discuss the complete organization of their society in general terms instead of constraining them to take account of its complex details.

- Creates a "universe of discourse" that permits technical specialists in unrelated institutional spheres, otherwise hedged within their own environment, to deal with each other on the basis of a common social theory.

- Offers men a fully articulated system of values against which to measure and judge social institutions. This system, in its original guise a defense of existing institutions, may also be used to criticize the way they actually work, to deplore the distance between ideology and reality; when the ideology is antagonistic to existing institutions, its "fully articulated system of values" can suggest basic institutional defects and point to means of removing them.

- Becomes a guide to suggested paths of social action, reform, change, or, if it is "conservative," the avoidance thereof.

Successful ideologies have never been inconsequential or impractical; those that came from the pens of men like John Locke, Friedrich Nietzsche, and Karl Marx were exceedingly potent in their far-reaching consequences. They have also been important in the individual life cycle of Western man.

Socialization and the Decline of Ideology

It has been the case in our culture for some time that, with adolescence behind us, our earning capacity goes up, and as it does, we find ourselves more deeply involved in existing institutions. Thereupon, we embrace ideologies that justify the status quo. Barring serious setbacks, age could traditionally be counted on to produce growing conservatism. Young people, deprived of the opportunity afforded their elders, impatient to succeed and innocent of experience, were and are still likely to make great demands on society. These demands are generally uncompromising; they call for quick fulfillment of ultimate ideals. Until recently, young people who found their society wanting in moral fiber and passed harsh judgment on the failings of their elders frequently did so by embracing new radical ideologies. They might be attracted to religious mysticism, democracy, socialism, communism, anarchism, or fascism—depending, of course, on the time and place. Older people continued to champion the radical ideas of an earlier age—after these ideas had become the ideologies of an established order.

This conflict between youth and age over the ideal and the actual, the desired end and the stubborn reality, is by no means new in Western society. Such conflicts between the generations are relatively open and clear-cut when the participants take the conflicting ideologies they espouse seriously. When those ideologies are corroded with doubt, the conflict that persists is much more complicated.

Even in a society whose formal ideologies are important, parents play a large part in the normative training of their children. Parents are required to explain the meaning of society and its institutions to the young. Thus, many of the ultimate values with which youth judges its parents and their institutions are drawn directly from parents.

There are inherently embarrassing possibilities in this situation—more so when formal ideology shrinks to its present proportions. Children, in their need to know, go on asking the same questions about the meaning of preestablished rules, surrounding institutions, and their place in society. Only now, parents are less able to answer such questions. There are "received" answers that they cannot offer their children with a whole heart. The mother and father who see their world as too big and too complex to be compassable may be obliged to give either honest but unsatisfactory answers or traditional answers that they either do not know very well or in which they themselves do not wholly believe.

The perennial dissatisfaction of children with their parents has a special quality in periods of feeble ideology, not usually present at other times. This quality is cynicism. It pervades the atmosphere, reducing the old cry for reform, revolution, or regeneration to a whisper.

Cynicism and the Rat Race

Among young people in the world about us, cynicism takes many forms, but typically, those who subscribe to it say that all ideals are absurd, all ideologies indefensible, all standards nonsensical. Only self-interest remains. Work, skill, the will to get ahead, the acquisition of technique and "personality": these things matter and the rest is phony. They will not fall prey to causes, beliefs, and convictions that smack to them of romanticism and sentimentality. These things are incompatible with their own tough pose. They refuse to be trapped in blind alleys or in booby traps or distracted by side issues that might deflect them from the main task of getting ahead. That task is arduous enough. It calls for a high degree of determination. Other pleasures must be suppressed lest they interfere with the only meaningful activity they know and recognize. Getting ahead in school (excellent preparation for getting ahead in life later on) means carefully completing one's assignments, doing one's homework, passing examinations by hook or crook in "the right courses," making sure of high grades that look good on the all-important academic record. It means deciding at an early age (as early as eleven or twelve in junior high) on a career, to the attainment of which one's energies may thereafter be devoted. Educators are more mindful than they used to be that an extraordinary amount of serious work can be accomplished by students in college and immediately after college in postgraduate studies. The youth who is assiduous and dedicated, whose mind does not wander too far afield but quickly and tenaciously finds its proper groove, is well on his way to becoming a successful professional man.

For this he must pay a price. Whereas he can master an amazing amount of material in his chosen field while still relatively young, he can do so only by ignoring all fields that do not lie directly adjacent to his career line. So we behold the young man as a highly educated ignoramus. The type is not so new, but the age is; it used to take an extended period of specialization to produce trained incompetence. Now cynicism, coupled with a sharp eye for "the main chance," has speeded up the rate at which this characteristic can stamp itself on a human being.

The "Angry Young Men" in the "Rat Race"

The "angry young men" of England—writers like Kingsley Amis, John Osborne, John Wain, and John Braine—have pointed to other consequences of the same situation. These authors are especially effective in portraying men without illusions, heroes who are the antiheroes of contemporary fiction. Passion, élan, enchantment, joy, and belief are alien to them as they beat their way up—preferably all the way to the top, always ready to sacrifice friends, relatives, love, and morality—just for the sake of getting there, and having gotten there, not knowing why.

"There's four ways of being successful," Golk liked to say, "and they go by way of the suits; hearts, spades, diamonds, clubs." If he was exercising the autobiographical mode, he would add, "I've known them all: I've loved up, worked up, bought up, and smashed up."[16] Golk is the protagonist of a recent American novel by Richard G. Stern, an author who knows how strenuous the "rat race" can be. Earnestness is essential, humor a handicap. The grim single-mindedness of young people "on the make" continues to surprise their middle-class parents and teachers, who look back with nostalgia to their ostensibly more light-hearted, idealistic, and romantic youth. To many members of the older generation, youth seems to be composed of young-old men, while to many of the latter, their elders seem woefully flip and irresponsible. (This reversal of a familiar pattern has not gone unnoticed by the novelists; indeed, some like Henry Green and Sinclair Lewis have built whole works around the theme.)

Partly in self-defense, spokesmen for the older generation often downgrade busywork as an inherent part of the rat race. They feel that excessive preoccupation with skills, methods, and techniques, may advance a man rapidly, but also converts him into a high-class clerk or a well-paid technician unfit for anything but routine work. These oldsters contend that really creative work is much more the product of unorganized idle curiosity, of rambling, poking, and stumbling in the side alleys of a field where, perforce, much time is wasted, but within which the individual can find a meaningful and original problem. A discovery of his own may at any stage help him to focus further work—even if he has to do without top grades, "the right courses," a safe career, and the rat race.

However much greybeards might admonish them, young people after World War II gravitated more and more toward the rat race. On the campus, it tended to supplant the naive concern with national politics, utopian ideologies, and the virtues of various economic systems. "Useless" debate, the interminable bull session, which once gave a peculiar tone to college life (although even then it was typical only of a minority), came close to being extinguished. In postwar America, quiet affirmation of the rat race is a dominant informal ideology for the young. It corresponds to the worship of efficiency among older people. But this impure ideological coin has an obverse side.

The Beat Rejection of the Rat Race

There are youngsters who categorically reject the rat race. If they fail to develop a positive ideology, we may call them, in the current jargon, "beat." Beats proclaim their disaffiliation from the rat race, their general disengagement from the meaningless hustle-bustle around them, from the dispirited pursuit of money and gadgets. They repudiate "respectable" public life, regular hours, mechanical discipline, a fixed routine, in favor of cultivating their private pleasures, their personal sensibilities, the fine arts, and the art of living. The beard, the blue jeans, the sandals, the unwashed T-shirt, the unkempt hair, the leather jacket, the all-around slovenliness are symbols—and they are meant to be. They announce for their wearer, "I choose not to compete in society; I prefer to remove myself completely from the rat race where victory can lead only to intolerable respectability. I proudly and defiantly announce my choice. Just look at me and you, all you squares who aren't with it, who don't swing, will know me for what I am." Lawrence Lipton, elder statesman and rhapsodic chronicler of the beat movement, quotes one of his "holy barbarians," Angel Dan Davies:

> Right now beards are being worn by young people who reject the rewards of the . . . dog-eat-dog society, who hole up in pads in the slums and listen to jazz music all night and get high on pot and violate all their sexual taboos and show up late for work in the morning or stay home all day if they've got a poem eating away at them to get itself written or a picture to be painted. It's putting all those other things first—man! That's what scares . . . them.[17]

But actually to write the poem or paint the picture—to put first things first in an artist's order—and to do so with distinction, will almost certainly take just as much energy, effort, discipline, and dedication as conventional people "squander" on other things. Rejection of the rat race because it is the rat race cannot be complete unless those who disaffiliate have an intrinsic interest to pursue, meaningful goals to achieve, real work to accomplish. Otherwise, the Beats are simply repudiating the ideological hypocrisy of their parents, and only that. Beats know what they dislike, and perhaps even what they would like to like, but not always what they do like. They are involved in the symbols of rejection. Although the dramatization of their withdrawal and dissent can be vigorous, they are frequently passive people, attracted to Zen Buddhism as the religion of passivity, but so far unable to find ideological substance anywhere.

Insofar as Beats engage in the production of ideas, novels, poems, plays, essays, paintings, music, and films (whether or not they are easily understood), it is hard to dismiss them with crabbed condescension. The lack of appreciation for their work may be only a mote in the eye of the beholder. But insofar as Beats represent nothing but a passive rejection of middle-class values, with no enterprise to give that rejection meaning, they differ from earlier Bohemians who, while at odds with society, were often able to achieve their own fulfillment. The arid "disaffiliate" becomes a twentieth-century romantic, and, as the years advance, he discovers that his life has been nothing but a pose.

The Hipster as a Symbol of Freedom from the Rat Race

The Beat is a by-product of the middle class against which he rebels. In his working-class origins, he differs from the hipster, who has no middle-class background to reject. The hipster is, in the purest form, a Negro jazz musician. Hipsters ignore the rat race; they do not have to disengage themselves from it. Theirs is basically a world of active, unsublimated masculine pleasure. Their behavior is not self-consciously designed to fulfill a theory; it is the natural expression of a sensuous way of life. Hipsters stay outside the rat race because they have other and, in their eyes, more important things to do. These things are mainly connected with sensual gratification—which hipsters find in music, sex, and marijuana.

If the hipster does not wear conventional clothes, it is because he does not feel the need. Wearing unconventional clothes is not a deliberate symbolic act by which he conveys his defiance. What he says is couched in his own idiom, but he is sparing in his use of words. "Cool" and relatively inarticulate, he has no great investment in the mind, in intellectuality. He has little respect for the legal code, but does not become a delinquent, for to do so systematically would also require him to repress his sensuality.

The hipster stands in a peculiar relationship to his beat admirer. The hipster is what the Beat would like to be, and would be, but for the circumstance that he grew up in a middle-class environment. The hipster, in his turn, if he did not have beat recognition and adulation, would simply be one of several types never directly exposed to the Protestant Ethic.

Criminals and Juvenile Delinquents as Conservatives

Neither Beats nor hipsters should be confused with juvenile delinquents and professional criminals. Lipton is explicit about this:

> The beat and the juvenile delinquent are only kissin' cousins. They have the same enemies, which is the slender thread that sometimes unites them in temporary alliance. Both are outlaws, speak a private language and put down the squares, but in beat circles the J.D. is regarded as a square, a hip square in some things, but still a square.
>
> He is a square because his values are the conventional American values: success, the worship of things, the obsession with speed and devil-take-the-hindmost attitudes in everything. They are "sharpies" always looking for angles. They believe everything they read in the ads. The "kick" they are looking for when they "borrow" a car for a night is the kick of making "a majestic entrance" in front of a chick's house. The juvenile delinquent wants a Ford in his future, but he wants his future right now. He can't buy it so he steals it. "My old man waited," one of

> them remarked to me, "and what did it get him? He's fifty and he's still driving a '49 Chevy."
>
> The names they give their gangs are indicative of their hunger for social status. In Venice West it's The Dages. Some of them pronounce it "dogs" but they know it means something like The Man of Distinction. (Wasn't "putting on the dog" once a slang synonym for distinctive?) If one gang names itself The Counts, the gang in the next block goes it one better with The Dukes. Such pretensions are abhorrent to the beatnik.
>
> Their "social protest," which is a common theme in liberal magazines trying to "understand" the J.D., is so much doubletalk in the beatnik's opinion. They are not victims of the society; they are its fruit and flower. The J.D. in a stolen car, dressed up in his sharp clothes, seated beside his chick and smoking the cigarette that is the choice of men who demand the best, is the ironic triumph of the adman's dream. They are not likely to yield to the lures of communism. In fact, many of the J.D.s of past generations are now among society's most successful businessmen. Their only protest is that it takes too long.[18]

Lipton's strictures apply as much to adult offenders as to juvenile delinquents. Except for confidence men, professional members of the underworld prefer not to work through any public business sanctioned by law. Nevertheless, their ideology affirms at least tangentially the very same values of contemporary middle-class society that members of the middle-class are precluded from achieving easily by the nature of their work. In this sense, delinquents and criminals constitute a true conservative group.

Social Maturity and Freedom in Modern Society

It was of the delinquent and criminal group and other ostensibly "deviant" types that Robert K. Merton wrote (originally in 1938) when he set forth a basic sociological paradigm for the understanding of conflict between means and ends.[19] Merton, in an analysis that has since come to be regarded as classical, argued that whereas there are always socially acceptable ends and culturally defined means to those ends, a disproportionate preoccupation with either set of norms may so eclipse the other as to produce serious problems. Thus, inadequate institutional means for the achievement of successfully transmitted social goals can lead to criminal "innovation." When everyone in a class society is "expected" to succeed by accumulating wealth, and only a few can actually do so within the prescribed rules, others will make their own rules. Far from scorning the common goals of their society, they passionately long to share them.

Merton's analysis was especially pertinent in the thirties, a period of great economic adversity when society had failed signally to provide adequate institutional means to attain socially acceptable goals. The sociologist could not help agreeing that "innovation," like other mechanisms (ritualism, rebellion, retreatism) noted by Merton, came into play as men struggled with this conflict.

The Mertonian model is not obsolete: we still have the problem of unequal access to desired goals. But in the 1960s, it has become equally clear that our society does not provide a coherent body of goals. There are now millions of people superbly equipped with the means to reach goals whose content and meaning have been too loosely defined for them to grasp.

Earlier, we suggested an analogy between our situation and that of the child in a toy shop who wants everything, and in consequence wants nothing very much or for very long. If our society has caused us to regress in some such way, then we have traveled farther than many men suspect from the ethics of our fathers.

Our fathers, bred on the Judaeo-Christian ethic, thought that they and their progeny should be adults. Their ideal was a grown man, free to make his own decisions, to correct them when they were misguided, to thrash about for better solutions. In one word, he was always to be morally responsible. When secularized, the ideal exalted rationality, a certain capacity to assess alternatives, and for the most part, to arrive at correct decisions. Politically, this meant that men could govern themselves through their chosen representatives. Indeed, liberal democracy rested on the assumption that increasingly rational, mature, responsible men were there to run it.

As the unified personality disintegrated, we strove for mastery of external and automatic means by which to make decisions. Failing that, we were annoyed at our inability to make free choices. This feeling of ethical impotence, and the dissatisfaction it can arouse, places the greatest possible strain on liberal democracy. The public relations gods of politics do not reduce this strain. They make it easier for us to surrender our critical faculties, to follow and accept their "hero" of the moment—whether he is a father figure; a young, energetic, efficient, and voluble champion; a Hitler, Stalin, or Khrushchev.

And yet, there may never have been another time in history when man so sorely needed the type of person who will not abdicate his critical self-consciousness, who will not allow himself to be led about by the manufacturers of a public profile. We are in the midst of an unparalleled crisis. Civilization is at stake. The species at this moment is capable of committing suicide with H-bombs—or of robotizing itself through administrative machinery now available to all would-be dictators. When men err in this crisis, the consequences are graver than before, and their serious errors are more likely to be irreversible.

Sociology arose as a field of study in response to the "senselessness" of human society. Countless philosophers and sociologists have labored to make sense of this apparent senselessness. Together, they have often made brilliant analyses of specific societies. Change within the societies has, however, regularly outrun their descriptions. The best efforts to make society intelligible have resulted only in an analysis of the history of continuously emerging society.

There was once a pristine vision of sociology as the discipline that would provide rational planning for the necessary renovation of modern society. We have lived to see its practitioners employed by various public and private bureaucracies under their particular jurisdictions. Rational planning of the entire societal process is so far no more than a vague possibility.

Sociology as a science has little to do with that possibility. Whether civilization, let alone a democratic system, survives is a (in fact, *the*) sociological question. But its resolution does not lie in the hands of sociologists. It lies rather in the capacity of ordinary citizens to become rational, free, critical, and mature. They must do this or perish (if not physically, then spiritually) at a time when many of their institutions, by design and by circumstance, conspire to render them into infants.

Notes

1. J. Huizinga, *The Waning of the Middle Ages* (Garden City, NY: Anchor, 1954), 9.

2. *Ibid.*, 12.

3. See "The Road Not Taken," in *Complete Poems of Robert Frost* (New York: Holt, Rinehart and Winston, 1964), 131.

4. John K. Galbraith, *The Affluent Society* (New York: Houghton, 1958).

5. Daniel Bell, *The End of Ideology* (Glencoe, IL: Free Press, 1960).

6. Quoted by Hal Draper in "Neo-Corporatists and Neo-Reformers," *New Politics* 1 (March 1961), 95.

7. *Ibid.*

8. *Ibid.*, 91.

9. Talcott Parsons, "Social Strains in America," in *The New American Right*, ed. Daniel Bell (New York: Criterion, 1955), 139-40.

10. Karl Mannheim, *Essays on Sociology and Social Psychology* (London: Routledge & Kegan Paul, 1953), 117.

11. Robert S. Lynd, *Knowledge for What?* (Princeton: Princeton University Press, 1945), 65-66.

12. See Edgar Morin, *The Stars* (New York: Grove Press, 1961), 54-56.

13. H. D. F. Kitto, *The Greeks* (London: Penguin, 1951), 195.

14. *Ibid.*, 196-97.

15. Allen Wheelis. *The Quest for Identity* (New York: Norton, 1958), 17-19.

16. Richard G. Stern, *Golk* (Cleveland: World, 1960), 95.

17. Lawrence Lipton, *The Holy Barbarians* (New York: Julian Messner, 1959), 26.

18. *Ibid.*, 138.

19. Robert K. Merton, "Social Structure and Anomie," *American Sociological Review* 3 (October 1938), 672-82.

16

Art and the Mass Society

Joseph Bensman with Israel Gerver

The withdrawal of artists from concern with social meaning during recent decades stems from two general sources: the *internal* rationalization of art, as found in technical and aesthetic systems; and the *external* orientation of art, as indicated in the changing social position of the artist. This essay addresses both.

The internal rationalization of art as an aesthetic system refers to art as *pure art,* art as a form. As a medium apart from other media, art develops rules, logics, and an internal economy of its own. The development of all modern art in the last two centuries is the history of explication, expansion, and development of "inner logics" both for the field and for schools of art. Over a long period of time, the aesthetic premises of the arts have become more rationalized, self-conscious, and self-consistent. Consequently, artistic fulfillment consists of expressing and exhausting the possibilities inherent in a set of aesthetic assumptions.

Among and within schools, there are rivalries between the partisans of divergent aesthetic assumptions and techniques. Such factions do not remain static. When the limits of the traditional philosophy

---

Published originally in a slightly different form in *Social Problems* 6 (Summer 1958), 4-10 [revised and expanded version of paper presented at the American Sociological Society annual meeting, Urbana, Illinois, September 1954].

are reached, new assumptions are posited and new techniques and modes of creativity are permitted.

The consequences of this process are:

> 1. The major problems of art become primarily technical, and the artist becomes primarily concerned with problems of technique.[1] As a consequence, the artist is constrained to focus his attention on methodological problems. The meaning of social experience becomes secondary or, in some cases, excluded from the scope of art.
>
> 2. As the rationalization of each artistic medium develops, its techniques, methods, conventions, rules, language, and logic become more elaborate and precise. The position of artist then requires a thorough, intensive, and prolonged training, indoctrination, and practice. At the same time, the appreciation of the artistic product increasingly requires knowledge of those highly sophisticated criteria on which the work is based. Since knowledge of such criteria can only be based on specialized and intensive training, art becomes more and more inaccessible and incomprehensible to those who have not acquired the aesthetic standards of appreciation. The work of art is alienated from the taste of the lay public, and artistic interpreters (critics, educators, publicists, managers, dealers) become important in determining the channels by which works of art are exposed to and accepted by an untrained public.
>
> 3. The development of self-conscious schools of art is not monolithic. The artistic and aesthetic foun-

> dations of a school are the results of acceptance and usage by producers of commonly accepted aesthetic propositions. Even though artists belong to numerous and competing schools, art is still peculiarly a means of personal expression. Specific artists of any one school will emphasize different tenets of a school. Given this situation, the general public is confronted with an overwhelming plenitude of artistic traditions presented side by side.

The relationship of artistic product to the social position of the artist has been studied and documented in the last century. One major type of analysis has been in the Marxist tradition.[2] It has emphasized the relationship of the artist to the means of production, to the class structure, and to markets. In general, the major thesis of Marxist analysis is that artistic production "reflects" the system of economic and industrial production. The Marxist argument stresses the problems of the market for works of art. Taste is defined as a reflection of changes in the composition and character of the supporting strata for artists, the purchasers of artistic production who compose the market.

Marxists attempt to demonstrate a parallel between the class position of the artist and themes, symbols, avoidances, and biases in his artistic production. This leads generally to a circumvention of aesthetic considerations. Moreover, overemphasis on external criteria of artistic productions results less in generalizations about art, and more in generalizations about society.[3] These limitations do not completely invalidate external analysis, so long as it is not used as a simpleminded approach. The same stricture applies to internal analysis.

In modern times, there have been many shifts in the relationship of art to society. The Renaissance entailed greater secularization. This occurred along with the rise of new classes and new financial resources for art purchases. The major change in the market relations of the Renaissance artist was primarily from religious to secular patronage.[4]

While the artist had lower social status, the relationship of the artist to his consumer was a close one. The artist participated in and knew the life of his patrons. There was a common universe of taste between artist and consumer generated by shared social existence and the special character of the patrons.

The rise of a large middle class in the eighteenth and nineteenth centuries resulted in a mass market for art. For example, portraiture was transformed into a middle-class art, but more significant than the class nature of such art is its mass character. With mass audiences whose obligation was the purchase of a ticket or a book, rather than employment of the artist, art reached monumental proportions. The full symphony orchestra became the characteristic expression of music; it performed for large audiences in architecturally appropriate halls.[5]

Nineteenth-century artists captured large audiences by adopting mass themes that expressed national, political, and social aspirations. Within mass audiences, scientific technology increased the scope within which the artist operated, and the artist was increasingly removed from his audience. Indeed, today, the musician may make a reputation on phonograph records before he makes a live debut. Major concert performers such as Arthur Rubinstein and Joseph Szigeti were introduced to the musical audience in this country via the phonograph recording. In the past decade, the long-playing record has accelerated this procedure of promoting performers and composers (both dead and alive) by records rather than by risking expensive live performances. Similarly, in painting, the reproduction of pictures has led to a mass audience, but the painter's relationship to the audience has been depersonalized.

The very impersonality of the marketplace removed the artist from the art consumer. As art consumption adjusted to the purchase price of tickets, books, and the like, the type and character of artistic consumer was further differentiated, making it more difficult for the artist to absorb and share the clients' world. Since appreciation of art is associated with the price of a ticket, the intellectual requirements for art consumption are reduced.

The newer art consumers of differentiated background with feebler critical criteria have replaced the stable patron groups of previous eras; correspondingly, the canons of art have become less stable. The artist, not confronting a particular patron, can choose his public from a plurality of possible consumers. He is not bound to fulfill the artistic demands of a specific consumer, nor does he necessarily face a public whose standards are either firm or highly developed.

When the artist appeals to a mass audience, he encounters certain economic gatekeepers: the impresarios, promoters, critics, and so forth, whose often erroneous stereotypes of the public may become demands on the artist.[6] In modern society, where artists have engaged in social commentary, they have more often than not rejected dominant social values. Serious art has generally been hostile or indifferent to industrialism and the middle-class way of life. This rejection has not necessarily been programmatic, utopian, or revolutionary, but it has been critical of the philistinism and shoddiness of materialistic society.

Serious arts may reject the world by avoiding it—in portraying a world in which formal aesthetic concerns are dominant (Impressionism, Cubism, abstract art, etc.)—or by portraying its most unseemly side (neo-Gothicism, surrealism, naturalism, etc.). In practice, the very term *naturalism* refers to the ugliness of the world.

Since the artist is not directly concerned with a mass audience, the absence of direct pressures based on personal contacts with a patron frees the artist from all external demands and forces him to develop his own perspectives. The internal standards most directly relevant to the artist qua artist are those of technique. From this, there emerges another set of consequences. Art is essentially *exploratory.* Each product is an extension of the past and a feat of *virtuosity.* Mere reproduction of past work is avoided. *Novelty* in virtuosity becomes an end in itself. Freedom from the patron and the particular public, the production for an impersonal market, tends to isolate the producer from the consumer socially and economically. The artist's life patterns are separated from the rest of society, and aesthetic concerns intensify this separation.

It is perhaps ironic that the development of the mass middle-class audience enables the artist to reject middle-class standards in asserting his independence. At times, such assertions of independence surpass the aesthetic reasons for independence, as in the phenomena of Bohemianism, in which the 'artistic attitude' transcends artistic production. As art becomes increasingly concerned with its own dynamics, the freedom of art to pursue artistic ends places serious art at tension with the society.

The serious arts, as described above, exhibit two major interrelated tendencies. Serious, self-conscious artists become primarily concerned with the creation, development, expansion, exploration, and criticism of their central techniques and methods. As a result of this attitude, artists either avoid the world in artistic self-preoccupation or reject the world because it ignores and rejects their central core of values. Thus, the artist forsakes the attempt at intellectual leadership in which his art would be an instrument to define or influence the society.

This pattern is not true of the mass arts. In the mass arts, the concern with technique is almost as great as in the serious arts, but the mass arts attempt to express themes and messages characteristic of either everyday life or more precisely what its consumers need or want to believe about everyday life. The mass arts communicate inaccurately with major distortions, but they do communicate.

Since the mass arts involve the use of vast and expensive communication networks, the mass arts are based on heavy capital outlays and fixed expenses. Even when unit costs are low, the mass arts can be profitable only when they have a high sales volume. This is especially true of the '*free*' mass arts—radio, television, and, to a large extent, the press—for, in these sponsored arts, circulation, surveys of readership, and Nielsen ratings are a substitute for sales volume.

Given this apparatus, the mass artists can only be viewed as technicians who are elements of vast and intricate administrative organizations geared to satisfying existing demands. They are assisted by market researchers, whether formally defined as such or not, and by promoters, publicity men, agents, financial and other analysts, impresarios, critics, and agency representatives.[7] Others supply the content of the artist's work, and he must execute the design within the limits of mass formulae. The genius in this field is the artist who is his own market researcher—that is, one who can predict when the largest market will be available for a given technical feat, be it the tough detective of Hammett et al. or the plastic models of religious figures that decorate automobile windshields as mass contemporary iconography.

Although the mass artist is as involved in problems of technique as the serious artist, there are differences. As noted earlier, the technical preoccupations of serious artists result from attempts to solve technical and aesthetic problems. By contrast, the mass artist can rarely define his own problems, because they are predefined for him by the keepers of the public taste. The solutions are necessarily simple, since they cannot go beyond public knowledge. This also holds for the means of presentation. The mass artist cannot go radically beyond established techniques, because this would violate the canons of established tastes. Instead, he must rely on the serious arts to establish and develop new techniques. When these become acceptable to sufficiently large audiences, they can be adopted by the mass artists.

The economics of the mass market determine the content of mass art and its form. Under the compulsion of the mass approach, the businessman of the arts must attempt to find stereotypes of publics that will support merchandisable products. This is not an easy task. It has been assumed by many analysts of mass mentality that *mass* means lack of differentiation, and that mass society consists of a vast number of undifferentiated people. This idea reflects an inaccurate derivation of the character of the audience from the standardized products that they consume. Actually, the mass society is a conglomeration of different groups—classes, occupations, perspectives, traditions, and geographical and cultural backgrounds.

The mass arts have to find "meaningful" themes that evoke the experiences of these diverse groups. The culture level of the mass arts is irrelevant. What is important is an audience large enough to justify a competitive return on an investment. In a society with a sizable population, there may be large enough "middle-brow" and even "high-brow" audiences to justify the costs of the relatively less expensive mass arts, such as the symphony and opera. When the specialized publics are sufficiently large, it is possible to make money with specialized mass productions addressed to different groups.

As the anticipated potential audiences increase in size, a number of limitations and restrictions are placed on producers. These have been analyzed elsewhere[8] and are only restated here.

> 1. The larger the anticipated audience, the greater is the care that the *thematic treatment should not alienate any interest group of the potential audience.* This

means that controversial subjects must be ignored, unless the resolution of the conflict is neutral. Such themes should be stated so that no pressure group is likely to attack the work and thereby influence large numbers of potential consumers to boycott the product.

2. Concurrently, characters must be created so that diverse groups can identify them. These symbols of identification are stereotyped abstractions. "Realism" consists of adding external details to the "abstraction" rather than developing the themes and figures from their internal necessity—for example, the use of folk-song flavor in movie background music in order to present a convincing rural background.

3. The mass media are constantly vulnerable to intimidation by legal censors and the would-be censors of pressure groups. The controllers of the mass arts must continually estimate and respond to the weights and influences of conflicting pressure and interest groups. The final product is almost always a compromise, an adjustment to these different estimates. It is this form of audience calculus, rather than the internal dynamics of the art form, the creative theme, or the internal logic of the characters and events portrayed, that largely determines the mass product.

4. Since the mass arts are the creation of semipermanent institutions and associations, the owners of any particular *art product* view its merits as less impor-

> tant than the maintenance of the institution. Thus, goodwill, good public relations, respectability, and a favorable public esteem are necessary. Artistic producers are always viewed both as technicians and as upholders of public, private, and political morality. Failure to measure up to these may result in catastrophe, even when no technical failure is present.
>
> 5. Because of the above factors, the mass arts are conservative. They rarely risk capital in presentations that are beyond the ascertained taste, experience, knowledge, and illusions of the audience. This is true of political as well as artistic areas. When large numbers of the members of society go in a new political direction, the mass media feasibly may move in that direction. The dynamics of such changes lie outside of the sphere of the arts, but, because of this tendency to conform, the mass arts can be used as a device for estimating the underlying state of public opinion.[9] While the principle governing the mass arts is one of conformity to established norms, when marked changes occur, the prescient mass artist (if he guesses correctly) can give public expression to a trend.

The rise of science fiction especially during the post-World War II years provides an example. The number of pulp magazines more than quadrupled, and the market spread to the slick magazines, which started to publish science fiction. With the public faced with the power of science in the form of atomic bombs, guided missiles, rocketry, space satellites, and so on, the mass market for literature involving futuristic possibilities of science was inevitable. Along with the popularity of science fiction, there has also developed a distaste for dealing with the harsher potentialities of science for this world.

We have until now emphasized the limitations of the mass arts. They cannot come to grips with reality in such a way as to alienate large segments of their calculated audience. Since in a complex society almost all "problems" are controversial (except where a predetermined solution is prevalent and respectable), the mass arts manifestly avoid these conflicts.

However, the avoidance of all problems per se would result in the economic collapse of art as an industry. The initial economic assumptions of the mass arts include their ability to stimulate interest. They must provide some points of relevance to the consumer. The mass arts, while they explicitly avoid the manifest problems of social experience, actually disguise it and mirror the psychological life of their intended audience.

Thus, the mass arts provide scope for identification. The identification symbol may either provide for wish fulfillment or for the release of aggressions and hostilities that the consumer cannot express. Hence, the identifying symbols tend to be wealthy, glamorous, and exciting and to have sexual access to desirable partners; at the same time, the protagonists are threatened by outside forces, cannot control their environment, and give expression to types of brutal, violent, and antisocial behavior that are not possible in the ordinary life of the consumer. Mass art production is similar to the world of dreams and fantasy as described by psychoanalysis. All of the elements of reality are present in disguised form. Psychologically, the mass arts are different from individual projections in that in modern society the projective mechanisms are alienated from their users. Modern man does not even manufacture his own illusions. Instead, they are manufactured for him by an elite corps of scientific mass producers. The primary act of mass art consumers is the act of identification, and modern scientific mass psychological techniques make such identification easy.[10]

Whether this tendency is desirable is beyond the scope of this essay. One can argue that such mass illusion and deception makes it difficult for the consumer to come to grips with reality and hence understand his social world and deal intelligently with his problems. It is also possible to argue that the mass arts tend to permit the gradual release and displacement of tensions that might otherwise be intolerable, that confrontation of reality where individuals lack the ability or the power to deal with it might lead to radical reconstructions of the society in directions that are not necessarily desirable.

These speculations aside, the dominant fact remains that the world dramatized by the mass arts is a world that manifestly does not exist. The symbolic apparatus of modern society does not adequately describe or clarify modern life. In the public relations sphere, man's experiences are interpreted in order to permit his manipulation. In the world of serious art, his experiences are avoided. In the mass arts, his experiences are transvalued so that he can respond in terms of controlled processes of reaction that lead only to relatively crude and synthetic emotions. Thus, all spheres of symbolic communication present man with deception and confusion. Man pierces the veil of the modern arts in their various forms, to glimpse the underlying reality, only occasionally and by accident or fierce determination.

Notes

1. See Rene Leibowitz, *Schoenberg and His School* (New York: Philosophical Library, 1949), xiii-xiv, 259-84.

2. Georg Lukacs, *Studies in European Realism* (London: Holloway, 1950); George Plekhanov, *Art and Society* (New York: Critics Group Series, 1937), No. 3.

3. For example, Lukacs, at chs. 1-3, describes Balzac as an analyst of "the true nature of the capitalist world." He also asserts, at 63: "Balzac depicted the original accumulation of capital in the ideological sphere."

4. See Jacob Burckhardt, *The Civilization of the Renaissance in Italy* (London: Phaidon Press, 1945); Arnold Hauser, *Social History of Art*, (New York: Alfred A. Knopf, 1951), Vol. I.

5. Cecil Smith, *Worlds of Music* (New York: Lippincott, 1952).

6. *Ibid.*

7. *Ibid.*

8. See Clyde and Florence Kluckholn, "American Culture: Generalized Orientations," in Lyman Bryson, Louis Finkelstein, and R. M. McIver, eds., *Conflicts of Power in Modern Culture* (New York: Harper Brothers, 1947), 106-28; Robert K. Merton, *Mass Persuasion* (New York: Harper Brothers, 1946); George Orwell, "The Ethics of the Detective Story," *Politics* (November 1944).

9. Cf. Leo Lowenthal, "Biographies in Popular Magazines," in Paul F. Lazarsfeld and Frank Stanton, eds., *Radio Research* (New York: Harper Brothers, 1943), 507-20.

10. Nathan Leites and Martha Wolfenstein, *The Movies* (Glencoe, IL: Free Press, 1950).

17

The Cultural Contradictions of Daniel Bell

Joseph Bensman with Arthur J. Vidich

In "The Cultural Contradictions of Capitalism," Daniel Bell has done an excellent job of defining and summarizing the attributes of the new sensibility, the postmodernist and antirationalist "psychedelic" culture that is actionist, antiestablishment, experimental, and obsessed with continuous change. Even better, he has elucidated the cultural and intellectual trends and movements that over the past two hundred years have led to the apparent dominance of the new culture. In fact, he has done such an excellent job of proving the cumulative power of the trend that we fail to see, on the basis of his evidence, why the new culture did not predominate in the 1950s instead of in the late sixties and why its impact was so sudden, shocking, and discontinuous. On the basis of the overwhelming evidence Bell cites, the growth in salience of the new culture ought to have been continuous and should have appeared in a slowly evolving way. Moreover, if all these factors have been operating for so long, the new culture should not have come as such a surprise to so many people.

To come directly to the point, we suspect that Bell is guilty of providing an overdetermination of causation, of providing enough

Published originally in a slightly different form in *Journal of Aesthetic Education* 6 (January-April 1972), 52-65. Republished with permission from University of Illinois Press.

causes to explain half a dozen cultural revolutions but no specific causes for the one that did occur. Moreover, we will argue that his central theme, the freeing of culture from its socioeconomic base, is not a cause for the current cultural revolution, which in fact did not occur as Bell describes it. To state it differently, Bell's central argument that culture is now free from its socioeconomic base is, at best, only partially true. Indeed, the major ways that culture still reflects the underlying social and economic reality have been wholly ignored in his essay.

It is true that an avant-garde that is critical of the bourgeoisie, "the establishment," and Western society in general has emerged. However, this avant-garde is virtually as old as the bourgeoisie itself and certainly much older than the term *avant-garde.* Cervantes, Simplicissimus, Rabelais, Molière, Rousseau, Beaumarchais, de Sade, Stendhal, Balzac, and, in fact, virtually all Western intellectuals have been antiestablishment and antibourgeoisie, regardless of their social origins and regardless of the label. Granted, only with the Symbolist movement and Impressionism did the experimental aspects of the new sensibility emerge, whereas the antirationalist tendencies emerged previously, with Rousseau and romanticism. Only in the late nineteenth century and early twentieth century did such tendencies become programmatic, arising with the *Salon des Refuses,* and with Expressionism, Surrealism, and Dada. Nonetheless, all of the revolutionary tendencies in art were present long before such self-conscious programs. The rationalistic and scientific tendencies in culture and intellectual trends were expressed (apart from the scientific theories of impressionism) only in the technological optimism of the ideologies of Saint-Simon, Marx, Comte, and their successors.

The freeing of culture from its economic and social base was itself a function of the growth of the bourgeoisie and of a market for culture occurring with the rise of printing, the subscription concert, and bourgeois mass markets for printing and sculpture. In this development, the artist was liberated from the patron, the guild, and the church and was free to seek his audience either in the mass market of bourgeois culture consumers or in the approval of other artists. Thus, mass art and "art for art's sake," either antibourgeoisie or purely aesthetic, experimental, technical, and obscure, emerged. This development began in the seventeenth century and has continued into the twentieth. Over this period of time, a freeing of the artist from some socioeconomic structures has thus occurred, but, since this occurred so early, it does not explain the phenomenon of the 1960s.

Bell does not define the socioeconomic institutions from which culture has apparently liberated itself. By referring negatively to Marx and Marxist ideas, he apparently means economic and productive institutions. Bell's rejection of Marx means that he chooses not to treat class as an operative part of the socioeconomic institution from which culture has achieved "autonomy." By thus treating culture as an autonomous flowing of ideas, techniques, and aesthetic systems and programs, Bell frees himself from referring to the classes that constitute the artists and audiences for art and culture.

We know by and large that the class origins of artists have been primarily in the bourgeoisie and the lower-middle classes. It is also clear that the customers and audiences of artists have been drawn from the upper classes and the bourgeoisie reaching as far down as the lower-middle classes. In Europe, these customers have not necessarily been exponents of middle-class values even when they have been part of the middle classes. In highly developed societies, it has always been the case, at least since the classical period of Greece, that antiestablishment ideologies have been produced in the upper classes, in segments of the middle classes, and in the intelligentsia.

In virtually all class systems, the achievement of upper-class status frees that class from the work and the discipline necessary for economic mobility. Quite frequently, enforced idleness and leisure deprive the upper and middle classes from social functions other than those of consumption and of political and military activity. The total number of people needed from the upper classes for the internal mastery and control of a society is actually quite limited in relation to the total size of the class. Frequently, economic and military expansion has provided the middle and upper classes outlets for the utilization of the stores of energy unexpended because of their social and economic privileges and predominance. Seen in this light, the pursuit of art, knowledge, and science is simply another avenue available to the upper classes by which they are able to expend the excesses of energy provided by their favored class position. But the very affluence of the privileged classes frees all but a few from both the necessity of mastering the arts in order to live off of them and the discipline required to achieve professional and craft standards. In fact, members of the upper classes usually become declassed if they pursue the arts professionally, because professionalization implies a necessity for work. As a result, the upper classes, if at all interested in the arts, are forced to become art consumers in order to pursue leisure conspicuously.

But art consumption alone has never been enough to absorb the time and energy of the idle upper classes. Alternatives have included participation in sports, gambling, racing, and hunting; sexual pursuits, carousing, and gluttony; and experimentation with alcohol and drugs. Historically, upper-class leisure-time activities have also included revolutionary, antiestablishment, and antibourgeoisie politics. Thus, the phenomena typical of the current cultural revolutions have been going on for more than two thousand years.

Certainly, during the latter half of the nineteenth century in Russia, the intelligentsia displayed the full range of political, cultural, and aesthetic libertarianism in almost the same forms as can be found in the present. Berlin, during the Weimar Republic, had its own versions of activist political alternatives, apathetic expressionism, and cultural and personal libertarianism, libertinism, and romanticism. The libertinism of the ancien régime in Paris and Versailles, despite the Enlightenment, included elements of a "sexual revolution," romanticism, political revolution, activism, and an emphasis on freeing oneself from all restraints. Most of this experimentation was confined to the upper classes, but after the Restoration the same liberation movements were carried on in the salons of the upper bourgeoisie, attended by artists, writers, and intellectuals. In both Restoration England, during the reign of George IV, and in Edwardian England, the same upper-class phenomena were prevalent. The coxcomb, the dandy, and Beau Brummell remind us of the class. Thus, middle and upper classes that were art consumers even when art was anti-establishment, that indulged in all varieties of pleasure seeking and participated in reform and revolutionary political movements of all sorts, were characteristic throughout European history.

Equivalent classes have been much less common in American history. At various times, America has had small, somewhat isolated, upper-class enclaves. Included among these have been Gramercy Park and Washington Square in New York, Beacon Hill in Boston, and Charleston and New Orleans in the South, which produced lifestyles and cultures similar to their European class counterparts. But these enclaves in America were small and were not part of the mainstream American civilization. The overwhelming mainstream consisted of commercial expansion, westernization, industrialization, and, for millions of immigrants, Americanization. The expansion and development of the United States served the same functions in using up the energy released by economic development as did the arts, self-indulgence, leisure, warfare, and politics in Europe. Moreover, in the United States, economic mobility, materialism, and political movements were not ideological in the sense that ideology characterized European political movements, not excluding Marxism. During America's expansionist frontier phase what dominated politics and public debate was the advance and defense of economic interests—in which the major political issues were interest rates, tariff rates, credit policies, and governmental subsidies and protection to farmers, railroads, and other major economic interests, such as the protection of free labor or the extension of slavery. *Ideology* in the sense that Bell defines the term was never an important American phenomenon, except among fringe groups in New York who related themselves to European issues. Thus, the "end of ideology," if it ever ended, would have ended in Europe. It never really began in America.

The concentration in the United States on economic interests rather than on ideological issues was in part a reflection of the absence of a relatively stable, traditionalized class system. In Europe, the class system became the focal point of all internal social conflict. In the United States, classes emerged and were prominent, but their privileges after the Revolutionary War were never legalized. Equally and perhaps more importantly, the continuous expansion and growth of the American economy and the continuous emergence of new class groups and class interests prevented the stabilization of classes and class interests. Moreover, continuous change in the composition and characteristics of the leading classes prevented the formation, despite Veblen's theories, of *stable* leisure classes that resembled the European upper classes in the characteristics described above. In the United States, the energies of the upper classes were, in general, absorbed by economic expansion or, as described by Veblen, in vulgar conspicuous consumption after fortunes had been accumulated.

Of course, as Bell notes, the Protestant ethic and Puritanism were involved, but this occurred especially in the nineteenth century. The

Protestant ethic was given impetus by the opportunities inherent in the American frontier and in the absence of aristocratic restraints on vulgar materialism in a new and rapidly expanding country. In England, for example, the presence of a court and a legal aristocracy served to deflect the interests of successful Scottish-Irish Puritans away from vulgar economic expansion and into elegant cultural styles, political service, and prestigious consumption.

Overall, the Protestant ethic had a highly limited territorial focus, though without doubt it has been important in its consequences. Certainly, it was extremely important in the early development of English commercial capitalism, primarily Scottish in origin, and in early industrial capitalism, as it was important much later in America. It was also important in Switzerland, Holland, and among French Huguenots, who early scattered to America and to Prussia. But it must be remembered that the Protestant ethic, a concept created by Weber, was already proclaimed dead in its religious sense by Weber by 1904.

With the passage of time in the United States, the Protestant ethic was absorbed into its service clubs by organizations such as the Rotary, the Better Business Bureau, and other booster clubs. Later, it was incorporated in somewhat more distorted form into the organizational structures of giant corporations that began to dominate the organizational life of America. But the decline and distortion of the Protestant ethic does not explain the new cultural revolutions of the 1960s and '70s, which occurred long afterward. Moreover, even apart from the Protestant ethic, the new culture is a worldwide phenomenon that has risen in every society where cultural freedom exists, whether or not such a society has been influenced by the Protestant ethic.

By the same logic, the failure of corporate capitalism to develop an ideology that would have given it legitimacy cannot be viewed as a cause of phenomena of the sixties and the seventies. The failure of corporate managerial capitalism to develop a legitimizing ideology was a central theme of the intellectual history of the thirties. Veblen, Peter Drucker, Robert Brady, Berle and Means, and James Burnham were only a few of the authors who pointed this out. And while some of these authors and others (including Bell himself) since the thirties attempted to create new ideologies that would replace the defunct ideologies of laissez-faire, no new theory or combination of new theories (all primarily based on managerial or technological trusteeship) received enough acceptance by even the managerial classes to provide ideological legitimacy for the corporate system. Yet American society has survived without an ideology. Without an overall ideology, the New Deal prevented a deeper American crisis by promising a reform in American institutional arrangements, and the Republican Party during the Eisenhower administrations accepted the fundamental premises of the New Deal. Moreover, World War II and the Cold War forced a moratorium on the ideological self-probing and doubts of the thirties: it appeared that American survival was at stake and that American ideologies of political freedom and conventional capitalism, regardless of imperfections and inconsistencies, were preferable to defeat.

Theodore Draper has advanced an intriguing theory that the Cold War forced American political leaders and the public to avoid the self-probing "self-doubts" of the thirties, since it caused each group to turn their attention and energy outward. Only with the apparent relaxing of the Cold War, according to Draper, has America been forced to face the fact that it has no ideological system that can withstand its own self-doubts. The end of a cold war psychology has thus caused a collapse of the psychological defenses of the American public and a failure of conviction and nerve on the part of its leaders. President Nixon can appear to be simultaneously a conservative, a liberal, and a revolutionary, but in each of these aspects, he appears to be rhetorically indistinguishable from what are often thought to be his more liberal political opponents.

Draper's thesis appears to be highly plausible as a political explanation. In its present form, however, it does not explain the new psychedelic culture, unless the latter is viewed as a means of filling the gap created by the destruction of the cultural defenses caused by the end of the Cold War.

In summary, our objection to Bell's thesis is that while his theories do explain a consistent antibourgeoisie attitude in the arts that has persisted in European society since the seventeenth century, it explains *nothing* that is particular to the cultural revolutions of the late sixties and the seventies. His theory not only ignores the phenomenon of class but especially ignores those classes in America and Europe that are the bearers of the "new" culture and consciousness. He posits the decline of the Protestant ethic to explain phenomena that occur in places where the Protestant ethic had long ago ceased to be dominant, if it ever had been. He argues that the end of political ideology results in a cultural but not a political revolution, but does not account for the fact that the "end of political ideologies" occurred some thirty years before the appearance of the cultural revolution. Most seriously, in our opinion, he has failed to prove his thesis of the independence of culture from the socioeconomic system.

In our book *The New American Society*,[1] we address the same problems posed by Bell in "The Cultural Contradictions of Capitalism." In that study, we arrive at a solution to the question of the relationship between culture and socioeconomic institutions that is exactly the opposite of Bell's. We describe and analyze the rise of the new middle class since World War II.[2] This new middle class is composed of people who are college educated, American born, and the children either of immigrants to the United States or of migrants from rural to urban areas within the United States. This middle class is employed in the professions and in the middle and upper levels of the giant economic bureaucracies that dominate American life. The emergence of the class position of this group can only be understood in terms of socio-institutional developments such as the rise of giant corporations, the acceptance of Keynesian economics by the federal government, the end of immigration in the twenties, and the rise of mass college education (particularly during and immediately after World War II) and of a highly technological society.

The lifestyles of this new middle class have not stabilized but have been in a continuous process of creation and re-creation since World War II. A significant feature of these lifestyles involves a repudiation of the cultural vulgarity that has traditionally been a dominant feature of American society. In this effort to create new lifestyles, the first (parental) generation of these new middle classes strove to emulate American and European models of an older upper class, endeavored to adopt styles embedded in high and elite culture, and became protagonists of ideologies of technological and managerial elitism. If they had been radical ideologists or political activists in their youth, they rejected both the ideologies and the activism and frequently replaced them with an emphasis on sophisticated cultural consumption or on managerial elitism.

The first generation of the new middle classes enjoyed success far beyond their expectations simply because the technological drift of their society rewarded the skills and training they possessed. In addition, that drift was so strong and the economic expansion in their skill sectors was so great that numerically they became the largest segment of the middle class as a whole, while all other classes declined relative to the increase of the new middle classes.

But this group was not the bearer of the new cultural and "political" revolutions. It was their children, the second generation of the new middle classes, who created and became the audience for these revolutions. The parental generation, many of whom were veterans whose careers were delayed by World War II, was caught up in making up for lost time in the quest for mobility and economic and professional success. In part, they were the silent generation, silenced by their dedication to nonpolitical goals. It was their children and their children's children, along with a small number of the older generation who "flipped out" of the old culture and into the new, who were the protagonists of new cultural revolutions.

The children, unlike their parents, were middle class by birth rather than by achievement. They, unlike their parents, could take for granted the affluence into which they had been born. The culture they acquired in the frequently suburban home was often acquired under the pressure and coercion of their striving parents who had themselves only imperfectly acquired that culture as a result of their own efforts. The children found it easy to accept the ideals and the culture of their parents, but did not have to temper either the ideals or the opportunities for cultural consumption with the struggle necessary to achieve economic mobility. Having already comfortably arrived, they found it easy to be critical. They saw their parents as bureaucrats, technicians and technologists, and sellouts to a corrupt society. If they acquiesced to this society, they saw themselves doomed to both military service in a senseless war and to menial bureaucratic service in organizations that, at best, had no other purpose than mechanical survival. If the new society was rational, it was rational only in a formal, institutional sense. If it was technological, the technology served materialistic and corrupt ends. If it required discipline, the discipline was to external, alien goals. If the established arts exhibited any of these characteristics, then the arts were irrelevant, as was a politics wedded to a corrupt establishment.

The rejection of instrumentalism, technological society, rationality, self-discipline, and self-control was thus a rejection of the framework of middle-class life, as they perceived it. The cultural revolution has taken place in the arts and politics. And it also has taken place in the conception of ideal models of personality. But if the political behavior of the New Left can be considered political, then politics and culture are not exclusive categories. Both are forms of rejection; both can coexist without contradicting each other. But the new culture, especially in its emphasis on pot, drugs, freaking out, and sexual, narcotic, and communal retreatism, do not constitute a basis for a disciplined, continuous political program. Apart from the Young Socialist Alliance, the new politics is neither disciplined nor a political movement.

We thus stress as a central issue the emergence of a new class that has arisen in response to fundamental economic and institutional changes in American society. This new class has many of the characteristics of the older, upper classes in European history and, though it has selected antecedents in the American past, it has emerged in large numbers for the first time as a result of structural changes in American society. Thus, American society for the first time will experience the problem of having in its midst a large alienated "upper class." In fact, the problem engendered by the emergence of this new class in the United States will be greater than in European societies, since the class from which the new culture draws its ranks is larger than comparable classes in the past. European societies are only now beginning to undergo industrial and bureaucratic transitions similar to those in the United States and hence also have begun to experience the growth of current forms of the new middle classes and the new culture, though this appears to be to a lesser degree than in the United States. Large sections of European society are still in the developmental phase, emphasizing technology, the new managerial elitism, and a new enthusiasm for social and economic mobility and for consumer durables that are taken for granted in the United States. However, in Europe, too, segments of both the old and new middle classes have already flipped into the new forms of avant-garde culture.

The implication of all this for the future and for social policy is not easy to assess. To the extent that the indicated trends represent fundamental structural changes in society and in the composition of class structures and cultures, social policy can only come to terms with the changes. We cannot abolish or "legislate away" the changes simply because the groups that are the representatives and bearers of the change constitute a significant segment of those who will be making or approving social policy. To imagine that the policy maker can abstract himself from the social structure and thus manipulate it is the highest form of elitism, worthy of Saint-Simon or Karl Marx himself. We can, however, project some possibilities concerning the extent of the forthcoming changes and their consequences for society, as we now know it.

We would expect a sizeable number of the new middle classes, especially the children of this class, to freak out permanently to narcotics and narcotics culture. Others will drop out in rural and urban communes, "villages," and slums, and will live as "lumpen proletariats" on remittances, panhandling, scavenging, and relief. They will rationalize their dropping out in terms of art, culture, utopianism, and a professed commitment to a higher sensitivity and morality. Included in this group will be the politically alienated, the heirs of the New Left and the SDS (Students for a Democratic Society) whose righteousness will remain unabated and productive of scattered violence, bombings, and "confrontations." But while the numbers of these groups will be large and the damage they will suffer (and cause) as a result of drugs, disease, malnutrition, neglect, and violence will be great, the percentage of population of the new middle classes so involved will not be large, certainly far less than 20 percent. Apart from the frightful human cost to individuals, a functioning capital intensive, technological society can withstand this amount of human wastage, since from a purely economic point of view labor shortages are not a problem for such a society.

A more serious problem would arise if the new consciousness would cause a sizeable proportion of the new middle classes, who, after all, are the managerial and technological underpinning of a technological society, to neglect technical education, abandon efforts at mobility, reject self-discipline, and subvert the technological and bureaucratic values on which our society is based. We do not expect this to happen to the extent necessary to cripple seriously the technical and organizational operations of the society. Our opinion is based on a number of reasons. First, the social and psychological dropping out that has already occurred has been among only a small percentage of the new middle classes. It has primarily occurred, as in other comparable historical periods, among those segments of the middle classes that were not initially oriented to disciplined, scientific, and technological work. Thus, the technological loss has been minimal because of self-regulated selection and recruitment processes. Second, a large but as yet undetermined number of those who have freaked out have already returned. These numbers have discovered that the freaked-out life is not as glamorous as it appears to be when viewed from the outside. Daily existence involves not only poverty and deprivation, but also idleness, boredom, and the absence of routines, which provide the means of externalizing one's life and of escaping the feelings of emptiness that impelled one to freak out in the first place.

A major reason for not expecting the freaked-out way of life to penetrate extensively is that enjoying and consuming the new culture is expensive. The enjoyment of music, new styles of clothing and adornment, restaurants, and even pot, when done with elegance, grace, and a sense of chic, all cost money, which can be acquired only by handsome remittances, inheritances, or from work. Finally, the vast majority of the new middle classes, regardless of their idealism, appear not to want to sacrifice the affluence to which they have become habituated for the ideals that cause them to reject in principle the society that provides the affluence.

As a result, we can expect a peculiar split in psychology of the new middle classes. The overwhelming majority of the new middle classes—and members of the ascending lower and lower-middle classes—will continue to serve as the technological and administrative cadres for the technological society. Once in the ambience of the industrial, governmental, and professional bureaucracies, a sufficient number will find that the aesthetics and inducements of leadership are attractive enough to provide the basis for a continuing administrative and technological elite. But even while this is true, the majority of the new middle class will find the pleasures and blandishments of the new culture sufficiently attractive to make this culture the dominant one in Western society. The new culture need neither weaken seriously nor destroy the administrative and technological structures that support it.

The new avant-garde music, art, theater, cinema, and literature will become dominant in both mass and high culture, but will not eradicate classical high culture. Great works in art and literature manage to retain their appeal regardless of current styles and fads. But avant-garde culture already has reached the stage where it predominates as a midcult in many of the arts and in the mass media.

Thus, we think that basic problems of social policy involve issues dealing with the wreckage and the waste caused by those who freak out seriously. However, one problem could affect our "optimistic" predictions. A deep depression could convert mild cultural disaffection into large-scale potentially dangerous political disaffection and into a violent and mindless radicalism. That radicalism could produce equally violent and mindless political movements from a burgeoning radical right. The new middle classes and the new culture have already provoked the hostility of the old, vulgar middle classes and of a new lower and lower-middle class that, on the basis of twenty-five years of relative prosperity, is just beginning to enjoy a stake in an American society that many of the new middle class have already enjoyed and rejected.

Thus, the central issue in contemporary social policy is that of avoiding a serious depression and of avoiding further political polarization of the society. For underlying the seemingly nonpolitical issues of art and culture lie the most divisive and explosive political and ideological issues of our time.

Notes

1. Chicago: Quadrangle Books, 1971.

2. See also Joseph Bensman and Arthur J. Vidich, "The New Middle Classes: Their Culture and Life Styles," *Journal of Aesthetic Education* 4 (January 1970), 23.

18

A Theory of the Contemporary American Community

Joseph Bensman with Arthur J. Vidich

The Key Problems and Findings in Springdale

Since working on *Small Town in Mass Society* ten years ago, we have been preoccupied with assessing the meaning of the small town in relationship to the evolution of American society, to its historic past, its present, its implications for the future of American society, and its significance for newly emerging lifestyles in the society as a whole. This has involved a review of other sociological, literary, and journalistic studies of which there have been an abundant number in recent times on the rural, suburban, urban, and university communities. Just as journalistic and literary studies of the suburb abound so also do studies of university towns, which have received a large share of "scientific" attention because they are easily accessible to the university professor and because they fascinate him in the light of his own particular existence.

In reviewing this literature and in working with it in detail with our graduate students at the City University of New York and the New School for Social Research, we have inevitably used our own fieldwork and our own study as a point of departure. The central questions

---

Published originally in a slightly different form in *Small Town in Mass Society*, rev. ed. (Princeton: Princeton University Press, 1968), 317-47. Republished with permission from Marilyn Bensman and Joseph Vidich.

and problems we raised for the data we gathered in Springdale and interpreted in our book have served us as a paradigm or outline for assessing the place of the community in American society. Before going to this broader topic, let us review the problems and findings of the Springdale study.

The central problem that evoked our study of Springdale was discovery of the relationship between Springdale and the larger society. In our initial contacts with the community, we had found that even those local accomplishments of which the people were so proud were the result of operations of the large-scale, impersonal machinery of outside organizations whose policies in most cases were not even addressed to Springdale as a particular place but to Springdale as one of hundreds of similar towns that fell in a given category. Thus, land-grant college programs, milk pricing decisions, and telephone company policies applied to all towns like Springdale, but Springdalers, of course, did not see these larger realities. Springdale could only respond to these outside forces, but quite often took its own response to be a sign that the town was being original and creative. When we first noticed that these processes of initiation and response were at work, we undertook a survey of all major cultural and institutional areas in the community for the purpose of isolating those aspects of the life and organization of the community that were intrinsic to it and those that were the products of the surrounding society.

Despite our attempt to find original and indigenous sources of the community's culture and values, we were unable to find any. Instead, we found external sources and origins for everything that the community cherished as being most genuinely representative of its own spirit. Moreover, we found that the community harbored genuine resentments against the urban centers and institutions that devalued, by their very pervasiveness, all that the community was, stood for, and believed in. The most original and creative elements in the community were these resentments and the attempts that the town made in collusion with other rural, upstate blocs (in legislative and lobbying activities), through gerrymandering and delays in legislative reapportionments, to encumber urban areas, especially New York City, with financial demands and political favoritism. In some measure, the town succeeded in these efforts, and such successes were especially enjoyed in the community.

As we pursued this line of analysis, we became aware of the fact that the community did not respond as a unit to the external institutions and forces that determined its internal structure and culture. There were significant differences in the way different segments of the community responded to different parts of the outside society. In some cases, like that of the expanding dairy farmers, the outside society (via favorable dairy marketing policies) provided opportunities for growth to Springdale dairy farmers. In other cases, like that of the centralization of merchandizing practices, the competition from the outside society (supermarkets in the county seat) caused local institutions (small businesses) to shrivel and decay. It was through such differential rates of growth and decline that the very character of the community itself was transformed.

The uneven rates of assimilation of external elements into the community resulted in considerable variety and differentiation in the community's culture, lifestyles, and institutional structure. For example, almost every period of American cultural history was actively represented by some segment of the community—ideologies of grassroots Jacksonian democratic populism existed in combination with idealistic, anticorporate, muckrakerism in the style of Lincoln Steffens, and, on top of this, one could find the latest forms and substances of sophisticated, college-bred, urban, upper-middle class lifestyles. In between these forms, the town still sang songs that went backward through the decades of the '40s, '30s, '20s, and World

War I. It was as if the town at the point in time when we studied it was a summation of the archeology of American history. In a word, the culture of the town was stratified in terms of various periods of American history and in its selective adaptation to contemporary institutions.

There are two ideas in *Small Town in Mass Society* that we think are innovations and that are especially relevant to a formulation of a theory of the American community. The first concerns the attempts of Springdalers to deal with the effects of the penetration of their community by new ideas, cultural forms, and lifestyles. These appear to be alien to the older ideas and lifestyles that have become part of their way of life. The second idea concerns the significance of the new cultural forms and lifestyles themselves.

Springdale's older traditions are part of the ideals of Jacksonian democracy, which properly belong to the tradition of the frontier, democratic populism, and the ideology of economic growth and expansiveness. This nineteenth-century complex of values still had considerable vitality in Springdale when we studied it. Springdalers believed in a democratic society that provides equal representation for all and equal opportunity for mobility based on individual effort and skill, friendliness, neighborliness, and mutual aid. However, we found that all of these values are at odds with the institutional realities of the community. If he were to look, the Springdaler would have found that:

> 1. Almost all aspects of his town were controlled by external forces over which he had little control; the idea of democratic self-determination had no basis in fact.
>
> 2. Even within the town, political life was controlled by a small clique of party professionals whose desire was to keep real estate taxes down even though this

> policy was contrary to the wishes and aspirations of the educated middle class. Instead of being expansive and investment-oriented, the town fathers were stingy and anal.
>
> 3. The avenues for opportunity, growth, and expansiveness within the town were severely limited. The Rotarian optimism of the Better Business Bureau had a hollow and false ring. Economic growth was limited to the prosperous farmers while small businessmen increasingly became franchise operators. Personal growth and opportunity for most people could be achieved only by leaving the town. For those in the younger generation who remained, inheritance of wealth, status, and position was the major basis of social and self-definition.
>
> 4. Social inequalities (inherited and economic) and sharp competitiveness within the community were in conflict with the cooperative, friendly, warm self-image of the inhabitants and of the town.

The dilemmas and contradictions that are a consequence of these differences between reality and belief resulted in complicated patterns of social and personal self-deception that permitted Springdalers to retain their system of belief while at the same time allowing them to act within the framework of those social realities that denied the tenability of their beliefs. What we saw in Springdale was an elaborate but routinely accepted set of social defenses that made it possible for Springdalers to live with their situation. The genius of these defenses was that it allowed for an accommodation between older traditions and beliefs and the newer institutional forms.

The second idea that we regard as increasingly important was the new lifestyles that were being introduced into the community at the time we did the study. This was our "discovery" of the emergence of the new middle class. This new middle class was composed primarily of college-educated professionals and white-collar and managerial workers. These people often deliberately, but sometimes involuntarily, underemployed themselves, and instead of seeking a meaningful existence in economic mobility and relentless work, addressed their lives to achievement of stylized consumption, cultural and prestigious social and recreational activity, and efforts to be sophisticated, smart, and urbane. All of these traits stood in contrast to the rural vulgarity, the materialism, the unrelenting work, and the lowbrow leisure of the traditional populist values and of contemporary mass media.

Springdale's new middle classes, small in size though they were, engaged in the process of importing sophisticated cultural lifestyles from urban society and from the nearby state-Ivy university. By doing this, they were engaged in a process of revolutionizing the lifestyles of the community. Even though they were an avant-garde minority in social and cultural affairs and even though they were active in social organizations and clubs, they were effectively excluded from political control of the town. In politics, they participated only as technicians and as voters in activities controlled by business leaders and farm spokesmen who were interested in holding the line on real estate taxes.

Springdale as a Microcosm in the Macrocosm

We have argued that Springdale imported and retained as its "own" elements from all historical and many cultural epochs in American society. We can infer that the same processes described for Springdale occurred and are occurring at various levels and localities in

American society at large. We wish to show how the major themes expressed in the life of Springdale are representative of larger themes characteristic of American life as a whole.

The dominant culture and lifestyles so remarkably preserved in Springdale were representative of almost all of the American past. They were so well preserved because of the attempt of the residents of the town to maintain a familiar way of life and a traditional ideology in the face of a society that devalues that way of life.

The living characteristics of Springdale were part of the characteristics of the late frontier, of nineteenth-century industrial and commercial culture, and of a belief in agrarian democracy and independence. The supporting ideology for this past was a simple, optimistic materialism that Mencken in the 1920s called Yahooism, boosterism, Rotarianism, and the ideology of the *boobus Americanus.* Sinclair Lewis etched the personality and culture of Main Street America in acid and unrelentingly barbed terms. Sherwood Anderson and Edward Arlington Robinson described the period and its ideologies in somewhat more sympathetic and tender but not essentially different terms. Despite these negative descriptions, the essential characteristics of traditional frontier democracy, apart from its naive and "uncultured" materialism, did involve a genuine development of local democracy, equalitarianism, friendliness, economic aggressiveness, mobility, expansiveness, and opportunity consciousness. Springdalers who upheld these values were correct in their insistence that their traditional values embody the central values of the American past in both its best and its most characteristic senses.

However, the changes in American society that have put Springdale on the defensive are changes that have occurred during the past one hundred years, while the ideology of Springdale is based on the period from 1810 to 1860. Institutional changes that negate the ideology are based on developments that began during and after the Civil War and continue to operate up to the present. Industrialization has led to opportunities in the urban centers while the population of the rural community and rural society has been increasingly depleted.

Governmental, business, religious, and educational super-bureaucracies far distant from the rural town formulate policies to which the rural world can respond only with resentment. The urban proletariat has replaced the rural majority only in turn to be replaced in numerical primacy by the new middle classes and by service workers who are not primary producers. The "family farm," though it still exists, is now a big business industrialized in its operations and administratively organized; for the most part, farming is now corporately organized. While decreasing in number, the units of production have greatly increased in size. Throughout the country, the commuting industrial, white-collar, and professional classes have invaded the rural countryside and old farmhouses. The older rural predominance is a thing of the past, a fact that is gradually being reluctantly acknowledged by the acceptance of reapportionment legislation.

Factors in the Emergence of New Middle-Class Lifestyles

After the Civil War, America was inundated with immigrants primarily from eastern, southern, and southeastern Europe. Escaping from poverty caused by overpopulation due to rising birth rates, by shrinkage in the size of agricultural holdings, and by slow growth in the industrial sector, these immigrants saw in America opportunities that either did not exist in their own countries or were denied to them. In responding to the opportunities that America offered, the immigrant affirmed the validity of and gave added impetus to the economic optimism and expansiveness that characterized an expanding frontier and later an expanding industrial society. In being converts to the American way, the immigrants supported and deepened the American dream. They became the true Americans, especially as third and older generations of Americans lost their naive enthusiasms because of a lack of success in American society or because, if successful, they emulated European rather than American models of upper- and upper-middle-class life. For example, in Springdale, it was Polish and Finnish immigrants and their children who in their escape from urban factory work and coal mining revived Springdale's agriculture in the twenties and thirties. The older generation of Americans had given up or accepted defeat due to the prolonged agricultural depression that continued from the early twenties to the late thirties. Springdale's older industrial and business classes that had emerged during the post-Civil War industrial expansion were already defunct. Those of their descendants who remained in the town were a declining aristocracy who lived off claims for status that were no longer recognized by the newer groups. In the case of one illustrious family whose name figures prominently in the historical annals at the turn of the century, the remaining descendants included an aged and destitute dowager who was supported by her middle-aged sons, the eldest of whom had a moderately successful military career, and the youngest of whom was for the most part unemployed and would have been considered "shack" if he had not had his name. The fortunes of this family spanned four generations between the Civil War and 1950. Where once they had been immigrants, they were now being replaced in income power and status by a newer set of immigrants who, in fact, saw opportunities where the older Americans did not see them.

When immigration ended in 1924, a major support for the continuous revitalization of the American dream was cut off. The end of immigration forced American society to live off its own capacity to renew its spirit from its own resources. As we shall see, American society has failed in this respect, but its failure has been masked because it usually takes at least three generations to produce either a gentleman or a total outcast. The second generation of the eastern and south European immigration now makes up a large part of the middle class and the lower-middle working and service classes. The third generation since the closing of mass immigration is just now entering into maturity.

Throughout American history, *successful* immigrants of the third generation have tended to adopt sophisticated culture and/or the degenerate lifestyles that are reminiscent of a European aristocracy. These third-generation lifestyles are opposed to the simple, direct, naive, democratic, optimistic, and vulgar materialism of popular democracy. These lifestyles are alien to the dominant tradition, just as that of the career military officer in the above example is a contravention of traditional values. Those in the third generation who are unsuccessful, the failures, either regress to an acceptance of a lower-class way of life or to the degeneracy of a backwoods "Appalachian," "Swamp Yankee" culture, whether in the city or in the country. If the third generation is not wholly degenerate or skid row, it desperately hangs on to tatters of past respectability by means of hoarding, penuriousness, and a defensive worship of the American past, even though such worship of the past in America is un-American. Springdale showed that the pre- and post-Civil War American traditions gave way in the face of immigrant Americanism. At present, the United States faces a problematic future with respect to the third generation of the last stage of immigration.

In the same sense that the end of immigration has weakened the American dream, the urbanization of American society and the decline in the proportion of the population engaged in agriculture as compared to those engaged in secondary industries and business has resulted in a shift away from frontier democracy. The vast waves of immigration into the United States were paralleled by an equally significant internal migration from the country to the cities. The sons and daughters of American farmers sought not only the economic opportunities of urban life but also its excitement, glamour, and offer of escape from country bondage. For the first generation rural-born urbanite, the city was the frontier, which offered hope, a sense of adventure and optimism, and an opportunity for mobility. But just as in the case of the foreign-born immigrant, the opportunities in the city were more salient to the first and second generations of rural migrants. The successful urbanite takes urbanism for granted and not only adjusts to new styles of urban sophistication but helps to invent wholly new forms of urban living that are not rooted in the American tradition. Failure in any urban generation produces the functional equivalents of Appalachian culture, the ghetto of outcasts. The city produces, in addition, unique patterns of bohemian, artistic, intellectual, homosexual, beat, hippie, criminal, and other "deviant communities" simply because individuals who would be isolated or noticeable in a smaller community can, in the size and anonymity of the metropolis, come together and form communities of deviants without being particularly noticed. The urban area thus creates centers from which lifestyles that have been historically deviant or nonexistent can be created, thickened, reinforced, and disseminated. In this latter respect, urbanism, as an established aspect of American society, not only provides for the weakening of the frontier tradition, but creates new and varied lifestyles that are alien to and replace the relatively more simple frontier tradition.

The creation of these new styles, it must be noted, is directly related to the nature and conditions of the American economy. Changes in the structure of American industry, in the amount and quality of government, and in the growth of new service, leisure, educational, and other institutions have produced a new class of white-collar workers, officials, managers, and professionals. The majority of these are employees whose working hours are limited by the nature of their jobs and by wages and hours legislation. This new class has more leisure available simply because the opportunity to exploit oneself through overwork is not as easy as it was when self-employment in agriculture, small business, or in handicrafts were the characteristic forms of employment. Changes in the methods, styles, and uses of leisure are thus a central aspect in the emergence of new lifestyles in American society. The availability of leisure is a function of newer forms of work patterns.

The simple, naive optimism of the frontier and earlier industrial capitalism, as Lynd, Warner, and Hunter have pointed out, was shattered by the Depression. In the thirties, this naive optimism became replaced by a defensive optimism in which the credo of the frontier and economic liberalism began to look backward rather than, as in the original frontier spirit, forward. But the defensiveness of the thirties was replaced in the fifties and sixties by a premature optimism celebrated by American intellectuals who glorified a new economic expansiveness, based not upon the expansion of the frontier or of primary industry, but upon the expansion of the consumption and service sectors of society, including the expansion of education, government, foundations, science, and military institutions. This newer optimism of the fifties and sixties was radically different from the optimism of earlier periods because it accepted a managed, bureaucratic, mass consumption and mass leisure society, whose leaders, rather than being self-made men who operated within the framework of a laissez-faire society, were business managers and government bureaucrats aided by university-trained scientific and managerial intellectuals.

The last major factor that influenced the production of new lifestyles is to be found in the mass education of soldiers during World War II and under the G.I. Bill of Rights, as well as in the subsequent trend toward mass higher education that these educational experiments spurred. Under wartime education, the G.I. Bill of Rights, and the later mass education of millions of youth, a significant portion of this group, which was to become the new middle class, was given a preview of its own future lifestyles as presented to them during their collegiate years by the university and by the college professor.

Millions of American students who rejected the parochialism and the immigrant status of their fathers as un-American thought they found a true Americanism in the university, though in fact the immigrant and rural traditions were more characteristically American. Until the 1930s, American university professors tended to be drawn from old stock, who had already made the transition to the American version of the genteel life. Art, literature, poetry, music, scholarship, book learning, and the cultural pursuits were rejected by the populist and frontier traditions and prevailed largely on the Eastern seaboard where the passage of generations had made these aristocratic European pursuits respectable. The next generation of professors, our present one, came mainly from the first generation of G.I. Bill students who assimilated their version of Americanism from professors of old American stock.

While still on the campus, these students were provided with a total way of life that included classroom study, social life, student politics, and culture. The contrast between this life and their past life in immigrant or rural American households only reaffirmed the desire already inculcated in them by their parents to slough off the ethnic and rural traditions that even their parents regarded with a degree of embarrassment. While on campus, these students were socialized only to the possibility of a different way of life. As these college students were graduated and entered the suburbs and the new, managerial, bureaucratic, professional, and service occupations, the new lifestyles and new culture became crystallized.

Again, these classes experienced enforced opportunities for leisure, if not in the first years of their careers, by the time of early middle age, though the age of enforced leisure seems to be getting younger and younger. The structure of work in large-scale enterprises and bureaucracies causes the new middle class to find alternative means for using its time. It is at this point that the new middle class reinvokes an interest in its collegiate experiences with culture, sports, and social life. While in college, these experiences may not have been particularly salient: the courses in music or art appreciation and tennis or badminton were thought to be pleasant but somehow luxurious when considered in relation to earning a degree in order to get a job. It was only later that this collegiate exposure to culture and recreational pursuits took on special meanings and became a reservoir on which to draw in order to fabricate a lifestyle to replace the ethnic and rural provincial traditions.

As a result, the new middle classes become culture consumers. They are interested in art, music, literature, plays, books, psychology, anthropology, and even popular sociology. They are self-consciously interested in good taste, modern design, and decorating. They have become interested in what previously were upper-class sports: tennis, squash, golf, boating. Horseback riding in the middle class is in the Eastern tradition of genteel leisure rather than the Western tradition of matter-of-fact work. The country club, the community center, and, ironically, the church have been major centers for an active, sophisticated, cultured social life.

Almost all other dimensions of the middle-class lifestyle have undergone revision. In sexual codes, there has been an increasing liberation from the Puritanism of the American Protestant past. In part, this is due to the decline of the ideologically supported image of hell and damnation under the increasing influence of secularism and science; even the last holdouts, the Baptist and Methodist churches, have moderated their earlier positions on sexual codes. Also, one cannot discount the impact of the notion of sexual freedom based on Freudian psychology and on cultural relativism, which has exposed several generations to the sexual life of savages and the inner fantasies and secret behavior of prudish Victorians. The idea of sexual liberation and sophistication is also a result, in part, of exposure to European models of sophistication especially as conveyed earlier by the Waughs, Huxley, and Noel Coward, and later by French, Italian, and Swedish images of la dolce vita. Finally, one cannot discount the importance of the simple fact of increased leisure time in permitting greater exploration and development in this area.

Religiously, this new middle class has abandoned all that the Bible Belt once stood for and has transformed the earlier forms of ethnic Catholicism into modern forms of American "churchgoing" and sometimes social action directed by priestly leadership, which itself sometimes expresses the new middle-class values by demanding a break with age-old celibacy rules. Fundamentalism is regarded as gauche, and all middle-class churches of whatever faith place a high premium on tone, style, architectural sophistication, and intellectualized religion.

Politically, the new middle class is infinitely more liberal than were the middle classes of the pre-1930s. However, these new liberals are not always active in national politics and are interested in local politics in quite special ways. They do not vote according to the older traditional patterns of Republican and Democratic bloc voting at any level—urban, state, or regional. If they are sons of farmers or businessmen in the North and the East, members of this class are more likely to vote Democratic than did their parents. If they are sons of immigrants who lived in urban Democratic ghettos, they are more likely to vote Republican in the suburbs. If they moved to the far West, there is no predictable pattern between how they vote and how their parents voted. If they are in southern cities, they begin to find it easier to vote Republican.

In short, the new middle classes are developing a perspective of their own focused on a liberal, cultured, sophisticated way of life. It is often independent of the traditional identification between voting and position in the economic structure.

The impact of the new classes on politics has made itself felt strongly with respect to political style. The older frontier style of politics involved personal warmth, "cornball" localism, vulgarity, and lowbrow anti-intellectualism. In the past, highly sophisticated, intellectual, cultivated, and broad-minded political leaders have had to pretend they were rustic boobs in order to retain their popularity with local constituencies. In urban politics, the ethnic politician was forced to retain his accent and his hyphenated Americanism, and he was forced to prove that he had not outgrown his ghetto roots. Neither of these older American styles appeals to the new middle classes.

The new middle classes have become devotees of literate, articulate, cultured, sophisticated, and vital "patrician-like" politicians. Representatives of the style most congenial to them are people like Adlai Stevenson, Averell Harriman, John and Robert Kennedy, John Lindsay, Nelson Rockefeller, Eugene McCarthy, and Charles Percy. These men are cast not as "lords" of the masses, as was the case with FDR, but rather as the distillations of new middle-class aspirations and styles. The middle class and its particular expectations have become sufficiently recognizable to call forth a leadership style willing to cater to it. Of course, this has not become a dominant style, but one that exists in proportion to the quantitative importance of the middle class. Recent examples of successful political leaders who show that the older styles continue to exist along with the newer one are presidents Truman, Eisenhower, and Johnson and mayors La Guardia, Wagner, and Daley. For the new middle classes, these older styles are regarded as uncouth, crude, and at times vulgar. Thus, for example, much if not most of the reaction against Johnson in the new middle class stems from his populist, Texan-frontier, uncultivated style. By the same token, much of his support is based on the consonance of his populist style with the personal styles of his constituencies. Eastern sophisticated middle-class-style "liberalism" wherever it is expressed in urban America is at odds with the older layers of frontier populism in the smaller towns and in the segments of urban populations that, though they live in cities, are still populist in mentality. A large part of politics in the United States is a reflection of one or the other of these orientations to political styles. The "educated" middle class would like to conceal its politics of identification with symbols by finding *issues* that express its identification, but, just as for the populists, issues are frequently less important to them than political symbols that allow them to identify with an image of dignified, educated reasonableness, which is all the more compelling if it is linked to "Ivy-collegianism."

In local politics, especially in the suburbs, the new middle classes have been intensely interested in municipal services, education and school affairs, the PTA, and, as a summation of all this, the school budget. For them, the idea of quality education has had the highest value, and they have shown little respect for traditional tax rates.

In their attitudes of irreverence toward the tax rate, which in America has been a sacred cow, the new middle class has made a major break with the tradition of local politics in the United States. In middle-class communities, the major and most emotional political issue is the size of the school budget. This issue is probably the major political issue in American society insofar as it involves more participation, more activity, and more personal involvement than any other issue, including foreign policy and, at the moment—1967—the war in Vietnam. While the middle-class demonstrations against American foreign policy and the war in Vietnam appear, because of the visibility of public protest, to be a central preoccupation, this is misleading. For the middle classes, the school issue is much more important, but, because this issue is fought at a local level and because it is a *local* issue for thousands of different and decentralized jurisdictions, it is rarely seen to be as central an issue as the more obvious political protests against national policy. Because of its local particularity, the impact on the public consciousness of this issue is hardly perceived. A mass demonstration on the Pentagon has the quality of a national drama, but such dramas occur at infrequent intervals. The new middle class lives with the school issue through the lives of its children, a process that commands their attention on a daily and weekly basis. While the new middle class may be capable of extreme expressions of moral indignation against national political policies, its material commitments are to the education of its children and to helping them avoid the draft. It is perhaps unfair to reduce middle-class politics to the issue of parental interests in children without offering more demonstrably conclusive evidence. When President Johnson proposed in 1966 that the draft be conducted on a lottery basis, all candidates irrespective of class having an equal chance of being selected, it was the middle class that appeared to have the greatest objections to this procedure. The issue of the lottery draft was quietly dropped, but it served as a reminder to the middle class that its sons have been protected (by attending the university) from the risks of war. When presented with an issue either of education or the draft that affects its children, the middle class responds not in terms of higher moral values but in terms of self-interest.

In describing this new middle class as we have above, we have described in somewhat more detail the same middle class whose emergence in Springdale we recorded. When we first noticed this class in Springdale, we were not fully aware of what we had encountered though we realized that it was a unique feature of the life of Springdale. Our awareness of what we saw at that time was heightened by the work of other sociologists and social analysts such as Seeley, Merton, Spectorsky, Mills, Dahl, Whyte, and Riesman who, in their work, were responding to aspects of the same phenomenon. In the late forties and early fifties, a number of different observers responded to the same reality, and each saw his discovery in terms of the problem that concerned him.

When we studied Springdale, we saw this new middle class in the process of expressing these new lifestyles in a small town. At that time, this class was unable to impose its "style" on the organizational and political life of the town. The middle class we observed was aggressive and defensive, never sure that it belonged in Springdale but unable to leave it because it had no other place to go. What we saw at that time was the avant-garde of that class, but it was so weak as to be hardly noticeable. However, in retrospect, the weakness of that middle class was a simple function of the fact that Springdale was removed from the urban centers of the United States. It rather represented earlier stages of American history that remained viable to the residents of the town because they were more committed to the past than to the future. Springdale represented an earlier stage in American society and was not in the mainstream of American history except for a tiny middle class that had then begun to appear in the town. At that time, Springdale had just barely begun to register what was a dominant fact of American life.

The Middle-Class Revolution in American Society

From our experience in Springdale as it was amplified by the works of other students of the middle class, it became clear that a revolution in American social structure and lifestyles had taken place. In comparing our own work with that of Mills, Seeley, Whyte, and Riesman, it is clear that the middle-class revolution has occurred at unequal rates in different communities. A community like Springdale at the time we studied it was further removed from the middle-class revolution than other communities like the new suburbs of New York, Cleveland, Milwaukee, St. Louis, and so on. The rate of penetration of the new middle-class style varies according to place and size of town. With time, the middle-class revolution has spread and penetrated into more and more communities, eventually touching even the most remote hamlets. By now, the new middle class and its styles have been felt in all communities in the country irrespective of size. However, this revolution has not been felt at equal rates and equal levels of intensity in all communities. The differences in rates and intensities account for many of the different types of communities that now exist in the United States. In general terms, we would specify four types of communities in which the middle-class revolution has expressed itself.

The Small Rural Town

Springdale at the time we studied it represented a traditional American community in which the middle-class revolution was working itself out. The new middle classes were *not* influential in a political sense, but were influential in their participation in social organizations and in their "way of life," which transmitted new styles to the community. They were in the process of revolutionizing the traditional habits of the town. The more remote a town from the centers of influence, the more removed it will be from the middle-class revolution. No doubt, there are communities in *all* parts of the country that still manage to resist the dominance of the new middle-class life and intellectual styles. However, it would appear that the small town in the long run will be absorbed into the middle-class culture. Springdale at the time we studied it was already a backwater. Those communities that are still like it now represent the last link in America to the nineteenth century and its values.

The University Town

In those American university towns that do not have industries, the new middle classes are personified by college professors, college administrators, and by other professionals who are attracted to the town as a place of residence because of the cultural tone given to the town by the university. Frequently, the university town is dominated by a middle-class lifestyle that is an academic variant of the new middle-class lifestyle in general. This lifestyle exhibits an emphasis on cultural consumption of the performing arts as provided by university sponsored music, drama, and art shows and an active political interest that reveals a parochial and sometimes self-righteous liberalism. In national affairs, segments of this group have been leaders in civil rights and peace politics, and other more substantial segments of this same community have been politically involved as experts, consultants, and propagandists for the White House and government agencies with respect to foreign, military, and domestic policies. In local politics, the university middle class has a greater unity of interest, which focuses on schools and public services; in its support of these activities, it departs from virtues and policies, such as parsimony in government and low taxes, traditionally promoted by small businessmen in small communities. These unique features are given a special emphasis to the extent that the university middle classes are self-conscious of their alienation from the ethos of their surrounding region; they stand out and are resented by other segments of the new middle classes. They wear their liberalism as a badge, but they cannot take their way of life for granted.

In some university towns, academicians acting as an interest group have succeeded in gaining control of the machinery of local government. They have done this either by directly taking control of a local party apparatus, by making political alliances with other like-minded groups, or by serving as "technical consultants" in solving the specialized problems of government, such as municipal finance, assessment policy, zoning, and so on. Wherever this shift in political control has occurred, it has had revolutionary effects on the political life of the communities involved, for it has resulted in the defeat of business leaders who traditionally have controlled local government in smaller communities. In larger and medium-sized cities where the university is only one of a number of interest groups, university members have had occasion to make alliances with ethnic and labor leaders and have shared and traded power with them. This has occurred quite frequently in traditionally Republican communities, which have now become intermittently Democratic. The size of the town in which a university is located is the critical factor in determining the capacity of professorial liberalism to place its stamp on the public political life of the community.

The Suburban Community

A similar revolution in middle-class styles has taken place in the suburbs of the great metropolises of America. The people who live in these bedroom communities are the managerial, professional, technical, and administrative staffs of the great private and governmental agencies whose offices are located in the central city. In fact, the growth of the suburbs and the new middle class has been proportionate to the growth in size of large-scale enterprises since the end of World War II. Hence, the commuter has become a major factor in American life. Large-scale commuting has also introduced new features into the living styles of the middle class. For regardless of the respectability they are constrained to demonstrate while at their work site, in their home communities they are "free" to develop lifestyles that play on a variety of themes and variations. The local themes around which these lifestyles have been built are:

1. The pursuit of socially organized high culture and leisure activities that are focused around a church or temple. Though the activities are not religious in character, the church provides the setting and legitimating tone for forms of sophistication that would have been alien to the ethnic church or to earlier Protestantism.

2. The organization of life around sports and a social life centered in the country club. Golf, dancing, fishing, tennis, bridge, boating, travel, and swimming are organized into a way of life that emphasizes physical fitness, activity, fresh air, and sunshine.

3. The development of refined interests and tastes in cultural activities that are organized in associations, groups, leagues, and clubs devoted to the pursuit of art, drama, music, and other cultural projects. Activity takes the form of attending concerts, lectures, exhibitions, classes; holding memberships in book and art clubs; and participation as performers, artists, promoters, organizers, and supporters of the arts.

> 4. The pursuit of gaiety and wit, modern living, and the fun morality. Life is active, informal, sophisticated, and broadly tolerant of modern moral and ethical codes. In this group, cultural tastes run to folk dancing and singing, the cocktail and costume party, and the discotheque.

These styles mix in different ways in different suburbs, but, in some cases, whole suburbs will be known for a single, predominant style. However, in spite of such differences in emphasis, these communities exhibit characteristic traits. A large amount of formal and informal group activity focuses on the schools, the PTA, and class mothers and on debate, discussion, opposition, and support surrounding the school budget. Specific issues arise that are part of the school budget: special courses, teacher salary schedules, technical facilities, and so on. Local political groups are organized and exist for one school board election because the issues involved do not parallel any other political issues. After the election, such groups disband only to be reorganized frequently along different lines for the next election. During the phase of overt school politics in these communities, a substantial portion of the community's attention will be absorbed by the school conflict. Newspaper advertisements are published in support of or opposition to the budget or the bond issue. These are written, financed, and published by voluntary committees, which also print and distribute handbills, petitions, and bulk mailings. Letters to the editor comprise a serious form of public debate. Public meetings, rump caucuses, and especially the meetings of the school board are scenes of oral debates, personal animus, and expressions of political passions. For short periods of time before and during the election of school board members and/or the vote on the budget or bond issue, these debates become the central focus of the public life of much of suburbia. Talk continues for a short while after the election.

In some cases, permanent personal animosities develop, leading to avoidance relationships. If a defeat is particularly humiliating, the loser may consider leaving the community. If the issue is particularly intense and lines are sharply drawn, the children in school may be drawn into the conflict, and their relationships with teachers and administrators may be affected. If teachers become involved, their involvement can affect their job status in the school. Short of sex, school issues touch most deeply the passions of suburbia.

Second in importance to school-oriented politics are civic improvement groups, which have an interest in reforming and modernizing the community; critical issues include street lighting, sanitation, sidewalk paving, stop signs, safety at intersections, architectural uniformity, preservation of historical monuments, library improvement, zoning, and community planning. In more recent times, the suburbs have been confronted with the suburbanite Negro who wishes to join the suburban community. This is a newer issue that has been added to the others and at times has involved as much passion for the whites as the school question.

The groups that make up suburbia react differently to the issues mentioned above. The newer middle classes and the recent arrivals in the suburbs are likely to support all issues aimed at improving the community. They care less about the tax rate and display a willingness to have the best services, the best facilities, and a cultured environment. On the other hand, the older groups who lived in the suburbs before the influx of the newer middle classes are more apt to oppose the innovations. For them, it may or may not be a question of taxes. If the older residents are locals who lived in what was previously a small town that became a suburb during the expansion since World War II, taxes are likely to be the issue because these older groups do not have urban sources of income; their income is apt to be derived locally, from industry or from small business, and is less apt to reflect recent inflationary trends. If the older residents are suburbanites from an earlier period—for example, prior to World War II—they are apt to be derived from different ethnic stock and are apt to be more secure and established in their style of life. Their sources of income are not only urban derived but they include some renters. In this case, taxes are not the issue. The issue is rather one of resenting the newer ethnic and arriviste aspirants whose exuberance and hunger for culture is alien to community tradition. They also resent the boisterousness, the energy, and the ceaseless activity of the new arrivals who appear to be pushing their way into organizations and institutions that were regarded as being securely held. The older strata of suburbanites had been accustomed to running the community and resent the new challengers. The new middle classes represent a style that upsets their stable ways of life.

Conflicts such as these are typical of the suburban way of life and its culture. How these conflicts are resolved is not predictable. Some suburbs—for example, the working-class suburbs—were created from scratch and do not exhibit these characteristics. Other suburbs are still dominated by the older middle classes and exhibit a quality of stability and tradition that may be the envy of the newer suburbs as well as a model for emulation. These older suburbs can survive in their accustomed style only if their inhabitants sustain their urban sources of income, but inevitably, because of age and death, representatives of the newer styles will replace them. In some suburbs, the newer middle class has been completely successful in imposing its style on the suburb and has taken over both the political and the social institutions in the community. In still other cases, the issue hangs in balance with no clear and decisive resolution in favor of either the new or the old. In such cases, opposing factions sometimes win and sometimes lose. What appears to be a victory may be only a temporary one because the losers had not sufficiently mobilized their forces at the time of their defeat. The suburban political drama takes a very large variety of forms.

The decisive factor in determining victory or defeat for the new middle classes in the suburbs appears to be based on the percentage of the total population that they constitute. When the new middle classes are a sizable minority, they color the whole life of the town, but they do not occupy the major institutional positions. When they are a small minority, they live out their lifestyles in social enclaves and barely impose their tone on the town, dominating nothing. When their number grows to a size sufficient to give them a feeling that they are unjustly unrecognized and deprived by official institutions, they are apt to make a bid to control the community. No one has yet measured what proportion is necessary for the new middle class to achieve dominance. However, at some point in the continuing conflict between older tradition and new middle-class aspirations, a struggle for the control of the public life of the town ensues. When the new middle class becomes dominant, it succeeds in imposing its style on other segments of the community. For the past twenty years, the new middle class has for the most part succeeded in asserting its style in hundreds of American suburbs.

The New Urban Middle Class

The same kinds of lifestyles and public issues characteristic of the suburbs occur in greatly magnified forms within the metropolis. Certain sectors of the city become the residential centers of the new urban middle classes—silk-stocking districts. These are areas in which high-rent housing and housing developments are concentrated. In New York City, for example, this would include Peter Cooper and Stuyvesant Town, the old (west) Greenwich Village and Washington Square, the upper west side, the east sixties, Brooklyn Heights, and, recently, Park Slope. In each of these areas, a major proportion of the population is college-educated professionals, managers, technically trained bureaucrats, and employed intellectuals. Being closer to the heart of things, they regard themselves as more sophisticated, avant-garde, and au courant than suburban counterparts who have opted for home ownership and a nonurban environment for their children. In fact, many suburbanites first resided in these urban middle-class enclaves, then, when their children reached school age, moved to the suburbs to avoid the complexities and expense of urban family living.

Within the new urban, middle-class enclaves, all of the variations in suburban lifestyles are exhibited, but are expressed with greater intensity, variety, and modern sophistication. For example, the urban "swinger" has a style that can be expressed more completely if the devotee lives in Manhattan than if he attempts the style while living in the suburbs. To some extent, the residential location of the urban segment of the middle class is determined by the age of children. The urban middle class is most apt to be quite young (with preschool children) or middle-aged (with college-enrolled children). The suburbanites tend to have school-age children younger than college age. Other observers have noted that there is considerable physical mobility between the suburbs and the preferred cliff-dwelling areas of the metropolis. Place of residence is thus not the critical factor in defining the new middle class.

However, members of the new urban middle class have introduced one major innovation into the middle-class lifestyle. A substantial number of them have entered politics as ideological and/or party activists. In their case, however, they have favored reform politics over the ethnic and bossism political style to which their immigrant parents were frequently committed. They have helped to create an image of reform politics as cultured, clean, and civilized. Thus, reform politics has been responsible for creating a new type of urban political hero whose image is based on cleanness as opposed to bossist corruption. Robert Wagner, the Yale man who was mayor of New York City and was dubbed an old-time boss by the reformers, was followed by John Lindsay, another Yale man, who "came up smelling clean." In New York City, the reform political club membership almost coincides with the membership of the alumni associations of City College of New York, Fordham, and New York universities. The politics of the urban middle class are liberal and focus on political honesty, integrity, antibossism, and a commitment to high municipal expenditures for improvements of a cultural, educational, and humanitarian nature. Under reform leadership, the City supports "happenings," park improvements, and cultural events and tries to make it a "fun city," as opposed to under, say, La Guardia, who limited his style to honest, efficient administration and to chasing fire engines and reading comics over the radio during a newspaper strike (which would now be regarded as "campy" by part of the less political urban middle class). The political problem of the urban middle class is that as soon as a reform politician is elected to office he is forced to make compromises with the older ethnic bosses and populist politicians in the national, state, or city administrations. As soon as he makes these compromises, the reform middle class becomes disenchanted and begins to look for new reform candidates, and the original reform candidate is likely to lose the support of his idealistic and liberal constituency. If the elected reform politician does not make these compromises, he finds it almost impossible to function as an urban politician in gaining support for his programs and his district. For the urban middle class, narrow *class interest* in the traditional ethnic and lower-class sense of the term is of less interest than are liberal and cultured orientations and the ideology of political purity. Political life, for the politically oriented segments of the urban middle class, is thus a continuous succession of defeats that are never accepted as final defeats because there is always the hope that reform will ultimately win. In the meantime, this middle class can sustain a sense of high-mindedness, reform, and purity while not substantially altering the total pattern of urban politics. Our analysis, of course, does not by itself help us to comprehend the older ghetto or the newer race politics of the metropolis. In part, however, the new radical and racial leadership is drawn from disaffected, college-trained, minority youth. On the urban political scene, the middle class has not and is not likely to become sufficiently powerful to dominate urban politics.

The Future of the Middle Class and Its Lifestyles

In the previous discussion, we have attempted to define the new lifestyles of the new middle classes. We have indicated the nature of these lifestyles at their most typical centers. We have further indicated that these lifestyles have become diffused throughout our nation's population and are triumphing over older styles as their bearers become a larger proportion of the population of an area. Due to changes in the educational and occupational structure of our society, which make America a more and more middle-class society, we can expect these lifestyles to permeate all areas of our society. In the short or long run, even the lifestyles of the rural community will be affected. We would, of course, expect them to penetrate middle-size communities, depending, again, on the proximity to centers of diffusion. We noted that even in Springdale the new middle class had already made a significant impact as early as 1955. At the other extreme, while the urban middle class has emerged as a distinctive phenomenon and has made an impact on urban society, it is less clear what its chances for future predominance are.

Insofar as urban areas are centers for diffusion of these lifestyles, they have an importance that goes far beyond their dominance in an immediate urban location. Knowing the centers from which diffusion takes place and the rates of diffusion are important in predicting the future. In general, the East and West Coast metropolises are the centers from which the diffusion takes place. In some respects, the West Coast has been more inventive and more modern in its cultural development than the East. This claim to cultural leadership by the West is one that is resented by the cultural and other leaders of the East Coast (a few years ago, this contest was fought in terms of population statistics, but, now that California clearly has a larger population than New York, the basis on which superiority is to be judged has shifted to other grounds). While the East and West Coast metropolises advance their claims against each other, the metropolises in the Midwest, particularly Chicago, strive hard to advance their own claims. However, they appear to be advancing their own claims primarily by self-consciously trying not to be impressed by either coast. So far, Chicago and the Middle Western urban metropolises have not been able to challenge the inventiveness and cultural sophistication of either of the coasts. Their claims have, for the most part, been unheard except by themselves.

However, within each of these dominant geographic areas, these giant metropolises have been the center for the development of new cultural and lifestyle themes, particularly in their suburban, exurban, bohemian, and silk-stocking neighborhoods. The concentration in depth of these lifestyles varies by region and by city size. In New York, Boston, San Francisco, and Los Angeles, the avant-garde middle class reaches its highest expression of "modernity" and sophistication. Places like Chicago are still once removed from the "creative centers." St. Louis, Dallas, Milwaukee, Cleveland, New Orleans, and other cities somewhat more distant from the center exhibit a striving, aggressive, somewhat provincial pretentiousness that rings hollow in the face of the "truly authentic" East and West Coast culture. The rural community and the small town that are most intellectually and culturally distant from the urban centers are farthest removed no matter how physically proximate they may be to the center of urban culture.

The university town, regardless of its size, is always a subcenter for these new styles because the university citizenry has direct access to them insofar as the styles themselves are products of the university. The university thus becomes a transmission belt to the rest of the immediate vicinity surrounding it irrespective of the density of population in the region. While the East and West Coasts set styles at a national level, each university town plays a similar role for a more restricted audience.

However, all areas including rural ones are not far removed from the centers of cultural innovation. The mass media, especially television, the film (particularly foreign ones), and magazines (especially *Life* and *Look*) disseminate these new lifestyles almost instantaneously to all sectors of the society, including the deep South, the Maine mountains, the Ozarks, and rural Appalachia. With the mass media, no area is more remote than another. However, the success of this cultural transmission depends a great deal on the receptivity of the population in the middle-sized cities and in the rural areas to this new cultural exposure and the new lifestyles.

There are two groups that are most receptive and hence most critical as points of penetration for the introduction of the new lifestyles in the rural areas:

> 1. The college-educated new middle classes in the 25 to 45 age group who live in tension with the populist culture of their communities. This group feels restricted and hemmed in by traditional small-town values, from which it escapes by identifying with external sophisticated styles. This group orients itself

> to the nearby university and the higher culture as it is transmitted by the mass media.
>
> 2. Teenage youth, especially the children of middle-class parents who are dissatisfied with the provinciality and narrowness of small-town life, look to the mass media for styles of rebellion against what they regard to be the complacency, hypocrisy, and dullness of their elders, particularly their parents. Thus, it is these young people who are the first in their communities to become aware of the new styles and to adopt them as a form of self-assertion; consequently, they are responsible for introducing them into the town and to their elders. The parents sometimes adopt the styles directly from their children: the miniskirt would be a case in point as would be the introduction of longer hairstyles and beards for men. When these young people go to college, they discover more personal and authentic forms and sources of rebellion and more accessible targets in the form of the university administration, the bureaucracy, and repressive professors.

To the extent that the remotest areas are thus penetrated, we can predict that the revolution from populist, frontier culture is in the process of being disseminated throughout the nation, even in the South, the West, and the "upstate" and "downstate" regions of all parts of the country. No doubt, such communities are less penetrated than those with multiple forms of access, but the penetration is quite deep and is likely to continue. It may take twenty-five to fifty years before such penetration is completed. But the fact of the penetration, its intensity, and its quality pose a number of problems.

The depopulation of the rural community is by no means complete. The intensification of large-scale capital investment in agriculture will continue to drive owners of what were formerly known as family-sized farms out of farming. Many of these farmers and particularly their children will seek work and opportunity in the city. But in "rural" areas, employed managers and technicians, many with university training, will become increasingly numerous and important not only in agriculture, but as officials in local branches of national and regional businesses that are increasingly being located in formerly rural areas. So, too, as Federal agencies penetrate more deeply and intensively, rural employment will include government officials, hospital technicians and nurses, military personnel, inspectors and investigators, and specialized educational and welfare personnel. Through these personnel channels, the residues of university training and culture will incessantly permeate the rural community with the urban middle-class styles.

Rural youth will continue as in the past to leave the rural community as the city and the university become more compelling magnets. While in the past the rural community has had an overage population because of the youthful migration, this tendency is now being corrected by the development of specialized communities for the aged which, with the help of Federal aid, depopulate the rural community of some of its aged residents. The desirability of Florida, California, and the Southwest as places for retirement communities has corrected somewhat the age distribution in small towns. This population redistribution will help to weaken the commitment of the rural town to its past traditions and will make it more accessible to modern forms of culture.

After all of these changes have taken place, what remains is the probability of a continuous and enduring battle between the proponents of populist culture and the bearers of the new urban lifestyles, for, wherever the latter group reaches sufficient size, it challenges the older, traditional group for leadership. In the threat to its leadership, the older group sees that it not only faces the loss of community leadership and higher real estate taxes but also the defeat of its entire way of life. This way of life, though on the decline, has long historical roots. It is identified with grassroots democracy, Americanism, and all the virtues of the American past. For those committed to the past and its values, this decline will be hard to digest.

The danger for the United States is that the hostility, defensiveness, and counteraggressiveness engendered by the imminence of defeat will become the basis for a backlash against the full sweep forward of American history as it develops in the present and the future. Populism gone sour could become the source of an antidemocratic, quasi-totalitarian reaction which in spite of its origins in an earlier democratic ideology could turn against the new cultural styles evolving in our society. There is thus the risk that in resisting these new lifestyles populist democracy may become the basis for new social movements that could subvert the foundations of the present by holding to romanticized images of the past. An organized nativistic movement based partly on a xenophobic isolationism could shelter under its cover not only defensive populists but also a variety of other groups whose resentments are less crystallized, but which could find a focus in some form of nativism.

We have indicated that the new lifestyles are not based on un-American ideas but instead have evolved out of fundamental organizational, economic, educational, and demographic changes in American society. These changes represent fundamental and perhaps irreversible trends in the very structure of American society. Whether or not one likes the direction of these trends, they cannot be wished away, abolished by law, or reversed by going back to the past without doing violence to the emergent society. The older populist classes must decide whether to accept defeat gracefully. The newer middle classes, for their part, must decide whether to accept success without exacting vengeance for real or imaginary defeats that occurred in the period prior to its victory. A direct confrontation based on these opposing orientations must be avoided if the United States hopes to cope with its other problems.

19

Freedom, Bureaucracy, and Styles for Dissent

Joseph Bensman with Arthur J. Vidich

Issues of quality of life, culture, and civilization reach beyond economic and political realities. The problem of how America is to realize itself in terms of the higher values has been raised by, among others, Adlai Stevenson, John F. Kennedy, and John Kenneth Galbraith, all of whom have placed a higher priority on the issue of the quality of American life than on brute economic expansion. We would imagine that American culture is something other than that displayed in the styles of the beautiful people, the radical chic, and the multimedia, communitarian, and countercultures.

The solution of economic problems does not automatically resolve the issue of what America is to become as a civilization. In fact, the very resolution of the economic problems creates new problems for the quality of American life.

The resolution of almost every world economic problem requires a greater harnessing of the world's populations and a tighter organization of individuals and groups. Bureaucracy is the major administrative vehicle of industrial society, in the United States as in the rest of the world. Thus, the solution of almost every specific practical

---

Published originally in a slightly different form in *The New American Society: The Revolution of the Middle Class* (Chicago: Quadrangle Books, 1971), 275-90. Republished with permission of Marilyn Bensman and Joseph Vidich.

problem in the United States involves the extension of bureaucracy and a broader and deeper penetration of its effects in all areas of personal, social, and cultural experience. Bureaucracy deprives individuals of freedom and autonomy, not necessarily by coercion but instead by creating a favorable system of rewards for compliance with dehumanized, technical, and efficient patterns of performance. The development of the bureaucratic machine, nationally and internationally, results in a kind of bureaucratic ideology that would deprive all individuals of any independence from it. Bureaucrats develop a sense of their power and have a tendency to affirm their bureaucratic function by exercising this power against the individual and his unique, personal creativity. When the bureaucrat expresses himself through the exercise of the bureaucratic function, he opposes the personal inclinations of others to express themselves.

The key personal, social, and cultural problems that flow from the processes of bureaucratization are the following:

> 1. *The development of pleasant, comfortable, premanufactured patterns of conformity that destroy personal autonomy and individualism.* The individual loses the sense that his life has any meaning apart from these stylized forms, or the sense that he can take his own identity for granted in a way that allows him not to feel that all he thinks and does is external to a real self that he cannot express. In trying to achieve a real identity, he seeks romantic escape into exotic behavior and attitudes. Included in such escapes are freaking out, self-delusion, self-destruction, and a senseless destruction of the "repressive" system without considering realizable alternatives.

2. *The bureaucratic overdevelopment of stylized patterns of opinion and tastes that deny not only the independence but also the capacity for independence to all individuals who are not members of the bureaucratic elites.* The elites have, as their job, the manufacturing of issues, opinions, thought patterns, and cultural tastes for the rest of society. It is in this function that co-opted intellectuals are most dangerous. If this process becomes efficient enough, all independent thought, opinion, and taste is blotted out in a glut of canned, premanufactured thought forms. The problem is one of maintaining channels that will allow authentic expression in a world that is becoming increasingly bureaucratic in organization. In our contemporary society, pseudoexpressiveness that expresses nothing but self-preoccupation and self-withdrawal from all realities, including spiritual ones, becomes defined as expressiveness.

3. *The development in the most general sense of a quality or tone of life that reflects the tone and quality of the bureaucratic milieu and becomes a dominant public style.* Since all major and most minor institutions in the society have been infused with the spirit of bureaucracy, there is little to prevent the spirit of the bureaucrat from attaching to all life experiences. Should the spirit of bureaucracy be brought into the private sphere, the truly private will be driven still deeper into itself. In this event, society would no longer have the resources of creative individuals, resources that it needs for its own

> creative regeneration. Again, pseudoindividuality enables empty persons to defend themselves against the standardization of a bureaucratic culture.
>
> 4. *The development of means by which the bureaucratic and administrative elites can use their key positions in their own interests.* Excessive ambition and the quest for autonomy on the part of the bureaucrats can only be achieved at the price of the freedom of the rest of society. The Soviet Union, as portrayed by Solzhenitsyn, is the best example of this problem. Potential solutions to these problems can only be sketched here. And as we are dealing with issues concerning the quality of American life, describing these solutions per se is of little avail. To the extent that there are any solutions, they must be lived and cannot be resolved by discussion.

The problem of conformity and one-dimensionality has more facets than has generally been imagined. As we have suggested, conformity is demanded by the objective, quasi-legal requirements of work in large-scale organizations, and by the opinion-forming and other mass media that provide premanufactured experiences and styles for individual consumption. Yet, in spite of this, the ambience of urban bureaucratic society offers opportunities for solutions to problems of identity and autonomy not found in simpler societies.

The freedom from work afforded by a short workday allows almost everyone except the overworked elites the leisure to develop personal styles, interests, and idiosyncrasies. Such leisure is not available in societies where the need for work and the length of the workday chain the individual to objective work that permits little individualization. But the simple availability of leisure is not enough.

One must know what to do with his leisure once he has it. In this respect, the mass media are neutral in that they can be ignored at will. One can insulate himself from the mass media simply by finding something better to do with his time.

Bureaucracy, in addition to being legalistic and precise in limiting the rights and duties of the official while on the job, implies that other forms of activity not covered by the rules are left to the discretion of the individual. The way in which the individual uses his private life before and after work is increasingly his own business, particularly in urban centers where one's work site and nonwork life are geographically separated. Frequently, however, the habits of blandness and compliance learned at work are carried over into the nonwork life. This happens not because the bureaucratic elites demand it but because the individual is unable to cope with the opportunities afforded him. If he wishes, in his nonwork life, the individual can pursue his own interests, talents, and tastes without regard for the external constraints of bureaucracy. In the middle class, as we have noted, individual bureaucrats sometimes develop enough independence to become swingers, Beats, hippies, beautiful people, and liberal and radical reformers. Unfortunately, these activities are often the expression of an attitude of negation and are therefore incapable of enriching life over any extended period of time.

The freedom available in bureaucratic mass society is only available to those who are capable of using it. The failure to use such freedom is less the failure of our economic institutions than it is the failure of the individual. In this respect, however, the failure of the individual is due partly to the failure of parents and educational institutions to take seriously these crises of identity and problems of conformity.

Because bureaucratic work appears incapable of channeling the creative energies released by favorable middle-class environments, forms of expression other than work must be found to absorb these emerging energies. This means that individuals must be taught or must somehow learn that self-expression and creativity can be realized in serious, nonvocational, but disciplined work. Parents and schools and colleges must in some way show the neophyte how to develop interests, skills, and tastes that are not necessarily vocationally connected. In the middle-class world, an education that prepares one only for work fails to prepare one for life, because the most serious aspects of life are no longer connected to work. If leisure and consumption are functions of life as well as economics, the truly significant aspects of life are neglected by occupational training. Our educational system has failed to demonstrate this to youth because it is primarily vocational in character. But it has also failed in a more serious sense by failing to set an example to youth of what it means to have a serious, disciplined, intrinsic interest in a subject. The new relevant education, consisting of rap sessions, T-groups, and communitarian freedom, accentuates the original problem because it accepts the fact that students will not and cannot make demands on themselves.

While teachers and parents are ultimately responsible for this state of affairs, youth is also implicated. The failure of youth to realize the opportunities inherent in the imperfections of the bureaucratic world is to a large extent a failure of consciousness and of nerve. The failure of consciousness means simply that individuals fail to recognize the amount of freedom that is available if they would choose to use it. The failure of nerve is an unwillingness to test seriously the limits of their interests and talents by doing positive, creative work.

It appears that the specters of conformity, restraints, adult hypocrisy, and the rat race have so dominated youth that they have chosen to combat everything en bloc without fully realizing what it is they are fighting. In choosing to combat the "culture of conformity" and the "establishment," they have failed to see the lack of unity and solidarity of adult society and of the symbols they are fighting. They appear to be more interested in attacking that world than in extracting the degrees of freedom that it offers. By concentrating on rebellious attack or withdrawal, they demonstrate by their behavior that they reject the very freedom they claim their society denies them. Whether hippie, radical, or "existentially honest," their rebellion is less an affirmation of independent autonomous values and beliefs than an affirmation of quite the opposite. Their ideas are transfixed by the image of the ideas they oppose. As a result, they achieve not the freedom they desire but only a symbolic affirmation of negation.

For the most part, these youth, not yet committed to a job and still in possession of the freedom guaranteed by parental support, do not have to make the distinction between work and nonwork life. If they could escape from their symbolic rebellion and withdrawal and could develop a sense of their own direction, it would release the energy necessary to create human or artistic cultures.

The failure of youth to do more than rebel (or lament), and the failure of their elders to do much more than conform, are based on an initial misapprehension of the pressures to conform. Conformism results from a lack of confidence in the ability to pursue one's own inclinations. If individuals can learn to pursue their own personal demons without regard to assumed pressures for conformity, self-assurance and self-confidence are likely to result from the act itself. Doing what one wishes to do will in itself remove the sting of conformist pressures. The failure to exploit the tolerance in repressive tolerance is a major crime. The failure to inform youth of that tolerance is an even greater crime.

Exploitation of the opportunities in repressive tolerance is not necessarily a solution to political problems in American society. The inability of youth to find opportunities for disciplined self-development has been defined as a political problem. We believe that opportunities for cultural and self-realization are available for middle-class youth, but that those youth have frequently failed to exploit these opportunities. We also believe that opportunities for the expression of the political idealism of youth are available but have not been exploited in a sustained and disciplined way—as we shall make clear later.

When the conformist sees his values violated by others who do so with confidence and impunity, he becomes less confident in his conformist behavior. In a complex, pluralist society, the very act of living an autonomous life creates the conditions that validate that life for others. Such men as Eric Hoffer, Irving Howe, Philip Rahv, Stanley Edgar Hyman, Meyer Schapiro, Harold Rosenberg, Kenneth Burke, Lewis Mumford, Wallace Stevens, William Carlos Williams, William Faulkner, and Paul Goodman have demonstrated the possibilities inherent in nonconformist work despite the demands of a conformist world. If the individual has confidence in his own lifestyles and values, he need not feel oppressed by others who may disapprove.

This notion that pressures to conform are brought against one is as much a product of the individual's own willingness to accept such pressures as it is the existence of the pressure itself. Failure to realize this results in conformity as well as the unnecessary rebellion against it.

David Riesman suggests that it is possible to accept the responsibility for determining and shaping one's own lifestyle. To do this, however, one must have confidence in one's own values, the self-discipline to acquire the skills and knowledge necessary to cultivate one's interests, and the nerve to try to be autonomous. A painter, novelist, poet, or artist of any sort who is productive acquires the skill, discipline, nerve, and industriousness necessary to the achievement of autonomy by the very act of his productivity. He discovers the possibility of autonomy by relentlessly doing his own work, the results of which, as they accumulate, provide him with a means for gaining confidence from the fact that he has already done something. Frequently, such individuals have been forced to live off earnings from routine, uninteresting work while creating works for which there is no audience. They may find approval only after they become successful, though there is no guarantee that such approval will be forthcoming. The landscape is strewn with novel, but unsung, failures. But in achieving either success or failure, the price paid for autonomy is the disciplined attempt to achieve it. One need not be a genius. Anyone with talent or who is strongly interested in politics, art, music, literature, and so forth, need only pursue his interests. Disciplined pursuit of the interest results in the acquisition of sensitivity, knowledge, skill, and discrimination that validate the initial interest. The validation allows one to live and grow within the framework of his own values, tastes, and interests.

One cannot pursue this style without paying a price, which at times is high. It may involve isolation from one's immediate social environment, loss of friendship with the rest of the herd based on the common denominator of the herd's interests, or being regarded as odd, eccentric, irascible, and difficult to get along with. To live against such threats of disapproval requires nerve. In this sense, the failure of nerve is equivalent to the unwillingness to acquire the discipline, self-confidence, and interest to be free. We believe it is this failure, more than the constraints of the Philistine, the community, or the commune, that is likely to produce conformity and the problems associated with it. Rebellion against the philistine or middle-class lifestyle is a rebellion that lacks both the nerve and discipline to act on the principles that evoke the rebellion. When one accepts the constraints of a radical cell or a new commune, he reasserts his conformity. Radical constraints can be violated by splitting. The new radical politics have as their major virtue the inability to organize anything.

Regardless of the possibilities, it appears that the number of individuals who are capable of living affirmatively within the framework of autonomous values is small. One of the most difficult of human tasks seems to be to summon personal reserves of interest, self-discipline, and nerve that will allow one to be at least partially responsible for his own growth and autonomous development. The upper-middle class, having been freed from economic necessity, seems to be particularly incapable of self-direction. Increasing numbers of middle-class youth have become aware of the demands for conformity placed on them, and increasing numbers rebel but fail in their rebellion—often with frightening results.

Finding solutions to these problems depends on the ability of the society to apply rationally resources and technology that are already available. But, in addition, self-discipline, self-control, and the development of personal and creative skills are means to self-realization and intelligent control of the social structure.

We have argued that segments of middle-class youth, whose very affluence has allowed them to avoid the discipline necessary for mobility and caused them to escalate their demands on the system, have developed an attitude of righteousness, mindlessness, and a quest for immediate and direct action. It is in this sense that radical, extremist youth is irrational. We have also indicated that past repressions and promises, followed by lack of fulfillment, have produced a black anger and rage that result in violence, riots, and uprisings that, no matter how understandable, produce no solutions to the problems that evoke the protests.

But neither of these problems of youths or blacks nor the failure to solve them, *in themselves*, need threaten American society. Each solution to major social and economic problems is likely to result in an increasing co-optation of the protesting groups, so that in the long run the granting of rights and social concessions may modify undesirable conditions and social injustices.

The more serious problem is that the action of radical youth and angry blacks may provoke the hostilities of lower-class, lower-middle-class, and middle-class whites, and create a backlash of irrationality that transcends its causes. Until the mid-sixties the old redneck, racist, lower-class and lower-middle-class culture of resentment was on the decline. The new middle classes—smug, liberal, and striving for culture—were the bearers of an ideology of liberalism, reform, political honesty, and government intervention in the solution of all major social problems. The black revolution and the youth revolution have frightened the new lower-middle class out of its apathy and its ethnic liberalism. The white working class and lower-middle class increasingly see the blacks as threatening their property values, their jobs, their safety, their tenure, and the success they feel they have achieved by hard work. The youthful radical, the upper-middle-class radical, and, increasingly, the lower-middle-class radical are threats to the very system that guaranteed their success. The new patriots want law and order, and if law and order means repression, an increasing number of middle- and working-class Americans want it. Since the 1968 presidential election, almost every state and local election in the United States has seen the proponents of law and order victorious. The response of blacks and white radical youth to the threat or actuality of repression is to become more destructive, provocative, and violent, which in turn stimulates greater counterviolence and repression.

As the hostility between the radical and reactionary forces in American society continues to polarize, it becomes more and more difficult to gain political support for solutions to the *original* problems. The middle classes become less liberal. Budgetary racism becomes more pronounced. Taxpayers' rebellions become something to be reckoned with. Emotional, irrational, racial, and political antagonisms have become the central issues of the day, and manifest problems that might originally have been solved are now ignored. They cannot be ignored indefinitely, for failure to solve them only worsens the irrationalities that produced the problems in the first place.

If the only solution to our current problems is repression, then neither radical students nor blacks nor liberals can win. A bureaucratic mass society can be permissive or repressive; if it becomes repressive, it can become totalitarian. The middle classes, along with the white working class and the upper classes, can be liberal, conservative, or totalitarian, depending on the state of their defensive anxieties. Under the impact of the black and youth revolutions, these classes are being driven to the right. Youth can be liberal or totalitarian; radical youth, under the banner of freedom, are becoming totalitarian and are driving other groups to adopt some versions of totalitarian repressiveness. If this process should continue, then the reason involved in Keynesian political economy will give way to an economy supported by police and domestic military budgets. We believe America is well down the road toward this state of affairs.

The other major problems of the quality of American life—that is, the destruction of an independent public opinion, the cancerous spread of a bureaucratic spirit, and the dominance of society by bureaucratic elites—can, for the purposes of discussing their solution, be treated as one problem. Its root cause is the use by centralized bureaucratic elites of the organizations that they control and the resources provided by giant budgets for their own interests. Through their control of the mass media, they can provide pleasant entertainment and national morality dramas that can be passively and comfortably consumed without recourse to independent effort or thought.

Television has abundantly demonstrated its ability to take the sting out of poverty, black revolution, youth revolution, drugs, and educational problems simply by presenting them in situational comedies or in serious dramas. The media can emphasize or minimize social problems; under pressure from, say, the vice president, they can play up or play down crime, race riots, student rebellions, and the successes or failures of presidential administrations. Programs that respond seriously to such problems are believed so long as their message agrees with the interests or reinforces the prejudices of their audiences.

Opinion-making institutions can present and diffuse ideologies that justify the dominance of bureaucratic elites and can withhold information that conceals incompetence, malfeasance, and self-serving. By virtue of their favored positions, they attempt to immunize themselves from criticism while developing justifications that entitle them to the highest rewards our society can produce. In these respects, modern bureaucratic elites are no different from all elites of the past, for the self-rewarding and self-justifying aspects of elitehood are generic to its nature.

What is unique about the past thirty years is the ability of the elites not only to command the machines of information diffusion and information control, but also their ability to co-opt the academic and intellectual strata into their public opinion and publicity organizations. Before World War II, the intellectual and academic classes were isolated from the elite establishment because there were no means to reward them for conformity to elite demands. The prosperity of America has provided—via gigantic corporation budgets and government, foundation, and university grants and positions—the means to grant the material rewards that have converted many American intellectuals into active technicians and self-satisfied extollers and ideologists for America's major organizations and institutions. Academicians and intellectuals have found these new social rewards pleasant. When the funds are cut back and rewards are no longer forthcoming, many intellectuals begin to make mindless, senseless attacks on the system that has heretofore kept them living in a style to which they have become only too accustomed. These intellectual critics are joined by youth who will later reach thirty, become professors, and accept the perquisites and emoluments of subsidized professorial life. They become highly principled in response to newfound idealism, empty leisure, and a quest for high-minded causes. The most gutless of professors and academic technicians have simply collapsed under the not-too-subtle threats and pressures of their students and have proved their sympathies by leading the students—to promotion and tenure for themselves, to jail sentences and expulsion for the students.

The idea of a democracy demands that intellectually independent and capable individuals scrutinize the operations of society and speak out against the excesses of its "self-elected," "self-appointed," and co-opted leaders and representatives. More than ever before, the conditions of mass democracy demand that intellectuals play the role of tribune (but not of Caesar) for the people.

Traditional democratic theory has assumed that the various interest groups in society will check each other. In addition, the free press, independent of all external pressure, is supposed to reveal abuses and excesses of power. In reality, several factors limit these traditional solutions.

The legal, administrative, and economic complexity of the modern bureaucratic apparatus makes it extremely difficult for anyone to scrutinize its informal operations. The social distance of the press (not to mention all other audiences) from the sources of decision make it difficult, though not impossible, for the press to overcome the problem of the management of news and opinion. The fear of retaliation by government agencies, when criticism of the press and television is made by such responsible figures as the Vice President of the United States, can and must be a major concern not only to the news media but to all those who hope to retain some form of democracy in America. Gaining access to privileged information and to organizational secrets would require forms of counterintelligence agencies that would be accountable to the public. The use of the ombudsman is a weak gesture in this direction.

A more difficult problem arises from the fact that the ethics of modern bureaucracy increasingly require that in situations of policy conflicts and other forms of organizational infighting, the responsible official solves his problem without recourse to the public and the press. The ethical imperative demands that differences be resolved in camera. By going to the press or to other outside pressure groups and audiences, the bureaucrat expands the scope of the battlefield and invites a counterattack that would expose his excesses and special privileges. Even Robert Kennedy and J. Edgar Hoover, who lost little love for each other, managed in 1967 to call a truce in their public argument over wiretapping. It seems clear that the various bureaucratic elites and the mass interest groups they represent are likely to try to prevent the public from gaining information that allows for independent, informed decisions.

Strong as these tendencies to secretiveness and allegiance may be, independent journalists, academicians, intellectuals, and congressmen have at times succeeded in serving as tribunes for the people. People like Ralph Nader, Jack Anderson, the late Drew Pearson, Harrison Salisbury, Martin Luther King Jr.; Senators Estes Kefauver, Eugene McCarthy, and J. William Fulbright; and Congressman

Wright Patman have at times dramatized issues and exposed abuses that would otherwise have been neglected. Authors of books and editors of small magazines are in a unique position. Due to the relatively low cost of producing a book or small magazine as compared with producing a newspaper, mass magazine, or television program, it is still possible for writers to study and report independently on issues that are not, and frequently cannot be, treated by other media. The means for maintaining independent sources of information and points of view rests on the willingness of a relatively few intellectuals and writers to remain independent in spite of countless opportunities to surrender their autonomy in return for higher rewards in the mass media. More than at any time in the past, American society offers untold opportunities to sell out—ideologically as well as financially.

As methods for selling out to large-scale organizations become more refined and perfected, the sellout as an act can become genteel, prestigious, respectable, and highly profitable. Yet it is some kind of tribute to the human spirit that the process of increasing the rewards for acquiescence and co-optability also generates a striving on the part of some for personal autonomy and independence that results in the continued expression of dissenting views. In spite of its lack of conventional rewards, our society depends on dissent. Whether such dissent will continue to reproduce itself is by no means certain or automatic. Its continued existence matters, not because it can sometimes correct the abuses inherent in any elite-dominated society, but as a symbol that can survive in spite of those abuses. In spite of all those forces organized to achieve a comfortable acquiescence or a forced, gutless radicalism, the simple existence of genuine dissent is the last significant symbol of the free society.

For the politically sophisticated who are aware of the full potential of bureaucratic constraints, and of those who oppose them, there is an ethical imperative to expose, oppose, and define human limits to organized repressions. To expose fraud and to oppose excessive ambition from both left and right becomes a major form of political action.

But exposing the fraud, the self-seeking, and the incompetence of bureaucratic elites is not enough. At best, it results in a correction of the random mistakes of bureaucrats. It cannot lead to changes in bureaucratic policy and structures. Yet radical structural changes do not offer a solution to the problems of American society either. A radical attack on bureaucracy is likely to result initially in vast bloodletting followed by the reinstitution of a bureaucratic terrorism more thorough and centralized than we can now imagine.

It is impossible for American society to return to a decentralized laissez-faire state, despite the wishes of young and old reactionaries. Government budgets will remain large, and bureaucracy will remain as the basic organizational feature of industrial society so long as industrial society is able to exist. The upper and middle classes will be composed of managerial, administrative, intellectual, technical, and professional personnel. Many members of these groups, because of their education and favored position, will have the problem of rising above the pedestrian and technical nature of their bureaucratic work. Cultural and political discontent is, and will continue to be, a chronic problem in all advanced industrial societies.

Political discontent can be resolved by providing substantive solutions—rather than vast structural changes—to the problems on which the discontent becomes focused. John Dewey, in *The Quest for Certainty,* suggested that the history of the world was a quest for ultimate and final solutions. A structural change, perhaps produced by revolution, or by one big blowup, has always appeared to promise a final solution to all the knotty and complex problems of society. But the very complexity of the issues in contemporary industrial society works against total solutions. This means that youthful idealism must be channeled into action on the dozens of political issues to which a solution is possible. Concentrating on these issues means concentrating on the acquisition of specific interests and information. It means that youth (and, of course, adults) must acquire the skills for political action. These skills include bargaining, organizing, and demonstrating, to be sure, but also running copy machines, knocking at doors, and being able to listen politely to those regarded as their inferiors. More than this, youth must learn that the political process is a continuous one in which there is no guarantee of victory. They will often lose battles, sometimes wars. At times, they will find it necessary to make weak compromises that will tarnish the sincerity of their efforts. Moreover, they will discover, as all political activists in the past have discovered, that their political victories may result in more opportunities for profit and exploitation by the Philistines they think they have defeated. They may have to face the even more disillusioning knowledge that victory by idealists may convert the idealists into self-serving, successful bureaucrats, hacks, or businessmen. Youth may recognize these metamorphoses when they see them in their friends, enemies, and parents. They may change their perspective only when it happens to themselves.

Having ideals and being willing to risk realizing them involves dangers. The only way to avoid these risks is through apathy, withdrawal from society, or the quest for violent self-destruction in the pursuit of total solutions.

A final note: Modern bureaucracies fall short of being thorough in their repressiveness. They are too inefficient. Whether their efficiency is more dangerous than their mistakes is an open question. Modern extremist political movements are even less efficient. They are as likely to purge their friends as their enemies, and, in the long run, if they are successful, their only friend is the executioner.

Note on the Editors

Robert Jackall is Willmott Family Professor of Sociology & Public Affairs at Williams College. He is the author of *Moral Mazes: The World of Corporate Managers* and *Street Stories: The World of Police Detectives*, among other books.

Duffy Graham is the author of *The Consciousness of the Litigator.*

Index

A

D

E

F

G

K

L

O

P

Q

R

U

V

W

X

Y

Z

www.ingramcontent.com/pod-product-compliance
Lightning Source LLC
Chambersburg PA
CBHW030632270326
41929CB00007B/39

* 9 7 8 0 9 8 4 6 4 4 5 9 9 *